ESSAYS IN APOCALYPSE

D0973361

TERRY JAMES

SOME THOUGHTS ON THE END OF DAYS

First printing: August 2018

ISBN: 978-0-89221-758-8
Library of Congress Number: 2018947240

Cover by Diana Bogardus

Unless otherwise noted, Scripture quotations are from the King James Version (KJV) of the Bible.

Scripture noted NKJV is taken from the New King James Version. Copyright © 1982 by Thomas Nelson, Inc. Used by permission. All rights reserved.

Scripture noted NIV is taken from the New International Version®, copyright © 1973, 1978, 1984, 2011 by Biblica, Inc.™ Used by permission of Zondervan. All rights reserved worldwide.

Please consider requesting that a copy of this volume be purchased by your local library system.

Printed in the United States of America

Please visit our website for other great titles:
www.newleafpress.com

For information regarding author interviews,
please contact the publicity department at (870) 438-5288.

New Leaf Press
A Division of New Leaf Publishing Group
www.newleafpress.com

Dedicated to my brother
Philip Robin James

Acknowledgments

Every book is the product, finally, of those who encircle the author as he thinks, composes, and writes. To do the best job of presenting the material in the volume, he needs the best possible professional help. He also needs loved ones surrounding him to nurture him, to give him validation and confidence.

In my case, I am most blessed. The professionals in the research and editing process *are* my daughters in the deepest regions of my heart. I'm thankful for all of my family.

As always, my love and thanks to Angie Peters — world's best editor.

Same love and thanks to Dana Neel, a world-class researcher and all-around assistant in many areas of the process.

To Margaret, Terry Jr., Nathan, Kerry, Jeanie, and Todd, thanks and love for staying close, yet not crowding, while the writing was in process.

Especially to my mother, Kathleen James-Basse, my love for all she has meant in my life through the years.

Many thanks to the talented people at New Leaf Publishing Group for masterfully working to shape the volume into a book qualified to be used in the Lord's service.

My gratitude and love to the Lord Jesus Christ, without whose guidance and insights, through Holy Spirit direction, all work on this book would have been in vain.

— Terry James

Contents

Foreword

Dare I say I am a fan of Terry James? I am — at least of his insight and writing style. I am always checking the Internet for his latest article so that I can post it to my various website locations. He and I have watched the same events unfold over a few decades. But only in the last decade have they "converged" and filled each day with anticipation as I would wonder what the breaking story might be as it concerned eschatology.

No one outlines these issues quite like Terry. He has issues analyzed even before the story breaks. Once it breaks, he connects the dots in simple language with concise and easy-to-understand logic.

We need more thinkers and writers like this. Many want to get lost in the weeds rather than keeping to the point.

In the last 20 years, we've seen an increase in aberrant eschatological theologies. In 2005, Hal Lindsey personally told me that those who would disagree with the basics of pre-Trib dispensationalism would do so in a very contentious way. One of the most grievous ordeals of ministry life has been contending with the contentious who are always coming up with a new way of doing Bible prophecy. And the new way is seldom biblically solid. It has been sad to see that, upon disagreement, division follows, and even unkind words are publicly spoken.

Sure, we should expect this when we take a stand for anything, but this world is falling apart, and we need to stick together and encourage one another. Thus, I am comforted that there are some teachers and writers who have not wavered in their theology and who faithfully encourage the flock with the truth. That is what Terry does with his writing.

Terry James may be physically blind, but he has eyes to see things spiritually that few do. You will see that in this book as he tackles the predicted issues that are coming to life. He will make sense of a lot of things.

Pay attention to his warnings and his writings. The world is spinning with things to come, just as predicted.

The King is returning, perhaps today.

— Jan Markell

A Note from the Author

As many readers know, I write a weekly "Nearing Midnight" column for the Rapture Ready website. When reviewed over time, these essays provide a unique opportunity to look back through issues and events to see ongoing, dated snapshots of the progression of stage-setting for fulfillment of Bible prophecy.

Beginning with chapter 4, the chapter titles reflect material I wrote *at the time of the chapter title date*, so when you see words like "last week" or "next month," please keep in mind that the references are to past, not current, events.

1

America: Babylon's Mirror Image

One of the most frightening descriptions of judgment found in Bible prophecy is set within the 17th and 18th chapters of Revelation. God's wrath is foretold to fall upon history's most blasphemous and wealthiest religious, political, and socioeconomic humanistic system.

Babylon the Great will be destroyed in a single hour. It will take place at some point during the last seven years of the age leading up to Christ's Second Coming.

One of the most asked questions by those interested in end-times matters is: "Is America in Bible prophecy?" — or "Why isn't America, certainly considered the greatest nation to this point in history in terms of wealth and material achievement, not in Bible prophecy?"

The most common answer given by teachers and others who view prophecy from the pre-Millennial, pre-Tribulation, *futurist* perspective is: "No." America is *not* found in Bible prophecy. That has most frequently been my own answer to that basic question. The United States of America isn't found within the pages of God's prophetic Word.

I can't answer for others who deal with biblical eschatology (the study of end things). I can only say that my own meaning within my answer is that the U.S. isn't mentioned *by name* anywhere in prophecy.

Whether this most materially blessed nation in history, despite the absence of its name, is or is not somewhere in prophecy is another matter. Regarding that matter, my thinking, based upon study of God's Word, has trended in more recent times toward "perhaps."

Babylon, the city second only to Jerusalem as far as the number of times it's mentioned in the Bible, is, of course, at the center of most controversy in the question of whether America is implied in Scripture. Is the United States *Babylon the Great*?

Despite the adamant answers to this query by some of my colleagues and friends on both sides of the America/Babylon matter, I must say they

9

cannot — nor can I — know for certain. Only history playing out can provide the answer. We don't know the future in detail when speculating upon such peripheral prophetic issues. Such is reserved exclusively for the God of heaven.

Time's unfolding, however, always draws things to come into focus so that prophetic detail can be more clearly discerned. It seems to me that recent times have provided ever-increasing magnification, showing America's possible inclusion within these "end-of-days" prophecies, as the secular world terms them.

I am not declaring that I think America is Babylon the Great. Like this chapter's title implies, however, our nation, in many ways, looks to me to be more and more like a *mirror reflection* of that prophesied entity.

Babylon the Great

Let's look here at the mysterious entity God called "Babylon the Great." Its total destruction assuredly describes how it will be the apex nation/city/commercial and religious system of human history:

> And the kings of the earth, who have committed fornication and lived deliciously with her, shall bewail her, and lament for her, when they shall see the smoke of her burning,
>
> Standing afar off for the fear of her torment, saying, Alas, alas that great city Babylon, that mighty city! for in one hour is thy judgment come. . . .
>
> The merchants of these things, which were made rich by her, shall stand afar off for the fear of her torment, weeping and wailing,
>
> And saying, Alas, alas that great city, that was clothed in fine linen, and purple, and scarlet, and decked with gold, and precious stones, and pearls!
>
> For in one hour so great riches is come to naught. And every shipmaster, and all the company in ships, and sailors, and as many as trade by sea, stood afar off,
>
> And cried when they saw the smoke of her burning, saying, What city is like unto this great city!
>
> And they cast dust on their heads, and cried, weeping and wailing, saying, Alas, alas that great city, wherein were made rich all that had ships in the sea by reason of her costliness! for in one hour is she made desolate (Revelation 18:9–19).

There have been great religious and commercial centers throughout history. Some of these were, no doubt, seen by the merchants of the time and others as wielding great seductive and controlling power like that described above. Some of these have been destroyed, usually by military action. Others — such as in the case of Pompeii, destroyed by the eruption of Vesuvius — have been almost instantly decimated by what many consider the judgment of God.

But, these were all in the past — mostly in the ancient past. There has been no such total devastation to such a powerful city or nation in modern times. And the destruction of Babylon the Great is prophetically scheduled to take place at a future time set within the context of the last seven years leading up to Christ's Second Advent.

If God's Word is true — and it is truth in every respect — there must be a city, nation, and commercial influence of tremendous magnitude during the time of what John was told to call the Apocalypse, the "Revelation of Jesus Christ."

We must then, if trying to understand whether the present generation is near the time of Christ's "Revelation" or Second Coming, ask whether a city-state commercial system as described in Revelation chapter 18 exists.

As a matter of fact, there is indeed such an entity. It is the only one on the scene as of right now. Far beyond that fact, the one presently on the scene is one unlike any to have ever existed throughout the history of mankind.

The United States of America is, in terms of human achievement and attainment of every conceivable development of material convenience, the absolute apex of all nations of all of history! This isn't being boastful of my nation. It's simply fact that even the most ardent America-hater can't truthfully deny. As my fellow Arkansan, that great philosopher Dizzy Dean, said, "It ain't braggin' if you can do it."[1]

America, blessed beyond all nations, materially speaking — and even spiritually speaking, in some sense — has done it. The United States has achieved greatness that is the envy of the world . . . and the hatred of the world as well, in many cases.

It is deflating, after that statement, to have to say that this once-great nation has become, perhaps, among the most debauched and debased of human history. Lord Edward Acton said it well: "Power corrupts and absolute power corrupts absolutely."[2] America has achieved power like no other nation-state. She has corrupted herself, possibly beyond redemption.

---

1. https://www.brainyquote.com/quotes/dizzy_dean_379853.
2. https://acton.org/research/lord-acton-quote-archive.

The primary cause of the fall into corruption is that American society and culture — its people, for the most part — have collectively turned their backs on God. The nation has grown rich and insensitive to God's blessings, His great purposes for bringing into existence this most unique experiment in liberty. Like the Lord's indictment of Babylon the Great, it might be said, "For all nations have drunk of the wine of the wrath of her fornication, and the kings of the earth have committed fornication with her, and the merchants of the earth are waxed rich through the abundance of her delicacies" (Revelation 18:3).

America is the richest nation that has ever been upon this fallen planet. Jesus told us that it is easier for a camel to go through the eye of a needle than for a rich person to "see" the Kingdom of heaven (Matthew 19:24). The spiritual heart — the minds of the rich — are easily turned from thoughts of the true God of heaven. These have a difficult time even "seeing" or recognizing things of the Kingdom of heaven. They, therefore, certainly have an almost impossible challenge in finding the only route to salvation — that found in Romans 10:9–10: "That if thou shalt confess with thy mouth the Lord Jesus, and shalt believe in thine heart that God hath raised him from the dead, thou shalt be saved. For with the heart man believeth unto righteousness; and with the mouth confession is made unto salvation."

Thankfully, Jesus followed up that dire "camel through the eye of a needle" assessment by stating that "with God all things are possible," meaning that the rich can attain salvation, because of God's love and grace.

The United States of America experienced that love and grace as a nation with the 2016 presidential election. This is a view I realize isn't shared by a vast number of Americans, even necessarily Americans who voted for the winner in that election. But my view is that God's grace, love, and patience are the reason for the sudden, unexpected turn of events in the direction the election took that night of November 8.

The 2 Chronicles 7:14 Scripture was on full display: "If my people, which are called by my name, shall humble themselves, and pray, and seek my face, and turn from their wicked ways; then will I hear from heaven, and will forgive their sin, and will heal their land."

Some theologians will argue adamantly that this declaration by God was only for the Jewish people — the nation Israel. It has, at best, only unknowably uncertain, peripheral application for today's Age of Grace (Church Age), they insist.

I disagree. God tells us that He does not change. He is the same yesterday, today, and forever. The 2 Chronicles 7:14 promise has not been abandoned by the God of heaven.

The essays within this book detail my view on how God's praying people helped cause the surprise — even shock — politicians, pundits, and people across the nation and world received when the election results became known at around 9:00 p.m. eastern time on November 8, 2016.

Not to be misunderstood, I am not saying or even hinting that I think the winning candidate for the presidency is a *godly* person. I am saying, however, that the winning candidate is *God's man* for this critical hour as this generation moves ever deeper into the last of the last days.

The United States — the world — received a sort of reprieve. The phenomenal turnabout in direction America took was like a child playing with a battery-operated toy car, reaching down and picking the toy up, turning it around, and letting it run in the opposite direction.

Well . . . that might be a bit of a weak analogy to what happened, but maybe it will suffice for illustrative purposes here. We consider at this juncture only the moral issues of the most basic sort, just to, hopefully, further make the point. America's obstinate turning from God's prescriptive way for humanity was on full display during the previous presidential administration. God said, through Paul the Apostle in Romans chapter 1 and in numerous Old Testament passages, that homosexuality is a sin. God seems to consider man lying (engaging in sexual acts) with man and woman with woman as among the most egregious of sins. Such is termed an "abomination" in God's Holy Word.

Not only did the practice of homosexuality ramp up during the years of the previous administration, it was given government sanction at every turn. We recall that the president had the White House bathed in the rainbow colors to show his support for those on the side of gay rights.

We remember, too, that Christian business owners were prosecuted and fined for refusing to bake cakes for homosexual "marriages."

And, to that point, the United States government, with full backing of the court system, slapped the Creator of mankind in the face by saying marriage is not the way God ordained. We infer from that decision that God was wrong in the opinion of America's court system. Same-sex marriage was normalized — or that was the attempt that was made.

God made male and female, we are plainly informed in Genesis. The courts and the "progressive" minds of America and the world tell us that, regardless of our birth gender, we can be whatever we want to be. The psychologists, psychiatrists, and other psychoanalysts of today agree. Some textbooks on such matters have been rewritten. They now say that homosexuality, transsexuality, and all other formerly aberrant sexual identities are now normal, alternative lifestyle choices.

While the new president — again, as I see as not a *godly* man, but as *God's man* — hasn't addressed to any great extent the particular issue of immorality concerning sexuality within the American culture, he has indicated strongly that he intends to see that Christianity is treated fairly. He has said he saw that the Christian faith was under assault and that he intends to rectify that inequity. I believe the Lord has seen fit to surround the president with a number of Christian men and women who will help guide him in the effort to "rectify" the inequities.

America has corrupted herself, as delineated above. However, she has been an instrument for righteousness in the hand of God as well.

From its beginning, despite the problems of infiltration by esoteric influences, America had at its conception principles that obviously were put in the minds of the Founding Fathers by the God of heaven. Those Judeo-Christian principles served the nation well. The gospel of Jesus Christ flourished as the dominant faith without its proponents acting dictatorially by suppressing or oppressing other religions.

While some such oppression might have on rare occasion attempted to so dominate, the Constitution was there to assure freedom of religious practice and expression. In the matter of sharing the gospel message of Jesus Christ, America was indeed that shining light on the hill about which President Ronald Reagan and others have proudly spoken.

Second only in importance to spreading the gospel around the world through missionary effort and through the fantastic technologies she developed is the nation's other divine purpose, in my view. America served as midwife for Israel's rebirth into modernity.

America was the primary mover in supporting the fledgling Jewish state when much of the world was indifferent or even antagonistic to Israel becoming a nation. The most powerful country on earth just happened to be there with a president, Harry S. Truman, who saw prophetic significance in what was taking place. It was a divine appointment, there is no doubt.

This nation, then, was once a *great* nation, considering the two main purposes it has served. In that sense, the desire to "make America great again" is a worthy and even noble ambition. However, it will never be made great again through political manipulations or economic revival. Only the God of heaven who gave the nation its commission in the first place can truly "make America great again."

When looking at the America/Babylon the Great question, do we see in Scripture any indication that the doomed religious and commercial city-nation system ever had redeeming qualities?

Perhaps — and it is a big "perhaps."

Based upon the fact that Bible prophecy often has dual reference, usually to a local or immediate circumstance and secondly to a distant circumstance, it is appropriate to wonder if the Babylon mentioned in Jeremiah is a future reference to the Revelation chapter 18 Babylon in the following: "Babylon hath been a golden cup in the LORD's hand, that made all the earth drunken: the nations have drunken of her wine; therefore the nations are mad. Babylon is suddenly fallen and destroyed: howl for her; take balm for her pain, if so she may be healed" (Jeremiah 51:7–8).

There is the possibility that this is a reference to mention by the Lord that the Babylon to be judged was once used by God in a good way. Babylon has been a "golden cup." Of course, the next statement is that Babylon nonetheless caused the whole world to drink of her evil, thus making all earth-dwellers "mad." There also seems to be some room here to believe that there is still hope for redemption. Jeremiah says, "Howl for her; take balm for her pain, if so be she may be healed."

I believe the declaration that this Babylon referenced has been "a golden cup in the Lord's hand" could easily describe America's usefulness in the matters of exporting the gospel and of serving as midwife in Israel's rebirth in 1948. I'm not prepared to say this is *definitely* describing the United States, but that it would serve as an apt description of the way God has used this nation. In that sense, America is a mirror image of the Babylon mentioned in the Jeremiah declaration.

It is easy then, as one who loves America, to take some comfort from the following words of the prophet: "Howl for her; take balm for her pain, if so she may be healed."

Admittedly, it is nigh impossible to see how Babylon the Great might ever have a chance of redemption from her gross sinfulness, as described in excruciating detail by John. But we remember that Saul, the mass murderer of the earliest Christians, found redemption by God's grace. As a matter of fact, we can look at our own sinfulness before coming to Christ to understand that the redemptive process is far above our own thoughts and ways. Praise God!

In the same way, we might take comfort from the thought of a balm for the healing of America. If it is indeed a mirror image of Babylon the Great, it is equally troubling to consider the corruption-laden imagery that reflects from that mirror.

America the Not So Beautiful

John announces the vision as he sees the crashing down of Babylon the Great:

> And after these things I saw another angel come down from heaven, having great power; and the earth was lightened with his glory. And he cried mightily with a strong voice, saying, Babylon the great is fallen, is fallen, and is become the habitation of devils, and the hold of every foul spirit, and a cage of every unclean and hateful bird. For all nations have drunk of the wine of the wrath of her fornication, and the kings of the earth have committed fornication with her, and the merchants of the earth are waxed rich through the abundance of her delicacies (Revelation 18:1–3).

Babylon, if it was indeed once a "golden cup" in the hand of the Lord, certainly is here described as having collapsed to rubble. We don't know exactly who this city-nation commercial system was (prophetically will be) in its glory days that made it Babylon the *Great*. It is part of the description of a "mystery" and is called just that in its hellish, religious aspect:

> And there came one of the seven angels which had the seven vials, and talked with me, saying unto me, Come hither; I will shew unto thee the judgment of the great whore that sitteth upon many waters: With whom the kings of the earth have committed fornication, and the inhabitants of the earth have been made drunk with the wine of her fornication. So he carried me away in the spirit into the wilderness: and I saw a woman sit upon a scarlet coloured beast, full of names of blasphemy, having seven heads and ten horns. And the woman was arrayed in purple and scarlet colour, and decked with gold and precious stones and pearls, having a golden cup in her hand full of abominations and filthiness of her fornication: And upon her forehead was a name written, MYSTERY, BABYLON THE GREAT, THE MOTHER OF HARLOTS AND ABOMINATIONS OF THE EARTH (Revelation 17:1–5).

It seems obvious that this future Babylon the Great has at its core a satanic religion. In its final throes of collapse, this religion has become an integral, inseparable part of doing business worldwide. All merchants, kings, and everyone else are required to worship within this religious monstrosity as directed by its religious leader.

We go to Revelation 13 to better understand this blasphemous relationship. This describes earth's last and most horrendous tyrant, Antichrist:

> And it was given unto him to make war with the saints, and to overcome them: and power was given him over all kindreds, and tongues, and nations. And all that dwell upon the earth shall worship him, whose names are not written in the book of life of the Lamb slain from the foundation of the world. . . . And I beheld another beast coming up out of the earth; and he had two horns like a lamb, and he spake as a dragon. And he exerciseth all the power of the first beast before him, and causeth the earth and them which dwell therein to worship the first beast, whose deadly wound was healed (Revelation 13:7–12).

We can understand from this prophecy that the final führer will have a sidekick, called here "the second beast." This will be a false religious leader who will force all the world to worship Antichrist, who controls all buying and selling. All of this is rolled up into the entity called Babylon the Great.

Looking in the mirror of the future at Babylon the Great, can we see resemblance to the current apex nation of history, the United States of America? Our country has put forth the gospel as no other nation-state. This is true if only because we have been blessed with the amazing technologies to get the message of Jesus Christ to the whole world.

America has been the champion of Israel, seeing to it that the modern Jewish state was reborn in the 20th century.

The U.S. has been at the forefront of kindness and generosity to the unfortunate peoples of the world at every turn. Whether in war-torn, postwar Europe and Japan or in the regions devastated by any given natural disaster around the globe, this country has been the first on the scene with tremendous amounts of money and supplies to help relieve the suffering.

Until the mid-20th century, America had at its core morality based upon Judeo-Christian values emanating from the Holy Scriptures.

Even though there was much immorality within the nation, and there was increasing corruption at every level of society and culture during the first half of the 1900s, any aberration or severe deviation from that core morality was so ostracized that such evil stayed locked in the shadows for the most part except for the era known as the Roaring Twenties.

If not a "golden cup" in the hand of the Lord, America was a nation that still embraced His way of comportment for the most part.

All changed, it seemed to me, in 1962–1963 and 1973.

Prayer in public schools was banned. Bible reading, too, was banished from the classrooms of America. Abortion became the preferred way of handling unwanted babies still in the womb with *Roe v. Wade* in 1973.

From the time of those years, most every form of evil seems to have been loosed upon America. It was as if Daniel the prophet's words burst in their beginning of fulfillment during that 11-year era from 1962 to 1973. Of the wrap-up of human history prior to Christ's return, Daniel said, "And the end thereof shall be with a flood" (Daniel 9:26).

A flood of evil has descended, to be sure.

John F. Kennedy was assassinated in 1963, followed by the start of the sexual revolution, and the Vietnam War that took more than 50,000 American lives. The drug culture exploded on the national scene and two prominent Americans in the news were shot to death, ostensibly for their political views — Martin Luther King Jr. and Robert F. Kennedy. The national debt arose to astronomical heights with Lyndon Johnson's Great Society, which unleashed unprecedented spending into his War on Poverty.

The liberal mindset swiftly overwhelmed more conservative thinking, bringing about legislation and judicial appointments and decisions that moved America away from the God who had so richly blessed the country.

That inevitable, future, national train wreck has not been stopped, or even slowed. It has accelerated, as a matter of fact. Upside down thinking of politicians, judges at every level, and presidents and their administrations have helped bring at least half of the American populace to the point described by Paul the Apostle:

> And even as they did not like to retain God in their knowledge, God gave them over to a reprobate mind, to do those things which are not convenient; being filled with all unrighteousness, fornication, wickedness, covetousness, maliciousness; full of envy, murder, debate, deceit, malignity; whisperers, backbiters, haters of God, despiteful, proud, boasters, inventors of evil things, disobedient to parents, without understanding, covenant breakers, without natural affection, implacable, unmerciful: who knowing the judgment of God, that they which commit such things are worthy of death, not only do the same, but have pleasure in them that do them (Romans 1:28–32).

The United States of America does not present a "beautiful" picture early on in the 21st century. Her image, sad to have to report, could be said to, in many ways, be a mirror image of end-times Babylon. Our nation's sins are reflective of the many things that God's Word prophesies will bring Babylon the Great crashing from its prideful heights.

How Near Is Christ's Return?

Today, there is an increased number of observers of prophecy who insist that America is scheduled to be the Babylonian entity of Revelation 18. Still, there remain the majority who hold to Babylon the Great as a city-nation religious and commercial system yet to form and be centered in the geographical area where ancient Babylon was located.

Both sides of the issue seem rather insistent that their view is correct. There are few I've noticed who hold that an alternate view could be found. Both sides use Scripture effectively as a basis for their viewpoints. Both sides have logical arguments to validate their perspectives.

As stated at the beginning of this chapter, my own thinking in answer to the question is a "perhaps," which I know is wishy-washy at first glance. I would, however, ask consideration of my reason for switching from "absolutely not" to "perhaps." I would like to try to explain why I think there is a possibility that America could be the mysterious entity that will absolutely dominate the world for a brief time.

There are great scholars, living and some now with the Lord, who have held that the Word of God places the Babylon of Revelation 18 in the land of Shinar. They present scriptural reasons they believe this. I respect them and their findings. However, I must say that, upon careful study, I don't find absolute, 100 percent assurance that this end-times, humanistic, conglomerate system can't be located, at least in part, in regions other than ancient Babylon.

Rather than go into all the scriptural reasons for supporting my thesis that "perhaps" Babylon the Great could turn out to be the United States, I will just offer what I believe to be a most logical speculation in that regard. I could present many Scriptures brought to the forefront of scholarship over the years to back any of the points of view, including my "perhaps." There are a number of fine works from which to glean such scholarship.

But, I'll postulate a logical argument, with one caveat. I'm convinced that the preponderance of evidence presented by the issues, events, and conditions of today's world indicate exceedingly that the time of Christ's Second Coming is very near. This is the premise upon which I base what follows.

Remember my words earlier in this chapter: "Time's unfolding . . . always draws things to come into focus so that prophetic detail can be more clearly discerned. It seems to me that recent times have provided ever-increasing magnification, showing America's possible inclusion within these 'end of days.' "

How near is Christ's return? Most relevant to the question we are examining regarding Babylon the Great is what is the present disposition of America, particularly in the geopolitical and socioeconomic global configuration? These are questions we need to look at in order to understand the common-sense logic I'll try to present.

In consideration of the first question — "How near are we to Christ's Second Coming?" — here are some facts.

1. There is today a turning away from God and His prescription for living, even among born-again believers. Apostasy has infected this generation. The seeker-friendly forms of service that are designed to increase church enrollment, but at the expense of sound doctrine, are rampant.

2. Nations are in the process of alignment and are continuing to align in the order they are prophesied to present at the time Christ's return nears.

Gog-Magog forces, including Russia, Iran (Persia), and even Turkey (Togormah) are coalescing. They are doing so north of Israel, just as God's Word predicts in Ezekiel 38 and 39.

3. Syria is in the news, at the heart of which is its capital city, Damascus. The Isaiah 17:1 prophecy could easily be fulfilled in the days, weeks, or months just ahead.

4. Israel is back in the land God promised to it, with Jerusalem in contention by all the nations of the region. Israel's enemies are threatening to destroy her, but have been thwarted at every effort to do so.

5. Globalists are foaming at the mouth to form a new world order that will forever throw off the shackles God has placed on mankind exactly as Psalm 2 foretells.

6. The economies of the world are in total disarray, causing great distress and perplexity as to how to solve the many problems caused by the global fiscal crisis.

7. Technologies exist that can track every individual on earth, if employed as is apparently planned in the near future.

8. That technology, linked by satellite from continent to continent, will undoubtedly be used to put all the world in electronic chains and at the same time create a system of EFT (electronic funds transfer), providing a solution to the financial problems of current monetary crises. Undoubtedly, this will eventuate in the Antichrist 666 marking system of Revelation 13:16–18.

Those of us who hold to the futurist, pre-Millennial, pre-Trib perspective believe Christ's return to be soon.

All of this combines to show that this generation is very near the time of Christ's Second Advent, in my estimation.

The thought I wish to share is that since Christ's return is so near, the entity known as Babylon the Great has to be on the scene in some major form. For this great system of influence on world commerce and in every other area to have its beginning now, then come together and grow to such influence in the last seven years of human history leading up to Christ's Second Coming, just doesn't make sense.

The region where ancient Babylon sat is for the most part undeveloped. Nothing is there to indicate any sort of potentiality for a suddenly developing, grandiose world center springing from that basically barren place.

Babylon the Great, as described in the Revelation 18 prophecy, is a religious, commercial, and cultural behemoth of monumental influence on the whole world. That influence could not possibly attain that degree, couldn't reach that spectacular height, within less than several decades. I believe it would take even much longer than that to become as all-encompassing as described.

However, the world has become exceedingly wicked. In this sense, the saturation point for blasphemy and evil behavior has already been reached. Sadly, as a nation, America leads the way in the perpetration of much of that evil. No caring American who loves the nation wants to think of her in terms of being guilty of producing the sinfulness Babylon the Great will export. But, there are things about this once God-influenced country that are frightening to consider.

My friend Dr. David Reagan, of Lamb and Lion Ministries and Christ in Prophecy television programs, provides troubling facts we must face. He wrote this in 2012:

> Think about it. Since 1973, we have murdered our babies in their mothers' wombs at the rate of 4,000 a day, totaling nearly 60 million, and their blood cries out for vengeance.
>
> We consume more than one-half of all the illegal drugs produced in the world, yet we constitute only 5% of the world's population.
>
> We spend $2.8 billion dollars per year on Internet pornography, which is more than half the world total of $4.9 billion.
>
> Our rate of cohabiting partners has increased tenfold since 1960, totaling over 12 million unmarried partners today.
>
> Our divorce rate is the highest of any nation in the world.
>
> Forty percent of our children are born to unmarried women.
>
> We spend over $100 billion per year on gambling.

Our number-one drug problem is alcohol, producing over 17.6 million adults who are alcoholics or who have alcohol problems.

Our nation has become a debt junkie, leading the world in both government debt and personal debt.

Blasphemy of God's name, His Word, and His Son has become commonplace in our media.

We are the moral polluter of planet Earth through the distribution of our immoral, violent, and blasphemous television programs and movies.

We have forsaken the nation of Israel, demanding that they surrender their heartland and divide their capital city.

We have become a nation that calls good evil and evil good. And we are paying the price:

Our schools have become arenas of deadly violence.

Our prison population is increasing exponentially, from 500,000 in 1980 to over 2.5 million today. Over 7.2 million of our people are under some form of correctional supervision.

Over 1.5 million of our women are reported victims of domestic violence each year, and it is estimated that the majority of cases are never reported.

We are currently averaging over 3 million child abuse cases each year, involving 6 million children.

We experience more than 12 million crimes every year, more than any other nation in the world.

Teen violence has increased exponentially, with youngsters killing each other over tennis shoes.

Gangs are terrorizing our cities.

Even the nicest of our neighborhoods are no longer safe, requiring us to protect our homes with security systems and weapons.

Our money is becoming increasingly worthless.

Our economy is being choked to death by a pile of debt that is beyond comprehension.

Our major corporations and labor unions are in bondage to greed.

Our society has become deeply divided, splintered among competing groups defined by racial, religious, and economic factors.

Our families are being destroyed by an epidemic of divorce.

Our entertainment industry consists of vulgarians amusing barbarians.

One of our fastest growing businesses is the pagan practice of tattooing and body piercing.

Our universities and media outlets are controlled by radical leftists who hold God in contempt.

Our federal government has become top-heavy with bureaucrats who are insensitive to taxpayers.

Our politicians have become more concerned with power than service.

All levels of government have become increasingly oppressive, seeking to regulate every aspect of our lives.

Taxation has become confiscatory in nature.

Our legal system has been hijacked by activists who desire to impose their will on the people, regardless of what the people desire.

Our freedom of speech is being threatened by "hate crime" legislation.

Our forms of sports are becoming increasingly violent, reminiscent of the gladiators of ancient Rome.

Our society has become star-stuck, more interested in celebrities than people of integrity.

Our churches are caught up in an epidemic of apostasy as they set aside the Word of God in an effort to cozy up to the world and gain its approval.

We are experiencing one major natural disaster after another in unprecedented volume and ferocity.

We have become afflicted with a plague of sexual perversion, producing an army of hard core militant homosexuals.

In summary, we are a people who have become desensitized to sin, and in the process, we have forgotten how to blush.[3]

Assuredly, the Tribulation, Armageddon, and Christ's Second Coming could be many years in the future. Such an extended period could provide time for Babylon the Great to develop from the ground up.

Again, however, the signals of Christ's return are converging at a phenomenal pace. Israel is in the land and at the center of great controversy. The potential conflict with its Muslim neighbors harbors the strong

---

3. Dr. David R. Reagan, "A Prophetic Manifesto: The Death of America," http://www. lamblion.us/2013/06/a-prophetic-manifesto-death-of-america.html.

possibility of the initiation of nuclear conflagration and World War III. Zechariah's prophecy of chapter 12:1–3 seems on the verge of exploding into the headlines of today's news.

Only one conclusion can reasonably be reached, therefore. Jesus is at the very door of heaven for His return to planet Earth. All these end-of-age prophecies must come to pass quickly.

One and only one nation-state in the world at present comes anywhere near matching the description of Babylon the Great as far as potential influence. As a matter of fact, America already has achieved similar influence and holds sway in a way not unlike that attributed to that end-times entity of Revelation 18.

Dr. Reagan's masterful exposé on America's contribution to planetary wickedness is self-explanatory. Tragically, in the comparison to Babylon the Great we've undertaken in this chapter, his findings show clearly that our nation is in many ways indeed a mirror image.

The United States of America is here and now, and fits much of the description of Revelation 18. Ancient Babylon at present is basically a land decimated by the likes of ISIS. Building any sort of worldwide commercial, religious, and socioeconomic headquarters like that prophesied to be destroyed isn't even on the drawing board of new world order architects, so far as has been released for public consumption.

It is true that Dubai and other cities of the Middle East have been constructed in amazingly short time. The great technological know-how and construction capabilities have accomplished astonishing building projects. But the outreach these sites have achieved so far as worldwide influence comes nowhere near that predicted for the doomed Babylon the Great.

Building from scratch such a city and national infrastructure could conceivably take place within relatively few years. But the building of such powerful influence on the merchants and kings of the world would take far, far longer.

Is America the nucleus of that great, humanistic system of religious and socioeconomic control? I don't know. But I think, based upon the fact that it is in many ways a mirror image of that prophesied entity, it's perfectly legitimate to conclude "perhaps."

2

The Building Economic Boom

There is coming an economic boom perhaps unlike any other in history. An economic *boom*, not a financial *bust*, the opposite of which you have been led to believe.

What I will propose here will, I hope, challenge things you've been induced to think about the immediate, biblically prophetic future. My neck, proverbially speaking, is stuck out there, I guess. My proposal is on firm grounds, however, so I'm not shy about sticking my neck out in presenting my thoughts on what I believe to be most immediately relevant in terms of Bible prophecy about to be fulfilled.

My confidence comes from the fact that the God of heaven — the Lord Jesus Christ — gave the prophecy upon which my proposal is constructed.

The matters I will present have not just recently emerged to the top of my thinking. Much of it I covered in what I wrote in 2010 and 2011 through a series of essays for our "Nearing Midnight" column on raptureready.com.

The series was entitled "Scanning a Fearful Future." Some of those articles were excerpted for my book *Rapture Ready . . . Or Not: 15 Reasons Why This Is the Generation That Will Be Left Behind.* Since the time of the publication of those essays, so much has taken place that I sense we must once again address the prophecy Jesus gave while sitting with His disciples that day upon the Mount of Olives. It is vital, in my view, that we do so.

A good deal of these things are chronicled, in detailed analysis, through the essays that follow. In these, I dissect much of the day by day, week by week, and month by month issues and events in the news that I believe have relevance, prophetically speaking.

Prepare for Economic Collapse

There has been for the past number of years the constant urging by those supposedly in the know for people to prepare for the imminent collapse of the national and world economies. "Preppers," as they are called, have set in supplies for the great financial catastrophe that hovers like the Sword of Damocles. Planet Earth is moving into the worst fiscal disaster in perhaps all of history, these believe. Certainly, it will be the worst since the Great Depression of the 1930s — so the warning goes.

As I wrote in the series of articles, I received at the time (and still do) emails that express fear that the collapse will come at any moment. I will say, though, that since so much time has now elapsed from the time the warnings began to first cause panic, the incoming emails have become fewer with each passing day. The little boy who cried wolf syndrome applies, I suppose.

Now, let me say that by all common logic, the world and American economies should have already come crashing down. The fiscal laws are in a state of surreal suspension. This isn't my opinion. The dynamics of how economics work at such stratospheric levels are far above me. But some of the great thinkers in such matters say even they are dumbfounded at how things can hold together as they are doing at present.

So, I'm not poking fun at the preppers. They, in most cases, are certainly wise to make some preparation for any emergency that might arise due to economic problems. All pointers indicate that the dam holding back world financial collapse should have long ago burst.

The astonishing fact, however, is that the horrendous collapse hasn't happened. The U.S. stock market gurus show no fear as they trade at all-time highs. Governments tax and spend at rates unseen in the annals of history.

Of course, the answer from the standpoint of supposed reality is that their wizardry through electronic manipulations can perpetuate the status quo indefinitely. The perception is that all is well. Everything is secure while they juggle the economic balls within the building bubble of trillions of dollars in debt.

There certainly appears to be no panic, despite underlying stresses that should tell the "experts" that they are like Wile E. Coyote in one of those *Road Runner* cartoons. They and their financial dealings are suspended in midair over a precipitous chasm. Nothing appears to be keeping them from plummeting into oblivion.

Despite the historical fact that every situation in the past with the troubling, economic indicators of warning prevalent today has bought calamity, the juggling continues. And the bubble grows. Everything should, by accident if not by purposeful action, have by this time brought a monumental financial collapse.

Running along a parallel course with the strange, midair suspension of an economic implosion is the matter of the rumors of war. Notice I say "rumors of war," not "war."

The Middle East is a powder keg. Asia is rife with situations that could explode into conflict. From Syria and the genocidal actions of dictator Bashar al-Assad to Iran and its Israel and America-hating ayatollahs to the North Korean despot Kim Jong-un who threatens South Korea and the United States with nuclear weapons, the world should have erupted in major war by now. But it hasn't.

In looking at things through the lens of Bible prophecy, it is incumbent to ask: What's up? What do these suspensions of cataclysmic results mean?

Man himself is incapable of preventing things from deteriorating and disintegrating into all-out economic turmoil and all-out war. Mankind's record in maintaining tranquility in these areas is abysmal, as the history books show.

Tremendous tensions exist that threaten world financial collapse and portend war at any moment — war of potentially catastrophic scope and scale. Yet there seems to be an unseen force that keeps Wile E. Coyote suspended above that chasm.

Only one force can suspend the physical laws, whether fiscal or other in nature. Jesus Christ is His Holy name. He is God the Son. He walked on the waters, instantly calmed the raging sea, and defied all laws of nature by performing countless miracles.

> For by him were all things created, that are in heaven, and that are in earth, visible and invisible, whether they be thrones, or dominions, or principalities, or powers: all things were created by him, and for him: And he is before all things, and by him all things consist (Colossians 1:16–17).

Diplomats, scientists, presidents, potentates, and others in authority in the humanistic sense might believe they, collectively or individually, are holding things together. But it is the Creator of all things, God the Son, who is doing so.

Jesus Christ is preventing the world systems from dissolving and sending all of humanity into the abyss of eternity. God the Holy Spirit (third person of the Godhead) is holding back absolute evil, according to 2 Thessalonians 2. He will do so until He removes from His present office of restrainer.

The time for the consummation of history is not yet. Jesus told His disciples as much when He sat upon the Mount of Olives and they asked Him when He would come back to earth and when would be the end of the age (world system):

> And Jesus answered and said unto them, Take heed that no
> man deceive you. For many shall come in my name, saying, I
> am Christ; and shall deceive many. And ye shall hear of wars and
> rumours of wars: see that ye be not troubled: for all these things
> must come to pass, but the end is not yet (Matthew 24:4–6).

God Himself, in the flesh as He faced His execution through crucifixion on
the Roman cross as supreme sacrifice for the sins of mankind, made it plain
for them and for our present generation. God alone will determine when
the end will come. Man will not destroy the planet or himself through
nuclear war or any other way. God's prophetic plan will run its course
undeterred.

God's Next Direct Intervention

So, perhaps we can begin to answer the questions. Why haven't the world
and American economic systems come crashing down already? Why hasn't
major war erupted in these tremendously tense times when nuclear weapons threaten our very existence? Why is all of this — like Wile E. Coyote
— still suspended in midair above that deadly chasm?

I am convinced that the answer to these gravity-defying matters
involves the extreme nearness of God's next direct intervention in the
affairs of mankind.

Jesus, I believe, again gave the explanation while prophesying before
His little group of disciples on the Mount of Olives.

He explained in considerable detail the exact world conditions at the
time He would next be "revealed" on the earth. That is, He told of His
coming back following His ascension into heaven. The disciples, of course,
had no idea at that time that Jesus would die on the cruel Roman Cross,
or that He would come back following His death, burial, and Resurrection
— even though He had told them He would have to die and be raised to
life in the eternal sense.

Jesus' prophecy giving these details is key to why worldwide economic
collapse hasn't happened. The truth contained within this prophecy is the
reason major war that would again devastate the world has not broken out.
All of this revolves around the fact that His next direct intervention in the
affairs of rebellious mankind is on the verge of taking place.

But what about all the other things Jesus prophesied in His Olivet
Discourse? The seven years of Tribulation, with 21 specific judgments that
will decimate the earth . . . doesn't all that horrendous wrath have to unfold
before His Second Coming?

This is where the pre-Tribulation view of Christ's two-phase return to earth makes understandable the things I propose as cocooned within the title of this chapter, "The Building Economic Boom."

The fact is that Christ, in His Olivet Discourse, is the same Lord who gave the Apostle John the details of judgment and wrath as John wrote the Revelation. John gave the glorious description of Christ's return to put an end to the war of Armageddon (read Revelation 19:11–12).

The carnage of the seven years leading up to that final war of the age will be so damaging, Jesus said, that all flesh on earth would die if He didn't intervene to put an end to that final battle.

But Jesus, as He sat with His disciples atop the Mount of Olives that day, gave another, completely different prophetic description about how world conditions will be when He next breaks into human history. The time He speaks of leading to the moment He is "revealed" in this case indicates no worldwide devastation prior to His return.

There is no mention of the four riders of the apocalypse — of huge, celestial bodies slamming into the sea, killing all life therein — and no mention of earthquakes that flatten entire cities. Nor is there reference to 100-pound hailstones that crush everything they strike. He says quite the opposite, in fact.

Let us look at this prophecy concerning earthly conditions immediately preceding His return. It is a prophecy that indeed describes conditions much different than those foretold by John leading up to the Second Advent as recorded in Revelation 19:11–12.

Jesus, rather than giving a fearful description of great Tribulation, said the following:

> But of that day and hour knoweth no man, no, not the angels of heaven, but my Father only. But as the days of Noah were, so shall also the coming of the Son of man be. For as in the days that were before the flood they were eating and drinking, marrying and giving in marriage, until the day that Noe entered into the ark, And knew not until the flood came, and took them all away; so shall also the coming of the Son of man be. Then shall two be in the field; the one shall be taken, and the other left. Two women shall be grinding at the mill; the one shall be taken, and the other left.
>
> Watch therefore: for ye know not what hour your Lord doth come (Matthew 24:36–42).

Compare this passage with the description given by John the Revelator in writing about the time leading up to Christ's return at Armageddon:

> And the seventh angel poured out his vial into the air; and there came a great voice out of the temple of heaven, from the throne, saying, It is done. And there were voices, and thunders, and lightnings; and there was a great earthquake, such as was not since men were upon the earth, so mighty an earthquake, and so great. And the great city was divided into three parts, and the cities of the nations fell: and great Babylon came in remembrance before God, to give unto her the cup of the wine of the fierceness of his wrath. And every island fled away, and the mountains were not found. And there fell upon men a great hail out of heaven, every stone about the weight of a talent: and men blasphemed God because of the plague of the hail; for the plague thereof was exceeding great (Revelation 16:17–21).

God's Word is absolute truth. It doesn't contradict itself. So, how to conflate these two entirely different descriptions of the times leading up to Christ's Second Coming is the task before us.

Jesus prophesies in His Olivet foretelling that things will be relatively business as usual when He next intervenes. Exactly like in Noah's day and Lot's day when those men were taken to safety, with business going on pretty much as normal, Jesus will at that future time make Himself known. Judgment, like in Noah's day and Lot's day, will begin to fall upon the world of rebellious people at that very moment.

Jesus, in His resurrected form, gave John the prophecy to put into the book we call the Revelation.

So, the Lord of heaven — God Himself — gave both prophecies for us to consider.

He tells us through John in the Revelation that when He comes back with the armies of heaven (Revelation 19:11–12), almost unimaginable judgment will be inflicted upon earth-dwellers. Jesus, through John, foretells in other places in this great book of prophecy that men will hide themselves in the clefts of rocks and even beg the rocks to fall on them in fear of facing God's wrath. No flesh — meaning all life — will survive that time, Jesus had John prophesy, if He doesn't return as He is expected to do at Armageddon.

These two distinctly different descriptions by the Lord Himself can't be adequately explained except through the pre-Tribulation Rapture position, in my view. Jesus is saying that His Second Coming consists of two separate phases. The first phase will be the Rapture of all believers at an unknown time while it's business as usual — in a fraction of a second, the "twinkling of an eye." The second phase will take place at least seven years later at Christ's Second Advent, when God's judgment and wrath have all but decimated the planet.

Jesus Christ will return above the planet in the clouds in the first phase, where He will receive all believers of the Church Age (Age of Grace), living and dead, and then take them back to the Father's house (John 14:1–3).

He will return all the way to the planet's surface at least seven years later, when He will put an end to the war of Armageddon. He will continue toward Jerusalem, where He will set up His Millennial Kingdom.

I believe a primary reason we can be certain that the Rapture will be pre-Tribulational is that Jesus tells us more in the Book of Luke account about the days of Noah and Lot:

> And as it was in the days of Noe, so shall it be also in the days of the Son of man. They did eat, they drank, they married wives, they were given in marriage, until the day that Noah entered into the ark, and the flood came, and destroyed them all. Likewise also as it was in the days of Lot; they did eat, they drank, they bought, they sold, they planted, they builded; but the same day that Lot went out of Sodom it rained fire and brimstone from heaven, and destroyed them all. Even thus shall it be in the day when the Son of man is revealed (Luke 17:26–30).

In this account, Jesus says that Noah and Lot were taken out first, and judgment began that very day. It will be exactly like that, He said, when He makes His presence known.

Just as Noah and Lot were removed, so will believers be. Then judgment will begin. The believer will not have to endure any part of the Tribulation, which is God's judgment upon the wicked (read 1 Thessalonians 5:9 and Revelation 3:10). The Rapture is a *pre-Tribulation* event.

Business *Better* Than Usual!

Now we come to the crux of the reason for this chapter's title, "The Building Economic Boom."

We've asked the questions: Why have the American and global economies not collapsed? Why hasn't world-devastating warfare broken out?

Another relevant question is in order, based upon the strange developments of our specific time in human history. It is a question that has the mainstream media and political pundits of every stripe bumfuzzled, if that's a word. Certainly, they are perplexed!

But to me, the answer to this question peculiar to our current circumstance is simple. The question: Why did Donald J. Trump win the U.S. presidential election against all odds? To understand the answer, I'm convinced you must believe in and understand Bible prophecy. More specifically, I believe you must understand it from the pre-Tribulational, dispensational viewpoint.

The Trump success, defying all odds, fits perfectly within the prophecy Jesus Christ gave in His Olivet foretelling. The strange, unexpected win also fits neatly within the mystery that is at the heart of the questions posed above.

Why haven't the national and world economies collapsed? Why hasn't global war broken out?

Essays within the following sections of this book — articles surrounding the time of the presidential election — dissect some of the dynamics that I think explain the Trump victory. A chief reason is that God's people — called by His name — prayed in the manner prescribed in 2 Chronicles 7:14. God honored those prayers. The election results make that absolutely clear.

Even though those essays cover the matters involved, I want, here in this chapter, to attempt to lay out what it all means in terms of where I believe we stand as a generation on God's prophetic timeline.

In that regard, it is the *business-as-usual* aspect of the "days of Noah, days of Lot" prophecy that I wish to explore with you.

Remember that for years many economic experts have been warning of the imminent collapse of the American and world financial systems. Those warnings continue, even though most are now scratching their heads in wonderment over what is preventing that collapse. Every crisis before — all of less magnitude — has resulted in a bubble burst that brought deep recession at the very least. At least one such crisis brought on world depression.

Again, few if any of these economic gurus understand what Bible prophecy has to say. None of the financial experts in the secular world I know of have any idea of the pre-Trib view of things to come. Few, if any, who are considered authorities on economics at that high level within the Christian world have any idea, either — or if they do, they haven't expressed that knowledge.

All mainstream business news "experts" I know of don't even address the impending economic catastrophe. They go on pontificating with their punditry as if no such crisis exists.

The mystery of what's going on with our Wile E. Coyote analogy (the American and world economies) hanging in mid-air rather than crashing into the chasm, I contend, cannot be understood apart from what Christ foretold that day on the Mount of Olives. Likewise, neither can it be adequately explained — apart from that prophecy — why Donald Trump is now president despite all the hate-filled forces of the world arrayed against him.

Recently, I heard Les Feldick, host and teacher of *Through the Bible with Les Feldick,* teaching about the Book of Isaiah. He was comparing the nation composed of Judah and Benjamin, which fought with the northern tribes called Israel, with America.

The United States, he believed when teaching that lesson in the early years of this century, was running in a parallel course to ancient Judah. They each moved in a direction away from God — and paid the price for it.

He said that he talked with someone who said that if God didn't slow down the things that were sweeping America in the wrong direction, the nation would go into total depravity.

Les then said that with everything else in view — the prophetic signs of the times — there didn't seem time enough to turn things around. The best that could be hoped for, he said, was that God would slow that movement into depravity.

Considering I was listening to his words at least ten years after he gave them, I was struck by their prescience. I am convinced this is precisely what is now happening with the strange presidential election results of 2016.

It all revolves around the prophecy Jesus gave that day on the Mount of Olives about the days of Noah and of Lot.

The previous administration had observably been complicit in moving America down a track directly opposite to God's prescribed way for individuals and nations. Most obvious was that the previous president not only championed the gay rights movement, he went to the ultimate limit of anti-God movement.

Homosexuality was officially made the equivalent of or even superior to heterosexual marriage. As mentioned before, President Obama even had the White House bathed in the rainbow colors of the gay rights movement to show solidarity and to honor his commitment to their depravity. It was as if the president and those he praised for their debased activity were saying that, while God gave the rainbow to show He would not again judge rebellious earth-dwellers for their evil with floodwaters, they were showing their defiance. They seemed to be mocking any impending judgment whatsoever that the God of heaven might bring.

America was on the fast track to total depravity. That movement certainly wasn't halted. But it definitely seems to have been slowed.

Again, this is in answer to many Christians praying the prayer at the heart of 2 Chronicles 7:14, I have no doubt.

Donald J. Trump has surrounded himself with many who appear to be born-again believers in Christ. This is a welcome fact while, admittedly, the president often expresses himself in ways not in alignment with ideal Christian comportment. He has, however, vowed to defend the Christian faith as once again representing that upon which America was at least partially based at its founding.

At the same time, I believe this movement into total depravity was slowed purposely by force of heavenly edict.

God alone determines when things will reach their consummation, just as Jesus told His disciples. The end will come when God, not any of the world diplomats or others, decides. He alone knows the end from the beginning. Call it His prophetic plan, or just His foreknowledge of the future; He has put in His Word how things will be as the time of His Son's return to planet Earth nears.

The Lord doesn't give specific detail about how things will play out in most cases. But, in the case of Jesus' "days of Noah and days of Lot" prophecy in the Olivet Discourse, I believe enough detail is given to postulate a relatively sensible possibility about prophecy likely to unfold in the near future.

According to God's Word, in Noah's day, "They did eat, they drank, they married wives, they were given in marriage." In Lot's day, they "did eat, they drank, they bought, they sold, they planted, they builded" (Luke 17:27–28).

Business was being conducted in a more or less normal manner in both cases. The times seemed to be in a state of upturn, not downturn, speaking strictly of economic circumstance. As a matter of fact, I suggest that business is going on much better than in normal times.

Jesus gave the disciples — and us — all the signals to look for as His return nears. He indicated that the signs of things going on would be so magnified in their reality that they would be unprecedented in violence and virulence. His Second Advent at Armageddon would prevent the destruction of all flesh. It would be far beyond normal destructiveness taking place.

In the "days of Noah and of Lot" prophecy, the Lord likewise, I am convinced, is indicating more than normal times. His words indicate a time of business — human activity — going on that is somewhat or even significantly elevated, economically speaking.

There is no worldwide economic collapse, no worldwide depression, as some "experts" are saying. There is predicted here, I think, a great economic uptick at the very moment Jesus next reveals Himself to the world. It will be in a catastrophic way, but unlike His intervention at Armageddon.

In the days that will be analogous to the days of Noah and Lot, His judgment will begin falling. When He returns at the end — Armageddon — He will put an end to the judgment and wrath, as well as to Satan's and Antichrist's evil.

As stated before, the election of Donald Trump surprised everyone. He is a businessman, an entrepreneur, an economic empire-builder. God obviously put Trump in the most powerful office on the planet — despite tremendous odds. With all the other signals of Christ's return in place, there must be significance to the strangely profound way this election unfolded. The Lord is up to something big with the selection of this particular man.

Satanic forces are in a rage against the Trump presidency as the news media — also against Trump's administration — fully attests, if you have been listening and watching. I believe this is because Satan's one-world plans have been stymied. The globalists who are desperate to build their long-awaited new world order are enraged. Yet Trump seems oblivious to their attacks. Although he can't be classified as a *godly* man, he is most definitely *God's man* for the hour.

Stock markets hit all-time highs following the Trump election. This, of course, is all on optimistic speculation. The economic bubble is at an all-time, precipitous state. All the economic structure should burst and bring the world down to rubble, fiscally speaking.

However, instead, we sense a growing optimism, even euphoria in some quarters, that a financial boom is building. I believe it will happen. Rather than the bust long feared to devastate the economy, I believe we are about to see a boom in national and worldwide economies.

It is just in the middle of such a boom that I believe Christ will call the Church (all born-again believers) to be with Him. It will be at a "think not" time (Matthew 24:44). It will be just like in the days of Noah and Lot!

3

Putin: Gog or Evil Twin?

The Gog-Magog coalition forming is a powerful signal of Christ's soon return. It is second in significance only to Israel being back in its God-promised land.

Russia is the leader-nation of that coalition. Vladimir Putin, president of that state that formerly headed up the now-defunct Soviet Union, is a profoundly interesting character. We will have a look at Mr. Putin and at this end-times agglomerate many of us who study Bible prophecy believe will fulfill Ezekiel chapters 38 and 39.

Here is what Ezekiel the prophet wrote under inspiration of God the Holy Spirit.

> And the word of the LORD came unto me, saying, Son of man, set thy face against Gog, the land of Magog, the chief prince of Meshech and Tubal, and prophesy against him, and say, Thus saith the Lord GOD; Behold I am against thee, O Gog, the chief prince of Meshech and Tubal: and I will turn thee back, and put hooks into thy jaws, and I will bring thee forth, and all thine army, horses and horsemen, all of them clothed with all sorts of armour, even a great company with bucklers and shields, all of them handling swords: Persia, Ethiopia, and Libya with them; all of them with shield and helmet: Gomer, and all his bands; the house of Togarmah of the north quarters, and all his bands: and many people with thee (Ezekiel 38:1–6).

The Holy Spirit was quite specific in revealing this assault on Israel in the "latter days." The names of Israel's attackers, although ancient, correspond to modern geographical locations. Scholars have studied these correlations intensively. Most agree so far as the conclusions are concerned.

It is appropriate — even expected — that the individual wanting to get to the truth would question why we think the ancient names represent the same geographical areas as the modern names for those regions. Again, the findings are the result of intensive study. Ultimately, however, it boils down to a matter of faith. In this case, faith in the honest scholarship of the researchers and their many years of research findings is necessary. Those findings must be accepted or not.

That said, let's see what most researchers tell us regarding the nations that God foretells will attack Israel in the end-times assault.

The Scofield Bible, first published in 1909, furnished notes on these prophetic regions that still are the standard for today. There have been nuances of further examination, but, basically, I regard those notes as central to identifying the regions in question.

Here are some briefs of those notes:

> Magog — "From Magog are descended the ancient Scythians or Tarters, whose descendents predominate in modern Russia."

> Tubal — "Tubal's descendents peopled the region south of the Black Sea from whence they spread north and south. It is probable that Tobolsk perpetuates the tribal name."

> Meshech — "Progenitor of a race mentioned in connection with Tubal, Magog, and other northern nations. Broadly speaking, Russia, excluding the conquests of Peter the Great and his successors, is the modern land of Magog, Tubal, and Meshech."

Dr. Jack Van Impe of *Jack Van Impe Presents* television ministry writes the following about this pronouncement of the Almighty against Russia's leader of this coalition arrayed against Israel:

> The word translated "chief" in Ezekiel 38:3 is *Rosh* in the Hebrew language. For centuries, prophetic scholars have generally agreed that the word *Rosh* is a proper name. Allowing this long-accepted conclusion in the translation of this verse would make it read, "And say, Thus saith the Lord God; Behold, I am against thee, O Gog, the Rosh prince of Meshech and Tubal."

But who is Rosh?

> That was the name of the tribe dwelling in the area of the Volga and is also the word for "Russia" today in some languages of the world. In Belgium and Holland, it is "Rus."

Here, abbreviated, it's "Russ," and often appears in that form in the headlines of newspapers. An understanding of this truth moved Robert Lowth, bishop of London 200 years ago, to write: "Rosh, taken as a proper name in Ezekiel signifies the inhabitants of Scythia from whom the modern Russians derive their modern name. The name 'Russia' dates only from the seventeenth century and was formed from the ancient name 'Russ.' "[4]

This "chief prince" of Meshech and Tubal, then, if the scholarship is on the mark, will be the leader of Russia. He will think to assault God's chosen nation. It is clear then that Ezekiel was delivering a warning to the Russian prince (leader) of Meshech and Tubal.

The prophecy informs further:

> Thus saith the Lord God; It shall also come to pass, that at the same time shall things come into thy mind, and thou shalt think an evil thought: and thou shalt say, I will go up to the land of unwalled villages; I will go to them that are at rest, that dwell safely, all of them dwelling without walls, and having neither bars nor gates, to take a spoil, and to take a prey; to turn thine hand upon the desolate places that are now inhabited, and upon the people that are gathered out of the nations, which have gotten cattle and goods, that dwell in the midst of the land (Ezekiel 38:10–12).

Ezekiel calls this Rosh prince "Gog." Should we look for a leader of Russia with the name that has some form of "Gog" attached if we expect that Ezekiel 38–39 prophecy to be fulfilled any time soon?

First, let's consider whether that assault upon Israel might be in view upon today's geopolitical horizon. I'm of the opinion that most reading this chapter are fully aware that, indeed, a coalition is developing that appears eerily like that given in the Gog-Magog prophecy.

Russia, no longer the nucleus of the USSR (Soviet Union), but an entity to itself — Rosh — is front and center in the daily news. The nation is not only making inroads into the Middle East, but has firmly established both naval and interior military bases in Syria. It is in a strengthening alliance with Iran (Persia). It is on increasingly friendly terms with Turkey (Togormah). It exerts powerful and growing influence over the entire

---

4. Dr. Jack Van Impe, "A Message of Hope from Dr. Jack Van Impe: The Coming War with Russia," *Perhaps Today* magazine, March 5, 2018, https://www.jvim.com/weekly-newsletter-march-5-2018/.

region to the north of Jerusalem. All of this portends the possibility of prophetic fulfillment of the Gog-Magog assault.

Gog, leader of the prophesied coalition, is foretold to "think an evil thought." It will be the catalyst that will bring the huge, combined force thundering down into the land God promised in perpetuity to His chosen people.

The devilish thinking obviously will involve the desire to gain great riches, to "take great spoil," as the Ezekiel prophecy puts it.

The question to consider, then, is whether Israel possesses any such riches that might put a larcenous thought into the mind of the Russian leader.

Why, yes it does, as a matter of fact. Israel has discovered enormous gas fields beneath its territorial waters in the Mediterranean. There are said to be tremendous reserves of both natural gas and petroleum in areas beneath Judea and Samaria — the Golan Heights region.

However, considering all of this in spiritual terms, the physical assets — the "spoils" to be had from Israel — are secondary and even tertiary in thinking upon the coming assault. The thoughts that will enter this Russian leader's evil mind will be satanically inspired.

If Satan can destroy Israel, God's promises to protect and preserve His chosen nation will be broken. Therefore, God will be proven to not be omnipotent and omniscient. Satan's own fate will not see its prophesied fulfillment — that of his being defeated and, ultimately, thrown into the lake of fire.

Satan's idea of "spoils" far exceeds in value what Gog will hope to plunder. Victory over God, the war Lucifer started with the rebellion in heaven, is at stake. Gog, like Antichrist, who will likely lead the Western coalition of nations at the time of the Ezekiel 38–39 war, will be merely a pawn of Lucifer. Both will be totally defeated by the Lord in a supernatural display of His absolute power. But, between now and the time of those heavenly victories, planet Earth — particularly Israel — will suffer immense destruction at the hands of these warring dictators.

Many who write about and speak out on Russia and the coming Gog-Magog war bring up the name of Russian President Vladimir Putin and note his potential for being Gog. I have in fact done so myself on occasion. We notice how the powerful Russian oligarch rules the roost from his Kremlin, dictatorial perch.

He is a former KGB officer who, it is more than obvious, has clung to his former KGB ways. His political opponents have a way of dying or disappearing. We have learned in recent times of men who think counter to Mr. Putin dying under mysterious circumstances — by strange maladies, in some cases. Putin is possibly one of the richest men in the world, his worth being estimated as much as $50 billion. This is considerably beyond his earnings capability while in the KGB during the years of the Soviet domination. While his nation's economy falters, the ruble has fallen precipitously; his fellow countrymen live at or near the poverty level. Yet, he fares sumptuously.

Putin's megalomania was in full display in recent years during his dealings with the Ukraine and the Crimea situation. His bravado and prideful self-image building is a narcissistic exercise he undertakes before the cameras on a seemingly regular basis. For example, he proudly displayed six-pack abs and dove into the sea to singlehandedly find treasure that salvagers working for years couldn't find.

His propensity for aggression and boldness in promoting himself certainly qualifies his personality as an archetype for the one Ezekiel terms *Gog*. His statements that threaten anyone who intervenes further in Syria's Bashar al-Assad regime indicate his intention to stay positioned to Israel's north indefinitely.

It is fascinating to place a string on a globe of the world, pinning the string directly on Jerusalem. Then, when running the string upward (northward on the same longitude line), you notice the string crosses the spot marked Moscow.

Ezekiel prophesied about this geographical positioning, saying to Gog, "And thou shalt come from thy place out of the north parts, thou, and many people with thee, all of them riding upon horses, a great company, and a mighty army" (Ezekiel 38:15).

To revisit the question posed above: Should we look for a leader of Russia with the name that has some form of "Gog" attached? Does the fact that that designation isn't a part of Mr. Putin's name mean he is disqualified as a candidate for being that evil leader from north of Jerusalem?

We will look to one of Bible prophecy's most acknowledged experts to help us answer this question. My long-time friend, Dr. Chuck Missler, has written many books and articles on the topic of the Gog-Magog attack of Ezekiel chapters 38–39. I can think of no more knowledgeable authority.

Dr. Missler says the following, in a most interesting discovery he made some years ago:

> We refer to Gog and Magog in our study of Ezekiel 38; from the context Gog is clearly the leader of Magog in that famous prophecy.
>
> But who is he? Where is he from? Amos 7:1 reads in English, "Thus hath the Lord GOD shewed unto me; and, behold,

he formed grasshoppers in the beginning of the shooting up of the latter growth; and, lo, it was the latter growth after the king's mowings."

What does that mean? I have no idea, because that's from the Masoretic text, which is written circa 900 A.D. But the Septuagint has some information that the Masoretic doesn't. Amos 7:1 in the Greek translation reads a little differently: "The Lord hath shewn me and behold a swarm of locusts were coming, and behold one of the young devastating locusts was Gog the King."

When I discovered this, Hal Lindsey and I dug into some research. The locusts in Revelation 9 have a king, Apollyon or Abaddon, but Proverbs 30:27 says that locusts have no king. So these locusts are not natural locusts; they are demon locusts. If that's the case, then Gog, who is the king of the locusts, is a demon king.[5]

Gog, then, Missler believes — as do I — is a demon spirit that presently resides somewhere in "the bottomless pit." This entity is leader of the supernatural demon-locusts that will be released as part of the 21 judgments when God's wrath is unleashed upon mankind. This takes place during the seven years of Tribulation outlined in the Book of Revelation. Here is that prophecy:

> And the fifth angel sounded, and I saw a star fall from heaven unto the earth: and to him was given the key of the bottomless pit. And he opened the bottomless pit; and there arose a smoke out of the pit, as the smoke of a great furnace; and the sun and the air were darkened by reason of the smoke of the pit. And there came out of the smoke locusts upon the earth: and unto them was given power, as the scorpions of the earth have power. And it was commanded them that they should not hurt the grass of the earth, neither any green thing, neither any tree; but only those men which have not the seal of God in their foreheads (Revelation 9:1–4).

---

5. Chuck Missler, "The Magog Identity," KHouse.org, https://www.khouse.org/enews_article/2014/2273/print/.

    It was with great sadness I heard of the passing of my friend Dr. Missler in May 2018 at his home in New Zealand. His popular and prolific teachings for over four decades inspired, informed, and encouraged millions. For more about his ministry and his legacy, visit https://www.khouse.org/.

The Gog demon spirit, we can conjecture, has freedom at some point to indwell the Russian leader and dominate his thinking. Gog will, we surmise, give that leader the "evil thought" and convince him to lead his coalition of nations southward toward God's chosen nation. It will be a fatal decision, for God will supernaturally destroy all but one-sixth of the Gog-Magog forces, according to the prophet Ezekiel:

> Therefore, thou son of man, prophesy against Gog, and say, Thus saith the Lord GOD; Behold, I am against thee, O Gog, the chief prince of Meshech and Tubal: and I will turn thee back, and leave but the sixth part of thee, and will cause thee to come up from the north parts, and will bring thee upon the mountains of Israel: and I will smite thy bow out of thy left hand, and will cause thine arrows to fall out of thy right hand. Thou shalt fall upon the mountains of Israel, thou, and all thy bands, and the people that is with thee: I will give thee unto the ravenous birds of every sort, and to the beasts of the field to be devoured. Thou shalt fall upon the open field: for I have spoken it, saith the Lord GOD (Ezekiel 39:1–5).

That future leader of Russia and his henchmen from Iran, Turkey, Libya, and others mentioned face the direct judgment of Israel's God. The hatred, no doubt a part of much of the coalition membership, will stem from the millennia-long satanic rage against God's chosen people. The religion of Islam will be at the core of that rage, I have no doubt.

While the Russian leader has quite other things in mind — such as the plunder of all the region for petroleum and for whatsoever other riches might be stolen — the Muslim world will have one thing in mind: the complete erasure of Israel from the face of the earth. This, after all, has been the rant of most every Islamic leader since the religion was founded.

All we have to do is consider the modern wars against Israel in 1956, 1967, 1973, 1987, and other assaults to know that the driving motivation of much of that Gog-Magog force will be to eliminate God's chosen people.

Even though we see the gathering of the Gog-Magog coalition today, I don't believe the Gog demon spirit has yet entered any Russian leader's mind. That, again, will involve the following:

> Thus saith the Lord GOD; It shall also come to pass, that at the same time shall things come into thy mind, and thou shalt think an evil thought: And thou shalt say, I will go up to the

land of unwalled villages; I will go to them that are at rest, that
dwell safely (Ezekiel 38:10–11).

The prophecy indicates that Israel's guard is down and it no longer fears its
enemy neighbors. That is certainly not the case at present.

It will be at that time, the prophecy implies, that the Gog demon spirit
will enter the top Russian leader. He will receive this evil whisper into his
already evil mind. Israel will look to this Russian leader to be "easy pick-
in's," as is said.

Great changes will have to have taken place by that time for conditions to put Israel in such a deluded state of confidence in their safety.
For this reason, I believe the Gog-Magog assault will take place following
the Rapture of the Church, that stupefying moment when all believers in
Christ who are living or have died during the Age of Grace will be called
into heaven by the Lord Jesus Christ (see Revelation 4:1–2; 1 Corinthians
15:51–55; 1 Thessalonians 4:13–18).

The Rapture will likely cause worldwide calamities we can't fully
comprehend or anticipate. Jesus said in His Olivet Discourse (Matthew
24:36–42 and Luke 17:26–30) that, like in Noah's day and Lot's day, His
catastrophic intervention will bring judgment. It will happen the very day
the Rapture takes place.

Again, we can know Jesus was prophesying about the Rapture and
not the Second Advent in that instance because He said the world will be
buying, selling, building, marrying, and planting — doing all the activities of normal living at the time He will be "revealed." That must be the
Rapture, not the Second Coming at Armageddon. The world will be in
total chaos at that time of His return to earth. Perhaps three-fourths of the
world's population will have perished by then.

Therefore, I'm convinced there must be a period of time between the
Rapture and when Antichrist confirms the covenant of Daniel 9:26–27.
The Gog-Magog war is most likely to take place within this period. It
might take many months or a number of years, but there are developments
that will have to take place.

Not only will Israel have to be convinced that its security is guaranteed,
but Babylon the Great must have sufficient time to develop into the astonishing religious and commercial center that is prophesied in Revelation 17
and 18.

That considered, everything regarding the coalition of nations that will
storm over the mountains of Israel is developing at an astonishing pace.
Geopolitical, religious, and socioeconomic conditions are almost in perfect

alignment for establishment of the global order that will be ruled by Antichrist for a time.

These conditions and developments are signals Jesus told us to look for while He sat atop the Mount of Olives and foretold how and when the end would come. They are harbingers of His return to planet Earth (Revelation 19:11–12). We are seeing these signposts everywhere we look around us today.

Chief among these is the daily movement of Russia into the Middle East as Vladimir Putin gathers to himself the henchmen of Syria, Iran, and all the others who seem to match Ezekiel's predicted coalition.

Russian chess master Garry Kasparov, now living outside of his native land, said, "Russia is the most dangerous nation in the world under Vladimir Putin."[6]

He went on to lay out the reasons he believed that to be the case — chiefly that the Russian economy is in a constant state of crisis. The Russian people are suffering much of the same sort of shortages as during Soviet times.

Putin, Kasparov said, threatens the United States and the world with military might because that's the only real strength he can show. That's why Russia has in the recent past been sending bombers to near-American waters off Alaska. It is a show of force that gets Putin headlines. He thus shows the Russian people how powerful and influential he is.

Certainly, treasures to his south must be in his bully-thinking, or will soon be so at some point.

Putin, of course, isn't necessarily the Russian leader who will hear the whisper of the Gog demon spirit. But, if not, he sure looks to possibly be an equally evil twin.

---

6. Fox and Friends, May 5, 2017.

*A reminder: The chapters from here on were written
at the time noted in the chapter title.*

4

January 2015: Walking with God

The year 2015 is already bringing tremendous challenges to the Christians of this quickly fleeting Church Age. Tragically, most within the Body of Christ are walking in lockstep with the world, not with the God who sent His only Son to redeem them.

It is infinitely easier to stroll the broad way, taking the path of least resistance, rather than walking the narrow way that is often fraught with devilishly placed obstacles of carnal pleasures. God's children are strangers in a foreign, deceptively dangerous land. It is imperative to understand the minefield and quagmires we must negotiate for our brief sojourn through this earthly life. All of that said, we could not be in safer hands than in those of the Heavenly Father, who also just happens to be Creator of all things.

The great comfort is that there is no way He will ever lose even one of those who are in His eternal family. Bible prophecy assures us a glorious future beyond all we can imagine. Children of God can, however, create some misery for ourselves here on earth by walking contrary to the way He has designed. His plans for our lives are perfect, but our headstrong rebelliousness can get us in trouble in the short term. It can, in fact, lead to loss of rewards when we stand before Christ, who paid the price to redeem us.

With these things in mind, I thought it good to review some things about walking with God the right way as we enter this new year. Let's look at this matter in a sort of Sunday-school lesson outline fashion.

God Created Man to Walk with Him

Genesis 3:8: "And they heard the voice of the LORD God walking in the garden in the cool of the day: and Adam and his wife hid themselves from the presence of the LORD God amongst the trees of the garden."

Enoch, the Example of Walking with God

Genesis 5:22–24: "And Enoch walked with God after he begat Methuselah three hundred years, and begat sons and daughters: and all the days of Enoch were three hundred sixty and five years: and Enoch walked with God: and he was not; for God took him."

Enoch Pleased God

Hebrews 11:5: "By faith Enoch was translated that he should not see death; and was not found, because God had translated him: for before his translation he had this testimony, that he pleased God."

What Is Involved with "Pleasing God"?

Micah 6:8: "He hath shewed thee, O man, what is good; and what doth the LORD require of thee, but to do justly, and to love mercy, and to walk humbly with thy God?"

Liberal theologians use this exclusively to say that God is love. They don't want to deal with the fact that sin must be judged by God apart from Jesus Christ and His redemptive act on the Cross. These commandments can only be followed once a person is saved. God sees all acts before salvation as unclean, apart from being in Christ. Once saved, the Christian is expected to walk as follows:

1. To do justly: This equates to doing righteously. We cannot "do justly," or righteously, unless we know God. We must be born into His family (born again). We cannot "please" Him without this as a beginning point.

2. To love mercy: This means to have the heart of God for others. God loved people so much that He sent His Son to die for their redemption. If we have His nature, we are to grow into showing the same kind of mercy. This is a process of transformation.

3. To walk humbly: This indicates that we should always put others before ourselves. Jesus had a servant's heart while on earth. Remember He told Peter that if he didn't allow Him to wash Peter's feet, Peter was not His.

The first commandment, according to Jesus, was to love God with all our hearts. And the second was very close to that: to love others more than ourselves. The Lord said there were no greater commandments than these two.

What Is the Result of Walking with God?

> 1 John 1:7: "But if we walk in the light, as he is in the light, we have fellowship one with another, and the blood of Jesus Christ his Son cleanseth us from all sin."

1. God's Holy Spirit light: God's light is the light from the Holy Spirit. It illuminates our minds and transforms us moment by moment into the likeness of Christ. The Holy Spirit gives us the supernatural ability (the light) to discern truth.

2. Becoming one with God: We become one with God, as Christ is one with Him, automatically, at the new birth, but it's a growth toward full understanding of that walk from that point. Jesus keeps us clean before God's throne throughout our earthbound life. (He is our advocate, our mediator; see 1 Timothy 2:5.)

The Transformed Life

> 2 Corinthians 6:16: "And what agreement hath the temple of God with idols? for ye are the temple of the living God; as God hath said, I will dwell in them, and walk in them; and I will be their God, and they shall be my people."

> Romans 12:2: "And be not conformed to this world: but be ye transformed by the renewing of your mind, that ye may prove what is that good, and acceptable, and perfect, will of God."

1. Believer's life transformed: Our lives are transformed moment by moment into the likeness of Christ, the one perfect life to have walked in the flesh upon earth. This is a process.

2. Believers must consistently and constantly seek God's will. This is what transforms our lives. The will of God is ALL that matters in the context of eternity (is the only thing that will survive this earthly existence).

This is what we will earn: hearing our Lord say, "Well done, thou good and faithful servant" (Matthew 25:21).

What Is the Will of God in Its Total Context?

> 2 Peter 3:9: "The Lord is not slack concerning his promise, as some men count slackness; but is longsuffering to us-ward, not willing that any should perish, but that all should come to repentance."

1. His will is that all people come to Him in repentance: When we seek His ultimate will, we fulfill our purposes to represent Christ, so that the world will see Him and people will turn to Him in repentance for salvation.

2. His will is that believers seek His kingdom and righteousness: When we carry out our duties within this divine framework, all the needs of this life — both spiritual and of the flesh — and the blessings that are best for us will be given to us. The following Scripture says, "But seek ye first the kingdom of God, and his righteousness; and all these things shall be added unto you" (Matthew 6:33).

3. His will is that we fulfill the Great Commission: Seeking His kingdom and His righteousness are tied up in the Great Commission Christ left with us at His ascension to the Father: "Go ye therefore, and teach all nations, baptizing them in the name of the Father, and of the Son, and of the Holy Ghost: teaching them to observe all things whatsoever I have commanded you: and, lo, I am with you always, even unto the end of the world. Amen" (Matthew 28:19–20).

Our Whole Purpose in Walking with God

> Ecclesiastes 12:13–14: "Let us hear the conclusion of the whole matter: Fear God, and keep his commandments: for this is the whole duty of man. For God shall bring every work into judgment, with every secret thing, whether it be good, or whether it be evil."

Let our resolution be to do our very best to walk with God for whatever time we have left on this earth — whether in our lifetime or before the Rapture.

Israel's Self-Delusion

Israel's media — at least its more optimistic base — is peering into this New Year through its journalistic crystal ball. It is, however, a crystal ball full of opaqueness as thick as those old crystal balls that, when turned upside down and shaken, produced a snowy blizzard within the otherwise clear liquid.

These well-meaning media pundits see the present petroleum downturn for their Arab enemies as a harbinger of things to come. The downturn of the fortunes of the Islamist governments surrounding the tiny Jewish state portends great things for their nation, they believe and forecast. Chief among the upturn in Israel's fortunes is the growing respect and welcome into the community of nations — according to our optimistic journalist friends. I wish I could share their bright optimism for this coming year and beyond for Israel. I cannot.

The optimism of which I write springs from the opinion piece, an excerpt of which follows:

> Op-ed: As the Gulf States are left with no money to spend and are experiencing internal shocks, the era of destructive Arab power is coming to an end; the Israeli mind and innovation era, on the other hand, is just beginning. . . . The Arab oil era is over, and so is the destructive power of the Persian Gulf's oil dictatorships. These dictatorships have disgracefully controlled the failing Europe: Buying politicians, bribing companies, taking over the economy and gaining political power which was also used against Israel. It will take a few months, but both the Europeans and the Americans will realize that the era of the destructive Arab power is over, because the Gulf States will have no money to spend. On the contrary, they will be rocked from the inside by social, ethnic, and terroristic shocks, as they will have no money left to continue satisfying terror.[7]

The pundits base their rosy outlook on the fact that market pressures have greatly reduced the dollars per barrel for petroleum. The belief is that the United States and Canada, in particular, are in the process of replacing the tremendous Saudi and other oil suppliers as the biggest producers of the world's petroleum.

They offer as proof that this replacement is already underway, the fact that America, Europe, and other nations now ignore Arab hatred of Israel in their call to sanction Israel in the UN. The world's nations no longer feel threatened by Arab extortion — held hostage to the threat to take drastic oil-supply action if the Arab countries and their oil lobby aren't obeyed.

This punditry holds forth that many nations who previously wouldn't do business with Israel because of the above-stated extortion now are eager to take advantage of the tremendous technologies and other goods and services Israel can provide. They list such nations as India, Japan, China, and South Korea as "close friends" in this new trade era, as they infer the immediate future to become. Israel's creativity fits well as a global trade model with these and other nations, according to the optimism these members of the pro-Israel media declare.

---

7. "The Arab Oil Era Is Over," Israel Opinion, Ynetnews, January 5, 2015.

As the excerpt above entails, much of their optimism revolves around the United States and Canada's replacement of OPEC and other Arab interests as primary producers and suppliers. These pundits see continuing fracking-technologies development as keeping petroleum prices low, thus making the Arab intimidation/extortion threat no longer in effect.

We can all wish this could be the course of 2015 and beyond. We would all like very much to see Israel accepted as the wonderfully and dynamically creative nation of people that it, in actuality, most certainly is in every respect. But, the optimism, although it looks to have validity for the moment to some extent, and maybe even for a number of months, is fraught with realities that will not allow the results these journalists desire and predict.

The first roadblock is the anti-Semitism that is literally exploding worldwide. Others are an American presidential administration and State Department overtly on the side of Israel's antagonists; terrorist Islamist states and organizations devoted to Israel's destruction; and, most important of all, Bible prophecy that has reported the end from the beginning.

The latter of these factors, of course, is not at fault for Israel's end-times marginalization and hatred by all of earth's nations (see Zechariah 12:1–2). God has seen fit to tell of these things. He doesn't cause them to come to pass. He is omniscient. His reporting is absolutely unfailing in its accuracy in every detail. Punditry can and most often does end in self-delusion, as we witness daily amongst the journalists of this world system.

Make no mistake, however; God, the omniscient reporter of history from beginning to end, says Israel — His chosen nation — will be the apex nation of the world, ultimately.

This Present Madness

Perhaps you will remember a novel by Frank E. Peretti published in 1986 with the title *This Present Darkness*. The story involved spiritual warfare engaged in by human protagonists and pitting God's angels against the demonic minions. It featured prayer and biblical prescription for battle as given in Ephesians 6:12 in particular.

The 1980s brought forth growing spiritual darkness on planet Earth, just as has every decade since the Fall in Eden. The issues and events of that decade provided more than plentiful fodder for the fiction conjured from Peretti's brain. Although the book dealt with and dwelled on spiritual darkness in a fictional way, the downward spiral of morality in America and the world during that time frame more than matched that portrayed by the novelist.

On the geopolitical level, the Soviet Union became increasingly brutal in exerting dictatorship over its East European client-states. All the while, its power was degrading because of the cost of maintaining and trying to further build upon its fanatic militarism. The USSR, being totally sold out to and invested in anti-God evil, suffered the weight created by communism's ideological gravity, which pulled freedom's light into itself in much the same way a star in the process of going nova collapses in upon itself. The last years of the decade, geopolitically, indeed imposed a dark presence.

Hatred for Israel grew in the mid-1980s as Islam's chief terrorist organizations were found to have massive arsenals stockpiled along Lebanon's southern border. Israel's avowed enemies within the Arab world obviously planned an all-out assault. The Jewish state's preemptive military action pushed back for decades the insanity that we are experiencing at present. Not only Islamist hatred led by a nuclear-ambitious Iran but anti-Semitism as well now seem an unstoppable malignancy spreading globally by the hour.

And this is where the "present darkness," as Peretti would have it, has become "this present madness," as is manifestly the case in so many ways.

Satan is the most cunningly evil of all creatures, and brilliant in stratagem, as tracing his footprints while he stalks back and forth like a roaring lion, seeking whom he might devour, clearly shows. But, he is also now insane — provable by truth found in God's Word: "And even as they did not like to retain God in their knowledge, God gave them over to a reprobate mind" (Romans 1:28).

The old serpent, the devil, who is the father of lies and hates any thought of God, has a mind that is totally incapable of seeing things as they really are. His thinking is upside down and incorrigibly wicked.

Proof that he is insane is found in the fact that he knows the Creator of all things is omniscient, omnipresent, and omnipotent. God cannot lie, and absolutely knows the end from the beginning in each and every excruciatingly minute detail. Yet, knowing that God has foretold Satan's ultimate destiny — that he will burn eternally in the lake of fire — Satan still thinks he will be victorious and escape his fate. That is the supremely arrogant essence of madness.

This Luciferian madness is more infectious than Ebola or any of most diseases one could name. Its effects, I contend, are seen most observably by considering, again, the number-one signal of where this generation stands on God's prophetic timeline. I'm referring to the nation Israel and God's chosen people, the Jews.

Specifically, I'm talking about the Christian Church — a broad, evangelical portion of which has adopted or is in the process of adopting the anti-Semitism that is metastasizing throughout the world.

Despite God's plain declaration that those who curse the progeny of Abraham, Isaac, and Jacob will suffer curses of eternal consequences, a vast number of pastors and their church bodies are taking up the rant of Palestinianism, which basically holds that modern Israel has no claim to God's promises to Abraham, Isaac, and Jacob.

Church leaders and their regimes that support Israel's enemies' right to the land God granted the Jews claim that Israel, in its modern incarnation, is illegitimate and an intruder. In this way, they are falling into the same satanic trap into which the people of Hitler's Germany fell. This is, in my view, madness that is much darker than the darkness Mr. Peretti portrayed in his best-selling novel.

This madness is swiftly bringing upon the world the greatest judgment ever experienced by those who defy the God of Abraham, Isaac, and Jacob. True believers in the Lord Jesus Christ — who was virgin-born a Jew, ministered and did miracles as a Jew, died on the Cross, and resurrected as a Jew for the salvation of all who will believe — should immediately leave any church that harbors this anti-Semitism.

This same Jewish Lord of all lords and King of all kings is coming again to rule and reign on the throne of David. It will be a Jewish throne!

5

February 2015: Antichrist Archetype Emerges

Let me say at the outset of this commentary that we are not to be looking for Antichrist to appear while history is within this dispensation — the Age of Grace. Christians are to be looking for Jesus Christ, the Savior of the world, not for its destroyer, the man of sin.

That said, there has surfaced an archetype of the leader to come who will be the first beast of Revelation 13. This generation is not yet in the Tribulation, but is experiencing precursors to those last seven years that make us know that a time of unprecedented trouble is just ahead. Likewise, a leader has arisen from the area of the reviving Roman Empire, one whose emergence makes the observant Bible prophecy student suspect ever more assuredly that Antichrist is waiting in the shadows of the immediate future.

He has burst on the scene at the center of perhaps the most pronounced economic crisis on earth at present. Not only that, but the crisis is at the heart of a troubled European Union, involving Greece, the tenth nation to join the EU in 1981.

Alexis Tsipras, 40, a leftist leader of the Syriza party, was elected prime minister of Greece. His party will, it appears, have 149 out of 300 seats in the Greek Parliament as a result of elections held Sunday, January 25. The party is expected to win 36.1 percent of the vote. This is 8 percent ahead of the conservative New Democracy party of Prime Minister Antonis Samaras.

The most relevant fact to consider, for our purposes, in Tsipras' sudden emergence out of the political turmoil is the root cause of the turmoil itself. Greece is the largest, most notable nation-state to suffer from economic chaos that has required massive bailout assistance from its fellow EU member nations.

Greece continues, despite those bailouts, to sink ever deeper into an economic morass. This has forced the Greek government to implement stringent — some would say draconian — austerity measures on every aspect of Greek life. Explosive anger and near anarchy by the populace have been the result.

The point is that the new government headed by Alexis Tsipras is the first Eurozone government openly opposed to the much-hated austerity the previous one had to agree to in order to satisfy the European Union and International Monetary Fund. They imposed on Greece severe requirements as a condition of its bailout.

The charismatic Tsipras told thousands of cheering supporters in Athens, "Greece leaves behind catastrophic austerity, it leaves behind fear and authoritarianism, it leaves behind five years of humiliation and anguish."[8]

He promised to negotiate the country's massive debt, almost assuring that there will be conflict with Eurozone partners. Many of Greece's fellow EU nations see that nation as the epitome of the problem that will bring on an insurmountable fiscal crisis, if not confronted and dealt with within a near, narrow time frame.

As for the new leader, he has, in effect, declared that he will chart his own course, ostensibly pitting himself against the EU powers that be. The new prime minister said Sunday that he would cooperate with fellow Eurozone leaders for "a fair and mutually beneficial solution." He said, however, that the Greek people came first. "Our priority from the very first day will be to deal with the big wounds left by the crisis," he said. "Our foremost priority is that our country and our people regain their lost dignity."[9]

The description of his elevation to high position is reminiscent of another European's rise to power following a crisis in post–World War I Germany. Even though the new Greek leader isn't surrounded by the depression dynamics on the level of those surrounding Adolf Hitler, similarities are there in the reactions he evokes from the people he purportedly champions.

This in itself makes him a person of interest. Any such leader rising suddenly and dramatically out of the nucleus of ancient Rome justifiably raises the eyebrows of Bible prophecy students. The visible, physical reactions of those who have put him on his pedestal are quite interesting.

Reports from Athens following the elections tell of glassy eyes filled with tears of joy as the people looked worshipfully at the man upon whom they're hanging their hopes. As a matter of fact, the slogan for his campaign was "Hope is coming!"

---

8. https://www.reuters.com/article/us-greece-election/greek-leftist-leader-tsipras-claims-victory-over-austerity-idUSKBN0KY00520150125.

9. Ibid.

Those reports certainly evoke memories of some of the black-and-white documentary films I remember seeing about times during Hitler's grand, oratorical promises to lift Germany out of depression and restore prosperity and dignity. This is in no way to imply that I believe Alexis Tsipras will grow to become Antichrist. But, his sudden rise, on the shoulders of people who are in great desperation for something better, points to how such a leader as described in Daniel and Revelation could suddenly vault to power.

I think we are looking at an archetype of the man whose name will add up to six hundred, three score, and six.

World War III: The Beginning?

Some observers of these troubled times say World War III has already begun. I'm not so sure I disagree. Dynamics for the roots of war are more prolific and far more volatile at present than those that generated both World War I and World War II.

Times preceding World War I were a tranquil era, relatively speaking, when compared to those leading up to World War II. Nonetheless, the seeds of war were there. Political events, spawned by nationalist movements and burgeoning industrialization, finally disrupted the tranquility of the late 1800s. This resulted in growing, bitter rivalries for coveted areas of expansion, both geographic and economic. The assassination of Austrian Archduke Franz Ferdinand is most often given as the cause for the beginning of World War I. But, it was only the sparking point.

Decades leading up to this infamous incident were fraught with extreme nationalism — people within the various nations of Europe being taught the superiority of their own countries. Also, the people were inculcated with paranoia that the competitor nations presented dangers that, if not defended against, would be harmful to the homeland.

Ferdinand's murder lit the fuse leading to the economic-based powder keg.

World War II began building from the moment hostilities stopped in World War I. The harsh reparations imposed — particularly upon the defeated, humiliated Germans — and the depression that forced Europe and the entire world into an economic abyss brought to the world earth's most infamous despot to this point in history.

Adolf Hitler eventually defied most every war requirement slapped on Germany, building the world's most powerful military by the late 1930s. He came to full power promising to rebirth respect for the Fatherland, restore monetary stability, and create prosperity.

The point is, both world wars had at their genesis severe economic conditions.

Some observers of such things, as I say, therefore proclaim that World War III has already begun. They see as the genesis of this conflict such things as the building economic bubble of world debt that must be constantly manipulated and massaged. To ignore the problems would bring catastrophe in short order, say most economists who will admit truth about the conditions the world faces at this critical hour.

The fuse for igniting man's final conflict, so the thinking goes, could be something like what is happening with Russia versus the money powers that be at this moment.

Russian President Vladimir Putin is faced with personal loss of power if Russia's economic woes continue to spiral downward. Sanctions against Russia for their hostile actions in Ukraine and in other areas under their self-perceived sphere of influence may present reason for the bear to act like, well, a bear.

Hitler, remember, used military buildup and action to get on the road to starting World War II. This is most often the way of tyrants when faced with backing down, thus losing, their dictatorial position. Remember also Saddam Hussein, when his regime was squeezed by the Middle East petroleum powers? He thrust his supposedly elite Republican Guard military force into Kuwait, and when forced to withdraw, began setting the oil wells on fire.

Mr. Putin faces similar squeezing by Saudi and the Western powers. He could be set to do something quite extraordinary, many observers conjecture.

The thing I hear over and over — particularly from economists in the know (and these are secular economists) — is that one incident or the other will likely be the catalyst for World War III. The incident in question will pop this building bubble that is unsustainable by all measures of economic sensibility. The cascade of collateral things involved will spark seen and unforeseen calamities, including the next world war, is their dire prediction.

One who understands Bible prophecy to any extent — from the dispensational, pre-Millennial, pre-Tribulation perspective — cannot help but agree with the basic tenets of these economists' postulations in this instance. Although the secular experts who make the predictions apparently have no biblical discernment in the matter of predictions for end-times conditions and outcomes, they assuredly have it right in general terms.

There is indeed coming one specific incident that can — and I'm still convinced will — bring on catastrophe as enumerated in Holy Scripture. When Christ shouts "Come up hither" (Revelation 4:1), the cascade of calamity will begin. It is clearly delineated in the following apocalyptic passage:

> And I saw, and behold a white horse: and he that sat on him had a bow; and a crown was given unto him: and he went forth conquering, and to conquer. And when he had opened the second seal, I heard the second beast say, Come and see. And there went out another horse that was red: and power was given to him that sat thereon to take peace from the earth, and that they should kill one another: and there was given unto him a great sword. And when he had opened the third seal, I heard the third beast say, Come and see. And I beheld, and lo a black horse; and he that sat on him had a pair of balances in his hand. And I heard a voice in the midst of the four beasts say, A measure of wheat for a penny, and three measures of barley for a penny; and see thou hurt not the oil and the wine. And when he had opened the fourth seal, I heard the voice of the fourth beast say, Come and see. And I looked, and behold a pale horse: and his name that sat on him was Death, and Hell followed with him. And power was given unto them over the fourth part of the earth, to kill with sword, and with hunger, and with death, and with the beasts of the earth (Revelation 6:2–8).

Moral Relativism

By now, most everyone has weighed in on President Obama's speech at the National Prayer Breakfast that stirred the already-boiling polemical pot. Obama attempted — in his own cutting, revisionist way — to behead Christianity while using the eviscerated corpse to rub sophistry-laden salve on the somewhat wounded religion of Islam, without ever really mentioning it by name. It was the most amazing dance around bringing up the name of that religion or its founder, Mohammed, I can recall, even for this president.

His defense of the religion, whose holy book commands that infidels be murdered (yes, especially by burning in some cases), came on the heels of the fiery execution of the Jordanian Air Force pilot who had been held prisoner for months by ISIS. Finally, it seems, the Arab world has been incited to the point of turning on its fellow Islamists. Jordanian King Abdullah saw the handwriting on the wall. His people were and continue to be agitated to the point of riot. They raged through the streets with the same degree of passion against the beasts of ISIS that much of Islamist populations of the Middle East demonstrated when they turned out to celebrate the destruction of the World Trade Towers when they fell on September 11, 2001.

Obama said while standing before the National Prayer Breakfast gathering in Washington, D.C., about claims to be under the banner of Christ, "Unless we get on our high horse and think this is unique to some other place, remember that during the Crusades and the Inquisition, people committed terrible deeds in the name of Christ. In our home country, slavery and Jim Crow all too often was justified in the name of Christ."[10]

Cast aside the fact that the man who was acclaimed as being like no other in intelligence and ability to be elected president of the United States demonstrated with the statement that he possesses almost no understanding of history involving either the Crusades or the Spanish Inquisition. What staggers sensibility is his audacity that is an in-your-face embrace of Islam and its violence at the expense of Christianity's message of love. His insult to Christians everywhere has for the most part been unanswered and is, to me, stunning.

There has been a degree of reaction, to be sure, but nothing compared to what would be the reaction of Muslims if, say, the president of an Islamist state had spoken in that manner about the Mohammed-spawned religion. Turning the other cheek, maybe, applies here. But, it seems to me that it's time to show the man who would slap us in the face, or spit in our face, the proverbial door.

Mr. Obama didn't mind saying the name of Christ while pointing out that it was in that name the Crusaders went about murdering people — Muslims, he meant — as a movement to enslave while they went forth conquering with the cross before them. His tirade left out the truth that it was Mohammed's murderous armies that had raped and pillaged while establishing their caliphate on behalf of Allah, and that the Crusaders' intent was to liberate and destroy the beastly Muslim hordes. The president never used the name of Mohammed or Islam in any of his castigating Christianity in the strongest terms — just short of calling Christ a devil rather than who He is.

I mean in no way to defend the Crusaders, who often were as beastly as the Muslims they meant to vanquish. Nor do I mean to absolve the

---

10. https://obamawhitehouse.archives.gov/the-press-office/2015/02/05/remarks-president-national-prayer-breakfast.

Catholic Church of all wrong. But the Catholic Church's part in the Spanish Inquisition was most often secondary to the secular, political horrors perpetrated. Fact is, Mr. Obama either didn't know the truth about all of that long-past history, or — I suspect — purposely intended to use that history in a totally misleading way in order to defend Islam, which again, he never mentioned by name.

All of this gets me to the point I hope to make. Having been alive during the early 1960s and in college, I recognize the insidious philosophy in which Professor Obama's mind has been simmering all his years in academia. I remember all the ideological mumbo-jumbo going on in those years, long before even our current president first stepped through the doors of higher education. Let me tell you: it is satanic tripe of the first order. I'm referring to the philosophical sludge churned up from times even before Voltaire and the so-called Age of Enlightenment.

By the time my classmates and I landed in the middle of the ultimate outcome time frame of the Age of Reason, the prime directive was, in the view of academia, to question everything. It was the time of no moral absolutes, values clarification, moral relativism, and situational ethics. Truth did not come just from the Bible. As a matter of fact, the Bible was, according to Voltaire and his ilk, a book of restrictive, draconian dogma that should be avoided. One should determine for one's self what is truth. As the term "situational ethics" implies, one should determine what is right for any given situation, based upon what seems most ethical or expedient at that particular moment.

Let me tell you that young people, with hormones and everything else raging, take to heart that kind of satanically engendered philosophy of life. "If it feels good, do it" was the very well-accepted apothegm during those years, and the philosophy is embraced even more heartily today.

It is easy for one who was fed that Luciferic philosophy — that would be me — to understand how a product of the academic world like Mr. Obama can now look at Christianity and militant Islam and see both as equally responsible for atrocity. However, what makes me know that he knows better in the deepest regions of his philosophizing is the fact that he refuses to include the name of Islam's prophet or even the name of the religion in trying to say he condemns the evil that burned the Jordanian pilot to a cinder while he was alive.

The president, without any doubt in my mind, embraces the philosophy of moral relativism. His philosophizing, however, is as phony, as specious, as the Marxist dogma he obviously believes — that ends justify means. He apparently believes it is okay to proclaim while in pre-election mode that he is a Christian, then, having no voter to answer to as he enters his third year of his second term, he can equate Jesus Christ to being founder of a religion as vicious as the Islamist murderers he is determined to protect and defend.

The Bible upon which he placed his hand and took the oath to protect and defend not Allah, but the Constitution of the United States, has some very strong warning for those who come down on the side of moral relativism: "Woe unto them that call good evil, and evil good; that put darkness for light, and light for darkness; that put bitter for sweet, and sweet for bitter!" (Isaiah 5:20).

6

March 2015: It's *Déjà Vu* All Over Again

My favorite philosopher, Yogi Berra, who provides the world such profundities as "If you don't go to other people's funerals, they won't go to yours," issued the most famous of all in 1961, after watching Roger Maris and Mickey Mantle hit back-to-back home runs: "It's *déjà vu* all over again!"

I'm getting a sense similar to what Yogi must have felt upon watching his teammates hit all those homers that year — except the feeling isn't as exhilarating as I'm sure was Yogi's experience. As a matter of fact, the sense is ominous — one of history repeating as the stage for prophecy fulfillment is being set by the grand deceiver of humankind.

My view of that earlier era, of course, is through the prism of the study of history. I wasn't quite on the scene yet when it took place. I'm referring to the time when Adolf Hitler was on the rise and made a pact with his nemesis to his east, Josef Stalin, the Soviet dictator. The German and Soviet tyrants signed the German-Soviet Nonaggression Pact in August 1939. Hitler roped in his bitter enemy in convincing him to sign an order that the führer not have to worry about being opposed by the Soviets in his assault on Poland. Stalin wanted to make sure his Soviet Empire was free from war to build his military into the powerful war-making machine it would one day become.

The *déjà vu* comes into the picture in recent developments taking place between the new Greek prime minister, Alexis Tsipras, and Russian President Vladimir Putin. It is a most fascinating *déjà vu*, to be sure. And, again, it is ominous.

Much has been made in recent days of the similarities between Tsipras and the Bible's description of the person who will be Antichrist. I agree with most of the comparisons. They are striking in some instances. However, there have been many striking comparisons to world leaders throughout the centuries to what the Word of God says about that son of perdition.

Hitler was, as most everyone who knows anything about the biblical description of Antichrist understands, a dictator who seemed to fill the bill as the first beast of Revelation in many ways. The German führer came and went, however, and the world yet wags on toward its fate, with its last seven years being ruled to great extent by the actual Antichrist.

To my way of thinking, Satan has at every pivotal moment in history had a personage prepared who might be the prophesied man of sin. We've all read of them. Antiochus Epiphanes, Nero, Napoleon Bonaparte, and both Axis leaders, Benito Mussolini and Hitler. In between such powerful "candidates" have been people like Saddam Hussein and others. Franklin Roosevelt, Henry Kissinger, and even Ronald Reagan have had their names dragged through that apocalyptic mud as well.

In the case of Greek Prime Minister Tsipras, the fact that he has emerged so dramatically in a time of building economic crisis that could be earth-shaking to European environs is highly significant. Likewise, he makes his appearance in Greece, the nation that in fact spawned the Roman Empire. Important, too, is the fact that Greece was the tenth nation to join the EU — in 1981.

All this economic turmoil is going on, with Tsipras and Greece at its center, while even more turbulence engulfs Israel, the nucleus of all Bible prophecy, so far as the wrap-up of human history is concerned. To that point, Israeli Prime Minister Benjamin Netanyahu is in the world — and Bible prophecy — spotlight this week, speaking before the United States Congress about war and peace and the survival of his nation — survival which, incidentally, is God-guaranteed!

Add to this the sudden coziness that Russia's Putin says is "a warming relationship" with Tsipras, and we have something akin to "*déjà vu* all over again."

Tsipras is opposing his own geopolitical association, the European Union, to embrace Europe's longstanding and stated enemy, Russia. He is, ostensibly, making a pact with Putin in declaring that the EU should make no sanctions against Russia because he agrees, in effect, with Putin's ludicrous charge that there are neo-Nazis who are making great mischief in Ukraine. Thus, Putin has every right to meddle in Ukraine, however he thinks best.

Tsipras' new pal, Vlad Putin, recently invited the new Greek prime minister to Moscow, where he gave him full moral support for Tsipras' demand that pre-1990 Germany owes Greece Nazi war reparations of more than 162 billion euros ($183 billion). This is apparently the scheme around which he plans to begin digging Greece out of the dismal fiscal hole it has dug for itself with its welfare state. Tsipras and Putin agree that the EU is treating Greece cruelly by demanding austerity be imposed if bailouts are to continue.

It all conjures, for the student of history and prophecy, the likes of Hitler and Stalin joining in their strange collusion, while cordite odors of some great, future conflict singe one's spiritual nostrils.

I'm not declaring herein that we are witnessing Antichrist and Gog embracing on the end-times stage of prophetic fulfillment. I'm just sensing *déjà vu* while our daily headlines continue to spell out how near we must be to Christ's call to His Church.

Iran and Nukes at the Brink

Crisis is building while Israeli Prime Minister Benjamin Netanyahu forewarns of the dangers of a nuclear-weapons-possessing Iran. The world of diplomats and geopoliticians, who are proclaimed as earth's smartest people, see Netanyahu as the instigator of the crisis, not the Iranian Islamist mullahs, ayatollahs, and war planners who have stated their intention of wiping Israel from the map. It is as if complete Chamberlain-like naiveté has metastasized in the brains of those who are supposed to know how to best govern and protect the rest of us.

The Iranian nuclear weapons development has been allowed to continue while the likes of U.S. Secretary of State John Kerry proudly blusters that he has been assured that Iran's nuclear weapons achievement has been postponed for ten years. This, he says, is "guaranteed" through the signatures of Iran's Muslim leaders. These are the same leaders whose "holy" book, the Koran, tells believers in Allah that they may lie, cheat, or do anything that is necessary if it puts forward Mohammed's directive that every person on planet Earth must be made to bow the knee to Allah or else die.

According to those in the know, all this deal-making has been done without the significant input of Israel, who is first in line to receive the terrifying products of the Iranian nuclear program, should it reach fruition. Likewise, it's relatively common knowledge among those possessing the wherewithal to know that verification of the ten-year pact of non-nuclear weapons production has at best a verification process that makes the many broken deals made with Russia and China over the years of the Cold War look like unassailable agreements made with the saints of heaven.

This administration has no comparable philosophy within its strategic planning that I've been able to detect like that of President Ronald Reagan when making deals with those who want to do away with you: "Trust but verify."

Reagan was reportedly a Bible reader and a believer that Bible prophecy is truth from the Creator of all things. He surely had at the center of his thinking in this regard the following admonitions/exhortations:

> Mark 3:27: "No man can enter into a strong man's house, and spoil his goods, except he will first bind the strong man; and then he will spoil his house."

> Luke 11:21–22: "When a strong man armed keepeth his palace, his goods are in peace: but when a stronger than he shall come upon him, and overcome him, he taketh from him all his armour wherein he trusted, and divideth his spoils."

Benjamin Netanyahu is a practicing Jew, thus he bases his beliefs on Old Testament teachings. However, he is said to conduct Bible studies within his home and includes thoughts from New Testament teachings. Doubtless, he has perused the above Scripture, which, after all, is based upon Old Testament truth. He knows beyond any doubt that you cannot "trust" unless you "verify," as Ronald Reagan put it. The very fact that Netanyahu came to the U.S. Congress to lay out the critical nature of dealing with Iran now rather than later shows that the Israeli government is very close to a devastating, preemptive attack on Iranian nuclear production facilities.

Implicit within his speech on March 3 was the intimation that he does not trust Mr. Kerry's version of how to "verify," in the matter of dealing with those who want more than anything to completely destroy every Jew on planet Earth.

It is just a matter of time, he forewarned, until not only Israel but all the West, including the United States, will be in the Iranian nuclear crosshairs. This should be a prognostication that is unnecessary to even verbalize. However, the fact of such a bleak future doesn't seem to register with this administration — even when plainly stated.

The Israeli prime minister came down adamantly against the Obama-Kerry deal with the Iranians. He gave clear, unequivocal reasons why he is so opposed to this "bad" deal, as he put it on several occasions during the speech.

The Obama administration's intention to lift restrictions after a ludicrous ten-year period of the Iranians agreeing to hold off on producing nuclear weaponry was met by Netanyahu's following response — each point given tremendous applause by most in the chamber:

Before lifting those restrictions, the world should demand that Iran do three things. First, stop its aggression against its neighbors in the Middle East. Second, stop supporting terrorism around the world. And third, stop threatening to annihilate my country, Israel, the one and only Jewish state.[11]

There is little doubt after this speech — directed at the Islamist hordes more than at those in Congress or President Obama — that Israel's security is his all-consuming intent. As Iran, with 119 nuclear centrifuges in action, is on the brink of producing weapons that could indeed accomplish their vicious leaders' goal of destroying the Jewish state, Netanyahu made his own determination unmistakably clear in his warning:

I can guarantee you this, the days when the Jewish people remained passive in the face of genocidal enemies, those days are over.

We are no longer scattered among the nations, powerless to defend ourselves. We restored our sovereignty in our ancient home. And the soldiers who defend our home have boundless courage. For the first time in 100 generations, we, the Jewish people, can defend ourselves.

This is why — this is why, as a prime minister of Israel, I can promise you one more thing: Even if Israel has to stand alone, Israel will stand.[12]

Again, we notice with great interest that the prophet Ezekiel foretells that Persia (Iran) will come with the forces of Magog (Russia and others) in an all-out assault on Israel. They do so with conventional forces, not nuclear. They obviously have not nuked Israel by the time they launch this attack. I conclude that, somewhere along the line, Persia (Iran) has either failed to develop nuclear weapons, or that capability has been neutralized in some way. If they get those weapons, they will almost certainly use them, and their first target will almost just as certainly be Israel.

Whether the Israeli Defense Force takes them out — an action that would almost assure Israel would instantly reach Zechariah 12:1–3 status — or it is an act of God, it appears from Bible prophecy that Iran and its grand plans to use atomic weapons against the Jewish state will never happen.

---

11. https://www.washingtonpost.com/news/post-politics/wp/2015/03/03/full-text-netanya-hus-address-to-congress/?noredirect=on&utm_term=.ff7abb82acea.
12. Ibid.

America is at a crossroads in its dealing with God's chosen nation. There is no such God-guaranteed prophetic protection given any other nation than Israel.

Our Congress — at least a great portion of that body — responded for the most part with tremendous approval of the things Bibi spoke on Tuesday, March 3, 2015. I'm encouraged by that response.

Antichrist Assumptions

Declarations about Bible prophecy's most evil (likely human) character are slashing through this time of end-of-the-age stage-setting. I say "likely human" because there is a looming question mark within my own cogitations about whether Antichrist will indeed be strictly human. Those who continue to hold to the beast of Revelation 13 as eventually emerging out of the revived Roman Empire are increasingly being viewed as in error. Many prophecy watchers now see that evil entity as a Muslim in waiting somewhere in the foreboding future. The deadly violence that is growing by the day, with ISIS (or ISIL) at the core of militant Islam's rage across the region that beastly horde infects, is proof that it will be an Islamist Antichrist who will one day soon be the man of sin of 2 Thessalonians 2:3 — the Muslim Antichrist chroniclers declare.

These Eastern-leg Antichrist adherents hold that the Bible prophecy students and scholars who have for centuries interpreted Daniel 9:26–27 as indicating the prince that shall come is to be of Roman geographic origin have been demonstrably wrong. The horrific events of today's Islamist, genocidal rampage as proof is implicit within their railing against the long-held Roman Antichrist view. These give as their scriptural proof the fact that the world's final, evil dictator is referred to as "the Assyrian." And, there is no denying it. God's Word does indeed call this coming tyrant "the Assyrian."

One such adherent to the Muslim Antichrist view gave the following Scriptures as proof the view is the correct one:

> Isaiah 10:24–25: "Therefore thus says the Lord God of hosts: 'O My people, who dwell in Zion, do not be afraid of the Assyrian. He shall strike you with a rod and lift up his staff against you, in the manner of Egypt. For yet a very little while and the indignation will cease, as will My anger in their destruction' " (NKJV).

> Isaiah 14:25–26: "That I will break the Assyrian in My land, and on My mountains tread him underfoot. Then his yoke

shall be removed from them, and his burden removed from their shoulders. This is the purpose that is purposed against the whole earth, and this is the hand that is stretched out over all the nations" (NKJV).

Micah 5:3–6: "Therefore He shall give them up, until the time that she who is in labor has given birth; then the remnant of His brethren shall return to the children of Israel. And He shall stand and feed His flock in the strength of the LORD, in the majesty of the name of the LORD His God; and they shall abide, for now He shall be great to the ends of the earth; and this One shall be peace. When the Assyrian comes into our land, and when he treads in our palaces, then we will raise against him seven shepherds and eight princely men. They shall waste with the sword the land of Assyria, and the land of Nimrod at its entrances; thus He shall deliver us from the Assyrian, when he comes into our land and when he treads within our borders" (NKJV).

The modern territories that encompass those geographic areas out of which the Assyrian (Muslim) Antichrist will come conquering like in ancient times — according to the adherents' view — include the following: Israel, parts of Iraq and Iran, Armenia, sections of Egypt and Turkey, Syria, and Jordan.

"The beast" will, they proclaim, emerge from the Middle East, not Europe. Scripture and current geopolitical, religious, and military trends are in agreement, they declare. Antichrist will be Muslim, or at least will initially hold to the religion of Mohammed and Allah as long as doing so is to his advantage while he acquires power.

Now to look at another currently metamorphosing geopolitical matter. It is a development that at least some of the major Muslim Antichrist adherents have come down hard on in recent days. I refer to the sudden, meteoric rise of Alexis Tsipras as prime minister of Greece. He is a young, physically attractive, charismatic leftist who has ignited the anti-austerity fire under the kindling that is the Greek populace. Some describe his appearances in conducting public rallies as very much like those conducted by the young Adolf Hitler while he was in the process of emerging during the 1930s within a Germany whose people were suffering dire economic circumstances.

I state again here so there is no mistake: I am not indicating that I believe this man is the one who will be Antichrist. I am simply stating that this seems to me to be the sort of man, under similar circumstances, who will one day erupt on the scene of a world quite desperate for an economic savior, one who will bring peace to a world about to explode in man's final war.

Alexis Tsipras, as I wrote previously, is an archetype of the man who will be Antichrist. Point is, he could, even if not likely, be that man himself. It is possible, based upon surrounding global circumstances and upon his origins.

This is not possible, according to the Muslim Antichrist adherents. Tsipras is Greek, not of Middle Eastern extraction. However, it was recently pointed out to me by an Egyptian Muslim scholar, no less, that the name Tsipras is not Greek, but Turkish. The professor wrote, "This causes a misspelling in several Western languages that adopt direct transliteration from Greek (Tsipras/Τσίπρας)."[13] In fact, in Turkish, this name is written "Çipras."

Turkey, of course, is the present state in the vast geographical area encompassed by ancient Assyria.

Alexis Tsipras, as is obvious, is not in a direct way part of the region once known as Assyria. He is a Greek citizen now elected to the nation's highest governmental position. He resides smack in the middle of the area from which the Roman Empire was spawned. Yet his ancestry is from that region with which Antichrist is associated, according to the prophets Isaiah and Micah.

The new Greek prime minister thus fits the Daniel 9:26 prerequisite. He has an ancestral resume compatible with Bible prophecy regarding the prince that shall come.

I concluded quite some time ago, after studying the Son of Perdition's genealogy — admittedly only in a cursory way — that Antichrist will be a Roman by geographical residence. At the same time, I've believed he will come from the Middle East (be an Assyrian) by ethnic extraction. This is precisely the model presented by this archetype named Alexis Tsipras or Çipras, as our Egyptian professor has informed.

I again emphasize that I'm not saying I think he will one day be Antichrist. I would never make such an assumption, as we as believers of the Church Age have no basis upon which to make such a claim. We are to look for our Lord and Savior Jesus Christ, not for the beast of Revelation 13. We will be kept out of the time when Antichrist wreaks havoc on a judgment-deserving world.

We are, however, commanded by the Lord Himself to "watch."

---

13. https://nevrapture.blogspot.com/2015/03/nearing-midnight-updates-from-todd.html?m=0.

We will keep doing just that while the road to Antichrist's regime continues to be paved by current issues and events.

China's Prophetic Action

Sino-American interaction — or perhaps better put, the lack of America's interaction — might have just taken on prophetic relevance. The nation, symbolized by the dragon, we know, will likely be one of the key players while rebellious mankind carries out the final acts of human history. There is some well-founded conjecture that China has prepared to fire the powerful volley that could eventually help bring America down as the greatest economic power on earth.

The story has yet to take on major emphasis by mainstream news, but look for it to grow in the near future. The news is not insignificant:

> BEIJING — At least 35 countries will join the China-led Asian Infrastructure Investment Bank (AIIB) by the deadline of March 31, the bank's interim chief, Jin Liqun, said on Sunday. Currently, India, Indonesia and New Zealand have expressed interest in joining the bank, he told a conference in Beijing, following a request by Britain, France, Italy and Luxembourg to become founding members. "By deadline, (we believe) 35 countries, or more, will become founding members of the bank," he said.[14]

The Chinese government has been rumored for many months to be working to undermine U.S. top-nation economic status and the American dollar's position in the monetary world. That there is a grab by China to secure as much gold as possible is no secret. They are making deals with Russia and others for buying gas and oil, thereby, it is thought, working to marginalize U.S. involvement and influence. It is believed they are attempting to set up an economic system, which they would, of course, head — totally separate from American interaction.

It is worrisome to many within the world of economics that China holds so much of America's debt. Fears are that their manipulation of a tremendous amount of U.S. Treasury bonds will one day be used to help crash America's economy.

One concern that China is doing all it can to gather world economic power to itself is its reaching out to traditional enemies such as South Korea and Japan. The three nations met recently, ostensibly to work out

14. Reuters, March 23, 2015.

territorial and diplomatic disputes. They agreed to continue to establish a trilateral series of meetings, and it is thought that the purpose of the meetings will be to secure stronger economic ties.

The dragon nation has proven to be one that is among the worst in the area of human rights. Its many atrocities show the leadership is led and inspired by a dragon of even more virulence — the great, red dragon, Satan.

Again, when considering the often-examined fact that America is mentioned nowhere in Bible prophecy, we must ask whether this current push by China to garner economic power at America's expense is yet another element of the end-times formula for bringing the United States down.

China, of course, is also not mentioned by name in Bible prophecy. However, is there much room for doubt that the dragon nation is there by inference?

I believe that China as the major end-times prophetic nation from the Orient is presented primarily in two places in the Book of Revelation. The first is found in the ninth chapter:

> And the sixth angel sounded, and I heard a voice from the four horns of the golden altar which is before God, saying to the sixth angel which had the trumpet, Loose the four angels which are bound in the great river Euphrates. And the four angels were loosed, which were prepared for an hour, and a day, and a month, and a year, for to slay the third part of men. And the number of the army of the horsemen were two hundred thousand thousand: and I heard the number of them (Revelation 9:13–16).

The prophet John expanded upon the foretelling in chapter 16:

> And the sixth angel poured out his vial upon the great river Euphrates; and the water thereof was dried up, that the way of the kings of the east might be prepared. And I saw three unclean spirits like frogs come out of the mouth of the dragon, and out of the mouth of the beast, and out of the mouth of the false prophet. For they are the spirits of devils, working miracles, which go forth unto the kings of the earth and of the whole world, to gather them to the battle of that great day of God Almighty (Revelation 16:12–14).

The king of the kings of the East — unless something very dramatic happens to change the configuration of things east of the Euphrates — has to be China. It could, by itself, have manned a 200-million-soldier army even as far back as the 1970s. Today, with the other nations of Asia and their massive populations, the 200-million figure presents no problem at all so far as potential for fulfillment of the prophecy is concerned. And, certainly, China exerts hegemony over all the other nations of its oriental sphere. Many within secular news media are beginning to recognize the same things those who watch Bible prophecy and current events have been recognizing for some time: China indeed looks like a major influence on factors that might bring about profound changes in the world.

Ironically, it is America and its rapidly fading wealth that has in effect funded the outfitting of that massive army that will one day destroy one-third of the world's population.

7

April 2015: Good Advice for Israel
— Sort of . . .

We remember how Vice President Dan Quayle was raked over the coals by mainstream media types who delighted in going on incessantly about each and every verbal gaffe he made. Actually, Quayle was an attractive young man who spoke well and was quite accomplished in life, serving, of course, as a senator from Indiana before joining the first Bush-Quayle campaign.

But, he is forever stigmatized as the guy who couldn't spell potato. For that and other insignificant verbal stumbles, he was assaulted in the press and through entertainment shows day after day.

The same thing was done earlier to Gerald Ford, Richard Nixon's vice president, who was then president when Nixon resigned. The mainstream news and entertainment venues made fun of Ford at every opportunity, like when he tripped exiting an airplane and was caught by a Secret Service agent or someone. Another time, he hit a golf ball off the tee and it went awry, hitting someone among the onlookers.

Chevy Chase of *Saturday Night Live* launched his comedy career mimicking Ford and his supposed clumsiness during those years. In actuality, Ford was, in his younger years, a superb athlete, starring at the University of Michigan in football.

Now we have a vice president who makes gaffes that make Quayle look like Shakespeare and Ford look like Mikhail Baryshnikov, the Russian ballet star. But, the media hounds, because Joseph Biden is of the same untouchable political ideology as they, say nothing more than, "Well, that's just Joe." It's much like they see him as an eccentric old uncle who amuses them, but as nothing about which to get political.

Mr. Biden weighed in on the nation of Israel, and his advice to Jews and their place in the world is, well, classic Old Joe.

Vice President Joe Biden told a gathering of prominent American Jewish officials last fall (fall 2014) that they should look to Israel — and not the United States — as the ultimate guarantor of their community's long-term safety.

The surprising remarks, made during a Rosh Hashanah celebration attended by government officials and members of Congress, were reported by *Atlantic* journalist Jeffrey Goldberg in a recent article about the future of European Jewry.

Biden said, "I had the great pleasure of knowing every prime minister since Golda Meir, when I was a young man in the Senate, and I'll never forget talking to her in her office with her assistant — a guy named Rabin — about the Six-Day War," he said. "The end of the meeting, we get up and walk out, the doors are open, and . . . the press is taking photos. . . . She looked straight ahead and said, 'Senator, don't look so sad. . . . Don't worry. We Jews have a secret weapon.'"

Then Biden recalled asking Meir what the secret weapon was. "I thought she was going to tell me something about a nuclear program," Biden said. "She looked straight ahead and she said, 'We have no place else to go. We have no place else to go.'"

"Folks, there is no place else to go, and you understand that in your bones. You understand in your bones that no matter how hospitable, no matter how consequential, no matter how engaged, no matter how deeply involved you are in the United States . . . there's only one guarantee. There is really only one absolute guarantee, and that's the state of Israel. And so I just want to assure you, for all the talk, and I know sometimes [President Barack Obama] gets beat up a little bit, but I guarantee you: he shares the exact same commitment to the security of Israel."[15] If a politician or anyone else of notoriety from another ideological mindset had said something about, for example, African-Americans and their ties to the continent of Africa, hinting that they should just go back there, I'll just leave it to the imagination what would happen to that person.

But, it was Joe Biden who said it, talking about the pariah state, Israel, so there's nothing to see here.

Biden knows Barack Obama's feelings about Israel. The president's attitude has been made transparently clear to all of us, as his administration's hashtag would have it. He is obviously determined to completely change American policy toward the Jewish state. Biden was being disingenuous in part of his remarks when he advised those Jews at the gathering on Rosh

---

15. Jpost.com staff, "Biden Told US Jews that Israel — Not America — Guaranteed Their Security," *Jerusalem Post*, March 30, 2015.

Hashanah that they should think about going to Israel — one supposes, in order to avoid some sort of coming trouble. His disingenuousness, however, did not include his advice that Jews think about leaving.

We remember the late journalist Helen Thomas, who, in a moment of senility, said the Jews should "get the he** back to the nations they came from." This is a mindset that pervades media and many within this administration. They, unlike Old Joe and Ms. Thomas, just haven't come to the point they can no longer govern verbalization of their dislike for Israel.

Actually, the advice to those of the House of Israel to think about going to Israel is prophetic in its import. There is coming a time when hatred for the Jews of the world will be greater than any previous time in history. Read Jeremiah 30:7, for example.

Jesus Himself said it would be a time worse than any that has ever been or would be again. He was speaking primarily of the time of Tribulation as it would be for Israel. Read Matthew 24:21.

We see that hatred building today across America and the world:

> On Monday, the Anti-Defamation League released its annual Audit of Anti-Semitic Incidents showing a slight increase in 2014 over the previous year in Florida and a huge jump nationwide.
>
> Middle East tensions may have exacerbated anti-Semitism, said Hava L. Holzhauer, Anti-Defamation League's Florida regional director. . . .
>
> In September, a banner outside of Miami Beach's oldest Conservative temple, Temple Emanu-el, was vandalized with swastikas. "The message is clear. It's a message of hate and intolerance," said Temple Emanu-el Rabbi Marc Philippe at the time. "And whenever you have intolerance, you have problems."[16]

The advice old Joe Biden gave totally misses the mark, as any well-grounded Bible prophecy student will understand. Israel — as all mankind — should not put our reliance for safety in security provided by the nations of the world. God is our only place of safety and refuge: "Behold, he that keepeth Israel shall neither slumber nor sleep" (Psalm 121:4).

Rebels with a Cause

Unlike the teenagers of the movie *Rebel Without a Cause* (starring James Dean), who didn't know why they were rebels, a growing number of people

16. http://www.miamiherald.com/news/state/florida/article16943411.html.

among this generation are rebels with a cause. That cause is an ancient one, led by the most hate-filled of all rebels. And the cause is twofold: hatred for mankind in general and for the Jewish race in particular.

Satan, the original rebel, determined that he had no equal. He could not abide the Creator bringing into existence a creature that would share his importance in the eyes of God. Iniquity was found in him, and he determined that he himself was equal in glory and magnificence to the Creator, thus was as powerful and would magnify himself and put himself above the throne of God. Isaiah the prophet tells the story:

> For thou hast said in thine heart, I will ascend into heaven,
> I will exalt my throne above the stars of God: I will sit also
> upon the mount of the congregation, in the sides of the north:
> I will ascend above the heights of the clouds; I will be like the
> most High (Isaiah 14:13–14).

This rebel has had as chief among his causes to destroy the creature he saw as his rival for preeminence. Once cast from heaven, he entered the Garden of Eden and set about to do just that. Our history books are replete with a record that traces the old serpent's trail. He has observably inflicted great damage, as is witnessed by our daily headlines. He has had no problem enlisting in his cause many of those who share in his rebellious hatred for anything and everything the God of heaven has set in place.

We, every hour, see his influence and his recruits' acquiescence to Satan's hatred for all things godly. Without reservation, I include in his army of rebels those who rage against anyone who opposes inflicting homosexuality on our society and culture. I include anyone who believes it is preferable to murder babies in the womb so that life can be more convenient for those who don't want the babies, only the carnal pleasure involved in procreating them.

Homosexuality and abortion bring to the war against humanity the insidiously clever methodologies Satan employs in conducting the battles he and his army wage daily. In each "cause" — homosexuality and abortion — the destruction of human life and prevention of human life through the perversion of sodomy are presented as nothing more or less than the right of the individual to choose what is right. Who is this God that He should interfere with man's business?

Part of the cause Satan has inspired his army of rebels to push in the war on mankind involves the whole matter of population control. Abortion and homosexuality aren't doing away with mankind quickly enough.

Here again, the evil genius of Lucifer is seen at work. Mankind must be taken off the planet so life can be better and survivable.

Officials within the United Nations are pushing the notion that the human population should be reduced in order to combat climate change. The longstanding notion has been continually pushed by Christiana Figueres, the executive secretary of the United Nations Framework Convention on Climate Change (UNFCC). In 2013, Figueres had a conversation regarding "fertility rates in population" as a contributor to climate change.[17] The other major assault in Satan's never-ceasing war against God and mankind is inspiring hatred against the Jewish race. This hatred is an easily traceable anger that began in Eden: "And I will put enmity between thee and the woman, and between thy seed and her seed; it shall bruise thy head, and thou shalt bruise his heel" (Genesis 3:15).

This, of course, is when God promised to send a Savior to redeem fallen man from sin. Satan and his schemes to oppose God at every turn and exalt himself above the God of heaven would be thwarted by this person who would eventually be born into God's creation called man. This happened when Jesus was born through the virgin birth to a young girl from the house of Israel. The Jewish people were chosen to bring the Christ into the world.

Satan hates all of mankind, but his hatred has been, throughout the ages, particularly focused on the progeny of Abraham, Isaac, and Jacob (whose name was changed to Israel). This is just as the prophet Zechariah foretold, as recorded in Zechariah 12:1–3. Hatred is becoming more violent the closer we get to the wrap-up of this dispensation (the Age of Grace).

This rebellious spirit against Israel, through whom the Savior was born, leaps at the observer more and more often through incidents such as the following:

> They were dressed in their team's colors and chanting passionately and excitedly — the only problem was they weren't in the stadium cheering on their team. Bosnian soccer fans who were in Vienna, Austria, on Friday for a match between Austria and Bosnia-Herzegovina chanted "Kill the Jews" alongside pro-Palestinian demonstrators in central Stephanplatz square before heading to the game. It was a frightening spectacle that proved anti-Semitism is still a jarring reality in Europe.

17. "UN Climate Change Official Says 'We Should Make Every Effort' to Depopulate the Planet," Rapture Ready News, April 8, 2015.

At first they stood calmly and shouted "Free Palestine" back and forth. Then, one can hear a single voice among the protestors shout out "Kill the Jews." The calls to violence swelled as the other protestors joined. In a swarm of rage, they began to jump up and down shouting "Ubij, ubij Zidove," which means "Kill, kill the Jews."[18]

The army of rebels is growing, and so is the scope and virulence of their cause — to fulfill Satan's end-times assault on Israel and, incidentally, on true Christians.

Israel in the Eye

It is striking, yet not much is said about it among prophecy observers, as far as I've found. A tremendous storm is brewing in the Middle East, and lesser, troubled winds are stirring all around the planet. What I believe to be the end-times hurricane is building. The one place where there seems a relative calm is within the focal nation of the world, from God's perspective.

Israel looks out upon the swirling winds that wreak deadly havoc upon regions to their north and east while the likes of ISIS (ISIL) beheads Christians and anyone else who doesn't agree with their brand of Islam. Saudi and others prepare to oppose assaults from a number of enemies who want their oil riches, while the terrorist organizations build and stockpile war-making tools.

Israel looks out upon Iran, while their once staunch ally, the United States, foolishly, as if under delusion, bargains away Israel's security from nuclear threat. Russia's Putin, stung by sanctions because of his aggressive behavior, glares angrily at Russia's neighbors and looks lustfully southward at the region where oil and gas fields diminish his own source of revenue to rebuild Soviet-style military might. America's president puts the Jewish state and its much personally disliked prime minister last on his priority list of things to do in trying to prevent conflict in the Middle East.

It's as if the whole world is pretending not to notice little Israel. Mainstream news media are complicit in deliberately looking the other way while Israel looks out from its precarious position in the calm center of the brewing storm and comments on its plight, unable to have its voice heard by those who count in terms of international community movers and shakers.

---

18. Courtney O'Brien, "Chilling: Bosnian Soccer Fans Join 'Kill the Jews' Chant in Vienna," *The Guardian*, Townhall.com.

The words seem calmly put, but beneath the surface utterances is an ominous undertone of the phrase "Never Again."

This portentous, subliminal message was made starkly manifest with last week's Iranian Army Days Celebration. Benjamin Netanyahu framed the objections the Israeli government has to things going on in regions all around his threatened country.

He protested, particularly, the Russians supplying the S-300 missiles to Iran when the Iranian regime is ramping up its threats. The Israeli prime minister derided the fact that there is no reference to Iran's stepped-up aggressiveness in the P5+1 major powers' dealing with Iran regarding their nuclear program.

The Iranian chess masters almost remind me of the Iron Sheik, a professional wrestler of the 1980s who was really an Iranian who defected from the despotic regime of Ayatollah Ruhollah Khomeini. The bad guy (Iron Sheik) would protest that he had nothing nefarious in mind while he tried to get past the referee to inflict damage on his opponent with illegal tactics.

Iranian President Hassan Rouhani, following the immensely enhanced 2015 version of Iran's military, which passed in review during the Army Day parade in Teheran on Saturday, April 18, said about the massive S-300 missiles from Russia, "[They are part of our] strategy of deterrence in order to prepare for peace and security in Iran and the Middle East. . . . Our method of action is defense and not offense."[19]

The intrigues in the matter of Iran vs. Israel are, of course, not a sports entertainment soap opera. It is a deadly serious, end-times chess game with potentially deadly serious consequences to the winners and losers.

The Israeli prime minister is not under the delusion that the rest of the world's leaders seem to be. He framed his clear understanding of the situation as it exists:

> "Yesterday we saw the military parade in Tehran and Iran's exhibition of weapons to the world," Netanyahu said. "Every year the missiles are bigger and enhanced — in accuracy, strength and deadliness. However, one thing does not change. What does not change is the inscription 'Death to Israel' on the missiles."[20]

Mr. Netanyahu's words were calm, without equivocation. He looks out upon the storm swirling about his beleaguered nation that sits in the

---

19. https://www.timesofisrael.com/iran-marks-army-day-with-cries-of-death-to-israel-us/.
20. https://www.jpost.com/Israel-News/PM-on-Russian-missiles-to-Iran-Every-year-the-missiles-get-bigger-more-accurate-more-deadly-398550.

storm's eye. But, the subliminal warning to the rest of the world must not be ignored: "Never Again."

We learned this past week that Netanyahu's claim is true that Iran could be as close as not even ten years to developing uranium enrichment for a bomb, but in actuality, it is only two to three months away from their goal. Now, the Obama administration is agreeing that that claim, scoffed at by media and by the administration, was exactly right.

The administration apparently decided to bring the truth of the matter to light because they want, due to the critical time the world faces for Iran's nuclear breakthrough, to pressure the Senate to rubber stamp Obama's deal with the Iranians. This, in some sort of ludicrous, convoluted rationale, supposedly convinces the administration that the deal will forestall the bomb's near-time production.

And Israel sits in the eye of the storm that is coming ever closer. "Never Again" is the refrain that can be heard eerily echoing within the increasing winds of war.

8

May 2015: Listening for the Midnight Cry

The purpose of the section of the Rapture Ready website termed "Nearing Midnight" is to chronicle issues and events of the current times in order to forewarn that the call of Christ to His Bride, the Church (see John 3:3), is near.

We can say this with certainty because of the many signals given off by those issues and events. These look to be the prophetic signs of the coming Tribulation period — human history's last seven years leading to the return of Christ to planet Earth at the time of Armageddon. Jesus said, "And when these things begin to come to pass, then look up, and lift up your heads; for your redemption draweth nigh" (Luke 21:28).

Paul the Apostle wrote about this moment of redemption: "For the Lord himself shall descend from heaven with a shout, with the voice of the archangel, and with the trump of God: and the dead in Christ shall rise first: Then we which are alive and remain shall be caught up together with them in the clouds, to meet the Lord in the air: and so shall we ever be with the Lord" (1 Thessalonians 4:16–17).

John, "the beloved disciple," wrote from his exile on Patmos about his vision of that moment of redemption: "After this I looked, and, behold, a door was opened in heaven: and the first voice which I heard was as it were of a trumpet talking with me; which said, Come up hither, and I will shew thee things which must be hereafter" (Revelation 4:1).

This shout from Christ Himself is likened to the moment when the midnight hour of human history has been reached. The black, boiling clouds of the Tribulation will have shrouded the whole planet in a veil of God's wrath because of man's rebellion. We see that moment as represented in the parable of the ten virgins: "And at midnight there was a cry made, Behold, the bridegroom cometh; go ye out to meet him" (Matthew 25:6).

Despite all the seminary-degreed protests to the contrary, this is the same moment Jesus prophesied in the Olivet Discourse, in what I believe is the most profound declaration about this midnight hour at which time He will next catastrophically intervene in man's history. I refer to the Lord's foretelling the coming judgment at the time of the Rapture, as given in the following. Note that Jesus prefaces His prophecy by saying, "But of that day and hour knoweth no man, no, not the angels of heaven, but my Father only" (Matthew 24:36).

The Rapture is an unknown time; it is imminent — can happen at any moment. The Second Advent can be counted down, because a precise number of days is given to the time Christ returns at Armageddon. The Lord then gives a description of what the world will be like at that hour unknown by anyone but His Father:

> But as the days of Noah were, so shall also the coming of the Son of man be. For as in the days that were before the flood they were eating and drinking, marrying and giving in marriage, until the day that Noe entered into the ark, And knew not until the flood came, and took them all away; so shall also the coming of the Son of man be. Then shall two be in the field; the one shall be taken, and the other left. Two women shall be grinding at the mill; the one shall be taken, and the other left. Watch therefore: for ye know not what hour your Lord doth come (Matthew 24:37–42).

Most of my theologically degreed friends — and I love them as my brothers in Christ — say that Jesus was addressing the Jews, not the Church. This, therefore, has to be addressing the time of His Second Advent at the end of the seven years of Tribulation. However, I believe, as did my good friend Dave Hunt, that the Lord would not speak confusion into prophecy. At the time of the Second Advent at Armageddon, as many as three-fourths of the world's population will have been killed through the terrible judgments given for that era. People will not be doing the things people in societies and cultures do during normal times. And the time of Tribulation will be by far the worst in human history, according to the Lord's own words (Matthew 24:21).

Dave Hunt spoke to these matters many years ago at a forum I attended. He started his presentation by talking about the title of the topic he was assigned:

[My] topic is "Is the Rapture in the Olivet Discourse?" Well, I'd like to talk on the topic "The pre-Trib Rapture in the Olivet Discourse." I couldn't quite handle that question. I couldn't justify why there ought to be any question at all. Why the pre-Trib Rapture, or the Rapture, or the Church, or anything else was in the Olivet Discourse.[21]

Dave, one of the most thorough and brilliant students of the Bible of my acquaintance, then talked about how the Olivet Discourse is declared by the seminary doctoral hierarchy to not address the Church or the Rapture in any way whatsoever. He went on to say that the Olivet Discourse, as he understood it, came about in response to specific questions the disciples asked Jesus. They wanted to know when the destruction of the temple and city would take place, and what would be the signs of His coming and of the end of the age. Dave said Jesus responded with the many signals He gave. Jesus didn't say that He was referring to His Second Coming at the time of Armageddon. Dave asked, "Why is it necessary to adamantly say that it couldn't be the Rapture Jesus was talking about in answer to their questions?"

A common reason given for the Rapture not being referred to in the Olivet Discourse, he said, was that the disciples there with Jesus couldn't understand about the Rapture, because they didn't understand about even the Church at that point.

Dave reminded that Jesus told the disciples at another time that He would go away, but would come again and receive them unto Himself and take them to heaven, where He will have prepared dwelling places (mansions) for them (John 14:1–3). The disciples didn't understand this, either, but it was about the Church, and Jesus told them about it. Dave said this coming for the disciples (the Church) couldn't be the Second Advent because He will return at that time of Armageddon with the saints — including the disciples to whom He was speaking. The disciples didn't understand that, it is true, Dave said. But Jesus was nonetheless speaking about the Rapture. The common sense of the things Jesus was saying fit perfectly — as His teachings always did.

Dave concluded,

I don't believe that His response had to be limited to what they understood. But I think He could tell them things that they didn't understand, and not necessarily in a way that they

---

21. Dave Hunt, "The Pre-Trib Rapture: Is It in the Olivet Discourse?" Pre-Trib Study Group, Dallas, Texas, December 1998.

would understand. . . . I can't think of any reason — rule of logic or exegesis — that would say the rapture can't be in the Olivet Discourse.[22]

Jesus expanded on His "days of Noah" analogy to the time when He would return at the Rapture:

> Likewise also as it was in the days of Lot; they did eat, they drank, they bought, they sold, they planted, they builded; but the same day that Lot went out of Sodom it rained fire and brimstone from heaven, and destroyed them all. Even thus shall it be in the day when the Son of man is revealed (Luke 17:28–30).

Be alert! Keep your head up and senses attuned to what the headlines are saying to your spiritual ears. The midnight cry might be the next words you hear.

Pre-Trib Rapture Unfair?

Emails continue to come to my inbox that in effect put forth that the view of the pre-Trib Rapture of the Church is leading people to be unprepared to face what evidence around us plainly indicates is coming. "New developments," as one writer puts it, now show that our pre-Trib view is wrong and we are doing God and those who come to the website great disservice by teaching such error.

We at Rapture Ready are ignoring those frightening threats to our families and nation, this emailer charged. Such things as the Jade Helm 15 operation the government is planning to conduct, for example, obviously is a plan to put martial law into effect as soon as a false flag event of sufficient magnitude can be created to make such intrusion upon our liberty seem justified.

My email correspondent then recommends numerous teachers I should seek out, those whom he has found to have the truth. I recently interviewed with one of these teachers on his TV program. (We discussed the Rapture to some extent, and the host seemed to agree with me at the end of our interview, by the way.)

We have always received diatribes against our belief in the pre-Trib view of the Rapture. But, recently, the "new evidence" slant on the rants has increased significantly. One element of the "new evidence" is interesting enough to be made the nucleus of this week's commentary.

---

22. Ibid.

Although the interesting element wasn't framed by the exact term "unfair," that was the tenor of the accusation against the pre-Trib view of the Rapture. The pre-Tribulational Rapture is an unfair proposition — rather, would be so, if the pre-Trib view were true, which, of course, it isn't, according to the "new evidence" that now overwhelmingly counters that possibility. That was our emailer's proposition.

The writer said he had studied the accumulating evidence and now must admit that he agreed with his new teachers. He believes

> . . . the pre-trib rapture needs a new and updated research. At this point it seems to me that to hold to this doctrine would suggest that the people in the very country that are support-ing and directly or indirectly are causing some of the greatest calamities upon the face of the earth (see articles stating the US funds ISIS) are the people who have not as yet suffered tribulation for Christ's sake, yet feel imminently prepared to be raptured.

He asked rhetorically, "What if the Christians in Iraq, Syria, and Northern Africa subscribed to the pre-trib doctrine? They were beheaded, martyred, not raptured. . . . How do we reconcile this to the doctrine, I humbly ask?"

Although a bit confused by the expression of his thought — and I don't mean to ridicule or be unkind — I presume he means that Christians in America who believe in the pre-Trib view of the Rapture support an American government that is causing most of the problems in the world. He goes on to imply (I infer), like such anti-pre-Trib emails always do, that since believers in the rest of the world are dying martyrs' deaths or at the very least suffering great persecution, Christians in America cannot expect to be raptured. This would be unfair — that is, run counter to God's right-eous character.

He apparently now believes that all Christians must suffer during at least part of the coming Tribulation. His premise about the nature of the Rapture of the Church, like all other such railing against the pre-Trib view I've received, demonstrates misunderstanding of the believer's position in Christ.

The following was, in part, my reply to him. I've edited it to some extent for making the point of this commentary:

> I'm responding because I want to — for the thousandth time at least — say that the Rapture of the Church is not a mat-ter of rescue from physical troubles so much as it is a salvation

issue. The Rapture is directly linked to belief in Christ for one's salvation during this Church Age. We are not to be called to be with Christ because we are deserving of rescue from a planet headed into Tribulation. We will be called to Him because of God's prophetic program. He will call the Church — His Bride — to Himself, then God again will begin dealing with Israel in all of His covenant promises to that people. This is what the Bible teaches about this prophetic truth.

Always the questions emailers such as you bring up is this: Why should American Christians not suffer, while the rest of the world's Christians are suffering greatly — even to the point of martyrdom?

Let me turn it around. Why is it necessary that any Christian suffer martyrdom or tribulation in order to be in God's good graces in terms of eternal security? Does the fact that millions of Americans have lived and died as believers in Christ mean that because they have not suffered through the seven years of Tribulation and martyrdom they will have to come back to life and go through those terrible things in order to be worthy to enter heaven?

Millions of believers have suffered and died, and are doing so even now, and it is terrible — tragic. However, that suffering has nothing whatsoever to do with the Rapture. The Rapture is a positional matter for the Christian. His or her position in Christ as Savior — as Redeemer — during the Church Age (Age of Grace) is what the Rapture is all about. The Rapture is a salvation issue, not an insurance policy of some sort against physical hard times and/or physical death. It is a matter of the soul.

Christians in America might yet suffer persecution and death. There are no promises in that regard. But, there are promises that Christians — in America and all over the world — will never suffer God's wrath or the seven years of His judgment. Wrath and judgment and dealing again with Israel is what the Tribulation entails.

You mention that "new developments" have you rethinking that these indicate Christians will go through at least part of the Tribulation. God's Word — His truth — is unchanging, no matter current circumstance. His prophetic program remains the same as He planned in eternity past.

The Rapture Ready website has many articles on the Rapture, containing all of the Scriptures relevant to the fact that the believer will be kept out of the very time of God's judgment that is surely coming to a world of wickedness and rebellion. (See Revelation 3:10.) The pre-Trib Rapture isn't unfair; it is truth from the Word of God.

Spirit Speak and Unholy Peace

In George Orwell's 1947 novel *1984*, the dictatorship that controlled much of Oceania rearranged news to fit the moment. The propaganda machine rewrote history on a daily, even hourly, basis to fit the narrative Big Brother wanted the hapless victims of the regime to receive. I believe one of the terms used for this journalism was "newspeak."

There was inflicted upon the citizens of this regional superpower the technique called "doublethink," in which everything that was reasonable and good was to be thought of as bad and evil, as long as it fit the Big Brother model for life in Oceania.

I'm getting the same feeling as when I read that novel for the first time so many years ago while in college. We are being fed, it seems to me, a line of newspeak aimed at creating doublethink, while this generation closes in on the very end of the age.

The term that comes to mind for what is being foisted upon a dumbed-down world of those who would rather be entertained than informed is something like "Spiritspeak." The world continues to move toward a time of an unholy peace — Daniel the prophet said "peace shall destroy many" (Daniel 8:25). Isaiah the prophet calls it a "covenant with death, and with hell" (Isaiah 28:15).

Recently the world's most noted spiritual leader spoke into the ear of the world this Spiritspeak. He gave his personal if not papal blessing to one of God's chosen people's proven enemies. The pronouncement came upon the Vatican's decision to formally recognize Palestine as an independent state. Although not a "spiritual" dictate from Pope Francis, it was issued in Spiritspeak language, with the Pope, in a warm embrace, declaring the Palestinian Authority head, Mahmoud Abbas, an "angel of peace."

The pronouncement was given as the Vatican is making moves to align with the European Union in getting firmly into the peace process in the Middle East. While the Obama administration and State Department appear to be stepping back from that process, the pope and the EU are bringing pressure to bear on Israeli Prime Minister Benjamin Netanyahu to accept the proposed two-state solution to the millennia-long conflict.

President Obama, practically at the same time Pope Francis was calling Abbas an "angel of peace," was again undercutting the newly re-elected Israeli prime minister, as has become his usual way. In his own newspeak way, Obama said the following in speaking to Al-Arabiya, the Saudi-owned, pan-Arab television station: "What I think at this point, realistically, we can do is to try to rebuild trust — not through a big over-arching deal, which I don't think is probably possible in the next year, given the makeup of the Netanyahu government, given the challenges I think that exist for President Abbas — but if we can start building some trust around."[23]

One doesn't have to be expert at reading between the lines; Obama put it right out there. Abbas is the one who has to put up with the subterfuge and with the sabotage against peace by Netanyahu. But, the president interjects, he hopes trust can be established, despite the Netanyahu government's evil mindset.

Both the pope and the U.S. president are rewriting history in this Spiritspeak that is from a direction other than heaven. God cannot lie (Titus 1:2). The pope and president are trying to dupe us all into accepting the equivalent of Orwell's doublethink.

God says such a phony peace will end up destroying many throughout the world. These "leaders" tell us such peace is man's salvation.

We can know of the unholy Spiritspeak taking place that calls good evil and evil good simply by understanding the real history of the PA leader, Mahmoud Abbas. Although admittedly presented from a pro-Israel viewpoint, the following is true, as an examination of real history of what is written here will verify:

> The only path forward for a two state solution to the conflict is for the Palestinians to be given statehood only after they have made peace with Israel and not before. Abbas and his predecessor, Yasir Arafat, have repeatedly refused Israeli offers of peace and statehood.
>
> To this day, he refuses to sign any deal that recognizes the legitimacy of a Jewish state no matter where its borders are drawn. That alone should be enough to deny Abbas the title of "angel of peace." But that isn't the only reason.

---

23. https://www.jpost.com/Arab-Israeli-Conflict/While-US-scales-back-Mideast-peace-goals-Europeans-talk-of-re-launching-diplomacy-403447.

Abbas was a longtime deputy to arch-terrorist Arafat and played a role in organizing and financing many acts of brutal terrorism. But unlike other world leaders who might have employed violence in his youth and then became a statesman, Abbas has never really changed. He is the same man who wrote a doctoral thesis that centered on Holocaust denial at Moscow's Patrice Lumumba University that was published in 1984. . . .

Just as important, though he occasionally makes statements about wanting peace when speaking to Western audiences or the international media, his official PA media incites hatred against Jews and Israel on a regular basis.[24]

It seems beyond ironic that Abbas, in the year 1984, had published his thesis denying the Nazi Holocaust against the Jews. It seems that Spirit-speak was particularly active that year, in preparation to the lead-up to the end-times unholy peace.

---

24. Jonathan Tobin, "Sorry, Your Holiness, You Are Dangerously Wrong," *Jewish World Review,* May 18, 2015.

9

June 2015: Progressive Thinking Prophetic

Progressive" is the term for the mindset most lauded by media today. The word, of course, is the label media and "progressives" themselves have pasted over the word "liberal" in order to distance themselves from the many failed policies of liberalism. Even those of the progressive mindset recognize that those failed policies within the arena of American politics and government has been proven to be — I don't know how else to frame them — *insane.*

We've all heard that one definition of insanity is to keep doing the same thing again and again, even though it fails every time. Nothing more aptly describes the liberal mindset in American politics and government than the policy begun by the Lyndon B. Johnson Administration in 1964.

Johnson's War on Poverty to create his Great Society was to eliminate poverty and assure that every citizen could become more equal in achieving a prosperous life. A noble thought, right? Well, yes. I'll concede that many — including the president himself — most likely really wanted that to happen. With liberals — I mean "progressives" — it's always the good intentions that count. But, it didn't happen. It still has not happened.

Our government has now spent more than $22 trillion in the same manner since 1964 — over and over again. Poverty is worse, and the welfare state has created and perpetuated a class of totally dependent people who for the most part are healthy, able-bodied, and capable of doing for themselves if not for the slothful element government has encouraged and exacerbated. I mention this economic fact only to show the insanity of the liberal — excuse me, "progressive" — thinking to which we are subjected every hour of every day. This mindset goes far beyond economic madness, as we will see.

Such thinking is prophetic. Paul foretold just such a mindset and where it would lead as the end of the age and the return of Jesus Christ nears:

> For the wrath of God is revealed from heaven against all ungodliness and unrighteousness of men, who hold the truth in unrighteousness; because that which may be known of God is manifest in them; for God hath shewed it unto them. For the invisible things of him from the creation of the world are clearly seen, being understood by the things that are made, even his eternal power and Godhead; so that they are without excuse: because that, when they knew God, they glorified him not as God, neither were thankful; but became vain in their imaginations, and their foolish heart was darkened. . . . And even as they did not like to retain God in their knowledge, God gave them over to a reprobate mind, to do those things which are not convenient (Romans 1:18–28).

Reprobate thinking, as we have seen before, is upside down thinking that can neither see a problem in a clear-headed way nor formulate a reasonably effective solution to a problem. Thinking that excludes God produces a reprobate mind — one that will, for example, keep throwing trillions of dollars that don't exist (because we are broke) at a problem that money only makes worse, not better.

The progressive mindset demonstrates time after time, again and again, over and over, that it wants to carry on with life apart from governance from the God of heaven. Humanistic government, in an ever-increasing grasp for power and control, is at the core of the liberal — excuse me, "progressive" — way of thinking.

The Creator God has said that marriage is for one man and one woman for life. The progressive says that this is a new time and place, and biblical thinking is old-fashioned, outmoded. We must *progress*. . . .

But, nature itself — the way males and females of all species capable of reproducing are constructed — shows plainly that it is male-female, not male-male or female-female, that constitutes the sexual union God (or, if you prefer, "nature") intended.

Paul, in His letter to the Romans, again puts a scriptural finger on the rebellion that festers within the progressive mindset:

> For this cause God gave them up unto vile affections: for even their women did change the natural use into that which is against nature: and likewise also the men, leaving the natural use of the woman, burned in their lust one toward another; men with men working that which is unseemly, and receiving

in themselves that recompense of their error which was meet (Romans 1:26–27).

God says plainly what He thinks about the killing of babies in the womb. He speaks clearly about shedding the blood of those who are a threat to no one because they are, in human terms, innocent: "These six things doth the LORD hate: yea, seven are an abomination unto him: a proud look, a lying tongue, and hands that shed innocent blood" (Proverbs 6:16–17).

The progressive says that, in effect, God — if there is, in fact, a God — doesn't know what He is saying in His Word. Life in the womb isn't life — at least, not yet human life. The progressives have the *right to choose* whether the child in the womb is to live or not. They have the *right to choose* what is convenient for their own life, and this includes the *right to choose* to execute a defenseless baby before it takes its first breath for expedience.

Entertainment media is the incubator for the progressive mind. In these last days, every thought of the heart is only on evil continually, as in Noah's day. The entertainment calls good evil and evil good, and the progressive mind becomes more reprobate by the hour.

One such example of the entertainment world incubating this reprobate mindset is a soon-to-be-released television production:

> The more subtle side of Satanism in Hollywood entertainment is now a thing of the past, as primetime television airs blatantly evil shows like the upcoming Fox drama *Lucifer*, which glorifies the goings about of the "lord of hell" after he fictitiously leaves the lake of fire and retires to Los Angeles. The premise behind the absurd drama, which is set to release in 2016, centers around so-called "Lucifer Morningstar" and his new life as the owner of Lux, an upscale nightclub located in the City of Angels. . . .
>
> Based on the show's trailer, the Lucifer character will be offered up to the masses who watch Fox as a likable character with moral and ethical convictions, fulfilling the biblical account of this insidious demonic entity. Described as the wisest creature that God ever created, Lucifer is said to be "full of wisdom, and perfect in beauty" — that is, before he was cut down and destroyed by his Creator for elevating himself in place of God.[25]

---

25. Ethan A. Huff, "Fox Network Launching New TV Series That Glorifies Lucifer; Marketed with Pro-Satan Tweets," *Natural News*, May 24, 2015.

Now, let me say as a caveat that political *conservatism* deserves little more praise than does progressivism. (Fox is claimed to be "conservative.") Humanism rules at the heart of all political and governmental entities upon this fallen and soon-to-be-judged planet. The greatest desire of all Christ followers should be to wage a campaign to win the hearts and minds of mankind for the Lord we serve:

> But the natural man receiveth not the things of the Spirit of God: for they are foolishness unto him: neither can he know them, because they are spiritually discerned. But he that is spiritual judgeth all things, yet he himself is judged of no man. For who hath known the mind of the Lord, that he may instruct him? But we have the mind of Christ (1 Corinthians 2:14–16).

Metastasizing Wickedness

The spread of cancer throughout the body is termed "metastasis." Indeed, medical science has it that 90 percent of fatalities from cancer are the result of metastasis rather than from the original tumor. It is a most dreadful diagnosis, and one that evokes many emotions in the victim, family, and friends. We have all been touched in one way or the other by such diagnoses and prognoses.

We will use the analogy for the moment that should make our environment-worshiping, progressive (liberal) friends at least take notice.

Planet Earth is looked upon by those who see the earth itself as sacred as a living organism, with body and spirit of its own. Anything that pollutes or disturbs Mother Earth is likened to disease within the human body.

Planet Earth, in this analogy, is suffering from a cancerous affliction that has no cure — no *humanistic* cure, that is.

Jesus prophesied that at the time of God's next intervention into the affairs of mankind, in terms of catastrophism, the earth would be in about the same condition as the planet was at the moment when the Flood of Noah's day began. Jesus named the sorts of everyday things that would be taking place at the time. People would be buying, selling, planting, building, and marrying — doing all the normal things most of the world does today.

But, the very fact that Jesus used the "Noah's day" reference makes the Bible student ask what caused God to intervene in such a traumatic way as to destroy the whole world?

The answer is found in the following:

> And God saw that the wickedness of man was great in the earth, and that every imagination of the thoughts of his heart was only evil continually. And it repented the LORD that he had made man on the earth, and it grieved him at his heart. And the LORD said, I will destroy man whom I have created from the face of the earth; both man, and beast, and the creeping thing, and the fowls of the air; for it repenteth me that I have made them (Genesis 6:5–7).

Jesus foretold that, in that future day, judgment would again begin to fall just like it did on the very day Noah and his seven family members were shut safely in the Ark. The causes of that earlier destruction were wickedness and violence filling the whole earth and the thoughts of man being only on evil all the time.

Flash forward to the time described by the prophet Zechariah, who prophesied a fascinating occurrence:

> Then the angel that talked with me went forth, and said unto me, Lift up now thine eyes, and see what is this that goeth forth. And I said, What is it? And he said, This is an ephah that goeth forth. He said moreover, This is their resemblance through all the earth. And, behold, there was lifted up a talent of lead: and this is a woman that sitteth in the midst of the ephah. And he said, This is wickedness. And he cast it into the midst of the ephah; and he cast the weight of lead upon the mouth thereof. Then lifted I up mine eyes, and looked, and, behold, there came out two women, and the wind was in their wings; for they had wings like the wings of a stork: and they lifted up the ephah between the earth and the heaven. Then said I to the angel that talked with me, Whither do these bear the ephah? And he said unto me, To build it an house in the land of Shinar: and it shall be established, and set there upon her own base (Zechariah 5:5–11).

The prophet, in his vision of the end of days, was doubtless astounded as he saw the strange birds, the big pot made of lead, and the terrible mixture that was thrown into the pot before they lifted off. *Where were they flying with this ephah? And why?*

Most interesting to me is that the angel said the following first, in answer, "He said moreover, This is their resemblance through all the earth."

The wickedness in that heavy pot, the angel was revealing, was the same as was all over the world.

We know this was the angel's assessment because of the verse that followed two verses later: "And he said, This is wickedness."

But where were the storks going with this ephah full of wickedness that now had metastasized throughout the earth? I contend they were taking the greatest concentration to planet Earth's most vital organ. We will call it the *heart* of the earth, the "cradle of civilization" for our anthropological, scientific friends.

The storks were flying the pot full of absolute wickedness back to the area called Shinar. This, of course, is the area of the Middle East most associated with the Tower of Babel in Genesis 11. That is the general area where this earth system — the Babylonian system — will meet its end.

This wickedness will cause the death of this present world system. The disease of sin and the wickedness it has produced since God's last catastrophic intervention into mankind's history is more virulent than any cancer that has ever afflicted man. Only the Great Physician can cure the disease. And, the surgery required will be very radical indeed. It will take place at Armageddon, then at the follow-up judgment of the sheep and goats described in Matthew 25.

When we consider where the most violent place on earth is at present, can there be any doubt that the storks have already flown with their concentrated ephah of wickedness and violence? Do the names ISIS, Iraq, Iran (Persia), Syria, Damascus, and Babylon itself sound familiar?

The whole planet is deathly ill with the already spreading cancer of wickedness. Rather, it is the planet's inhabitants who suffer with the sin that has reached the terminal point.

Thankfully, although the cure will be painful, God is about to begin the supernatural surgery only He can perform. He will first remove the only *good* as seen through His holy eyes — the Church, the born-again believers in His Son, Jesus Christ. The radical operation will then begin, during the era called Tribulation.

It should seem to even the casual observer that the surgery is needed sooner rather than later. Even so, come, Lord Jesus.

Marching toward the Mark

I preface what follows by saying that, in understanding economics on the scale needed to truly make heads or tails of what is coming at us, I am woefully educationally challenged. Even thus, however, I can clearly envision what lies in the not-too-distant future for America and the world. There is coming a collapse of unprecedented magnitude, and the ramifications will bring about worldwide calamity, the nucleus of which will involve famine and military conflict. This much I know from what Bible prophecy tells us about the wrap-up of human history, a time in which I'm convinced we find ourselves at the present hour.

Even the neophyte student of economics, after a quick look at how things are shaping financially, comes away with the foreboding sense of gloom and doom. The whole thing — the financial structure undergirding the system — is made not of steel and concrete, but of faith based upon . . . nothing. Why it hasn't already collapsed into a heap is puzzling.

A prime example of the smoke and mirrors involved in the state of the monetary world can be seen in microcosm with a statement by Alan Greenspan, former chairman of the Federal Reserve. He said a Social Security Trust Fund does not exist and that the U.S. is "way underestimating" the size of its national debt: "The notion that we have a trust fund is nonsense — that trust fund has no meaning whatsoever. . . . That means the trust fund is a meaningless instrument that has no function . . . it's exactly the same thing as current expenses."[26]

Greenspan was saying with his characterization of what's been going on with Social Security for decades that it has been and is now all a big lie. There is no "trust fund" to guarantee Social Security payments to recipients. The program is subject to collapse at any moment of crisis.

The same vulnerability is true of the whole economic system of this nation and the world, all nations of which are intricately linked to the U.S. economy in one way or another. The dollar, despite its problems and rumored problems to come, continues to sit atop the global monetary structure.

Our current money system began in 1971. It has survived many credit crunches since that time, but the currency is no longer backed by substantial gold reserves because Nixon took the United States off the Gold Standard in that year. Paper currency, therefore, is based upon nothing more than a credit system — i.e., it is a system built on who is willing to give and receive credit based upon faith that the dollar, unbacked by tangible assets, has purchasing power.

Adding to the worrisome reality that any breach of this credit system along the way in which the buying and selling would no longer be accepted

---

26. "Greenspan: Social Security Trust Fund 'Nonsense' and 'Meaningless,' " Newsmax, June 8, 2015.

in good faith — thus setting in motion a global financial collapse — is an even bigger, building problem.

As bad as the 2007–2008 financial collapse was, the next crisis could be very different. Worldwide debt, again, based upon nothing but smoke and mirrors, according to experts, presents a recipe for economic cataclysm:

> According to a recent study by McKinsey, the world's total debt (at least as officially recorded) now stands at $200 trillion — up $57 trillion since 2007. That's 286% of global GDP . . . and far in excess of what the real economy can support.
>
> At some point, a debt correction is inevitable. Debt expansions are always — always — followed by debt contractions. There is no other way. Debt cannot increase forever.
>
> And when it happens, ZIRP and QE [manipulative monetary processes] will not be enough to reverse the process, because they are already running at open throttle.[27]

My understanding in these matters is very limited from the standpoint of how the economic intricacy fits together. However, the authorities who claim to understand predict that cash to buy and sell will be in critically short supply when all this collapses in upon the world of consumers. They liken it to a tsunami.

The cash will first be sucked almost completely out of circulation, when a massive tidal wave of inflation-driven depression will crash upon all nations of the world.

Sounds very much like something of which I am somewhat a student. It sounds very much like the third rider and his black horse of Revelation 6.

All of this, of course, could easily set up apocalyptic things for the man with the plan who will ride in on the white horse described in that same chapter.

The complexities that have created this tsunami will be dealt with, no doubt, by computers, satellites, bioelectronic chips, and a system of buying and selling using numbers within a cashless system involving electronic funds transfer (EFT).

That smacks of Revelation 13:16–18, does it not? Indeed, this generation is marching toward the mark.

---

27. Bill Bonner, of Bonner and Partners, "Literally, Your ATM Won't Work," Zero Hedge, June 7, 2015.

10

July 2015: Persia, Prophecy, Pulpits, and Pews

President Barack Obama's nuclear nightmare negotiations with Iran are almost assuredly a done deal. It is highly unlikely that Congress can override his wishes, or that they even have the belly for it.

He has that powerful veto pen, you know — and that terrible telephone, about which he has informed us. These are weapons in his hand that apparently are, according to any who might oppose him, as fearsome as the possible nukes in the hands of the Persian mullahs he has just assured us we don't have to fear.

With even the nation's top general, the chairman of the Joint Chiefs of Staff, saying just before the nuclear agreement was announced that under no circumstance can Iran be allowed to have ICBMs with nuclear warheads aboard them, we learn that ICBMs were not mentioned in the agreement as prohibited in any way.

But, never fear. Inspections will make sure the experts can verify that compliance with the agreement that nukes won't be developed will be followed. But, wait — there are no guarantees in the agreement stipulating that Iran must allow inspectors in at a moment's notice if cheating is suspected.

It is true that there are dissenting voices. These opinions, for the most part, however, are muted to a large degree by mainstream media, and are always presented in a slanted way that takes the watcher of news right back to the fact that the president and Secretary of State John Kerry have really held the Persians' feet to the fire. Mr. Obama, it is said by those who cheer for him no matter what, is finally showing why he received the Nobel Peace Prize at almost the same time he became president of the United States. Everyone who was truly enlightened knew that the young, articulate black man (as Joe Biden called him, saying that finally there was such a man to offer as candidate) would quickly earn the prestigious award, so why not just give it to him up front.

The voice truly crying in the wilderness is marginalized to the point of being considered irrational even by some of the supposed fair and balanced voices on Fox News. I, for example, heard Shepard Smith agreeing with a pundit, an Obama sycophant, that Israeli Prime Minister Benjamin Netanyahu calling Obama's agreement with Iran a terrible thing was just repeating the mantra he has always ranted because he sees most everyone as Israel's detractors. The man added (and Smith didn't disagree) that those who *really* know the details of the Obama deal with Iran in the Israeli-secretive Mossad think Netanyahu is ignorant of the facts and simply is a contrarian. All of this against Mr. Netanyahu, without a follow-up interview with the supposed Israeli clandestine operatives in question — i.e., there was no proof of such criticism within today's Israeli Mossad.

Some within Congress are making noise that if the details of the agreement just announced don't contain guarantees that Iran won't continue working toward a bomb, they will do all within their power to see that it doesn't get final approval. Wanna bet?

Fact is, most of those in Congress have remained for the most part on the sidelines during all of the negotiations that were basically veiled — as are most things in which this presidential administration engages. They have had their heads in the proverbial sand.

Even more troubling than our representatives in government being willfully in the dark, however, is Christian leadership being even more so.

This is the truly egregious malfeasance that gets to the heart of why such a president can make such a deal with such a diabolist state.

This is why studying Bible prophecy is not just important; it's absolutely critical. The majority of pastors and teachers in churches — and I'm referring to those that preach the gospel and are led by those who are born-again believers — deliberately avoid even a cursory mention of prophecy found in God's Word. They are willfully ignorant and keep their parishioners in the pews dumbed down by their neglect.

Things going on involving Israel, Iran, and America have prophetic implications — with consequences to follow. One of the most focal regions of the world in Bible prophecy is at the heart of what we have witnessed the past week. Iran, of course, is at the center of ancient Persia, which is prophetically scheduled to be in cahoots with Russia during the Gog-Magog attack of Ezekiel chapters 38 and 39.

Israel is to be the target of that attack. All of this is shaping in a way that cannot be missed except for those with no spiritual understanding and/or interest in God's foretelling details of the end of human history.

Pastors and Bible teachers who avoid these things have performed a disservice that is incalculable in the amount of damage done.

The spiritually dark powers are hard at work. They have blinded the eyes of those charged with handling America's foreign-policy matters. There is a real Prince of Persia, and he is alive and well and aiding the Persian chess masters as they completely hornswoggle U.S. negotiators at every move on the nuclear chessboard.

Pastors and teachers who should know better are like dispensable pawns on that chessboard, as they are useless to warn either our politicians or the people in the pews of their ever-more extravagant theaters of worship-entertainment. They refuse to help prepare their flocks for defense against Satan's assaults against Christians and Christianity.

While key prophecies for the end of the age, such as the rise of Iran/Persia, are obvious on the horizon, the shepherds in their pulpits turn the minds and spiritual hearts of those in the pews more and more inward, choosing to insulate the flocks and themselves from the reality that is on the verge of devouring them.

The Apostle Paul's inspired exhortation should resonate in the spiritual ears of all of God's people as we see that day approaching: "But ye, brethren, are not in darkness, that that day should overtake you as a thief. Ye are all the children of light, and the children of the day: we are not of the night, nor of darkness. Therefore let us not sleep, as do others; but let us watch and be sober" (1 Thessalonians 5:4–6).

11

August 2015: Apocalyptic
Axis in the News

Ezekiel's unveiling of the end-times coalition that will constitute a catastrophe second only to the destruction at Armageddon seems a page of history that is in process of being turned at this very moment.

The protagonist nations making up the apocalyptic horde of Ezekiel 38 and 39 rumble ominous forewarning across the face of the modern Middle East. Their threats flicker in lightning-like shards against the increasingly darkening clouds of long-ago prophesied evil. While the end-of-the-age stormfront gathers exactly as Jesus and the Old and New Testament prophets foretold, only a few see the danger coming.

You who are reading this commentary are among a very limited number of prophetic weather observers. Few, even within the evangelical church, want to think on things that every indicator screams in siren-like fashion is coming upon this generation that is ripe for God's judgment.

Pastors have life lessons to prepare, marriages and funerals to preach, and building and church administration budgets to oversee. People in pews have children to raise, college tuitions to worry about funding, and the many cares of daily life in America in which to engage. The young and not-so-young have their cyber entertainments and other forms of amusements and business activities to conduct. Romances are to be nurtured and engaged in, while preparation for long lives of living on earth takes up every waking moment.

There observably is no time for God's people to think on what He wants His children to know about things to come. And those things are on the very cusp of happening.

This is all in consideration of life in the most blessed nation ever to grace the earth. Things across most of the rest of the world are much, much different for the most part. Many in those regions are longing for their Lord to intervene on their behalf.

Areas of the world other than North America and some parts of Europe especially have populations that face daily struggles even the poorest of Americans cannot fathom. As the just-released book by Robert L. Maginnis, *Never Submit,* points out in vivid description, genocide against Christians and others is taking place like in ancient times. The raging tide of militant, satanically inspired Islamists threatens anyone in their path.

Jesus' admonition was, I'm convinced, issued particularly for this generation — a generation of people who are doing anything but what the Lord exhorts in His forewarning: "And what I say unto you I say unto all, Watch" (Mark 13:37).

If you are watching, you cannot miss the apocalyptic axis forming at this very moment. The horrendous force, with Islam at its center, will, when the Lord Himself allows, bring cataclysmic destruction. Preachers and teachers of the Bible who believe it to be the inerrant Word of the Living God should be watching and understanding what is happening while prophecy is preparing for fulfillment. But they aren't. They are as willfully ignorant of what the headlines portend as are this presidential administration and the world of diplomats who are supposed to be the smartest people on the planet.

U.S. presidential administration operatives and the world's diplomats have an excuse for not having a clue. They don't know the Lord, who knows the end from the beginning, and who has told of this great invasion of the Middle East, which is building by the moment.

The people who have been commissioned by the Lord of heaven to shepherd the flocks have no such excuse.

Briefly, to bring these woefully and willfully ignorant shepherds up to date, it is the Ezekiel 38 and 39 prophecy that should not be missed.

The Russian, Iranian (Persian), Turkish (Togarmah) coalition is forming at an amazing rate. The following brief excerpts bring this stunning end-times prophecy starkly into view. I don't go into the Turkish part of the axis in this commentary, but suffice it to say that Turkey is in the news for its growing hegemonic influence in the Mideast region as strongly as are Russia and Iran:

> Two Russian warships have docked in northern Iran for a series of naval training exercises with the Islamic Republic, according to Persian-language reports translated by the CIA's Open Source Center.
>
> The two Russian ships docked in Iran's Anzali port on Sunday and will hold "joint naval exercises during the three-day

stay of the warships in Iran," according to a Persian-language report in Iran's state-controlled Fars News Agency. . . .

Russia and Iran have grown close in recent years, with delegations from each country regularly visiting one another to ink arms deals and other agreements aimed at strengthening Iran's nuclear program. . . .

Last week, a senior Iranian naval commander warned the United States against ever taking military action on Iranian interests, claiming that the response would be "unpredictably strong." . . .

The military leader went on to claim that "Iranian Armed Forces are now at the highest level of preparedness" and that "only the dead body of the American troops realizes the power of the Islamic Revolution."[28]

Month of Destiny
Part I

September 17, 1940, brought the end to Adolf Hitler's World War II assault on the United Kingdom termed "Operation Sea Lion." The Battle for Britain, as it has been dubbed by historians, failed after British people had absorbed a terrible pounding from Hitler's Luftwaffe bombers. Each day it seemed that the end had come for England.

When the nightly assaults finally ended, British Prime Minister Winston Churchill, in the grandiloquent way only he could say it, broadcast to the English people and the world: "This is not the end. This is not even the beginning of the end. But, it is, perhaps, the end of the beginning."

Yet another September of notoriety has arrived. I in no way equate my situation to that suffered by the British people of World War II, or to any other people of any other era who have suffered in such war. But I do feel bombarded after many months of things of fearful nature predicted to likely devastate the United States and the world beginning in the month of September 2015.

The articles and emails have increased the closer that month gets. And now we are there, the dreaded September. I'm suffering from pre-Trib war jitters.

To admittedly attempt to couch it coarsely in the masterful language of the great Sir Winston Churchill, we know it is not the end of the end.

---

28. Adam Kredo, "Russian Warships Dock in Iran for War Training," *Washington Free Beacon*, August 11, 2015.

It is not even the beginning of the end of the end. But we wonder if it is, perhaps, the end of the beginning of the end.

Jesus said that the things He foretold must come, but the end will not be yet (Matthew 24:6). But, He said that when we see the things He forewarned, the end would have begun, and our redemption would be drawing near (Luke 21:28).

I suppose we will shortly find out regarding this much-ballyhooed month whether all the apocalyptic possibilities conjectured from every quarter — religious and secular alike — will be borne out as planet Earth lurches into the fall. Many believe September will be a month of biblically prophetic destiny.

The chatter flows in unending analysis by those on the secular financial websites. Some are straight out of kooksville, with every conceivable theory ranging from aliens of Planet Kriptonia having stolen all of America's gold supplies to every Walmart in the United States having vast tunnels linking them one to another, where those aforementioned aliens will conduct business with the Illuminati devotees in a post-nuclear system of barter. Others are well-respected economic experts who have correctly predicted financial collapses such as that experienced in 2007–2008. Everyone of this latter sort — all for whom I certainly have respect because of their track records — have been proclaiming unabashedly that this immense financial bubble will burst very soon. It will be, they say, far worse than collapses of every other time in history.

It is more than interesting that these secular financial experts have in recent weeks been mentioning the *Shemitah*. Many of those who have never included religious thought of any sort within their analysis of what's going on now mention this "mystery" that Jonathan Cahn's books have brought to light. And, I have listened carefully. Many, many of the "experts" are now saying that the repetition of the cycles involved is just too prevalent and consistent to be coincidental.

At the same time, television economic gurus seem almost oblivious to the fear that there is a problem of Vesuvius magnitude about to blow. These certainly display no knowledge of Cahn's books or of the *Shemitah* postulations. As a matter of fact, many of these are observably committed to the Obama administration's mantra that a national economic recovery is in full swing. The concern expressed by the Internet experts and apparently dismissed by the broadcast and cable experts is for September 13.

This year of 2015 is the *Shemitah* year, called also a *Sabbath* or *Sabbatical* year. It is the seventh year of the agricultural cycle, which ends at sundown on the 13th of September. The whole matter is tied to God's covenant with the Jewish people.

Regarding the trepidacious thinking of the secular, non-mainstream financial marketeers, it is associated with financial issues, debt forgiveness, economic problems, recession, declines in the stock market, etc.

On top of this, it is the beginning of a *Jubilee* year, which is the end of 49 years of the seven-year cycles, and the start of the 50th year.

The 50th year involves requirement that all of Israel focus on God, the cancellation of debts, and restoration of land to the original owners, among other stipulations.

God promised blessings for Israel when the people kept the covenant to let the land lie fallow on the seventh year of each cycle. He warned of severe punitive ramifications if Israel didn't keep the *Shemitah* year covenant. Israel failed in keeping the covenant and has suffered many adverse circumstances. Bible scholars contend that the Jews are still suffering from failure to keep the covenant.

Jonathan Cahn, a Christian who is a Jew and a rabbi, in his book *The Mystery of the Shemitah* writes that he believes the United States and the world could have economic (and other) problems around the time of September 13 this year. He doesn't say it will happen for sure, but, based upon the pattern of past years when the *Shemitah* has been in play, the evidence (severe economic upheaval), he submits, seems to overwhelmingly suggest that something involving God's interaction might be scheduled soon.

Critics of Cahn's books most specifically point out that God's covenant regarding the *Shemitah* was between the Jews (Israel) and God. They contend that America and all Gentile nations are therefore not part of either the blessings or the punishment in the matter.

However, it cannot be denied that, over many years, the seven-year cycles have, almost contemporaneously, matched downturns in finance affecting national and global economies. As I say, so strangely intertwined is all of this that the *Shemitah* matter has captured the attention of non-mainstream news economic experts who are truly non-religious in forming their analyses.

With going on $19 trillion of national debt, and the Treasury printing money to throw at the impossible-to-ever-repay IOUs, and considering all the dynamics of economic insanity on the fiscal horizon, something has to give. Many other portentous matters are also impending in the month of September that have prophecy watchers glued to their calendars.

The Jewish holy days run concurrently with the *Shemitah*, further causing frowns of concentration for Bible prophecy observers. For example, one Bible prophecy authority and author writes,

> Sept.13–15: Rosh Hashanah (also called the Jewish New Year or the Feast of Trumpets) begins at sundown on Sept. 13 and ends at sundown on Sept. 15. Some (not all) prophecy teachers believe the Rapture could occur at the end of Rosh Hashanah this year or next year or some year.[29]

He writes further on an important matter happening around the time of the *Shemitah*:

> Sept.15: The 70th UN General Assembly will begin meeting. During this session (not necessarily on the 15th), France is expected to present a resolution to the UN Security Council to divide the Promised Land (Two-State Solution) and to force a peace treaty on Israel and the PA. If the UN does this, their decision will lead to the beginning of the Tribulation period.[30]

September 2015 — which will bring the last of the *blood moons* that have transfixed many — is seen by many as a pivotal point in God dealing with this world of anti-God rebels. In many circles of Bible prophecy, students and observers practically insist that dramatic and traumatic events will take place that will begin a new phase of His plan for fulfillment of prophecy.

Next week, we will look in depth at what the future for September and beyond might hold.

Month of Destiny
Part II

September 2015, a month that has received attention from Bible prophecy students like only two others I can remember, is upon us. The others were December of 1999 and December of 2012.

December 1999 brought much speculation and not a little fearfulness that Y2K — the turn of the millennium — would be accompanied by world-rending upheaval. December of 2012 came after many months, even years, of built-up hoopla involving the "prophecies" of the Mayan calendar, which predicted global cataclysm, according to some.

---

29. Daymond Duck, "Newest Articles," RaptureReady.com, September 15, 2015.
30. Ibid.

Both of those scythe-wielding, Grim Reaper speculations came and went without incident for the most part. Some argue that there were some major problems when the calendar rolled over to 2000, and there would have been disaster, had billions of dollars not been used to fix the problem ahead of time. Fact is, despite the dire predictions, there were no disasters.

So, with somewhat of a history upon which to call in the case of such anticipated date-oriented calamities, what are we to make of this September specter before us?

For those who view my tone to this point as flippant or laced with sarcasm, I assure that isn't my frame of mind. I simply want to remind that predictions that engender similar levels of worry have approached, then dissipated within the relatively recent past.

Although these impending prospects for significant prophetic impact are thought by many to be unprecedented, specific prophetic manifestation might not necessarily result — i.e., all the dates and other ingredients within the mix of anticipation that something spectacular will come of it all this month might not come to fruition.

Even if this turns out to be the case, faith that the Lord is beginning to move within these times so near the end of the Church Age should be strengthened, not weakened. As He has told us,

> For my thoughts are not your thoughts, neither are your ways my ways, saith the LORD. For as the heavens are higher than the earth, so are my ways higher than your ways, and my thoughts than your thoughts (Isaiah 55:8–9).

God's foreknowledge is perfect; thus, His timing is flawless. Although pundits of every sort have framed the many strange September 2015 dates and their various, ominous possibilities into a coalition of likely probabilities, these might well not eventuate.

No matter how many elements seem in alignment for triggering judgment-like occurrence, it is good to pause and consider the following: circumstance doesn't control God; God controls circumstance.

I believe we are witnesses to this providential control in the arena of national and global economies.

For months, the wizards of finance have, by violating every known rubric of economic theory, printed money with nothing to back it. They have thus thrown trillions of dollars at the building national debt through "quantitative easing." The Federal Reserve has kept interest rates at artificial lows to prevent the U.S. economy from imploding.

Early in the week, following a steep fall in stock market numbers the previous Friday, the economic pontificaters were out in force. One said that there is "concern," but the world isn't at an end. He said that although the high-tech stocks had been "smashed," they would rebound. He offered that China wasn't totally coming apart economically, like many feared, but that the Chinese were experiencing an eye-opening correction. The expert said that things happening were nothing at all like the collapse in 2007–2008. This week's activity, he said, was a change of "attitude." The 2007–2008 collapse was a change of "direction." (No, I don't know the difference; just telling you what the "expert" said.)

Even with the unprecedented chicanery practiced by those who are supposed to promote the general welfare of the nation, most in the know say the financial system of America and the world should have long ago collapsed. Nothing like what has been happening has ever been the case, as I, in my admittedly low I.Q. in these matters, understand. The U.S. economy is in uncharted economic waters, and the country is on the precipice of collapse.

But it hasn't collapsed, no thanks to the ineptitude of those throwing everything but the proverbial kitchen sink at a massive problem no one can even understand, much less make go away. The "experts" are baffled. There seems no explanation for why the bubble keeps building. All they know is a collapse of monumental destructiveness is coming. It will be world-changing, and almost instantaneous.

They don't know how close to right they are. We will explore this in a subsequent article.

While this hand-wringing is going on within the pantheon of high finance (privately, of course, where mainstream media is concerned), the world wages on, oblivious to impending cataclysm.

The spiritual seismometers of those who believe this generation is at the end of the Age of Grace (Church Age) sense something big is about to shake the world. Many who study Bible prophecy believe that the things pointing toward September as a month of prophetic destiny will coalesce to bring God's judgment on America and possibly all the world.

At the same time, most within that group are as oblivious to anything that might be seriously wrong as those in the general population. There is a sense of some uneasiness because of the evil of ISIS and occasional acts of evil by other bad actors. But, overall, it is business as usual in the pulpits and pews of America's churches, including the evangelical ones.

Where God's people such as Jerry Falwell and the Moral Majority would once have fought with all within their power against same-sex marriage and the absolute evil of things Planned Parenthood perpetrated against babies in the womb (and out of the womb in some cases), the preachers and their congregations are now, in fact, a *silent minority.* I must commend Glenn Beck, who, although a Mormon, thus not a person with full knowledge of biblical truth, is a patriot and common-sense man who is leading in protest against the evil within the likes of Planned Parenthood.

There remain courageous pastors and churches who speak out strongly against such abominable things. John Hagee of Cornerstone Church in San Antonio and Dr. Robert Jeffress of First Baptist Church of Dallas come to mind as two such pastors. But most are silent, and many have signed on to the anti-Israel movement, taking the side of those who want to divide that Jewish nation, thus to establish a Palestinian state.

For these reasons, and because of the calendar of events they see as in alignment, many who view Bible prophecy believe that God's judgment is about to fall upon America. That judgment, many are convinced, will begin in September 2015.

However, remember that circumstance does not control God; God controls circumstance.

Lord willing, next week we will further delve into what this long-fretted-over month might hold. One thing is sure — we have only a very few days to find out!

12

September 2015: Is This Gog-Magog?

Zola Levitt and I were talking privately, and Zola was thoroughly exercised about the topic of replacement theology. Some mainline denominations were beginning at the time to adopt the rising theological position termed "progressive dispensationalism." The "doctrine" put forward that Christ's throne had been transferred to heaven when the Lord sat down at the right hand of His Father. Therefore, the throne of King David was also transferred from an earthly throne to heaven. This meant, according to the progressive dispensationalists, that Israel had, in effect, been replaced in matters involving God's promises to the nation.

This was not much different than pure replacement theology, and Zola was about to address, as I recall, the pre-Trib Research Center group at Dallas that December on this topic. Such once-conservative seminaries as Moody and Dallas Theological had begun to go strongly toward the progressive dispensationalist viewpoint.

Zola, as anyone who knew him will attest, was passionate like few others about Israel and God's dealing with the Jews. I have never seen him quite so animated as during that conversation somewhere around the turn of the century, as I recall. He said that he and Dr. J. Vernon McGee had once "gotten into it" on a television program over whether Israel was back in the Middle East for fulfillment of prophecy. Dr. McGee held that while it was interesting that Israel had its nation restored after more than 1,900 years in its geographical homeland, he didn't believe this meant that Israel was necessarily there for the final time. They could yet be put out of the land and return at a later date.

This, of course, was like throwing gasoline on a raging fire. Zola said they really got crosswise. Zola held that Israel was there for the final time — for the wind-up of this dispensation (Age of Grace) and into the Tribulation. I told him that Dr. McGee knew the truth now, his having gone to be with the Lord at age 84 in 1988. Zola's only comment was, "Well, I would hope so."

Boy! Would old Dr. McGee have done a 180 on his view of the situation if he could suddenly be shown developments since getting his — as Zola would later say of his own impending going to be with the Lord — promotion to that magnificent realm. As a matter of fact, I sometimes have wondered if they have not again had their conversation, with both now being in complete agreement on the veracity of God's Word in regard to His promises to His chosen people.

Every day that passes brings into focus that truth. Israel is like a laser pointer indicating that these must indeed be the closing days of this Church Age. Stage-setting for fulfillment of Bible prophecy, as we have pointed out many times, literally fills today's geopolitical, socioeconomic, and religious landscape. Culture and society aren't just headed toward the cesspool; we have arrived in the septic tank.

The world's economy is poised to implode, with those in charge of the Fed not knowing which way to turn. Raising interest rates will bring the world's economy crashing down. Not raising interest rates means that dynamic exigencies as part of the intricately linked world monetary system will heat up even further, making the ultimate crash far worse than any in history when it happens.

The pope is traversing the world, apparently spouting strange doctrinal changes in his Catholic system and sticking his papal nose in every free nation's business. He seems to me in cahoots with the Marxist ideology espoused by those who are said to have mentored the current U.S. president.

Russia looks to be making alliances that will one day, perhaps sooner rather than later, form a coalition like that forewarned by the prophet Ezekiel in his Gog-Magog prophecy. Iran occupies the geographical area of ancient Persia. This Israel-hating state of satanic rage is Putin's client-state, as is Syria — these and other nations of the Islamist sort prophetically destined to be part of a horrendous end-times event.

Specifically, we must ask whether the most recent movement by Vladimir Putin might be, in fact, the actual staging for this great conflict of Ezekiel chapters 38 and 39.

Those who hold to the likelihood that a Psalm 83 war will precede the Gog-Magog attack will say this cannot be the time of that great Ezekiel 38–39 conflict. I continue to respectfully disagree with the proposition that such an inner ring of nations, as given in what I believe to be an imprecatory prayer by God's chosen nation in Psalm 83, indicates a separate military action. I continue to believe that the prayer offered in Psalm 83 will be answered powerfully and unequivocally by the God of heaven with the all but total annihilation of the combined Gog-Magog forces of all surrounding nations who come against Israel.

That Russia has inserted itself into the Middle East in ways that trouble America's top military generals goes without saying. The Russians have said they won't hesitate to send a large contingent of ground troops into Syria if the request is made by the Syrian regime.

The AP reported September 17 that Syrian Foreign Minister Walid al-Moallem said Damascus wouldn't hesitate to ask for Russian troops if needed. At the same time, he denied that Russian combat troops were already fighting in Syria.

Proof continues to accumulate that the Russians are moving in to stay in the region. Many military and other intelligence officials are asking in television appearances what the buildup means. Ezekiel, we remember, said some would be asking the same question as the Gog-Magog invasion began to take shape.

One respected intelligence advisory wrote the following:

> The Russian military deployment to the Bassel al Assad air base in Latakia, Syria, is continuing at a rapid tempo, Stratfor can confirm. Previous imagery of the airfield, taken Sept. 4, showed significant engineering works underway. New imagery from Sept. 15, provided by our partners at All Source Analysis, reveals the completion of several large concrete aprons that were previously under construction. A large amount of Russian military equipment has also arrived at the airfield. A battalion-sized Russian contingent now appears to be located at the base, along with artillery and attack helicopter support. Several large Russian transport aircraft are also visible on the runway and the nearby ramps.[31]

With American fighter jets and other military assets in the same general area, there is growing concern that an incident of a dangerous sort could happen whether by accident or by instigation. The Russian and American officials have been shown to be engaging in meetings over developments in the war-torn region.

Are we seeing the beginning of a Russian buildup for the fulfillment of the Gog-Magog assault?

---

31. "Russia Fortifies Its Position in Syria," Stratfor, September 17, 2015.

I believe this is indeed a point in the staging for that prophesied war. Just *what* point is anyone's guess.

My own thinking is that the Gog-Magog assault will take place some time after the Rapture of the Church. This is because this will be a world-shaking, cataclysmic event. Many other lands besides just this region will be affected. This war, in my view, will take the world out of the business-as-usual state that Jesus prophesied will be prevalent at the time He next intervenes into human history in a catastrophic way. Judgment will fall, the Lord said, that very day, just as in the days of Noah and the days of Lot (again, read Matthew 24:36–42 and Luke 17: 26–30).

We see developing a sure signal that the Tribulation period is fast approaching. It is time for believers to work hard to bring as many of the lost into God's family as possible. At the same time, we must remember to lift up our heads and keep looking up!

Despisers of Good

Something is going on that I believe can no longer be considered an anomaly. It smacks ominously of forewarning found within the Apostle Paul's "perilous times" prophecy of 2 Timothy 3: "This know also, that in the last days perilous times shall come. For men shall be . . . despisers of those that are good" (2 Timothy 3:1–3).

Although the signs have been on the cultural and societal horizon for years, the manifestation of Paul's forewarning became clearer during the school shooting in Columbine, Colorado, on April 20, 1999. It was the first time in such a nationwide way that hatred for Jesus Christ raised its monstrous head, producing martyrdom for the cause of Christ in America.

An article about Rachel Scott, a 17-year-old Columbine student says:

> Three weeks before the shooting she had witnessed to the shooters Eric and Dylan. Eric and Dylan were the odd pair out and students mostly stayed away from them. But Rachel tried to talk to them and encouraged them to leave their hateful feelings and turn to Jesus. But they hated her the more and even made homemade videotapes mocking her Christian faith.
>
> On the day of the shooting, Rachel was outside the school building having her lunch. Eric and Dylan entered the school campus and first shot Rachel. They shot her in the leg twice and shot her again in the back. They left but returned seconds later. On noticing that she was still alive, Eric walked over to

Rachel and grabbed her by the hair, lifted up her head and asked her *"Do you still believe in your God?"* Her response was unflinching and unwavering, "You know I do," and that provoked Eric and he responded, "Then go be with Him," and shot her in the head.[32]

That singular, direct act of murder because a Christian wouldn't deny her Lord might be considered no more than an aberration. The slaughter of Christians within the church of mostly black congregants in Kentucky a couple of months ago could, perhaps, be chalked up as merely an insane man coincidentally choosing a group of believers in Christ in his rage to kill. But, the deadly attack on the college in Oregon this past week should take all growing hatred for those who claim Christ as Lord out of the realm of anomaly and coincidence.

With this most recent shooting it should be considered undeniable that we have witnessed a key prophetic indicator. It is as if God's finger is pointing directly to the fact that these are the "perilous times" to which Paul referred:

> A gunman singled out Christians, telling them they would see God in "one second," during a rampage at an Oregon college Thursday that left at least nine innocent people dead and several more wounded, survivors and authorities said.
>
> "[He started] asking people one by one what their religion was. 'Are you a Christian?' he would ask them, and if you're a Christian, stand up. And they would stand up and he said, 'Good, because you're a Christian, you are going to see God in just about one second.' And then he shot and killed them," Stacy Boylen, whose daughter was wounded at Umpqua Community College in Roseburg, Ore., told CNN.[33]

The phrase "despisers of those that are good" is more than obvious in its application to this news story in thinking on the Apostle Paul's prophecy. This young, demented man *despised* Christians by his own admission through his words and actions. But, the word "despiser" takes on a much more condemning meaning for the evil day in which we live when considering the treatment of the horrendous event.

---

32. Sachin, "Rachel Joy Scott — Her Story Must Be Told," FreeHeartDay.com. April 20, 2013, http://www.freeheartday.com/rachel-joy-scott-her-story-must-be-told.

33. Chris Perez, Danika Fears, and Natalie Musumeci, "Oregon Gunman Singled Out Christians During Rampage," NYPost.com. October 1, 2015.

In almost all mainstream accounts of this story, the reports never mention that the shooter asked the specific question "Are you Christian?" and they never include the statement that because they are Christians they will die in one minute. In nearly every case, the mainstream reported only that the shooter asked what *religion* the victims were.

This is blatant bias in trying to keep the public from recognizing that Christians were specifically chosen to be murdered. This is, in my opinion, the mainstream press showing its own collective disdain for Jesus Christ, for Christians. By omission, they demonstrate they despise those who are good.

Why do I say those who were murdered in cold blood were "good"?

Jesus, when called by a man "Good Master," asked the man why he had called Him "good." Jesus told the man there was only one who was good: God (read Matthew 19:17). Jesus wasn't scolding the man; rather, He was pointing out that all people are fallen, but God is without sin. He is the only good. Jesus was and is God. He said as recorded in another passage, "Before Abraham was, I Am" (John 8:58). Jesus was saying that He is God. He is the only good there is.

To further dissect the perilous-times prophecy in question, we next consider why we can legitimately point out that the shooter in the Oregon massacre of Christians was a "despiser of those that are good" (2 Timothy 3:3) and why the media's deliberate refusal to mention that Christians were specifically targeted seems to indicate that they, too, are "despisers of those that are good."

Jesus, time and time again, declared that those who believe in Him for salvation because of His death on the Cross for them are "in" Him. The believer is *one* with Jesus just as Jesus, the only begotten Son of God, is one with the Heavenly Father. (Read John chapter 17, and this becomes absolutely clear.)

This means that the true believer in Jesus Christ is in God's family for eternity. They will be in heaven forever after this life.

The only reason God the Father sees any human being as good is through His Son. When the shooter murdered the Christians, he showed that he despised those who were good in the holy eyes of God.

Not only the American mainstream news conglomerate but many in this nation's political domain have demonstrated beyond much doubt that they are "despisers of those that are good."

The attitude of Mr. Obama and the tenor of his time in office demonstrate disdain for Christianity, as far as I'm concerned:

> At the National Prayer Breakfast, President Obama reminded attendees that violence rooted in religion isn't exclusive to Islam, but has been carried out by Christians as well. . . .
>
> "Unless we get on our high horse and think this is unique to some other place, remember that during the Crusades and the Inquisition, people committed terrible deeds in the name of Christ," Obama said. "In our home country, slavery and Jim Crow all too often was justified in the name of Christ."[34]

This has been his consistent treatment of the subject of Christianity. He continually praises the godly attributes of Islam, but hasn't lifted a presidential finger to help stop the genocide against Christians in the places where ISIS (ISIL, as he puts it) are butchering even women and children, including infants.

I remember vividly the National Democratic Convention leading up to the 2012 presidential elections. In three separate voice votes, delegates were asked whether they supported the inclusion of God and the recognition of Jerusalem in their party's guiding policy document. Three separate times, loud shouts of "no" all but drowned out the sound made by the chairman's gavel. Chairman Antonio Villaraigosa ultimately just declared that the "ayes" had it — despite that there was nowhere near the two-thirds "ayes" voice vote sounded in the hall. As God and Jerusalem were inserted back into the Democratic platform, the hall erupted in boos — proof that despisers of good were there in abundance.

Recent Supreme Court decisions and other court actions against principles from God's Word, even going so far as to put Christians in jail and strap others with fines that caused loss of livelihoods, makes it clear that we are in perilous times. We are in the satanic process of being surrounded by despisers of those who are good.

---

34. Charlie Spiering, "Obama at National Prayer Breakfast: 'People Committed Terrible Deeds in the Name of Christ,' " Breitbart, February 5, 2015.

13

November 2015: Temple Mount Turbulence

With stage-setting for fulfillment of Bible prophecy during this Church Age winding up for the final throes of satanic hatred against Jews, turbulence surrounding Mount Moriah shouldn't surprise. It comes right on schedule with things shaping up for the Gog-Magog assault foretold to come against Israel. The winds of conflict into which the seeds of Islamist rage have been sown, nurtured by the likes of the United Nations and the international community, will soon cause the whirlwind of man's final war to be reaped.

The great military hero, Israel's General Moshe Dyan, following the June 1967 Six Day War, it is sad to say, prepared the way for seeding the disastrous storm to come. He turned over the Temple Mount to the Jordanian waqf, or Islamic trust, that continues to administer the site. He did so after a thorough victory had been won over a much greater in number combined Arab world army determined then, and determined still, to wipe Israel off the Middle East map. Dyan's action has given a sense of possession to the Islamist world that should not, in my opinion, have been allowed.

Increased violence in Israel, in east Jerusalem, and in the West Bank has marked recent days. So-called lone-wolf attacks have apparently been ordered on Jews by militant factions within the Palestinian Authority (PA) and other organized terrorist commands.

The proclaimed reason for the attacks is the lying charge of Jewish encroachment upon the Temple Mount compound.

The "lone" assassins use knives, screwdrivers, or anything they can get their hands on to stab Jewish people whenever opportunity arises. Israeli authorities have taken subsequent action to deal with the attacks. Not surprisingly, it is the Israeli authorities' actions to stop the assaults that draw the ire of the world press, not the heinous, unprovoked attacks by the Islamist militants against innocent individuals simply trying to go about their daily lives in peace:

> At least 52 Palestinians, half of whom Israel says were as-
> sailants, have been shot dead by Israelis in the West Bank and
> Gaza since Oct. 1. Nine Israelis have been stabbed or shot dead
> by Palestinians.
>
> In the latest incident, a Palestinian was shot dead on Satur-
> day after he tried to stab an Israeli security guard at a crossing
> between the West Bank and Israel, Israeli police said.[35]

Palestinians were prohibited for a time by Israeli police, who have law enforcement authority, from worshiping on the Temple Mount, some-thing Jews are not allowed to do at any time. The temporary prohibiting of worship due to the stepped-up attacks against Jewish civilians brought stone-throwing and other acts of violence by the Arabs.

American Secretary of State John Kerry entered the fray surrounding the rage over the al-Aqsa mosque compound, the third holiest site in Islam, which Jews call the Temple Mount and the Islamist world calls the Noble Sanctuary, or *Haram al-Sharif.*

Kerry, after talking with PA President Mahmoud Abbas and Jordan's King Abdullah in Amman, Jordan, said the Israeli government had agreed to the "excellent suggestion" of King Abdullah that the Temple Mount compound be monitored 24 hours a day by intensive video surveillance. He said that Israel had assured that there will be no change in the status quo. I interpret that to mean that things will continue as agreed to by Dyan in 1967 for the most part. If so, the "settlement" assures only another brief lull — possibly — in a conflict that is destined to grow to be earth's final conflagration.

As examined many times before in these commentaries, the Temple Mount matter is the most contentious on the planet. The reasons for the unsolvable tensions are rooted in the very creation of man.

When man fell victim to the serpent's lie in Eden that he would become like God if he disobeyed the Creator's prohibition against eating the forbid-den fruit, Mount Moriah — the Temple Mount — became paramount in man's redemption. Satan (the serpent of the Garden of Eden) knows it is the one place on earth that is truly God's touchstone to humanity. That is where redemption — salvation — was to come into play. That is where, in fact,

---

35. Arshad Mohammed and Ori Lewis Reuters, "Kerry Lays Out Steps to Ease Israeli-Pales-tinian Strife," Reuters, October 24, 2015.

God's redemption plan was completed when His Son, Jesus Christ, laid down His life as the sacrificial Lamb that takes away the sin of the world.

Lucifer the fallen — Satan — desires beyond all else to take charge of the Temple Mount, the location of the Holy of Holies and the Ark of the Covenant.

Upon Christ's death, the veil was torn from top to bottom, ripping apart the curtain between God and mankind. We now have access directly to God's throne through belief in His only begotten Son.

Satan will one day, according to Bible prophecy, have his man called the "prince that shall come" — Antichrist — stand exactly where that Ark once sat on Moriah. He will indwell that man — whom I believe might be a Nephilim — and have the beast declare himself God.

The turbulence atop Moriah has just begun.

Israel's Strange Silence

Middle East maliciousness is literally exploding, igniting fires of death and fear across the world. Europe feels the heat of the Islamist rage as ISIS turns up the rheostat of hatred in France and other places.

Europeans, particularly the Scandinavian countries, the favorites for Muslims who set their sights on migration, are becoming desperate for ways to close borders forced open by European Union dictates.

Polling statistics show that Americans are increasingly concerned that soon the incendiary, religious fanaticism will infect this nation. "Lone-wolf" actions by ISIS wannabees are, in fact, bringing the more fanatic brand of Islam to this continent, which was insulated from that religious fervor prior to the 1993 bombing of the World Trade Towers.

ISIS propagandists are making it known beyond any doubt that they view America as the place they most wish to spread their special brand of terror.

This is all going on simultaneously across the world. All the while, governments and military authorities are nearly at a loss as to how to deal with the Islamic beast. At the same time, there is an almost complete lack of mention of the one entity most of the world considers the prime reason for this voracious activity by the likes of militant Islam.

It is downright eerie.

That entity itself is inexplicably silent for the most part about the rage to its north. I'm talking, of course, about Israel, the tiny Jewish state that is claimed by practically every diplomat in the world to be, in one way or another, at the heart of the ever-more-dangerous situation in the Middle East.

For decades, Israel has been at the center of almost every action and reaction to Muslim terrorism in the region. From the time of the murders of the Israeli athletes in the 1972 Munich Olympics, to the downing of the World Trade Towers and damage to the Pentagon during the 9-11 attacks, and until just recently, Israel has continuously been at the center of things. Not so now. Israel is silent; the world doesn't seem to be noticing that tiny nation for the moment.

Why is this so? Why, after decades in modern times — after thousands of years in the battle of Israel versus its enemies — is the modern Jewish state seemingly off the radar screen of the ongoing conflict?

This, I realize, could change instantly at any moment. Israel could be thrust in the middle of dire crisis before this column appears. It is an almost-unnatural situation, if I may use that phraseology. The almost-"natural" state is for Israel to be constantly and consistently blasted by its enemy, Islamist antagonists, and by the world community at large.

There have been, of course, occasional reports lately of Temple Mount turmoil about which we and others have commented. But, about the larger involvement of the entire Arab-Islamist world, and even Iran in the conflict with hated Israel, I find scant mention these days.

While Israel remains basically mute, and everyone else's attention is turned to ISIS and the turbulence it is kicking up in Syria and around the world through its proxy "migrants," Vladimir Putin and the Iranian mullahs are cooking up plans, the intentions of which only the Lord knows at this point. But, be sure of one thing: all of this means that the stage is rapidly being set for the final act of this pre-Tribulation program that is about to begin.

It almost seems like predators are circling around the intended prey. The prey is being temporarily ignored while the pecking order is arranged for who will get the first spoils of the intended victim — this I mean from a prophetic perspective.

In the nebulous background, there seems to be a power juxtapositioning of the apex predators and the scavenger types to determine what comes next regarding the end-times assault against the nation God chose long ago to remain standing when all others are vanquished.

It's as if Benjamin Netanyahu and Israel's government are flummoxed as to what it all means, this violence that is on display to Israel's north and, increasingly, around the globe. But one thing is sure: the Israeli prime minister and other Jews of good, common sense and an understanding of history know that it somehow all means that they — the Jews, Israel — are the intended prey. Somehow it will all come down to them having to consider invoking the Samson Option, in geopolitical terms of "them versus us."

Israel is silent, but not asleep. Netanyahu and the Israelis who have that sense of foreboding know that soon the hungry eyes of the predators will turn back to them just like they always do. Their deeply committed vow is "Never again!"

The blame for the problems of the Middle East is always directed at them. A news story this past week clearly indicates that satanically directed attitudes against God's chosen people are as deluding as ever. Sweden is under attack by the so-called migrants from Syria and other areas that ISIS seeks to dominate in its determination to establish a worldwide caliphate. Swedish women and even young girls are being raped by the invading horde, it is reported. Despite this, one top Swedish government official manages to point a finger of blame at the strangely silent Jewish state:

> Swedish Foreign Minister Margot Wallström linked Palestinian grievances with Israel to the Islamist terror attacks that killed 129 people in Paris.
>
> "Obviously, we have reason to be worried, not just in Sweden but across the world — because there are so many that are being radicalized. Here, once again, we are brought back to situations like the one in the Middle East, where not least, the Palestinians see that there is not a future. We must either accept a desperate situation or resort to violence," Wallström said in a television interview.[36]

That Israel is responsible for the Islamist rage is the message. Zechariah's forewarning can be heard thundering, even if present-day Israel is for the most part silent:

> Behold, I will make Jerusalem a cup of trembling unto all the people round about, when they shall be in the siege both against Judah and against Jerusalem. And in that day will I make Jerusalem a burdensome stone for all people: all that burden themselves with it shall be cut in pieces, though all the people of the earth be gathered together against it (Zechariah 12:2–3).

---

36. "How Original: Sweden Blames Paris Attacks on Israel," Israel News, November 17, 2015.

Almighty's Analysis of America

What is your religious persuasion? The question is standard in the census polling process.

America's population was 318.9 million as of 2014, according to Census Bureau statistics. Polling numbers that year showed that 70.6 percent of Americans identified themselves as Christians. This was a significant decline from polling done in 1990, in which 86 percent of Americans said they were Christians. Wikipedia states that America has nearly 247 million Christians, the highest number of any nation, although there are other nations with higher percentages of Christians.

So, when asking people their religion, the response most often is *Christian*. Or, they answer by giving the denomination within Christianity with which they identify.

Such is the *natural* response in this land that was founded on Judeo-Christian principles. But, it is not the *natural* response that the Grand Poll Taker is seeking, but the *supernatural*. Based upon God's analysis of His polling statistics hangs the fate of cultures, societies, and nations.

We can get a sense of heaven's polling methodology, I think, by looking at a specific case in which such census taking was employed — to an extent, at least. It is a fascinating exercise considering planet Earth's apex nation, so far as superpower status, in human terms, is concerned.

The twin cities of Sodom and Gomorrah were powerful commercial societies of their time. These, of course, are infamous as their fate is the stuff made of legend.

During the course of almost any week, I come across one TV documentary or another that goes into great detail about these cultures. Most often, the documentarians spend their time debunking the true biblical account, choosing instead to give every conceivable reason these great commercial centers no longer exist. The filmmakers tell the biblical story, in their own usually warped versions, then give natural reasons Sodom and Gomorrah were obliterated.

Until relatively recent times, historians most often scoffed at the biblical story of Sodom and Gomorrah. The cities were considered mere legends. But digs at the southern end of the Dead Sea that continue to bring that civilization to the salty surface make it crystal clear. These places were devastated by fire and brimstone, just as God's Word proclaims.

Now, what does all of this have to do with America and statistics on the number of Christians in the nation? Remember the statement by Billy

Graham's wife, Ruth Bell Graham, we've all heard many times: "If God doesn't judge America [for its wickedness], He'll have to apologize to Sodom and Gomorrah."[37]

Many of us totally agree with her assessment. The reason is that America, it can be argued, has in some aspects gone beyond the sinfulness of those two ancient cities. We could examine any number of ways this is true. We've looked at two of these in great detail a number of times in these commentaries.

The most glaring similarity is the matter of homosexuality. That was the great sin emphasized in the Genesis account of God's judgment of that culture.

I don't have to go too deeply into the similarity because we are all familiar with what has been going on in the past couple of years in this country. First, God-ordained union between a man and a woman has been changed by the courts of this land to pervert the God-given institution called marriage. Sexual activity that the Creator calls abomination, the lawless, God-defying people of America call gay. And this is not to diminish the equally abominable sexual activity within the heterosexual world — fornication and adultery.

Secondly, the matter of abortion comes front and center in the comparison. Babies in the womb and small children in that ancient society undoubtedly cramped the style of the deviants of the time. The products of the unbridled sexual activity made it easy to sacrifice those babies upon the altar of convenience. The deeper people went into debauchery, the more self-absorbed and willing they were to go to any lengths to make their next thrill more exhilarating.

In Sodom and Gomorrah, we are talking about cities of thousands; in America, we are talking about an entire nation of more than 300 million. They could have aborted only thousands; we abort more than a million per year. Recent undercover video evidence flashes proof in our faces for all to see. Planned Parenthood and its like give irrefutable evidence that we have gone beyond that ancient people in the degree of unrighteousness perpetrated.

And the term "unrighteousness" is the heart of the matter in the polling question: What is your religious persuasion?

The nation is, according to the answers given the pollsters, overwhelmingly Christian, even considering the drop in the numbers from 1990 until 2014. We are supposed to believe that 70.6 percent of America's 318.9

---

37. https://billygraham.org/story/billy-graham-my-heart-aches-for-america/.

million people are Christians. Again, that's more than 247 million claiming to be Christians.

Now we come to the title of our commentary this week: "Almighty's Analysis of America." People can say they are anything. The human pollsters must take down what they are given. The term "Christian" is accepted at face value and marked on the polling sheet. The Lord of heaven, however, goes infinitely more deeply into His polling process. To Him, the precise definition of the term is of eternal importance.

"Christianity," in heaven's economy, is tied to "righteousness." To be a Christian, one must be righteous. But, the Bible says the following: "As it is written, There is none righteous, no, not one" (Romans 3:10). How, then, can anyone be a Christian? That is, how can anyone be considered righteous?

God's grace gift provides the answer: "But God commendeth his love toward us, in that, while we were yet sinners, Christ died for us" (Romans 5:8).

God sees as righteous only those who have believed in His Son, Jesus Christ, for salvation from their sins: "For the wages of sin is death; but the gift of God is eternal life through Jesus Christ our Lord" (Romans 6:23); "For whosoever shall call upon the name of the Lord shall be saved" (Romans 10:13).

When one is "saved," he or she is "righteous" because God sees righteousness only in His beloved Son, who died as sacrifice for all of mankind.

Now we will get back to this matter of America and the percentage of those who say they are Christians. These figures don't compute. Mrs. Graham was right. America's degree of depravity, by any stretch, doesn't come under God's definition of righteousness. Revisiting our thoughts on Sodom and Gomorrah, God spoke with His servant Abraham. He informed Abraham that he was going to have to destroy those wicked cities of Sodom and Gomorrah because of the great sins. The account is found in Genesis 18:23–33.

Abraham was terribly grieved, and pleaded with the Lord. He asked that if God could find 50 people who were righteous would He spare the cities. God agreed, but could not. Abraham then pleaded for God to search for 45, then 40, then 30, then 20, then 10 righteous people to justify not destroying those places. In each case, the Lord tried but couldn't find even 10 among many thousands in Sodom and Gomorrah who believed in Him — which was required to be "righteous" in His holy eyes.

As I said, the documentarians are still reporting the findings of the archaeologists who are digging up the destruction of those doomed cities.

More and more I'm wondering, like Ruth Graham, about the possibility of America's ultimate fate being like that suffered by the city prophesied in Revelation 18. An encouraging truth is that God found the man named Lot, a citizen of Sodom, to be righteous in His holy eyes. A few of Lot's family members were obviously seen likewise because the Lord removed them from Sodom before the fire and brimstone fell. God said to Lot about that removal to safety, "Haste thee, escape thither; for I cannot do anything till thou become thither" (Genesis 19:22).

The Lord said that His judgment couldn't fall with its total devastation until the righteous Lot was first taken out of harm's way — until Lot and his family were completely removed from that wicked city.

Be encouraged, those of you who are righteous: Jesus Himself, in His ascended position at the right hand of His Father, promises a future generation, one I believe is alive today: "Because thou hast kept the word of my patience, I also will keep thee from the hour of temptation, which shall come upon all the world, to try them that dwell upon the earth" (Revelation 3:10).

The Lord counts you among those who will, perhaps very soon, hear the words of the Lord Jesus Christ: "Come up hither" (Revelation 4:1).

14

December 2015: Sovereignty and Climate Change

One priority heads the list that the principalities and powers in high places of Ephesians 6:12 must achieve in order to build the neo-Babel tower of world control. There can be no doubt of what that geopolitical goal is after considering what's going on within the COP (Conference of the Parties) held in Paris November 30 through December 11. That was the 21st get-together of the globalist organization with a membership now numbering more than 190 nations.

Their declared intention is to establish global agreement on what to do about so-called climate change in order to reduce greenhouse gas emissions brought about by human activity. Their proclamation of such danger to the environment through continuing sophistry that includes falsifying data on supposed global warming has been debunked over recent years.

These "de-growth" environmentalists nonetheless continue to shout through their worldwide media accomplices that greenhouse emission-caused global warming will bring an end to planet Earth — thus, even though they've had to alter their fearmongering rant to call it "climate change" because of scientific proof to the contrary.

The most recognizable religious figure on the planet is all in, too. Pope Frances, flying on the papal plane when leaving Africa, weighed in when asked to comment on whether anything constructive might come of the COP gathering: "I'm not sure, but I can say that it is now or never," he said. "We are on the edge of suicide . . . but I am sure that just about everybody meeting in Paris is aware of this and wants to do something."

He concluded, "The other day I read that in Greenland the glaciers have lost billions of tons. . . . In the Pacific there is a country that is buying another country in order to move, because in 20 years it's going to disappear. I believe in these people [the COP leadership], that they will do something. I hope so, and I pray for it."[38]

The climate change/environmental save-the-planet social engineers intend to change human consumption patterns in every possible way. They plan to reduce private land ownership to the point that all will be forced to live in restricted communal areas. This is what is meant, in part, by the "de-growth" mentioned earlier. The ultimate outgrowth of the "de-growther" plan is to reduce the population of earth to 500 million or less.

Talk show host Mark Levin, in chapter 7 of his recent book, *Plunder and Deceit,* mentions America's own neo-Babel de-growther in addressing the environmentalist movement:

> Much of the so-called environmental movement today has transmuted into an aggressively nefarious and primitive faction. In the last fifteen years, many of the tenets of utopian statism have coalesced around something called the "de-growth" movement. Originating in Europe but now taking a firm hold in the United States, the "degrowthers," as I shall characterize them, include in their ranks none other than President Barack Obama. On January 17, 2008, Obama made clear his hostility toward, of all things, electricity generated from coal and coal-powered plants. He told the *San Francisco Chronicle*, "You know, when I was asked earlier about the issue of coal . . . under my plan of a cap and trade system, electricity rates would necessarily skyrocket."[39]

Recently we have learned they are determined to eventually do away with air-conditioning and other comfort/convenience technologies. We in the West must be brought down to the same level of the Third World societies and cultures. Equality will then be achieved and Utopia established. They will have created their version of heaven on earth.

The real story behind all of this, of course, is the matter of *sovereignty.*

The plan of the builders of the end-times Tower of Babel know that to begin to achieve their goal of de-growth, the apex nation of the world must be stripped of her sovereignty. The United States is the holdup. Europe, the one-time bastion of civilization, has all but given its sovereignty over to the

38. Thomas D. Williams, "Pope: Climate Change Agreement 'Now or Never,' Humanity on the 'Edge of Suicide,' " Breitbart, December 1, 2015, http://www.breitbart.com/national-security/2015/12/01/pope-climate-change-agreement-now-never-humanity-edge-suicide/.

39. Mark Levin, *Plunder and Deceit* (New York: Threshold Edition, 2015), chapter 7.

socialistic, globalist, would-be masters. Now, we are seeing America being channeled into that European model. Sovereignty must be and is being stripped. Barack Hussein Obama has been chosen to be instrumental in the stripping process.

That's what this climate change mantra and drive is all about. It's what the incessant call to get the guns out of the hands of average Americans is all about. Sovereignty can be maintained only when it is defended by force. Armed Americans stand in the way. That is what the open borders and invitation to a massive invasion from our south and from the Middle East is all about. No more borders — i.e., *no more sovereignty.*

But of course, all this is but the tip of the proverbial iceberg of impending destruction.

The real *sovereignty* issue is that of the true sovereign — the Creator of the universe and of all things. The master of the would-be one-world engineers — the neo-Tower builders — wants, as he did from the time of the war in heaven, to overthrow the sovereignty of God.

Lucifer has brought today's globalists to the point of the Psalmist's predicted end-of-the-age arrangement:

> Why do the heathen rage, and the people imagine a vain thing?
>
> The kings of the earth set themselves, and the rulers take counsel together, against the LORD, and against his anointed, saying,
>
> Let us break their bands asunder, and cast away their cords from us.
>
> He that sitteth in the heavens shall laugh: the LORD shall have them in derision.
>
> Then shall he speak unto them in his wrath, and vex them in his sore displeasure.
>
> Yet have I set my king upon my holy hill of Zion (Psalm 2:1–6).

Even so, come, Lord Jesus.

15

January 2016: Piercing the Perils of 2016

Never in my own memory has a new year appeared to be more prophetically interesting. Never has one portended more perilous times, as the Apostle Paul would have it. Yet I wouldn't trade my time on this darkening planet with anyone of any other generation.

The fact that the Lord of heaven has put me here at this strange, ominous, yet immensely fascinating time in history makes it all the more intriguing in terms of wanting to know what happens next. He has put you here, too, at this time when the final curtain is about to fall. He has trusted you to be an actor in at least part of the final scenes of this great, cosmic play called human history. No illustrious personages of the past — not Julius Caesar, not Napoleon Bonaparte, not Alexander the Great, not even Winston Churchill, Franklin Delano Roosevelt, or Ronald Reagan — were so privileged. We are about to serve as active members of an especially commissioned cast who populates the end-times stage.

A schism — a separation — of cataclysmic proportion is about to occur. It will rend one part of humanity from the other. It will not be a natural catastrophe that will inflict the humanity-dividing rift. It won't be great political upheaval in America and around the world that will cause the tearing apart of life upon the troubled planet. Those things will certainly happen. But it won't be acts of nature or man that will bring about the very last scene of the age. That last act will be orchestrated by the Master director of all creation, the Lord God of heaven, who is the final judge of good and evil.

The excitement presaging that grand climax of the age is building. Momentous events written on the pages of Holy Scripture are about to come alive. The final curtain will rise when Jesus steps out on the clouds of glory and calls all believers — His Bride, the Church, to Himself. If you believe in Christ alone for salvation, you will catch the grand finale as you watch from the luxuriant balconies of heaven.

We see the drama building all around us for the tumultuous scenes set to play out during the times just ahead. The year 2016 is cloaked in the fog of malevolence this world continues to wrap itself in, an increasingly anti-God, anti-Christ vesture that embraces humanism forewarned about in Psalm 2:1–3.

A quick scan of the news just this past week exposes, I believe, the arrogance of those earth-dwellers who incessantly strive to break asunder the governance God rightfully placed upon His creation called man. The reports are laden with prophetic indicators.

One such report is seen in the prideful claims by a U.S. State Department spokesman, as the boast involves the increasing call for peace and safety. While the situation in Syria grows intensely worse by the hour, with the Syrian people torn violently between the forces of Syrian dictator Basher al-Assad and the hordes of ISIS murderers, Secretary of State John Kerry is lauded as bringing about a peace that just isn't happening and will never come to pass.

State Department spokesman John Kirby wrote under the headline "Bringing Peace and Security to Syria," "Under Secretary of State John Kerry's stewardship the United Nations passed a U.S. sponsored resolution to create a road map for Syria." Again, the problem is that, like in all of the humanistic efforts at bringing true peace, the only peacemaker is kept out of the peacemaking. Jesus Christ, the Prince of Peace, is denied at every turn by the president of the very country that speciously purports to be making the peace. (President Obama, remember, upon his very first week in office, proclaimed that the United States is not a Christian nation.)

The president of the United States of America, in effect, proclaimed, "Let us break their bands asunder, and cast away their cords from us."

We can believe what that omniscient, omnipotent, governing authority has to say about such arrogance and willfulness. The message is chilling for the planet's inhabitants who will be left behind when the great schism takes place.

Details of what is about to take place in 2016, of course, lurks in the murkiness of an ever-increasing pall of trepidation. But, for those who are secure within the unshakable, impenetrable shelter of their Lord and Savior, there is no reason to fear. Piercing that black uncertainty is an effulgence that lights the path to the brightest of all possible futures. It is that blessed hope of Titus 2:13!

America's Contribution to Armageddon

I caught the tail end of an interview featuring a former general saying on Fox News that this administration is helping to pave the way for a Third World War. Such a statement from a top military commander who is recently retired grabs one's attention as does few others. The retired officer went on to talk about the upheaval in most all of the Middle East caused by American withdrawal in so many key areas of the region. The vacuum created, the general was saying, is setting up the world for a war of unimaginable scope.

Particularly, he was commenting on the growing threats and actions between Saudi Arabia and Iran, which has flared following the Saudi's execution of a high-profile Shiite cleric and a number of others.

Iran's response was to take over the Saudi Embassy building and loot and ransack its contents. The reaction on both sides continues to escalate, dividing Islamic nation from Islamic nation along Shiite/Sunni religious lines and threatening a war that could spread into a global conflagration, according to the general and others.

President Obama has come under consistent criticism from military officers who have either resigned because of differences with the administration's way of handling military involvement around the world, or who have been forced out because of conflict with advice offered the president on military matters.

Those retired or resigned officers who continue to criticize Obama's use of military and his dealings with America and Israel's destruction-vowed enemies point to the danger to the nation and the world in the administration's actions, paving the road for Iran to build a nuclear force.

This, they say, is insanity, giving the very Islamists who want to bring on their version of Armageddon the capability to do so through acquiescence to Iran's demands on nuclear development and their demand that sanctions be lifted and access given to $150 billion as part of lifting those sanctions.

The protests of America's military experts seem to make no difference whatsoever, any more than the advice the generals gave in warning the president against first telegraphing the removal of American forces from Iraq, then in actually removing those forces. Such action was all but unprecedented in modern American military strategy. The result has been a power vacuum that is igniting the whole region in a conflict that is almost certainly unstoppable.

As written about before in this column, Israel remains strangely silent as all the Arab and Iranian states around the tiny Jewish state begin to burn like a grass fire surrounding a log cabin. But Israel is no such inanimate, ordinary spectator. Israeli Prime Minister Benjamin Netanyahu and the IDF know that Israel is the actual target when these wild men — as the Bible terms them — finally zero in on their most-hated enemy. Israel's trigger finger is on the ultimate weapon and will pull that trigger to defend itself.

Thus, there is a cry for peace and safety by the likes of American Secretary of State John Kerry. It is really, however, a demand that Israel be disarmed and marginalized. This is so Kerry's new friends, the Iranian mullahs, can have their way, bringing, he and the rest of the world's diplomatic fools believe, peace at last.

It is arguable to contend that the whole Middle East region would have been far better off if America had never gotten involved there. This is said time and time again by those who want to blame George W. Bush and his father for committing troops to the region in two military actions. This is, at least in part, a mistaken contention, however. The Lord Himself determined that the United States would be a major part in the founding of modern Israel and a major physical agent of Israel's protection.

The current American president and his ideological, leftist bedfellows display the reprobate thinking that comes from anti-God rebellion as forewarned in chapter 1 of Romans. A prime example of this upside down lunacy is on display when thinking on the situation in the president's dealings with both the nation of Iran and the American people.

In the matter of Iran, Mr. Obama and his ilk indicate they think it is just fine to arm the Armageddon-planning mullahs with nukes — despite the fact that these madmen have stated repeatedly that they plan to destroy the "Great Satan" and the "Little Satan" (America and Israel). At the same time, the president and his leftist, political associates indicate they think it will make America safe by disarming citizens through threatened executive action on gun control. The Iranian mullahs can be trusted with nuclear weapons and their delivery systems that can destroy the world, but the American gun owner can't be trusted to have a Second Amendment-guaranteed right to own and bear arms.

Such insanity almost certainly is in the process of making our nation culpable in helping bring on man's final war.

Thankfully, all of this means, as always, that Christ is about to call His Church to the safe shelter of their heavenly home.

It is imperative, therefore, that all who belong to Jesus Christ determine to lift that name that is above every other so that many who are lost will be drawn to the Lord. He is the only hope for those who are heading into the worst time in human history.

Satan's End-Times Surgery

Academia, it is becoming more apparent each day, is serving as the devil's workshop. For example, Yale University is being sought out to serve as Satan's operating room to excise truth in an area that is most troubling to him in restricting his end-of-days stratagem.

A report I received the past week from a friend and fellow watchman on the wall immediately impressed scriptural implication upon my spiritual senses: "This know also, that in the last days perilous times shall come. For men shall . . . [have] a form of godliness, but [deny] the power thereof" (2 Timothy 3:1–5).

My friend's email provided two letters to the editor that were recently sent to his local newspaper. He lives in Connecticut, near Yale University, the curriculum of which is the target of the letter-writer's proposals.

The letters to the editor encapsulated a stratagem of the old serpent I have for some time been observing. He seeks desperately to destroy the true, unvarnished witness of the veracity of God's Word. Mixing biblical truth with the false religions of the world seems to be key to his strategy. On some levels, it appears that he is succeeding.

Lucifer has "enlightened" (seduced) the world's religionists to a large extent to his seductive whispers proclaiming God is love. Anyone who denies that God is love must be put within the theologically and politically correct detention camp — the gulag — where haters must be dealt with appropriately. Anyone who claims that God condemns is a hater, a bigot, a person filled with an inhuman phobia of one sort or the other.

All within humanity are on the heavenly highway to salvation, no matter their sin — which, Satan whispers, doesn't exist. That is, all are on that salvation highway except those who insist there is but one way to heaven. Those who preach that God is judgmental, vindictive, and vengeful are haters.

The Bible and other "holy books" show — Satan whispers to the theologically and politically correct — that God is *only* love. The parts that indicate He judges humanity for sin other than that of failing to take care of the physical needs of fellow man are to be disregarded — spiritualized as meaning something other than what the hate-filled bigots who hold to the fundamental, evangelical view say it means.

This is the surgery Satan is attempting to perform — cleaving the love portion of religiosity from the judgmental. And this brings us to the letters to the editor concerning that prestigious academic institution, Yale University.

The writer, from Vermont, is, he informs, a former student of Yale's School of Theology. He points to apocalyptic prophecy as the primary reason for all of mankind's problems today. That a loving God would condemn anyone to suffer eternal punishment . . . well . . . let's allow his own words to explain:

> Yale shouldn't simply change the name of Calhoun College to that of an alumnus who is not a white supremacist. It should re-examine the mission of the Divinity School (where I received a Master of Divinity degree in 1980) which treats eschatology like a benign academic theological category, instead of the dangerous and incendiary belief-system that it is, in whatever religion it appears.
>
> It is not Christianity or Islam which is responsible for many of the mass killings we have seen in my lifetime. It is the unchallenged belief in eschatology (end time; final judgment; apocalypse) which has produced Jim Jones, David Koresh, the Tsarnaev brothers, Army psychiatrist Nidal Hasan, and the San Bernardino husband and wife shooters, all in the last half-century.
>
> It is time for President Peter Salovey's challenge for Yale to engage in soul searching to be expanded to include the Divinity School on a topic equally as poisonous as institutional racism: the belief that God will punish mankind for not obeying his sacred word, by imposing a final judgment in an end-time of hellfire and torment or of eternal bliss.[40]

The writer later replied to a response given his charge by the dean of Yale's School of Divinity. The dean explained how Yale and other such institutions were working with the U.N. to "remove all religion as a rationale/cause of extreme violence." The dean said he wasn't certain eschatology was the cause of the violence.

The letter writer wrote,

> Isn't Dean Sterling missing the forest for the trees? All religions which include Armageddon belief-systems, throw gasoline on the inflamed minds of wannabe martyrs, terrified of

---

40. Paul D. Keane, "Letter to the Editor: Yale Needs Deeper 'Soul Searching,' " *New Haven Register*, December 10, 2015; www.nhregister.com.

eternal torment and hungry for eternal bliss, from Jim Jones in Jonestown, Guyana, and David Koresh in Waco, Texas, to the Tsarnaev brothers in Boston, Army psychiatrist Nidal Hasan in Fort Hood, [Texas], and the husband and wife mass murderers in San Bernardino, California.

Armageddon should be banished from the religious canon as a paranoid delusion, not taught as benign theological embroidery. That would assist "the UN to try to remove religion as a rationale/cause for extreme violence," as Dean Sterling puts it.

At the least, scholars at Yale's distinguished divinity school should pursue the truth wherever it leads, without fear.[41]

Lucifer's attempted surgery is focused upon those who present end-times matters to the world. The old serpent has a volcanic rage against prophecy from the Bible because such prophecy tolls his soon-coming doom, and because that truth might resonate with anyone who looks around and sees how world conditions align perfectly with biblical eschatology. The world today demonstrates the veracity of God's Holy Word. Satan has decided on the brilliantly evil tactic of lumping all who preach and teach that truth with the likes of the murderous mullahs and jihadists who, as part of their madness, have to bring on their version of Armageddon so their prophesied Mahdi can rule the caliphate they seek to establish.

Anyone who thus puts forth that Tribulation, an Antichrist, and God's judgment for rebellion and sin are coming are wicked and no different from those who are raping, murdering, and beheading people by the thousands.

The stratagem is working within academia and even within the pseudo-Christianity held by many of today's liberal theologians.

God's love, however, cannot be cleaved from His judgment. It is all part of the same divine plan for the ages. Sin must be dealt with in final judgment so that pure, unadulterated love can reign throughout eternity.

That love is a person, and His is a name like no other. Jesus Christ is coming to make all things new and righteous. The first phase of that return — the Rapture — is on the very brink of taking place. We must not and will not be silent regarding prophetic truth.

Rapture-Resistance Reasoning

While those who truly grasp the lateness of the hour and what the issues and events of these strange, troubled times mean, a majority hasn't got a

---

41. Paul D. Keane, "Letter to the Editor: "Eschatology Fuels 'Inflamed Minds,' " *New Haven Register,* January 8, 2016.

clue. This is neither surprising nor unexpected, because a vast part of the world's population is in spiritual darkness, without Christ, therefore without the Holy Spirit to guide thinking and comportment.

Millions upon millions of others claim to be under the umbrella of Christianity. Most of these, statistics bear out, would not qualify as "Christian" under the definition of being "born again" because they haven't truly "believed," as described in Romans 10:9–10:

> That if thou shalt confess with thy mouth the Lord Jesus, and shalt believe in thine heart that God hath raised him from the dead, thou shalt be saved. For with the heart man believeth unto righteousness; and with the mouth confession is made unto salvation.

It is not my place nor that of any other person to say which individuals are and are not saved. However, we are to hold to biblical qualifications for becoming a child of God who will spend eternity with Him in heaven. In the sense of discernment, we can say that those with those biblical qualifications are saved and those without are not.

We will deal in this essay with those who are born again as defined above. I would like to get even more specific. Among those who are truly born again, there are many views of how things will play out prophetically. At the same time, there are also many who don't know and many who don't care about what God has foretold about their future. They are too busy living out their increments of life one heartbeat and breath at a time.

Sadly, the latter by far constitutes the majority. That is, most don't know about Bible prophecy, and most don't care. They are aided and abetted in their willful ignorance by the pastors and Bible teachers within their church bodies in this disregard for the prophetic portion of God's Word. That prophetic Word is almost one-third of the Scripture the Lord has given us through His love letter to mankind.

Even more specifically, I want to concentrate for the moment on the doctrine of the Rapture of the Church, that twinkling-of-an-eye moment Paul wrote about as recorded in 1 Thessalonians 4:13–18 and 1 Corinthians 15:52–55.

Of those who have truly been born again, few know about the Rapture in concrete terms or grasp that they will be called into heaven by their Lord. In America, even those who do understand that the Rapture is an event prophetically scheduled according to the Bible resist embracing that promise. That is, rather than desire to hear Christ's call, "Come up hither" (Revelation 4:1), they want to first live life on earth and fulfill all of the anticipated pleasures it offers. It is primarily this group of believers to which I address the thoughts that follow.

Notice, please, that I wrote as a qualifier, "in America." It is in America that this attitude of not embracing the Rapture among Christians is most pronounced. Proof of that is made clear through the thousands upon thousands of sermons preached each week. The number of prophetic messages among those thousands of sermons are infinitesimal. People don't want to hear that Christ's call is imminent. The pastors, in overwhelming numbers, demonstrate that they don't want to delve into that portion of Bible truth — even if they, in fact, believe that the Rapture is imminent.

Not desiring the Rapture is, for American believers, as natural as breathing. Life in the United States is not bad, and for the most part, it's pretty comfortable. Compared to living as a Christian in, say, the Middle East, Africa, or other parts of the world, being a Christian requires no heavy price. That is what I mean when I say it is as natural as breathing.

Christians in America, unlike their counterparts in less blessed, heavily oppressed, persecuted parts of the world, rather than worrying about whether they will be able to provide food for themselves and their children for the day, look forward to their upcoming marriages, vacations, or new purchases that will satisfy their latest comfortable lifestyle aspirations. These physical and psychological wants and needs are the natural outflow from abundance. Longing for the Rapture is a spiritual (supernatural) exercise that requires, for most, effort that seems to offer no tangible, immediate gratification. Such effort is just too taxing for most of America's Christians and their pastors. It takes them out of their comfort zone, much like prayer and Bible reading.

When American Christians in this category do think of the Rapture — which, again, they believe will happen, but somewhere in the hazy years of the future — they fear it will take them away from the pleasures of this earthly life and snatch them from their comfortable American lifestyle. It will present a completely changed paradigm, causing them to lose homes, family closeness, friendships, other relationships, and their "stuff" — all of which provide familiarity and pleasure.

This is especially true among the younger people. Their disinterest in prophecy in general and in the Rapture in particular is more than obvious in the makeup of those who attend prophecy conferences. I can no longer see due to a retinal disease, but am told that the conferences are almost without exception attended nearly exclusively by those with gray hair.

Perhaps I've been too harsh on Christians in America. However, we are approaching the very end of this Church Age. The overly stern exhortation is intended to focus attention on the reality that we might within months, weeks, days, or even hours look our Lord in His holy, omniscient eyes. He said He was going to prepare a place for us and would come again and take us there with Him (John 14:1–3). That place is something we can't even begin to fathom in its wonders and luxuriant surroundings. All the relationships in this life we thought we might lose in the Rapture will be magnified in their joy and intimacy a million times over. We are going to find that all earthly treasures we so valued are as trash compared to things the Lord has prepared for those who love Him.

I sense that the newlywed couple who belongs to Christ will find their relationship with each other dazzlingly more intimate than anything planet Earth could have nurtured. The stuff left behind will be instantly forgotten when we behold the heavenly treasury that holds us spellbound. The best days of our lives in this earthly confinement will seem as a time of terrible, debilitating paralysis. The Rapture will instantaneously bring life unencumbered by gravity and all laws of what we know as physics. The Lord put us here to enjoy the many good things He provides. There's nothing wrong in living life to its fullest. But, this is not our home. We are travelers in a foreign land. We are here for, at best, 70, 80, 90, or 100 years, then we slip out of these surly bonds.

We, as God's children, should not resist the doctrine of Rapture, but anticipate that glorious instant when the whole purpose of our being born into this universe reaches fruition. We will at that incomprehensible moment understand what it means to be joint heirs with Christ. Even so, come, Lord Jesus!

16

February 2016: Gog Incentive

One recent day's headlines combine to produce a picture that brings the lateness of the prophetic hour into focus:

- China's Xi Calls for Creation of Palestinian State

- Tunisia Declares Nationwide Curfew as Violent Protests against Unemployment and Poverty Spread

- Syria Conflict: "US Expanding Air Strip" in Kurdish North

- Saudi-Iranian Proxy War over Syria Spreads to World Economic Forum Meeting

- French Prime Minister Warns Europe Will Be "Totally Destabilized" if It Takes All Refugees

- This Is What the Death of a Nation Looks Like: Venezuela Prepares for 720% Hyperinflation

- Haiti Postpones Sunday's Presidential Election as Violence Erupts

Nations are in distress with perplexity. The seas and waves of peoples around the world are roaring. All signals point to the soon-coming Tribulation outlined in the greatest of all prophetic books, the Revelation. All the while, it is pretty much business as usual within the confines of the United States while the country prepares for another presidential election.

The global financial powers that be are in disarray equal to that of the national leaders around the world who are in the aforementioned distress. The international stock exchanges appear to be set for massive collapse, yet the trigger point for that Humpty-Dumpty fall seems to be held up by some unseen hand of fate. All appears to be in configuration precisely as Jesus foretold for the time of His next catastrophic intervention into the affairs of mankind. This is not referring to the Second Advent of Revelation

19:11–14, but to the Rapture, as described by Paul in 1 Thessalonians 4:13–15 and 1 Corinthians 15:52–55, and even by Jesus Himself in John 14:1–3.

Surrounding these stage props for the final act of the age, the handwriting is appearing on the walls of human history, perhaps beginning to clarify how the Ezekiel 38–39 scenario will play out. The nation Israel, as the student of Bible prophecy might expect, is in the middle of these interesting developments.

News reports have for some months reported the many intrigues of the oil industry while the cost per barrel has been tumbling since Saudi reduced its prices. It is believed by many "experts" that the oil-rich nation's royal family, in concert with the United States presidential administration, cut prices to undercut Russia's upsurging involvement in oil production and sales around the world.

The undercutting worked. The value of the ruble fell precipitously, and although the Russian currency unit is now up to around 85 cents against the U.S. dollar, Vladimir Putin's budding Russian empire continues to suffer. And, while he and his country suffer, he remains resolute in presenting the image of being able to project power in the manner of the Soviet regime at the apex of when it was able to threaten the world.

Despite great concerns that Putin indeed has the military resources and other assets to truly threaten his neighbors and the rest of the world, experts with firsthand knowledge of Russia's capability provide interesting perspective to the contrary. Bill Browder, chief executive officer of Hermitage Capital and a former champion advocating for Vladimir Putin, now believes the Russian president leads a nation in such great peril of likely collapse that the situation portends danger for the world. Browder's ire against Putin was generated as the result of two of his colleagues who opposed Putin's rule being killed, Browder supposes, by Putin's henchmen. Browder himself was expelled from Russia in 2005 after criticizing alleged endemic corruption in the country.

Browder told CNBC that Russia is in severe recession and could very soon descend into chaos if money in Russia "runs out."

"I don't think you can underestimate how bad the situation in Russia is right now, you've got oil below any measure where the budget can survive and you've got sanctions from the West. Russia is in what I'd call a real serious economic crisis," he said on Thursday [January 21].[42]

---

42. Holly Ellyatt, "When Russia's Money Runs Out, The 'Real Trouble' Starts," CNBC, January 21, 2018; https://www.cnbc.com/2016/01/21/when-russias-money-runs-out-the-real-trouble-starts.html.

He told CNBC while attending the World Economic Forum (WEF) that Russia's Central Bank is "running out of money." He added, "Eventually they're going to run out of that money and when they do, that's when the real trouble begins."[43] So, perhaps the Gog "evil thought" of Ezekiel 38–39 begins to become understandable to the diligent student of Bible prophecy. Russia's movement into the Middle East is itself an astounding development. Astonishing oil and gas discoveries off the coast of the Jewish state and within the Golan Heights area truly add prophetic intrigue in the minds of those who observe. These things, combined with reports of Russia's dire economic straits, give food for thought, indeed. Does it all add up to the incentive that will put hooks in the jaws of that prophesied leader termed "Gog"? Stay tuned. . . .

God Bless America Again

A country song from way back in the1960s and 1970s, during the Vietnam War era, plays through my mind these days. The chorus goes as follows:

> God bless America again. You must know the trouble that she's in. Wash her pretty face, dry her eyes and then . . . God bless America again.[44]

The war was raging while Walter Cronkite read the mainstream view of the news to us at dinnertime. Film of bloodied American GIs and corpses of black-pajamaed Vietcong projected from our TV screens while we downed our evening meals.

B-52s dropped hundreds of thousands of tons of explosives, carpet-bombing an unseen enemy many thousands of feet below. Rolling Thunder, as it was called, churned up killing fields of earth mixed with flesh and blood night after night, day after day.

More than 50,000 American soldiers and airmen went through the horrific, grinding process of becoming casualties of war their country's leaders, it turned out, never intended to bring to total victory, giving their last measure of devotion for America the Beautiful. At the same time, the ugliness of political warfare was being uncovered and displayed in a media orgy of, in my view, pro-Communist gleefulness.

A U.S. president of the United States was turned out of office in disgrace, and rightfully so. "Watergate" became forever an ingrained term within the American-English lexicon.

---

43. Ibid.
44. Bobby Bare, "God Bless America Again," by Bobby Bare and Boyce Hawkins, recorded September 18, 1969, track A on *God Bless America Again*, RCA Victor, Vinyl.

Would America ever recover? Would the curse that had descended since the time of Korea, with America's young men and women dying in a "police action" purposely fought to stalemate rather than to complete victory, ever lift from our nation?

There have been moments of seemingly possible national egress from the plunge into the abyss of political corrosiveness. It looked like the nation might pull away from the cultural rot begun in earnest during the sexual revolution of the 1960s and the legitimization of murdering babies in their mother's wombs.

The Moral Majority appeared for a brief, shining moment to be making headway in engendering movement toward moral sanity. Somehow, however, a national, cultural darkness began descending following the Reagan years. An almost tangible veil separating America's formerly flawed but Judeo-Christian-governed morality from a new immorality fell with the Clinton years, the White House intern's stained blue dress and all the rest.

Jeremiah Wright, Barack Hussein Obama's black-liberation theology "pastor," spewed from his Chicago pulpit a venomous rant that America's chickens had come home to roost and implied that the Lord of heaven should damn America — using God's name in vain with the invective. Wright was, I infer, talking about the Islamist attacks on the World Trade Center towers in New York and the Pentagon in Washington, D.C.

As much as I detest "Reverend" Wright's hate speech against the United States, I must admit that indeed, America's chickens appeared to have come home to roost, suffering on that September 11, 2001, Tuesday at least some degree of God's judgment. In my view, the past seven-plus years of Wright's best-known parishioner's time in the Oval Office has intensified that judgment.

The year 2016, I sense strongly, is going to be a pivotal year for this nation and the world. It is proper, I believe, to wonder whether God's judgment is now on track to preclude that of the corrective sort, such as in the past. I'm thinking of times like the Great Depression of the 1930s, which followed the debauched era of the Roaring Twenties.

Is God's judgment now entering a destructive phase rather than another corrective one? Is it entering a time like that when Sodom and Gomorrah came to their end? Is it possible that God will ever bless America again?

Like that country song tells throughout its lyrics, I, too, love America and don't want to ever let it fall because I haven't done my part in helping keep it upright in every sense.

All of this said, spiritually enlightened Bible students know that neither the leaders of this nation nor of any other will rectify the rapidly mounting problems. Only Jesus Christ will solve the otherwise unsolvable, sinister evil that is at humanity's core.

There are, within the community of Bible prophecy observers, those who wonder whether America is the most likely candidate for being the Babylon of the 18th chapter of Revelation — according to the Bible, the country that will be the most materially accomplished of all nations in history. I am one of those who ponder this possibility more seriously with each passing news headline involving America's president and State Department dealing with Israel.

God, it is abundantly clear, has, through His dealing with America, more than lived up to His promise to bless those who bless the progeny that would come from Abraham through Isaac. America, acting as midwife in the rebirth of the Jewish state into modernity in 1948, has received bountiful material blessings beyond measure. God has truly blessed America.

Conversely, He has promised to curse those who curse His chosen nation, Israel. The cultural war is causing the loss of America's former effort to promote the Judeo-Christian values the Founding Fathers infused into the Constitution. Just as troubling is the obvious disdain this president and those around him have for Israel, even choosing to champion Israel's enemies at every diplomatic opportunity, it seems.

Such continued folly will certainly bring national disaster the likes of which our previously blessed nation has never experienced. If indeed forgiveness of our national sins is possible given the lateness of the prophetic hour, let us implore God to bless America again. This must be done, however, without vain repetition of the idle words "God bless America" often used by presidents and politicians when ending their meaningless speeches.

There is but one heavenly prescription for obtaining an answer to such a prayer:

> If my people, which are called by my name, shall humble themselves, and pray, and seek my face, and turn from their wicked ways; then will I hear from heaven, and will forgive their sin, and will heal their land (2 Chronicles 7:14).

God does not change. Jesus Christ is the same yesterday, today, and forever. That call for His people to repent is still in effect — and it is for Church Age saints just as it was for His chosen people of ancient Israel. But time is swiftly fleeting.

"We will make America great again!" is a current presidential political proclamation. No, "we" won't. We've proven, through our actions and lack thereof, that as a people, we want to take America in the other direction. "We" didn't make America great in the first place, and we certainly can't make it great in the future.

"God bless America again," when offered in genuine spiritual, obedient humility — not in politically prideful demand — before the throne of Almighty God, is the only petition that has a prayer of a chance to save our nation.

Supreme Decision

Just as suspected, the year 2016 is on track to be a pivotal year in shaping biblically prophetic destiny. The sudden loss of Supreme Court Justice Antonin Scalia will produce ramifications far beyond those posed by this sitting president further stacking that court with yet another justice whose thinking is similar to his own ideological bent.

The ultimate decision involving replacement of the constitutional champion that was Scalia will perhaps, in one way or another, help determine the future course of all of mankind.

American Founding Fathers, whether fully aware in every case that they were listening to the directives of the Almighty, gave Americans yet unborn a republic based upon Judeo-Christian principles. And, indications are overwhelming that almost all of them — even the deists like Franklin and Jefferson — knew that Providence had a divine hand in victory in the War of Independence and in composing the liberty-laden U.S. Constitution.

The writings of the Founders show they recognized that it was not merely an existential deity that started the national ball rolling then left America to its own devices. It is more than obvious that the one and only God's mighty hand has been on this most materially blessed nation to ever exist throughout its coming up 240 years of nationhood.

Antonin Scalia was a Supreme Court justice who, with each decision he rendered, demonstrated that he believed our God-influenced Constitution should be defended and preserved. With his passing, we face the possibility that it is in danger of degeneration to ineffectiveness at best, and complete disregard at worst.

The Supreme Court has teeter-tottered on the fulcrum of cultural dichotomy, particularly since 1963, with the decisions to eliminate Bible reading and prayer from public schools. By this, I mean the traditional,

God-fearing part of America was on one side and the America that wanted no such constraint was on the other. Anti-God, humanistic gravity has consistently been tugging the nation downward with succeeding Supreme Court decisions. We witnessed a dramatic increase in the latest such tugging during the past year.

And now we face action by a president who, immediately upon Scalia's death, announced he will nominate a replacement within the ten-plus months left of his presidency. We don't have to wonder very deeply about the sort of nominee that will eventuate. All that is necessary is to consider Mr. Obama's ideological forays into jurisprudence at the Supreme Court level over the past seven years.

With decisions of the land's highest court steadily slanting toward the anti-Constitutional side, and now the loss of perhaps that court's strongest voice for preservation of the document the Founders gave us, we indeed face perilous times.

America, I put to you, is now moving rapidly downward on the slide into national oblivion. It is agonizing to have to say it, but the facts are staring us in the nation's rebellious face.

The Supreme Court and its problems are but a reflection of that rebellion. We have sown to the winds disregard for God's biblical guidelines for upright comportment. We are beginning to reap the whirlwind of reprobate thinking and conduct warned about by the Apostle Paul in Romans chapter 1.

Perhaps the final straw for heaven's Supreme Court is we the people allowing a wicked leadership to turn America against Israel and take up the cause of those who are vowed to destroy the Jewish state. Even more compelling as evidence of the nation's rebellion are the so-called Christian churches of America joining in cursing Israel. We hear every day about churches that have joined in the BDS (boycott, divestment, and sanction) movement to punish Israel for "occupying" land that they say doesn't belong to Israel.

To add insult to injury, they proclaim that the Church has replaced Israel as inheritor of the promises God gave Abraham, Isaac, and Jacob. Israel, they declare, has forfeited the claim to the promises and is no longer God's chosen people. The Lord is finished with them.

That is what these would-be usurpers of God's promises say. But here is what the Lord God of Israel says in His Holy Word:

> This is what the LORD says, he who appoints the sun to
> shine by day, who decrees the moon and stars to shine by

night, who stirs up the sea so that its waves roar — the LORD Almighty is his name; "Only if these decrees vanish from my sight," declares the LORD, "will Israel ever cease being a nation before me" (Jeremiah 31:35–36; NIV).

Just as the above promise is still in effect, so is God's warning of Genesis 12:3. America, if national repentance is not forthcoming, faces a Supreme Decision far more serious than the replacement of a U.S. Supreme Court justice.

17

March 2016: The Crisis Awaits

President Obama recently stated, in effect, that anyone who tells us the economic situation in the United States is not getting better is "peddling fiction." He said this despite the fact that the debt clock is ticking at a rate that will soon have Americans and generations to come owing beyond $20 trillion. Extrapolated over an extended number of years, some economists are saying unfunded liabilities of this nation amount to more than $200 trillion.

Like it or not, believe it or not, you and I are being swept along by the tide of human history toward something profoundly ominous. Hourly news accounts, no matter how much they've been doctored to try to present a recovering national and global economic picture, engender fearful concerns about things to come. It is almost impossible to grasp the causes and effects of the evil that is shaping and moving America and the world toward a destiny the supposed best minds on the planet can't determine. However, that inability to define the problems, much less find solutions, doesn't stop them from making seemingly wild stabs at trying to channel all of us into a drastically changed economic national and world order.

But are their attempts really wild stabs, or is there a method to their madness? History is replete with attempts to reshape national and global economic realities. Money equals power, and power exerts control upon this fallen planet. Power is the ultimate end game of all who seek it for themselves. Henry Kissinger put it this way: "Power is the ultimate aphrodisiac."[45]

The declaration can be understood in recalling the most ancient of accounts of an infamous personality seeking the greatest of all power:

> For thou hast said in thine heart, I will ascend into heaven,
> I will exalt my throne above the stars of God: I will sit also
> upon the mount of the congregation, in the sides of the north:

---

45. http://www.constitutionpreservation.org/articles/october-7-2011/power-ultimate-aphro-disiac.

I will ascend above the heights of the clouds; I will be like the most High (Isaiah 14:13–14).

Humankind's determination to do the same — acquire the power to which the angel named Lucifer aspired — hasn't changed since the serpent first told Eve that she and Adam would be like God if they ate from the fruit of the forbidden tree (see Genesis 3:5). Tracing the serpent's trail of power madness to a later time recorded in the Bible (Genesis 11), Nimrod was the would-be one-world-order builder of his day, following the Great Flood of Noah's time. Nimrod, like every megalomaniac since, lusted for God-like power.

Man's lust for power continues to grow; he has not learned the lessons of the past because, as a whole, he regards the Word of God as being irrelevant to governing the earth. One philosopher, George Santayana, put it this way: "Those who cannot remember the past are condemned to repeat it."[46]

The corruption God saw and condemned in antediluvian times, which caused Him to destroy all upon the earth except eight people, has again reached a dangerous level. Dictators prove the truth of another bit of philosophical wisdom, this by Lord Edward Acton: "All power tends to corrupt, and absolute power corrupts absolutely."[47]

In my estimation, we see this level of power being sought in the words and actions of the current presidential administration. Circumventing the U.S. Constitution at every opportunity because this president has "a phone and a pen" poses a danger to this republic. To, at the same time, have another branch of government that is supposed to act as a check and balance to an out-of-control executive, yet does nothing to present opposition, creates real and present danger to this nation.

While mainstream media seemingly sway acceptingly in the mesmerizing economic flute notes of the charmer, the real peddler of fiction, the immediate future looks ominously bleak, according to true financial experts who are without the benefit of the mainstream's ubiquitous microphones and cameras to get out their warning. The world is about to experience economic collapse the likes of which has never occurred, they say.

These people almost all agree that there will come a tipping point, one moment, that will prick the immense financial bubble that the money powers that be have manipulated to this point of crisis we face.

My own belief continues to be that God's great hand of control, rather than the would-be economic masters, has prevented the bubble from

---

46. http://bigthink.com/the-proverbial-skeptic/those-who-do-not-learn-history-doomed-to-repeat-it-really.
47. https://acton.org/research/lord-acton-quote-archive.

bursting. The crisis awaits the moment when the Lord Himself will burst the bubble. Careful study of the latest news makes it clear that the term "cashless system" is more and more in vogue. The economic gurus at the highest levels — in human terms and in supernatural, satanic terms — seem to be preparing a system of electronic funds transfer (EFT). They want to do away with physical currency and go to the cashless computer system so they can carry out their sleight-of-hand monetary machinations electronically.

The marks-and-numbers system of economics of Revelation 13:16–18 is more than just on the drawing board. We are seeing it come to pass in our daily news. All that is required for its implementation is the crisis that will bring it forward. I am convinced that crisis will be created by the Rapture of all who name the name of Christ.

Rapture Delayed

We have looked many times in this column at those who mock the end-times message and the topic of the Rapture in particular. Because those who scoff have been of the abrasive, unbelieving variety for the most part, I usually employ a standard Bible verse reply to let those who are mocking know that they are actually fulfilling Bible prophecy:

> Knowing this first, that there shall come in the last days scoffers, walking after their own lusts, and saying, Where is the promise of his coming? for since the fathers fell asleep, all things continue as they were from the beginning of the creation (2 Peter 3:3–4).

Lately, however, this isn't quite an appropriate response because the questions are coming weekly from genuine believers in the pre-Trib Rapture of the Church. These Christians are worried — some are very worried.

They look around and on every side they see and feel the satanic pressures from this fallen sphere closing in. Issues and events, the very ambience in which their lives are engulfed, generate thoughts that their circumstance is beginning to look much like the Bible's description of the Tribulation itself.

One such Christian brother wrote this past week, his words pretty much right to the point of the many other emails expressing like emotion. Here is his note in its entirety:

> Why is the Lord delaying the rapture? It should have happened years ago. We would be in the millennium now enjoying

> true peace and prosperity without the suffering. I don't get it.
> It's God call, of course, but 58 million aborted babies in the
> US since 1973, Christians tortured and murdered worldwide,
> people who believe in Jesus longing for his return suffering im-
> mensely. I don't get it where is our Lord and Savior?

The emailer didn't use any soft nuances of greetings or any other niceties. He just laid his spirit-distressed emotions right out there.

You don't answer such gut-wrenching concern with the Apostle Peter's prophecy as given above. This child of God is worried, puzzled . . . per-plexed. It's the kind of questioning I've heard in my own kids' anxieties when they were young and felt disappointed by one or another of my fail-ures to keep a promise. *"Dad should never let me down like that."*

Only, this perceived unkept promise isn't from an imperfect, human father. The error is in the question of the imperfect child asking it. Our Perfect Father will, as always, be 100 percent faithful to keep every promise made.

The Lord Jesus Himself, in His ascended position, said the following to John the Revelator:

> Because thou hast kept the word of my patience, I also will
> keep thee from the hour of temptation, which shall come upon
> all the world, to try them that dwell upon the earth (Revelation
> 3:10).

Jesus said it, and that means the Heavenly Father said it — promised it! Jesus said that He and the Father are one. They are inseparable, one and the same, the first and second persons of the Godhead, the Trinity.

God cannot lie, the Scripture tells us. Jesus is the Way, the Truth, and the Life. God keeps His promises. So, this brother in Christ, like all the other believers who look to the "blessed hope" of Titus 2:13, who are in fear and worry while watching this fallen world closing in, need an answer from the Word of God.

The Heavenly Father gave the answer to Peter to pass along to us just a bit farther on in Scripture. The answer to why the Rapture hasn't occurred as soon as almost all of us wish it would occur is, at least in part, wrapped up in the following:

> The Lord is not slack concerning his promise, as some men
> count slackness; but is longsuffering to us-ward, not willing
> that any should perish, but that all should come to repentance
> (2 Peter 3:9).

The Tribulation that will follow this Age of Grace will be filled with horrors that even John, under divine inspiration, had trouble describing. The Lord wants to provide every moment possible during this present dispensation for those lost in their sin to come safely into the shelter of His beloved Son, Jesus Christ. God wants this for the lost because, following the Rapture, making the decision to accept Christ for salvation will be more difficult by a multiple of factors. Facing beheading is but one of those factors!

That is the reason — at least a primary reason — the Rapture hasn't yet occurred in this generation, according to God's Word.

That said, I take notable exception to the emailer's contention that God is "delaying" the Rapture. You can take this to the bank: God is not delaying the Rapture. It will happen in the twinkling of an eye at precisely the moment the Father has determined. Jesus said, "But of that day and hour knoweth no man, no, not the angels of heaven, but my Father only" (Matthew 24:36).

God knows the instant He will send His Son to get His Bride, make no mistake. There is no delay.

On that note, issues and events closing in on us show that we are almost certainly very near the moment we instantaneously find ourselves face to face with the Lord Jesus. Just how near we are to the Rapture — if we could indeed know — would likely allay all fears.

Presidential Political Purulence

An infection is spreading among the American populace. It isn't bacteriological or viral in the biological sense, but it is an epidemic in some ways more virulent, more septic. It seems to have contaminated society at every level — even Christian pastors I thought would have been biblically vaccinated against the anti-God strain.

Unrestrained by apparently any prophylactic inhibitor, such as media censorship or even Moral Majority–type protective shielding, the salacious show goes on. It's made manifest before the nation and the world in an observably, unabashedly shameless display.

It shouldn't surprise, one must suppose. We've had hints of such lasciviousness within the White House, particularly since JFK's passing — that is, since enough time has passed that historical spelunkers have exposed the sexual trysts in the White House of Camelot's leader way back there 50-plus years ago. A president was later deemed a "crook" by the Watergate inquisitionist. But other than often-expletive, deleted language discovered on the infamous recordings of the Nixon White House, nothing even remotely approached the sexual goings-on like during the Kennedy White House years.

Many accounts of LBJ and his rather raw and rowdy approach to the presidency have since produced accounts of sexual debauchery in the White House. But until Bill Clinton, all was kept in the Oval Office closet. That closet was opened for all to know when that president's activities with the young intern within the small study just off the oval room were uncovered.

That down-and-dirty activity — a paraphrase of how Obama's preacher, Jeremiah Wright, put it — opened the once-high office of the presidency to the cesspool humor and conversation once reserved for the porn magazines and shops where only the most derelict would openly venture.

Now, on the presidential election debate stages where once the all-important issues and events of our time were heard, we are subjected regularly to debased topics once only discussed in forbidden books.

Talk of male and female genitalia are thrown about in today's political discourse in vulgar, slang invectives as readily as Richard Nixon might have once thrown accusations that John F. Kennedy was too young and inexperienced for the presidency.

It is astonishing to consider the Nixon-Kennedy debates (or any other) against what we are seeing now.

I remember the kind of gutter talk we are hearing by presidential candidates today thrown about by teenage boys during junior high and high school when I was in the ninth grade or so. Back then, those lunkheads — of which I was much too often one — would never bring that sort of conversation out into the light of adult society.

Now we have presidential wannabes talking about such things right in front of the bright lights and cameras, proudly airing their salaciousness for the world to hear.

There is, according to the polls, a vast, reality-show-type audience that is entertained by this new "populist" political trash-mouth talk. Those who aren't necessarily amused or entertained by it sit in silence for the most part, overlooking the degree to which the once most-respected office in the land is being debased and degraded.

Some of this silent sort are names recognized within evangelical Christianity, it is distressing to acknowledge.

This isn't to put down any presidential candidate or build up another. My only exhortation is to use much discretion and pray for godly discernment during this crucial election season. We are in prophetic times, I have no doubt. America is subjected to this presidential political purulence at a time when powers and principalities in high places intend to assert their wickedness upon a generation ripe for the coming Antichrist rise to power.

The Scripture that comes to mind should serve as a mirror into which we, the voters, should look, while doing our best to move in a direction other than the one of the once-condemned people depicted here:

> Were they ashamed when they had committed abomination? nay, they were not at all ashamed, neither could they blush: therefore shall they fall among them that fall: in the time of their visitation they shall be cast down, saith the LORD.
>
> I will surely consume them, saith the LORD: there shall be no grapes on the vine, nor figs on the fig tree, and the leaf shall fade; and the things that I have given them shall pass away from them (Jeremiah 8:12–13).

Prophetic Lull

Despite such terroristic actions as witnessed in Brussels this past week, like it does from time to time while lurching toward the end of this troubled age, the world seems to be pausing to catch its breath.

We sometimes call it a "lull" because prophetic progression appears to be on hold. It's kind of like in the South when a severe springtime storm is about to produce a big tornado. Everything gets eerily still.

What is happening, I'm told, is that the big super-cell thunderhead is sucking the surrounding atmosphere into its building vortex. All turns a greenish-yellow color and not a leaf is rustling.

One of the mistakes we make with regard to Bible prophecy is viewing things too much from our American perspective. Things may seem to be whirling around us, but the larger picture presents a different view.

We hear the rumbling and see the lightning flashing on the black horizon, but all is perfectly still, as if the complexion of the earth has taken on a sickly pallor. It seems that this humanistic system is holding its collective breath in somewhat of a perceived pause in these scary moments.

Presidential politics right now in the United States, on the other hand, are anything but eerily calm. For example, the campaign rhetoric and vitriol are raw rough and tumble. Americans who see things through a strictly political prism believe this storm we are in will determine where our world will be torn apart, depending upon who wins the presidency. The atmosphere is turbulent. We are in the midst of a terrible, national storm with the nation's future at stake.

That might all be true but, on a global basis, there seems to be an environment surrounding us with an ominous pallor that harbors far greater lethality. There may be far greater dangers than those given off by the political winds that are whipping us all into a frenzy here in America. Internationally, the powers and principalities of Ephesians 6:12 are working quietly behind the scenes, striving harder than ever to bring about that great, end-times tornado called the Tribulation.

One can sense the corruptive atmosphere of fallen man being drawn into the coming Tribulation vortex. Yet there seems to be for the moment an eerie calm, despite evidence of trouble brewing everywhere we look.

The president of the United States is reportedly working with the United Nations to bring about a two-state solution to the "Palestinian-Israeli problem" before he leaves office. Israel itself remains in a lull, while looking in every direction at a storm gathering against it. Russia and its headstrong president are making strange, unanticipated withdrawal gestures and movements in and around Syria and other entry points to the Middle East. North Korea blusters ahead with nuclear and missile tests, actions intended to threaten its immediate neighbor, South Korea, and the rest of us as well. China builds islands in international waters then claims them as their territory, while building military bases upon the newly formed land to threaten anyone who dares question its intentions.

Iran continues to silently work on a nuclear program that it no doubt thinks will one day be used against the "Great Satan" and the "Little Satan" — the United States and Israel.

The world's building economic disaster expands by the hour like an embolism within the human brain. The silent bubble could erupt explosively at any time, bringing the global, financial catastrophe that many fear.

Agents of the father of lies work incessantly to implant within the fallen minds of mankind that Christianity is a viper's nest of hatred. Just to our northern border, Canada's supreme judicial body has ruled in a number of cases that biblical text can be construed as hate speech that will not be tolerated. One pastor spent ten years and more than $200,000 to finally get a reversal of such a charge against him. Americans would be foolish to assume that a devilish invasion of evil jurisprudence isn't in Satan's plans for this nation. As a matter of fact, we've already experienced that kind of evil at some level. The cases involving the homosexual agenda and bakeries and flower shops that refuse to provide services for same-sex marriages come to mind.

All the above and much more give evidence that the atmosphere of liberty we've enjoyed since the country's founding is being sucked into the building thunderhead that will produce the greatest storm in human history.

While the world catches its breath, the power of the storm continues to build. Satan seems as if he will have his way against all of humanity in this great destructive era that now rumbles upon earth's angry horizon.

But Jesus said,

> These things I have spoken unto you, that in me ye might have peace. In the world ye shall have tribulation: but be of good cheer; I have overcome the world (John 16:33).

The Lord promised believers who are alive at the time this end-times storm threatens,

> Because thou hast kept the word of my patience, I also will keep thee from the hour of temptation, which shall come upon all the world, to try them that dwell upon the earth (Revelation 3:10).

It is altogether fitting and appropriate to echo the words of John the revelator: "Even so, come, Lord Jesus" (Revelation 22:20).

18

April 2016: End-Times Petri Dish

Sin infection spawned from man's disobedience has metastasized globally at this late point in the final dispensation leading to Christ's return. It is not far-fetched to think of things that are happening in such biological terms, or to express them as such, while two major players in Bible prophecy bring the terminal situation into focus.

The European Union (EU), thought by many observers of prophecy in Scripture to be the nucleus out of which will come a revived form of the Roman Empire in accordance with Daniel 9:26–27, is front and center in relevant news. The most central national entity of eschatology for the wind-up of human history, Israel, is the other key player in today's prophetic news. Of all developments in the milieu of end-times things going on, it is as if some master pharmacologist has upon his lab table a petri dish in which broils a deadly mixture prophesied to explode in a breakout of human history's deadliest era.

Effervescing within that dish are the virulent ingredients that threaten to take peace from the earth in the form of war unlike ever before. That war will not be brought about by the players most often believed to be the instigators of man's final war. Quite the opposite.

Armageddon will be brought about by the One the false religionists of the world of Christendom proclaim could never judge sin harshly. They promise that He is love, and no loving God could react with such hateful, punitive action. Here, again, is what God's Word says about the end-times activities taking place within that petri dish:

> For, behold, in those days, and in that time, when I shall bring again the captivity of Judah and Jerusalem, I will also gather all nations, and will bring them down into the valley of Jehoshaphat, and will plead with them there for my people and

for my heritage Israel, whom they have scattered among the nations, and parted my land (Joel 3:1–2).

That, my friends, is Armageddon that the Lord is prophesying through Joel. The nations of the world are going to pay a terrible price for their rebellion against Him and for the treatment of His chosen people, the Jews — Israel.

The intention to divide God's land — which He gave to Israel forever — is at the heart of the prophesied simmering brew. The world, including much of Christendom, is turning against Israel in the boycott, divestment, and sanction (BDS) piling-on. This, of course, involves economically punishing Israel because they refuse to give up land in order to give the Palestinians a nation within current Israeli borders — land won by Israel in several wars that already belonged to them by divine promise.

Many prophetic observers believe the Antichrist will emerge from the European Union, and it is presently speaking out of both sides of its official mouth. Its spokesman seems to obliquely defend Israel, while at the same time holding the Jewish state responsible for the holdup to a peaceful solution to the Israel-Palestinian "problem." We learn more about all this within the following excerpts:

> Without the Israeli-Palestinian conflict there would be no Boycott, Divestment and Sanctions movement, the European Union's envoy to Israel said Monday, arguing that the best way to fight BDS is to take steps to advance a two-state solution.
>
> "The most effective antidote against the BDS movement is to solve the Palestinian issue. If there were no Palestinian issue, there would be no BDS movement," [EU] Ambassador Lars Faaborg-Andersen said at a conference in Jerusalem.
>
> Earlier during the conference, which was organized by the Yedioth Ahronoth daily newspaper, Faaborg-Andersen expressed the EU's desire to see Israel thrive and said the union completely rejects any efforts to boycott Israel. "Let me make one thing 100 percent clear: The European Union is against BDS. Our policy is totally opposite of BDS. Our policy is one of engagement with Israel."
>
> But it is important for Israel not to be seen as undermining a two-state solution, he said. "If more effort is put into showing

a will to move forward and to obtain progress in this process, it would greatly weaken the BDS movement."[48]

The all-out effort to "divide" God's land is underway. America's president has chosen to put the United States at the center of this dangerous petri dish mixture. Certainly, the world must be near the time when the final prophecies will begin manifesting. That means the Rapture of all born-again believers is even nearer!

Supernatural Storm Shelter

Springtime in the Arkansas-Louisiana-Oklahoma-Texas region evokes precautionary thought of nature's most singularly powerful storms. By that, I mean storms that can do the most complete devastation within the areas they sweep across.

These, of course, are the huge tornadoes almost certain to occur in one or more of those states from April through June. Oklahoma, particularly, is prone to produce the most powerful of the twisters. We remember a couple of 300-mile-per-hour tornadoes within the last several decades in that state. One contained the strongest wind ever recorded on planet Earth — I believe 318 miles per hour was the figure.

My friends just outside Oklahoma City lost everything except their lives in one such monster storm a few years ago. Some of the readers of this column very generously contributed to a fund to help those folks, the family of a great personal friend of mine who is part of a team that heads a major prophetic ministry in Oklahoma City.

When I was last in that city, someone with me pointed out a company that manufactures and sells tornado shelters that was very near the TV studio where we taped some programs. It was a stark reminder of the fact that we were right in "tornado central." Without a "'fraidy hole" (as we in the South call them) to go into, one is on his or her own. People are subject to the vicissitudes of the winds that "come sweeping down the plains" in springtime, as the musical *Oklahoma* would have it.

As we point out consistently in these commentaries, a storm is brewing. It is supernatural, and it is a certainty. It will strike. It can be clearly seen gathering on the prophetic horizon.

Whether considering matters involving geopolitics, socioeconomics, religion, or any other aspect of the human condition, the forecast

48. Rapheal Ahre, "Boycotts Will Disappear When Israel Advances Peace, EU Envoy Says," *The Times of Israel*, March 28, 2016.

looks bleak indeed. No human-manufactured shelter can protect against the boiling, chaotic tempest that the Lord Himself predicts for times just ahead.

Daniel the prophet forecast the storm that approaches:

> And he shall confirm the covenant with many for one week: and in the midst of the week he shall cause the sacrifice and the oblation to cease, and for the overspreading of abominations he shall make it desolate, even until the consummation, and that determined shall be poured upon the desolate (Daniel 9:27).

Jesus zoomed in more specifically to forewarn about the power and destructiveness of the coming supernatural storm:

> For then shall be great tribulation, such as was not since the beginning of the world to this time, no, nor ever shall be (Matthew 24:21).

The entire Book of Revelation, of course, is a detailed, blow-by-blow description of the coming Tribulation tempest. John outlines 21 specific destructive aspects of the storm in a series of seven scrolls, seven trumpets, and seven bowls of judgment.

Again, no human manufacturer can produce a safe place against what is certainly scheduled to be the worst time of destruction the planet has ever known (and that's saying a lot, considering that all life was destroyed by water in the Flood of Noah's day). But, thankfully, there is a superhuman shelter that is readily available to every person alive today.

In thinking on that shelter, my own ruminations caused me to wonder more deeply about God's promises.

Jesus prophesied that, the next time He intervenes into the affairs of mankind, the world will be exactly like it was in the days of Noah and Lot (see Matthew 24:36–42, for example).

Like in those two instances, God's children who are alive at the time of the Rapture will be taken out of harm's way. The terrible storm of His judgment will then fall. All believers will go into the supernatural storm shelter prepared for them in heaven while there is great chaos and carnage on the planet that is ripe for God's wrath.

Many new believers left behind when the Rapture happens will come out of that Tribulation storm, some as martyrs and others as flesh-and-blood survivors to repopulate the millennial earth during the reign of Christ upon His Second Advent.

And there is a second supernatural storm shelter that will be provided during the Tribulation tempest itself. I believe the following prophecy applies to both the saints who will be raptured and another group of believers, the believing remnant of Jews who will find shelter through God's divine direction. This protection will likely include Tribulation-era Gentile believers to some extent, too:

> Come, my people, enter thou into thy chambers, and shut thy doors about thee: hide thyself as it were for a little moment, until the indignation be overpast. For, behold, the LORD cometh out of his place to punish the inhabitants of the earth for their iniquity: the earth also shall disclose her blood, and shall no more cover her slain (Isaiah 26:20–21).

Jesus Himself points the way to the supernatural storm shelter. It is the ONLY way to assure that we can be safe while the coming Tribulation tornado ravages a judgment-deserving world:

> Jesus saith unto him, I am the way, the truth, and the life: no man cometh unto the Father, but by me (John 14:6).

On Being Rapture Ready
Part I

Note: This April 22 is the fifth-year anniversary of the Good Friday trip I was given to somewhere on the perimeter of heaven. It remains as vivid in my every waking moment today as right after it happened.

I wanted to again present the articles I wrote at the end of that year — 2011 — because I believe we are so very near the time of Christ's call to us, "Come up hither" (Revelation 4:1).

Here, then, is Part I of my thoughts in December 2011 following that April 22, 2011, Good Friday event.

Being prepared to meet Jesus Christ face to face — as far as trying to make that my constant state of mind is concerned — has been part of my every waking moment since Good Friday of this year. Not wishing to go over it in a public forum like this one ad nauseam, nonetheless, I've been considering the relationship between my near-death moments of April 22 and being Rapture ready, as is the thought wrapped up in our website's name. So, here goes yet again. . . .

This is intended to be an exhortation for all of us who name Christ as our Lord — urging us individually and collectively to hold Him close to our spiritual hearts during this Christmas season. It is not meant to dwell upon my personal experience as an overriding point of focus. Many who read this column on a regular basis know some of the details of my heart event on Good Friday of this year. I'm often corrected by my wife, Margaret, for not calling it a heart attack. For some reason, that description just doesn't register within my aging gray matter. Others have heart attacks, not me.

I remember thinking at the time it was occurring that this wasn't possible. The EMT working on me told the hospital dispatcher that he had a "coronary in progress." It didn't register then, either. There I was, however, being rushed toward Saline Memorial Hospital, gasping for breath, the pain behind my sternum feeling as if it would explode my chest at any second.

I remember arriving and the gurney being tugged toward the ER outer doors. Then, there was the computer-like blip, and I was suddenly before a large heavenly throng of young, beautiful, cheering men and women. The ambiance of my surroundings was dazzling, and I wanted to join them. There was no recollection whatsoever of where I had been — no memories of this planetary existence.

I was, the doctor later told Margaret, dead on arrival.

They hit me with the defibrillation paddles — yes, just like you've seen in the shows where they say "Clear!" and then apply the paddles, making the body nearly jump off the table.

I felt nothing, but the action did cause me to leave the place I never wanted to leave. I remembered thinking, "I want to stay here forever in this perfect place." But everything turned dark, and I awoke in total darkness on the gurney. This is because I'm blind due to a retinal disease, as many who read the account know. The pain behind the sternum grew worse, and I heard the blip twice more. Each time, I was before that cheering, enthusiastic throng of vibrant young people. The sights were astonishing, colors of every description emanating from somewhere I could neither determine nor cared to investigate. The third time I was among them, we were all racing or being drawn by some powerful energy toward a destination I would never know. I was again in the hospital, this time on the cardiac unit's procedure table. I had again been hit with the paddles.

I had survived the "widow maker," an artery blockage that I was told only 5 percent of victims live through. I was clinically dead three times, my heart having stopped each time. I had been given a journey and return trip that few are privileged to experience — and I say that meaning it as humbly as it is possible to express the fact.

The reasons for and meanings of this experience have been confirmed and affirmed in my spiritual understanding. I've dealt briefly with those impressions from the Holy Spirit in a previous article, "HeavenVision." God willing, there will be a more in-depth presentation on these matters in a book we have planned for release early in 2012, entitled *HeavenVision: Glimpses of Glory.*

I continue to be given insight into what it all means. As stated at the beginning of this commentary, my thoughts have been turned toward being ever ready to meet the Lord Jesus Christ face to face since that Good Friday when my heart ceased to beat those three times. One of the things constantly on my mind is that my heart could fail again at any moment.

My rehabilitation has been an amazing success story. And, in that regard, I thank so many of you whose prayers were obviously heard in the throne room of heaven. I honestly haven't experienced one moment's problem, in any way, with my heart or anything else of consequence regarding my health. In fact, I was given the "Arkansas Cardiologist Association's Patient of the Year Award for 2011" on November 18. I was asked to speak to their convention and I told them that I don't know why I should be honored. All I did was survive. My Lord, Jesus Christ, deserves top honors because He holds the keys to death and hell. I then said that they, the wonderful medical professionals, also deserve honors for being the ones God chose to put me back into this race.

The only problem has been cracked teeth and one crowned tooth broken completely off that resulted from being hit with the paddles those three times. Nonetheless, the thought is there that one's last heartbeat can occur at any moment. Each time my heart stopped, I stood not before Jesus Christ, but in front of a cheering cloud of witnesses as given in Hebrews 12:1–3. This simply means I have been assured in my spiritual understanding that this wasn't really death. It was a preview I was given for reasons the Lord has determined. But, I will, when God's timing has come to fullness for my life, stand before my Lord and Savior. It will happen just as instantaneously as did my near-death trip to the fringes of glory. I am ready for that moment because Jesus saved my soul with His work of redemption on the Cross at Calvary nearly 2,000 years ago. When my heart beats that final time, I will, in the twinkling of an eye (see 1 Corinthians 15:52), stand before Him and be with Him for all of eternity.

But my heart has not stopped for that final time. When Christ calls all believers, living and dead, to Himself, I will, if still alive, stand instantaneously before Him just as I stood instantaneously before that cheering cloud of witnesses on Good Friday, April 22, 2011.

Being Rapture ready is being ready, period. It means you are prepared to meet the Lord at any moment — at all times. Every believer has the same promise — to be present with the Lord when life on earth is over:

> We are always confident, knowing that, whilst we are at home in the body, we are absent from the Lord: (for we walk by faith, not by sight): we are confident, I say, and willing rather to be absent from the body, and to be present with the Lord (2 Corinthians 5:6–8).

Next week we will go in-depth, examining details about what it means to be Rapture ready.

On Being Rapture Ready
Part 2

Note: This April 22 was the fifth-year anniversary of the Good Friday trip I was given to somewhere on the perimeter of heaven. It remains as vivid in my every waking moment today as right after it happened.

I wanted to again present the articles I wrote at the end of that year — 2011 — because I believe we are so very near the time of Christ's call to us, "Come up hither" (Revelation 4:1).

Here is Part II of that December 2011, "Nearing Midnight" article.

There is no specific signal that presages the Rapture of believers in the Scriptures. That calling by Christ to those who know Him as Savior will be unannounced and instantaneous. The Apostle Paul's words inform us of that stunning event:

> Behold, I shew you a mystery; We shall not all sleep, but we shall all be changed, in a moment, in the twinkling of an eye, at the last trump: for the trumpet shall sound, and the dead shall be raised incorruptible, and we shall be changed (1 Corinthians 15:51–52).

Paul says further,

> For the Lord himself shall descend from heaven with a shout, with the voice of the archangel, and with the trump of God: and the dead in Christ shall rise first: then we which are alive and remain shall be caught up together with them in the clouds, to meet the Lord in the air: and so shall we ever be with the Lord (1 Thessalonians 4:16–17).

The website Todd Strandberg began in 1987, before the Internet was making an impact to any extent on life in America and throughout the world, encompasses what Christ expects every born-again believer to become. Todd gave it the name "raptureready.com," defining a spiritual condition eternally crucial to every living individual.

All who have died during this Church Age (Age of Grace) are now beyond getting "Rapture ready." They are either "Rapture ready" or not. People alive now, if they don't know Christ as Savior, still have the opportunity to get Rapture ready. All who are saved (know Jesus as their Savior) are Rapture ready in one sense, but might not be Rapture ready in another. We will try to clarify these matters. It is most important that we do so.

I testified in my commentary last week of instantaneously standing before a throng of heavenly witnesses (Hebrews 12:1–3) the moment my heart stopped beating. This happened three separate times. Each time my heart ceased to beat, I was somewhere in eternity. God the Holy Spirit's assurance of where I was and who the beautiful, cheering young people were becomes more strongly burned into my own spirit by the day.

The only action I have taken in my life to warrant being instantly transported to that heavenly realm was to accept Christ as my Savior. There is no other action I could take while in this physical life to assure my instant transport into those stunning surroundings. While my near-death experience wasn't the Rapture, of course, I believe with all that is within my spiritual understanding that it was a type of what awaits the generation of Christians alive at the time of that great event, as described by the Apostle Paul's prophetic words as given above. At that future moment of Rapture, all who have died during the Church Age, or who are living at the time, will stand not before a throng of witnesses as I did, but before the Lord Jesus Himself! "Beloved, now are we the sons of God, and it doth not yet appear what we shall be: but we know that, when he shall appear, we shall be like him; for we shall see him as he is" (1 John 3:2).

All who are living today who do not know Jesus Christ as Savior stand in mortal danger. When their hearts beat the final time, they will find themselves in the same, unimaginably horrid place as the rich man described by Jesus in the story of the rich man and Lazarus (read Luke 16:19–31). Likewise, the moment Christ says at the Rapture, "Come up hither" (Revelation 4:1), the person who hasn't accepted Christ will be left behind on earth to face a time in human history of which the Lord Jesus Himself said, "For then shall be great tribulation, such as was not since the beginning of the world to this time, no, nor ever shall be. And except those days should be shortened, there should no flesh be saved" (Matthew 24:21–22).

Being Rapture Ready

So, it is imperative to make clear what it means to be Rapture ready. Our eternal souls hang in the balance of God's impending judgment. The Lord of heaven must judge sin, because He cannot abide sin in His holy presence. No sin can enter the gates of heaven. And this is where God's magnificent love comes to the forefront of His dealing with each of us who are sinners.

He loves you and me so much that He sent His Son — God in the flesh, Jesus Christ — to come to earth to be the perfect sin sacrifice, the Lamb slain from the foundation of the world, whose blood takes away the sin of the world. To be Rapture ready, you and I must be "saved" from our sins and made pure in the righteousness found only in Christ. When we believe God and accept Christ as Savior, we become Rapture ready in the eternal sense. We will go to heaven upon our death, or will be raptured when Jesus steps out on the clouds of glory and shouts, "Come up hither."

But there is another meaning of being Rapture ready. Each Christian is responsible for being Rapture ready in this sense. To be Rapture ready as a child of God means we are to be living our lives in a way pleasing to God. We are to lift the name of Jesus so that men, women, and children will be drawn to Him for salvation. We are to be watching for His any-moment return in the Rapture.

Let me make it clear. I believe the Word of God tells us that every person who is saved through the redemptive blood of Jesus Christ will go to be with Him at the moment of Rapture, no matter the state of his or her fellowship with the Lord. We will ALL stand before Him, Paul tells us.

However, to be truly Rapture ready as a Christian means that we are living life in such a biblically prescribed way that when Jesus calls us we will not be ashamed to look Him in His omniscient eyes. We should desire above all else to hear Him say, "Well done, good and faithful servant; thou hast been faithful over a few things, I will make thee ruler over many things: enter thou into the joy of thy lord" (Matthew 25:23).

End-times world conditions today are unmistakable. That face-to-face meeting could take place at any moment!

19

May 2016: Control Means Everything

Road rage has always confounded me. My first exposure to the phenomenon came in a humorous fashion. It was presented on *The Wonderful World of Disney* in animation. One of Mickey Mouse's close pals — the floppy-eared, buck-toothed Goofy — was the featured character.

The narrator talked about Goofy while the humanlike canine went about preparing for work one morning. The narrator told the viewer that this was the gentlest of creatures, a person who wouldn't harm a fly.

Goofy was polite to his wife and children. He peacefully read his newspaper at the breakfast table while sipping his coffee at a leisurely pace.

Goofy got up from the table, wiped his mouth with a napkin, folded the newspaper, and put it beneath his arm. He grasped his briefcase, put his fedora on his head, kissed Mrs. Goofy goodbye, hugged the little Goofies, and opened the door to his garage.

All the while, the narrator was telling the viewer just how soft-hearted and, indeed, how wonderful a husband, father, and citizen was our about-to-be work commuter. Mr. Goofy opened the driver-side door to his sedan and sat in the seat — all the while a tranquil, pleasant half-smile on his mug.

Then it happened! The moment he grasped the steering wheel, a profound transformation took place. His face contorted into a vicious, snarling countenance. His smile became a fang-bearing scowl of evil. His eyes widened and became red with bulging blood veins popping to the surface, his black eyes shifting angrily while drool seeped from the sides of the jowls and he snorted flames and smoke from his big snout.

Goofy became the supreme picture of rage. The narrator described the transformation and gave the viewer the complete account of Goofy the maniac's trip into the city of his workplace.

Soon after that program aired, I became a regular driver, having turned old enough to get a driver's license. However, I can't recall at the time having experienced road rage myself, or even having seen it take place in the real world. But the creators of that Disney program obviously had experienced the phenomenon.

A little later in life, I certainly witnessed the fact that road rage exists. It seems to be less and less a phenomenon; rather, it has turned into a "new normal" for driver comportment.

The latest incident we might recall is when a former NFL football player was shot to death while he and a female passenger were on a city street. The former player apparently bumped a car in front of him for blocking him from proceeding. He then steered his car around the car he had bumped.

The driver of the car that was bumped sped after the offending vehicle. When he caught up with the former player's car, the offended driver fired several shots into the other car, resulting in the former player being fatally wounded.

Such reports are not at all uncommon today. It's as if the human mind has lost all control of reasoning ability while behind the wheel. I believe this kind of road rage might be part of the Apostle Paul's "perilous times" prophecy of 2 Timothy 3. There seems little doubt that today drivers are increasingly "fierce" and "incontinent," as the KJV puts it. That people are without ability to govern their tempers is a bottom-line characterization of the human condition that could legitimately be concluded. Angers flare out of control over the slightest perceived personal disrespect. Too often, such incidents end with bloodshed.

All of the above is but a microcosm of the larger manifestation of the ferocity and lack of control raging across the world at present.

On a much more profound scale of uncontrolled fury, a corpulent little tyrant in North Korea starves his people while pouring money into military and nuclear technology with which to threaten the world. The mullahs of Islam incite hatred, encouraging all-out jihad against Israel and all who won't bow the knee to Allah. In American inner cities, organizations devoted to anarchy and mayhem for the sake of acquiring and/or maintaining power over their ethnic masses go about tearing down the societal fiber of America's culture. Total chaos appears to be but a major crisis away, perhaps in the very near future. Deteriorating economic conditions on a national and global scale could well be the catalyst for producing such crises, many experts warn.

Everything looks to be out of control, while elitists who want to bring all people back to Babel and a one-world order of absolute rule search for avenues to reach their utopian goals.

Uncertainty is the disorder of the day, however, no matter how far reaching are the programs and manipulations of the would-be globalist masters. This world, with its myriad building troubles, should have by now imploded from untenable, economic pressures or else exploded in nuclear fire because of road rage–like insanity in planetary conflict.

But, planet Earth wags on. The uncontrollable is for some reason still under control.

God raises up kings and nations, and He brings them down. Nothing within all of creation is ever beyond His controlling hand.

Whether considering worries about the upcoming presidential election, fear of North Korea and its nukes, ISIS and its barbarous terrorism, or the fearful diagnosis of a devastating illness or loss of those we love, all is under control at all times. There is no situation, no matter how profound or how personal, that the Lord of heaven doesn't control.

The key to being at peace within the safety and assurance of God's control of all circumstances is to be within the Heavenly Father's family.

This relationship is achieved, of course, only through acceptance of Jesus Christ as Savior (Romans 10:9–10). The Lord appeals to all of mankind to consider the matter of His absolute control and authority over all that exists:

> Have ye not known? have ye not heard? hath it not been told you from the beginning? have ye not understood from the foundations of the earth? It is he that sitteth upon the circle of the earth, and the inhabitants thereof are as grasshoppers; that stretcheth out the heavens as a curtain, and spreadeth them out as a tent to dwell in: that bringeth the princes to nothing; he maketh the judges of the earth as vanity. Yea, they shall not be planted; yea, they shall not be sown: yea, their stock shall not take root in the earth: and he shall also blow upon them, and they shall wither, and the whirlwind shall take them away as stubble. To whom then will ye liken me, or shall I be equal? saith the Holy One. Lift up your eyes on high, and behold who hath created these things, that bringeth out their host by number: he calleth them all by names by the greatness of his might, for that he is strong in power; not one faileth (Isaiah 40:21–26).

America's Most Dangerous Time

I once wrote the following in an article titled "Israel Betrayed by U.S.?"

> Israel today stands in the bull's eye of rage. This is true in the case of being targeted by the Jewish state's perennial antagonists, the Arab and Persian Islamist enemies. It is true in the case of the entire international community, whose constituent nations see Israel as the congestive blockage to regional and world peace. But it is the growing antagonism by United States presidential administration operatives that is most disconcerting while this beleaguered planet wobbles toward a time of unprecedented trouble.
>
> As a matter of fact, that coming time of unparalleled strife that will bring all nations to Armageddon is termed "the time of Jacob's trouble" by Isaiah the prophet: "Alas! for that day is great, so that none is like it: it is even the time of Jacob's trouble" (Jeremiah 30:7).
>
> And, it is Jacob's trouble — the prophesied end-of-days dastardly treatment of Israel by the nations of earth — that will cause the God of heaven to bring them to Armageddon. This is what the prophet Joel foretells: "I will also gather all nations, and will bring them down into the valley of Jehoshaphat, and will plead with them there for my people and for my heritage Israel, whom they have scattered among the nations, and parted my land" (Joel 3:2).

Will America Betray Israel?

> We come to the question "Israel Betrayed by U.S.?" The article's title is in the form of a question because, like so much of this American administration's dealings, the "transparency" presidential candidate Barack Obama and then President Obama promised is not forthcoming. Obama's intended dealing with Israel is wrapped in an impenetrable fog of political doublespeak. . . .

Since the time of that writing, a number of years have passed. Mr. Obama began his administration almost from the very first day by treating Israeli Prime Minister Benjamin Netanyahu like a White House exterminator — having him come in a door other than the front entrance reserved for dignitaries who are honored with official reception by the president.

The president, shortly after that first meeting with Netanyahu, abruptly left the prime minister and went to have a private dinner, presumably with his family. It was an undeniable snub.

This was apparently meant to be within his promise to have "the most transparent administration ever." It was certainly transparent that this president has an utter disregard for Mr. Netanyahu and for Israel, our number-one ally in the Middle East, if not our top ally in the entire world.

Subsequent snubs and disrespectful attempts to bully the Israeli leader and the Jewish state are too numerous to get into. Obama's attempts to intervene within the sovereign affairs of Israel have not abated as of this late hour in the Obama administration. In fact, they have increased dramatically.

While there is less than nine months of his time as president remaining, Mr. Obama is said to be planning many interventions into Israeli autonomy.

In yet another audacious display of intrusion into the affairs of Israel's dealings with its internal enemies — many of whom plot and carry out deadly attacks against Jewish citizens — America's diplomatic enforcers are at work. Ordered to do so by Barack Obama, America's State Department minions join with those determined to force Israel to bow to international demands in the matter of housing construction in volatile areas of contention.

One news item reports:

> WASHINGTON (AP) — Diplomats say the U.S. will endorse a tough new tone with Israel in an upcoming international report. The report is to take the Jewish state to task over settlements, demolitions and property seizures on land the Palestinians claim for a future state. . . .
>
> The harsh language marks a subtle shift. Washington has traditionally tempered statements by the so-called "Quartet" of mediators with careful diplomatic language.[49]

Early in the first Obama administration, the pressure to force Israel to give in to diplomatic pressures of land for peace became a driving force in U.S./Israeli relations. The effort has only ramped up since that time. It is as if this president has an obsessive compulsion to impose his will before his time is ended in the White House.

My personal sense is that the president's compulsion is indeed in play. Because it is Israel we are considering, however, there are also far more powerful intrigues involved. Ephesians 6:12 is at the center of this

---

49. Matthew Lee and Bradley Klapper, "US to Take Tougher Tone on Israeli Settlements in New Report," *Associated Press*, May 7, 2016.

last-minute drive to make the rearrangements that Israel's greatest hater wants accomplished.

But my personal sense of all this vitriol pointed toward Israel is of little consequence. What matters is what the prophetic Word of God says about His chosen nation and its destiny, both in the near term and in the ultimate sense.

In that regard, what we will see develop in these days and months leading up to the November election and beyond can be of profound significance. And in the America and the world-versus-Israel struggle, we can find little reassurance that anything good can come forth.

America has entered a most dangerous time.

Reviving Roman Empire Gestapo Growing

Thinking on the rise of Adolf Hitler to power in the Germany of the 1930s immediately produces realization that bringing together ruthless enforcement entities was key to establishment of der führer's dictatorship.

It started with the brown shirts, headed by Ernst Rhome, a homosexual thug who did Hitler's bidding in creating chaos and fear in a failing German republic. When the future führer began to consolidate power through eliminating opposition, the German Wehrmacht (Germany's army) soon had to share controlling authority with the Waffen-SS, the black-uniformed, select group of supposedly Aryan troops assigned as Hitler's personal body guard. The brown shirts were eliminated and the SS, headed by the now infamous Heinrich Himmler, began the implementation of the final solution — the genocidal war on all Jews in Europe.

At the same time, the civilian police establishment was turned into the dreaded Gestapo, the police force that locked the Nazi regime into place. The Nazi military and civilian policing establishment became, in effect, a single force against which there was little resistance.

And this brings us to the crux of things going on in that same geographical area from which Hitler terrorized the world.

Some have seen the development of a movement to establish similar tyrannical controls within the European Union. A recent article frames the growing threat the concerned observers fear. It states the following to begin the piece:

> As the European Union and the establishment behind it become increasingly totalitarian, paranoid, and unstable, the EU super-state is raising up and training its own transnational military-police force. According to reports and its own

propaganda material, the EU "Gendarmerie," as the force is known, will apparently be charged with putting down protests and civil unrest, raiding illegal political meetings, propping up foreign governments, and even confiscating weapons.[50]

The article states that the EU's military-police force is merely one component of the broader transnational police-state apparatus being quietly imposed on the formerly sovereign peoples of Europe. The force includes the bringing together of "transnational police" with "transnational army units" and "EU air and naval operations."

The bringing together of the forces has all been accomplished in the shadows, but is now being thrust into the light of geopolitical reality, according to the concerned observers reporting — those of Breitbart's U.K. operation.

It was a controversial training operation taking place in Germany's North Rhine-Westphalia in April that sparked concern and alarm within Europe and beyond.

Media reports stirred fears of the rise of a tyrannical, controlling force. According to those reports, the training consolidated 600 troops and police officers in order to prepare for crises of the international and civil war sorts.

The EU military-operation information branch reported about its training scheme that the aim of the April 15, 2016, Comprehensive Live Exercise will be capacity building of police and gendarmes who will participate in international stabilization missions and projects with a police component. The force is aimed at preparing the hybrid military-police force for "future" missions.

The troubling reports said that forces from Islamic Turkey and Tunisia, as well as the African nation of Cameroon, participated in the "scheming."

There remains, of course, considerable resistance to the reuniting of Europe. There is at the same time a strong trend toward nationalism. The threat from the Islamist world, with deadly attacks such as that in Brussels, make the populations, if not the one-world order leaderships of EU nations, deeply concerned about a reviving, unified, European empire that takes protection against dangerous Islamist "migrants" out of the hands of local and national authority. Yet, crises that loom, particularly involving Greece-type financial meltdowns and rioting, make probable over-arching EU police controls and military involvement inevitable.

---

50. Alex Newman, "EU Building Potentially Tyrannical Military-Police Force," *The New American*; http://www.thenewamerican.com/world-news/europe/item/23163, May 10, 2016.

Remember, it was severe fiscal crisis, along with his all-controlling military/police monstrosity, that brought Hitler to power. There are those who agree with George Santayana that "those who cannot remember the past are condemned to repeat it."

God's Word foretells that history repeats time after time. Every empire has eventually fallen, even, arguably, the greatest of all world empires, the Roman Empire. The same basic ingredients have constituted most every such collapse.

While Santayana's bit of philosophy has been proven true time after time, he left out a key element in phrasing his thought. It should be: "Those who do not acknowledge God and cannot remember the past are condemned to repeat it."

Every world empire has ignored the true God of heaven. Prophecy tells us that the final empire — that of Antichrist, the Roman prince of Daniel 9:26–27 — will be the most God-hating empire of all history.

Along with all other signals of Christ's soon return on the world scene today, the reviving of the Roman Empire is more and more coming into view. It is a sure signal that this generation is at the end of the Church Age and that Christ's call to His Bride must be near indeed.

Where's the Comfort?

Pre-Trib belief antagonists are on the rise. Rapture critics, even among those who claim to believe in the eventuality of a Rapture, just not the pre-Tribulation view of that event, purport to present evidence on every side that our times trumpet the obvious: the world is about to enter the Tribulation. Christ's call to believers, they say, just isn't going to happen before Christians suffer at least part of the terrors of that beastly era.

They offer that anyone with knowledge of issues and events going on should recognize that the New World Order bunch is transforming America and the world into the kingdom of Antichrist. All is about to come together for the Gog-led invasion into the Middle East. As a matter of fact, many hold that World War III has already begun.

Advanced computer and other control technologies and instrumentalities are in place for locking everyone on the planet into fiscal bondage and physical slavery to the final empire as prophesied by Daniel.

Those of us who believe there is coming a supernatural Rapture-escape from these judgments on sinful mankind are just living in fantasy land is the collective message I infer from emails and articles that increasingly assault my senses. That we should begin prepping with food, water, gold, silver, and finding a good bunker in which to hunker down during these upcoming days seems to be what these Rapture naysayers are presenting. Seldom do I hear them admonish us to be trying to witness with all our might the gospel of Jesus Christ. I guess there will be plenty of time for that once the Antichrist regime is firmly in place.

While the pre-Trib proponent holds at the heart of our efforts winning as many souls to Christ as possible so they won't go through that time of horrors, many of the anti-Rapture antagonists want to make sure they are more comfortable while trying to survive that hellish time.

Coincidentally, or perhaps not, these just happen to, in some cases of TV and other ministries who openly disdain the thought of Rapture, offer for sale all these things for survival. The packaged food items invariably are proclaimed to have shelf lives of three decades or longer. So, we can, if we survive, have these supplies to partake of well into the Millennium, I suppose. This is based upon the general theme that they believe the seven-year Tribulation, not the Rapture, is imminent. Over the past few years, there have been a number of debates taking place about whether there will be a pre-Trib Rapture. The best I've heard was the one at the pre-Trib study group meetings when Dr. Mark Hitchcock destroyed the anti-Rapture arguments of the Bible Answer Man.

There are some such debates scheduled for prophecy conferences in the near future. These will perhaps offer new food for thought, but I doubt they will change minds on either side of the controversy.

Personally, I believe the time for debate on this matter is past. It is now time to just offer the assurance of that soon-to-come, exhilarating moment when Christ will say, "Come up hither" (Revelation 4:1).

There are so many scriptural assurances of the pre-Tribulation Rapture that we could fill many articles with them. As a matter of fact, we have done just that on the Rapture Ready website.

I wish to mention only one Rapture factor here because I believe it is the most reassuring. Here we interject the question proposed in our title: Where's the Comfort? By that we ask: what comfort is there in the argument that Christians will go through the Tribulation?

Paul the Apostle first assures us of this fact: "For God hath not appointed us to wrath, but to obtain salvation by our Lord Jesus Christ" (1 Thessalonians 5:9). But it is the next thought from the mind of God that should cause warm reassurance in the spiritual heart of every believer: "Wherefore comfort yourselves together, and edify one another, even as also ye do" (1 Thessalonians 5:11).

Get it? We are to "comfort" ourselves, not wring our hands looking for these things to destroy us, or look for Antichrist. We are to be looking for our "blessed hope" (Titus 2:13).

There is no comfort — nor is there directive in God's Word — to be had in anticipating going through the time of God's wrath and almost certain martyrdom (probably by beheading). There is no comfort in looking for the worst dictator in the planet's history to hunt us down and lop off our heads.

Here is what God's Word promises instead of the dreaded scenario proposed by the Rapture antagonists:

> For this we say unto you by the word of the Lord, that we which are alive and remain unto the coming of the Lord shall not prevent them which are asleep. For the Lord himself shall descend from heaven with a shout, with the voice of the archangel, and with the trump of God: and the dead in Christ shall rise first: Then we which are alive and remain shall be caught up together with them in the clouds, to meet the Lord in the air: and so shall we ever be with the Lord. Wherefore comfort one another with these words (1 Thessalonians 4:15–18).

20

June 2016: Peace Quest Continues

Today's date of posting this article is the 72nd anniversary of D-Day. On June 6, 1944, the Allied forces wanted to accomplish two things as they steamed toward the coastline of France. They were intent on defeating and destroying the Nazis' ability to make war. Thereby, they were determined to establish peace that had been taken from the world on a global scale — primarily by the Germans — for the second time in less than a half century.

In reality, however, the world has never been completely free of war. That includes the earliest biblical history. Cain first went to war with his brother, Abel, over jealousy that created rage that ended in the first murder. Man has been killing man ever since, with the slaughter continuing to manifest even on our city streets on a growing scale. I give you as example the streets of south Chicago, where, during weekends in particular, black-on-black killing is horrendous.

Governmental authorities, both in the city of Chicago and in the present federal government, at whose heart sits the current presidential administration, hardly even acknowledge that a problem exists in the inner cities. The news conglomerate dutifully also ignores the deadly problem.

There is a satanic cover-up on the war that is raging, taking peace from life in America. The same forces covering up our domestic conflict are dedicated to keeping the world at large from knowing about the true causes and effects of the war in the Middle East. That conflict is destined to bring all of mankind to history's final war of this quickly fleeting age.

God's Word tells us that the quest for such a peace will eventuate in the most terrible time in human history. Jesus said in the Olivet Discourse that it will be a time so terrible that it would destroy all flesh on the planet if He did not return to end the warfare.

Daniel the prophet said the peace the world will seek will be produced and enforced by the "prince that shall come" (Daniel 9:26). It will be, the prophet Isaiah said, a covenant made with "death and hell" (Isaiah 28:15, 18). It all involves the Middle East, and, as I said, the news media as well as our government (and for that matter, the governments of the world) refuse to acknowledge the true causes and effects of the conflict that make the quest for peace necessary.

This peace is in the making this very moment.

This quest for peace, as I and other prophecy observers have mentioned many times, is the number-one signal of where we stand on God's prophetic timeline. We are watching prophecy in the process of fulfillment. The Gog-Magog forces are coalescing; the religions of the world are beginning to amalgamate, agreeing that there are many ways to heaven; and the effort to establish one-world order is on the move through Agenda 21, 30, and in other ways.

But, again, it is the desire for a Middle East peace, with Israel held up as the sticking point, that the world intensely desires. The diplomatic community and the global news conglomerate refuse to hear or propose any narrative other than that which declares the tiny Jewish state guilty of holding up the peace process.

The following excerpt proves the point:

> The Arab league supported on Saturday France's Middle East peace initiative and all international efforts to create lasting peace between Israelis and Palestinians, AFP reported. . . . Speaking before the ministers, [Palestinian president Mahmoud] Abbas said that the time has come to "mobilize Arab and international wills" towards creating a Palestinian state, however said in order to do so Israel would have to make serious policy changes.
>
> Abbas called for NATO forces to replace the IDF in the West Bank as part of any peace deal that leads to the creation of a two-state solution. He also rejected the idea of recognizing Israel as a Jewish state.[51]

The pressures are great on Israeli Prime Minister Benjamin Netanyahu and his government to give in to world diplomatic insistence that Israel give land for peace. That is something, of course, God says will bring war upon

---

51. Tovah Lazaroff, "Arab League Supportive of French Peace Initiative," *Jerusalem Post*, May 29, 2016.

the whole world (see Joel 3:2). This will be the cause and effect of that great, fearful conflict we have come to know as Armageddon.

It will be the result of seeking a false, deadly peace, rather than that lasting and perfect peace that can only be instituted by the Prince of Peace.

Rapture "Mystery" Revealed

With so much controversy involving the topic of the Rapture boiling today, I thought it would be good to look a little more closely at that event internally. That is, it might prove interesting to examine the Rapture within the pre-Trib view to look at a divide that exists.

Mostly, preachers don't want to address prophecy or, in particular, the doctrine of the Rapture at all. Since the call of Christ to His Church is next on God's calendar of events, in the view of pre-Trib proponents, ignoring this great promise of rescue from human history's most terrible time is something that both baffles and disturbs.

We who are familiar with that great future event know, at least cursorily, the differences within the various views of when the Rapture will occur. Whether it will happen post-Trib, mid-Trib, pre-Trib, etc., is sometimes hotly expressed by the various proponents. However, the vast numbers of preachers in America's pulpits today would tell you that the Rapture is a mystery to them, as is most of Bible prophecy.

Indeed, it is a "mystery" to them because they never have opened their Bibles with the thought toward looking into the Rapture — the very thing Paul said is a "mystery" he was showing us. They like to use the joke: "I'm a *Pan-Millennialist*. I believe it will all just *pan* out in the end."

Again, it isn't the hot debate between the pre-Trib, mid-Trib, and post-Trib views of the Rapture I wish to address. To me, the debate is over. The pre-Tribulation view is the only one in total context of what the Bible says about that great promise that makes sense. Paul's "mystery" unveiled, from the pre-Trib perspective, is what I hope to dissect a bit.

The Scripture, of course, that sets up this great event is as follows:

> Behold, I shew you a mystery; we shall not all sleep, but we shall all be changed, in a moment, in the twinkling of an eye, at the last trump: for the trumpet shall sound, and the dead shall be raised incorruptible, and we shall be changed (1 Corinthians 15:51–52).

Paul says he is presenting a "mystery." That is, he is dealing with a heretofore unknown matter — one not understood by believers in Christ. The "showing" of this "mystery" is the nuance of truth I wish to examine within the pre-Trib view of the Rapture.

The seminaries within fundamentalist-evangelical Christianity hold mostly that the Rapture was never dealt with in any way whatsoever until Paul "revealed" it. The most academically inclined will say this "mystery" was never alluded to in the Old Testament. They go on to say it was never mentioned in any way by Jesus and the prophets. It is, they say, only in the Pauline epistles that the Rapture is unveiled.

I believe this is untenable, except by those who refuse to consider that Paul was "showing" the mystery of the Rapture that had already been made manifest. He was explaining it, not just pulling it out of the hat for the first time. Paul was unveiling the truth about what Jesus Himself indeed had alluded to as given in the Gospel accounts.

The first mention of this "mystery," the Rapture, by the Lord was recorded by John:

> Let not your heart be troubled: ye believe in God, believe also in me. In my Father's house are many mansions: if it were not so, I would have told you. I go to prepare a place for you. And if I go and prepare a place for you, I will come again, and receive you unto myself; that where I am, there ye may be also (John 14:1–3).

Jesus said He will "receive" us to Himself, exactly like Paul reveals in 1 Corinthians 15:51 when he says we will be transformed because flesh and blood cannot inherit the kingdom of God (1 Corinthians 15:50). Paul further unveils that translation into Christ's presence in the following prophecy:

> Then we which are alive and remain shall be caught up together with them in the clouds, to meet the Lord in the air: and so shall we ever be with the Lord (1 Thessalonians 4:17).

The next words of our Lord about this "mystery" Paul is "showing" us is found in the Gospel of Matthew, in the Olivet Discourse:

> But of that day and hour knoweth no man, no, not the angels of heaven, but my Father only. But as the days of Noah were, so shall also the coming of the Son of man be. For as in the days that were before the flood they were eating and drinking, marrying and giving in marriage, until the day that Noe entered into the ark, and knew not until the flood came, and

took them all away; so shall also the coming of the Son of man be. Then shall two be in the field; the one shall be taken, and the other left. Two women shall be grinding at the mill; the one shall be taken, and the other left (Matthew 24:36–41).

Jesus further gave prophecy regarding that future, catastrophic break-in on human history as recorded in Luke 17:26–30. It is unfortunate that the most purely academic among fundamentalist theologians within the ranks of pre-Trib Rapture proponents can't see Jesus' *mysterious* mention of the Rapture in the Gospels — the "mystery" Paul is plainly unlocking for understanding for all believers.

I believe we are very near the moment of being the generation of believers who will be beneficiaries of that twinkling-of-an-eye moment when the Lord shouts, "Come up hither" (Revelation 4:1).

Glorious Change Coming

Something sinister lurks just ahead within this world of darkening uncertainty. The forewarning thought simmers beneath daily life that change is coming that will make these hours seem like the good old days for the inhabitants of future earth.

Princes and presidents, potentates and populations at large, sense gnawing dread spawned by the seemingly unstoppable spread of murderous, racial/religious hatreds. Proliferation of nuclear weaponry among the most violence-prone among us appears on the brink of unleashing man's final war.

The term "Armageddon" is regularly used to describe man's greatest fear during hourly newscasts. To quote Shakespeare, it is becoming clear that "something wicked this way comes."[52]

For the believer in Jesus Christ, however, the near horizon that is a harbinger of the worst of times in man's history presents just beyond that apocalyptic storm front a magnificent future beyond imagination.

Indeed, glorious change is coming. It will happen in a stunning moment of dazzling transformation and transport for the born-again believer. It will be a dynamic intervention by the one and only Creator-God of heaven — so long seemingly silent to rebellious mankind.

My commission is to proclaim to this generation that the very end of the age is at hand. Heaven is trumpeting the final siren of appeal for all to come within the shelter offered by the Savior who died and resurrected so that all who trust Him for salvation will be spared the horrors about to occur.

---

52. William Shakespeare, *Macbeth*, Act IV, Scene 1.

"Don't spend eternity apart from the Heavenly Father" is the profoundly important message that must be disseminated and accepted. He desires above all else that everyone come into the safe harbor of His family through His only begotten Son — the Lord Jesus Christ.

Whether one is *Rapture Ready . . . Or Not* (the title of my new book), the disappearance of all true believers is about to occur. The thrilling time of that long-ago prophesied call of Christians to join with Christ will happen at any moment!

I believe that I was prompted to relay the urgent message that the door to the Age of Grace (the Church Age) is on the very brink of closing to a Christ-rejecting generation.

This presents me with no pleasure. Neither, of course, does it please the God of heaven who must, following the closing of that door, unleash His wrath and judgment upon the world. Jesus shed His last drop of blood on the Cross at Calvary so that no one needs to spend one moment in that hellish time on earth we call the Tribulation or spend eternity in the place prepared for the devil and his fallen angelic horde.

Being Rapture ready is (1) knowing Christ for salvation through following this admonition:

> That if thou shalt confess with thy mouth the Lord Jesus, and shalt believe in thine heart that God hath raised him from the dead, thou shalt be saved. For with the heart man believeth unto righteousness; and with the mouth confession is made unto salvation (Romans 10:9–10).

Once a person complies with this way (the *only* way) to salvation, that person becomes (2) Rapture ready through living life according to direction given in God's Word.

One of the best verses to summarize this Rapture readiness is found in the following: "Trust in the LORD with all thine heart; and lean not unto thine own understanding. In all thy ways acknowledge him, and he shall direct thy paths" (Proverbs 3:5–6).

In this way, we will hear our Lord say, "Well done, good and faithful servant" (Matthew 25:23) when we see Him face to face at the moment of Rapture. To avoid any questions about whether I am saying we have to live above sin in order to go in the Rapture, I will be clear: every person who truly accepts Christ is going to leave the planet at the time Jesus calls the Church (Revelation 4:1). Not a single believer, whether he or she is walking "worthily" or not, will be left behind at Rapture. But, to be truly

Rapture ready in the sense of being "worthy" (in order to receive every reward the Lord wants to give us at the *bema,* the *Judgment Seat of Christ*), each Christian must be walking according to God's precepts as taught in His Holy Word.

In that glorious, twinkling-of-an-eye moment of translation from mortal to immortal, from corruption to incorruption, we will each realize the magnificence that is our Lord and Savior: Bridegroom. We will know Him in the same way He knows each of us. We will, in that eternal moment, want to have lived righteously for Him.

The change that is coming is spectacular beyond all that our imaginations can conjure, the Apostle Paul has informed us:

> But as it is written, Eye hath not seen, nor ear heard, neither have entered into the heart of man, the things which God hath prepared for them that love him (1 Corinthians 2:9).

Let us do all we can in Christ's service while opportunity is ours. Let us do all within our power to be truly Rapture Ready!

21

July 2016: Somebody Needs to Cause Craft to Prosper

Europe and the world continue to reel economically from the fallout of Brexit, the British pulling out of the European Union. Fear of financial freefall into the abyss of global depression is igniting fires of protests that something must be done. One such protest comes from the very heart of Europe, the area most associated with Bible prophecy and the reviving Roman Empire.

Italian Finance Minister Pier Carlo Padoan warned that "the unthinkable is happening. A double reaction to Brexit is under way, one financial, one political. The financial one, at least until now, is limited. I am more worried about the political one. There is a cocktail of factors that can lead to various outcomes, including a further push towards disintegration."[53]

Padoan lectured that those in authority in Europe must begin to listen to the people and their worries over out-of-control immigration, unemployment, and increasing inequality. Austerity measures, he said, exacerbate the problems, and something must be done to change those budget rules Rome considers to be fueling the crisis.

He said, "Inequality is growing in Europe because growth is weak." Further, he said, "We have had proposals on the table for months that say employment, growth, well-being and equality have to be the priorities . . . the situation we are in now is exceptional. We have to change."[54]

There is a sense that Mr. Padoan's call for new leadership is rising among the common people not only of Europe, but of the whole Western world. The message, it is equally observable, is being missed by those who hold the financial reins at the highest echelons of power. Rebellion seems to be building among the common folk against the elite who display a wanton disregard for the rest of us.

---

53. https://www.timesofisrael.com/italy-to-eu-after-brexit-change-or-risk-collapse/.
54. Ibid.

When thinking on what Bible prophecy has to say about the ultimate outcome of all the machinations going on in the arena of international power politics these days, the prophet Daniel comes to mind. He was given some very specific information to pass along to us by the messenger sent from the throne room of God. The message had at its heart a directly pertinent point regarding world economic conditions that will produce history's most all-controlling leader.

Daniel was given a profile of the one who will be Antichrist. That beast of Revelation 13, Daniel was told, will be a "king of fierce countenance" who will prosper greatly:

> And through his policy also he shall cause craft to prosper in his hand; and he shall magnify himself in his heart, and by peace shall destroy many: he shall also stand up against the Prince of princes; but he shall be broken without hand (Daniel 8:25).

The first part of the prophecy is most notable for our purposes. This last and most powerful political/military leader will "cause craft to prosper." He will apparently take a terrible economic situation that exists on a world-wide scale and turn it around in a mighty way.

Adolf Hitler did exactly this, students of recent history will recall. The German economy was in freefall — had hit the bottom. Hitler turned it around.

But we remember how he did it! All-out war-making, exactly how the angelic messenger told Daniel the final führer, Antichrist, will accomplish the economic turnaround: "by peace shall destroy many" (Daniel 8:25). The red horse of war, remember, follows immediately the rider on the white horse (Revelation 6).

We again remember the perhaps overly used words of Henri Spaak, secretary general of NATO from 1957 to 1960: "What we want is a man of sufficient stature to hold the alliances of all people and to lift us out of the economic morass into which we are sinking. Send us such a man, and be he god or devil, we will receive him."[55]

The world, particularly the stress-torn EU, certainly appears to be in an economic morass. A central figure from the exact center of Rome is calling for leadership to again cause craft to prosper. According to all other signals that are everywhere the prophecy student looks today, that man — who really is a devil — must be waiting in the shadows to step into the spotlight of history when the call comes.

---

55. https://www.christianstogether.net/Articles/319656/Christians_Together_in/Christian_ Life/Christians_and_Politics/EU_architect_would.aspx.

That call will come just after another one resounds across the earth's atmosphere: Christ's shout, "Come up hither" (Revelation 4:1).

Godlessness Groupies

Antichrist, the coming beast of Revelation 13, will be the most attractive, charismatic personality ever to step foot on the planet. His following will defy imagination. His magnetic personality and, no doubt, striking appearance will be the antithesis of Jesus Christ in every way when he "magnifies" himself, as the prophet Daniel foretold.

Jesus was meek. He came as a Lamb. The Bible tells us that He had no outstanding physical features or characteristics that would set Him apart from the rest of humanity. The exceptions were when He was on the Mount of Transfiguration when He was said to shine like the sun, and when He was said to be the most "marred" of all men at the time of His crucifixion.

Antichrist, that man of sin, will literally have a worldwide, totally devoted following.

I'm a "back number," as Dr. Vernon McGee used to say, referring to his own naïveté when it came to keeping up with the pop culture of his time. But it was brought to my attention the meteoric career of a singer who started out as Katy Hudson and now entertains under the stage name Katy Perry. She went from singing as a Christian recording artist to becoming a secular, recording/entertaining phenomenon. Her Christian album under Katy Hudson sold only 2,000 copies or so. She switched to secular recording and soared to the top of the charts. According to Wikipedia, she became the first artist with multiple videos to reach one billion views on Vevo with the videos for the songs "Roar" and "Dark Horse." Her following on Twitter and other social media forums indicates that she has at least 90 million fans.

Those numbers are stratospheric. Neither ol' Elvis nor the Beatles ever reached those heights, although they had their share of groupies, to be sure.

Antichrist, according to Revelation 13, will be worshiped by the whole world. Those who don't worship him will have their heads lopped off and worse. His numbers of followers will put Miss Katy's numbers in the category of infinitesimal by comparison.

We know of the Democrat Party's incessant coming under pressure to remove any reference to God from their party platform. When the convention began for the 2012 presidential nominating process, we remember that the nays were much louder than the yeas when the question was put up for continuing to use God's name in official language of the party's doings.

Just over a week ago, there was a report of an entertainer demanding that the song "God Bless America" be no longer sung at half times or at the beginnings of sporting events. He wants that "offensive anthem," as he characterized it, forever discarded. Even in the Congress of the United States, there is a constant drumbeat from some of the "progressive" quarters to do away with prayer to open sessions and to remove "In God We Trust" from coinage and other governmental officialdom. There has been much progress, as they would have it, in getting vestiges of God, such as the Ten Commandments, removed from public places. Prayer and Bible reading have long since been forbidden in public schools and other public places, as we know.

The perverting of human sexuality at every level and the slaughter of countless millions of babies assault our senses daily.

There is an ongoing effort to rewrite America's founding history. The champions of godlessness revisionists insist that the Founding Fathers wanted a totally secular nation, devoid of any moralistic governance. When confronted with the facts of those founders' own words in this regard, they, in effect, put the palms of their hands over their ears, close their eyes, and start humming one of this debauched culture's musical atrocities.

While engaged in research for my book, *Rapture Ready . . . Or Not: 15 Reasons This Is the Generation That Will Be Left Behind*, I looked into what the founders of America spoke and wrote on the matter of God's influence in their nation-creating efforts. I included many of their quotes in the book and could have put in hundreds more. Here are a few.

John Adams — second president of the United States, said,

> The general principles on which the fathers achieved independence were the general principles of Christianity. I will avow that I then believed, and now believe, that those general principles of Christianity are as eternal and immutable as the existence and attributes of God.
>
> I have examined all religions, and the result is that the Bible is the best book in the world.

John Quincy Adams — sixth president of the United States, said,

> In the chain of human events, the birthday of the nation is indissolubly linked with the birthday of the Savior. The Declaration of Independence laid the cornerstone of human government upon the first precepts of Christianity.

Samuel Adams — governor of Massachusetts, signer of the Declaration of Independence, and ratifier of the U.S. Constitution, said,

> I conceive we cannot better express ourselves than by humbly supplicating the Supreme Ruler of the world . . . that the confusions that are and have been among the nations may be overruled by the promoting and speedily bringing in the holy and happy period when the kingdoms of our Lord and Savior Jesus Christ may be everywhere established, and the people willingly bow to the scepter of Him who is the Prince of Peace.

Benjamin Franklin — signer of the Declaration of Independence, diplomat, printer, and scientist, said,

> As to Jesus of Nazareth, my opinion of whom you particularly desire, I think the system of morals and His religion as He left them to us, the best the world ever saw, or is likely to see.

Thomas Jefferson — signer of the Declaration of Independence, diplomat, governor of Virginia, secretary of state, and third president of the United States, said,

> The practice of morality being necessary for the well being of society, He [God] has taken care to impress its precepts so indelibly on our hearts that they shall not be effaced by the subtleties of our brain. We all agree in the obligation of the moral principles of Jesus and nowhere will they be found delivered in greater purity than in His discourses.

George Washington — judge, member of the Continental Congress, commander-in-chief of the Continental Army, president of the Constitutional Convention, first president of the United States, and "Father of his Country," said,

> While we are zealously performing the duties of good citizens and soldiers, we certainly ought not to be inattentive to the higher duties of religion. To the distinguished character of Patriot, it should be our highest glory to add the more distinguished character of Christian.[56]

---

56. George Washington, *The Writings of Washington*, John C. Fitzpatrick, editor (Washington: Government Printing Office, 1932), Vol. XI, p. 342–343, General Orders of May 2, 1778.

George Washington also said,

> I now make it my earnest prayer that God would . . . most graciously be pleased to dispose us all to do justice, to love mercy, and to demean ourselves with that charity, humility, and pacific temper of the mind which were the characteristics of the Divine Author of our blessed religion.[57]

How far we have strayed by allowing the groupies of godlessness to determine that Jesus Christ is anathema, but that the gods of entertainment in this world are to be glorified and followed into the abyss of national destruction. There is time to turn things around if we will follow the godly directive of 2 Chronicles 7:14. Sad to say — to put it in terms the groupies of godlessness will understand — the trending is in the opposite direction.

Let's continue to do our Christian duty in carrying out the Great Commission. Let us also vote the right way to the best of our ability. But, at the same time, let's keep looking for the glorious appearing of our "blessed hope" (Titus 2:13).

God Governs the Globalists

Some years ago, for one of my books, I wrote a chapter titled "Globalism's Siren Song." The chapter began as follows:

> *Come, young citizens of the world, we are one, we are one.*
> *Come, young citizens of the world, we are one, we are one.*
> *We have one hope, we have one dream, and with one voice*
> *we sing: Peace, prosperity, and love for all mankind.*[58]

> The lyrics are set to an enchanting, rhythmic melody and are sung by a chorus of sweet-voiced children. Soon you are humming, then singing along. What could possibly be wrong with those sentiments so innocently expressed? Peace, prosperity, and love for all mankind — are these not among the most noble of objectives?

> Powerful humanistic allurements beckon seductively, promising a golden future if all of earth's people will come

---

57. Quoted in David Barton, "The Founding Fathers on Jesus, Christianity and the Bible," https://wallbuilders.com/founding-fathers-jesus-christianity-bible/#.

58. Roger Whittaker, "I Am but a Small Voice," recorded 1980, track A on *I Am But A Small Voice*, RCA, Vinyl.

together as one. Such a glorious world order, long dreamed about and even fervently pursued, seems at last achievable. Those who hold the worldview that national boundaries must fall and sovereignties must diminish because we are all citizens of planet Earth passionately embrace the earth-shrinking technologies that science continues to produce. For example, the Internet. Yes, the Utopian dream at last seems achievable. However, while the sirens of globalism — like the twin sisters who lured unwary sailors to their deaths in Homer's *The Odyssey* — sing their lovely, mesmerizing songs of New World Order, the words pronounced by the Ancient of Days reverberate through the corridors of antiquity and leap at this generation from the pages of God's Holy Word:

> Behold, the people are one and they have all one language, and this they begin to do; and now nothing will be restrained from them which they have imagined to do (Genesis 11:6).[59]

One-world order was, at the time of that chapter's writing, a strong factor to consider in looking at where the world stood on God's prophetic timeline. Like for most of the latter part of the 20th century and the beginning of the 21st, the drive to return to Babel was in the news at least on a weekly basis.

The Soviet Union had dissolved after President Reagan's demand: "Mr. Gorbachev, tear down this wall!"[60] There seemed to be great optimism then that the building of that new Tower of Babel could begin in earnest.

The many developing conflicts, however, as the Middle East lit up with increased Islamist fanaticism and terrorism, required that the globalists go from singing their siren song in a joyful *Kumbaya* fashion to one sung with somewhat dampened enthusiasm. "We Are the World" and all such anthems seemed to lessen into a holding-pattern hum while the new world order builders were kept busy putting out fires that might ignite wars almost as dangerous as those that could have erupted in days of the Cold War.

For a time, there was a disjointed effort on behalf of what might be considered the *civilized* nations to deal with the Middle Eastern madness. But, with the coming of the felling of the World Trade Towers on September 11, 2001, there was an almost instantaneous coalescence of the

59. Terry James, *Foreshocks of Antichrist* (Eugene, OR: Harvest House, 1997), p. 25
60. http://www.historyplace.com/speeches/reagan-tear-down.htm.

global powers with many lesser powers. Operation Iraqi Freedom, you will remember, was the result.

While there appeared to be a new, powerful drive toward the new world order the first President George Bush talked about so much, America was the holdup. The United States was so overwhelmingly powerful in dealing with the Desert Storm campaign and later with the following war by President George W. Bush to oust Saddam Hussein from Iraq that the globalists' dream of a one-world power was impossible to form.

Sovereignty and autonomy of nations were the order of the day. God's hand moved upon the world of geopolitics to prevent the singing of the one-world anthems with increased vigor.

We come to the present hour. To the observer of the world scene today — and I'm not talking about the vast number of Americans or citizens of other nations, but the experts who watch for political rearrangement — the major roadblock to achieving global order is being dismantled as quickly as this presidential regime can manage. America is having its foundation chipped away as Barack Obama and all in cahoots with him around the world are striving for the fundamental transformation of America from being a constitutional republic to becoming, well, it remains to be seen. . . .

America must be brought down so the new Babylonian order can be built. Mr. Obama is in high gear at every turn, using the presidency of earth's most prominent nation to make the "hope and change" he promised before his election — a promise the true nature of which few in this country comprehended. That transformation is to be the removal of America as a hindrance to the larger order within which the powers that be can rule and reign as a central governing authority.

One report captures this president congratulating himself and his one-world order builders for their transformational efforts during the seven and a half years of his presidency:

> Globalist elite cooperation can defeat the "chronic violence" that is caused by real jihadist in France and supposed racism in police forces, President Barack Obama told a roomful of foreign ambassadors July 15.
>
> "Overnight in Nice [France], we witnessed another tragic and appalling attack on the freedom and the peace that we cherish . . . [and] it's been a difficult several weeks in the United States," Obama told the ambassadors gathered in the White House. . . .

After urging them to join in the effort to increase the policing of such "non-Islamic" terrorism, he patted his fellow global elitists and himself on the back.

"I want to thank so many of your countries for the partnership that we've forged and the progress we've achieved together over these past eight years in rescuing the global economy and securing vulnerable nuclear materials. A comprehensive deal to prevent Iran from obtaining a nuclear weapon. Halting the spread of Ebola, and thereby saving countless lives. In Paris, the most ambitious agreement in history to fight climate change. A new sustainable development set of goals to end extreme poverty and promote health and education and equality for all people."[61]

What he did not say was that every one of these "accomplishments" of his administration has caused problems that might never be undone. Also, he used executive fiat in almost every case, bypassing a nonresistant Congress and the U.S. Constitution at every turn.

So, the Obama administration has almost singlehandedly — so the globalist elite must think — begun the process of dismantling the roadblock to taking the world back to Babel. This, of course, is all preparation for Antichrist, the globalist of all globalists, to step onto the stage of human history for the final curtain call.

The God of heaven says that will not happen until the Church of Jesus Christ is removed. For it is the Holy Spirit indwelling the Church, not America, that is governing the globalists' efforts to establish one-world order.

In writing the chapter I mentioned in the opening of this commentary, I closed that chapter with the following, as I will do with this article.

The Lull Before the Storm

Thankfully, even though God's judgment upon sin is sure, He is also slow to anger and His mercy is great. It is my opinion that we are currently in a lull that God has graciously granted just before the prophesied end-of-time storm that will devastate a wrath-deserving generation. Even so, a brisk wind is already snapping the flag of warning that apocalypse approaches.

---

61. Neil Munro, "Globalist Obama: Terrorists, Racist Cops Are 'Chronic Impulses' to Be Defeated by Global Elites," Breitbart News, July 15, 2016.

God the Holy Spirit earnestly and tenderly beckons all who will heed His call to take shelter within the only harbor where protection from the deadly whirlwind to come can be found.

That safe harbor is Jesus Christ. Those who refuse to accept the haven or safety offered by Christ will perish beneath the raging, crashing surge as surely as did the antediluvians during the judgment of Noah's day.

22

August 2016: Devil Seeks to Warm Mankind

Satan is often portrayed, or at least thought of, as ruling over a Dante's *Inferno*-like domain. He is in his red union suit, his barbed tail wagging as his tight grin of evil is framed between his goatee and horns that protrude angrily above devilish eyebrows and red, glowing eyes.

Hades smolders around him as he relishes the next human victims he can entice into his hot, sulfurous kingdom. His intention is to see all of God's creation called man forever suffer in this eternally hot abode.

Truth is that only the last part of that portrayal has biblical validity. The devil does want every human being to suffer eternity apart from his or her Creator. The abyss (Tartarus) and eventually the Lake of Fire will be the final destination for lost humanity. Lucifer, the fallen one — the devil — however, will not rule over hell. He will be the one there who suffers most, according to God's truth about the matters involved.

The old serpent, however, is at present dealing with issues of heating things up and trying to lure people on board. Tragically, many are falling for his call to jump aboard the global warming (now changed to climate change) bandwagon.

I've written about it in my book *Rapture Ready . . . Or Not: 15 Reasons This Is the Generation That Will Be Left Behind* and in many articles. The lie that global warming (climate change) will make earth uninhabitable is the rallying cry for the push for one-world order. It indeed is at the heart of the blueprint the globalist elitists are using to construct Antichrist's hell on earth.

America's secretary of state and the U.S. Environmental Protection Agency forces are raging ahead full-blast to bring this nation into the blueprint, knowing that the Obama administration has less than one half-year to do so. America, as I have also written many times, must be brought down from its superpower status. The United States must be made to conform with the misery the globalists have helped much of the world achieve in order to make all on the planet look to them for solutions.

John Kerry, unknowingly, is doing his dead-level best to do the devil's work, in my humble view. He wants to warm us up considerably to somehow attain the utopian dreams he and the new world order builders want to construct.

Science proves almost hourly the lie that is global warming/climate change, about which Kerry and the others are wringing their hands as they fearmonger. They, with the help of national and international media, nonetheless move forward at foolhardy, breakneck speed.

Like the other reprobate (upside down) unreasonableness they foist, they believe that making us warmer by taking away the comfort of our air conditioners is part of the answer. Despite the great heat they say is about to make planet Earth like Venus or some other hellish planetary orb, they want to do away with the very thing that can make us comfortably cool — although, again, science continues to prove in every instance that the earth isn't heating up, but actually is cooling.

All we must do to understand the truth is to remember the global warmists who got caught in a growing field of solid ice a few years ago. They had to be rescued by ice-breaker ships as they moved toward the Arctic Circle in an attempt to gather evidence that the earth is warming.

Yet John Kerry, on behalf of this lame-duck administration, is doing all possible to bring America's sovereignty down so the global order can proceed uninhibited. He, like Mr. Obama, gives this insanely wrong matter — global warming — greater priority than the true threat we face: Islamist terrorism. The following excerpt frames the madness:

> Secretary of State John Kerry said in Vienna on Friday that air conditioners and refrigerators are as big of a threat to life as the threat of terrorism posed by groups like the Islamic State.
>
> *The Washington Examiner* reported that Kerry was in Vienna to amend the 1987 Montreal Protocol that would phase out hydrofluorocarbons, or HFCs, from basic household and commercial appliances like air conditioners, refrigerators, and inhalers.
>
> "As we were working together on the challenge of [ISIS] and terrorism," Kerry said, "it's hard for some people to grasp it, but what we — you — are doing here right now is of equal importance because it has the ability to literally save life on the planet itself."

Environmental Protection Agency Administrator Gina McCarthy was also present at the negotiations and is serving as lead negotiator for the United States. McCarthy has said that her goal is to enact the HFC agreement by the end of the year.

The EPA rules along with the global deal would ban HFC in the United States and would push for alternative chemicals for use in appliances.

The negotiations are part of President Obama's climate agenda to combat global climate change.[62]

That old serpent, Satan, wants to warm us all, apparently, even before the lost, wretched souls among humanity reach that final, ultimately fiery-hot destination. The globalist would-be masters, wittingly or not, are carrying out Lucifer's blueprint for constructing his Antichrist's world disorder.

God's Word has forewarned of this present state of last-days danger. The Lord is in control, but He has given us good sensibility and the marvelous privilege in this still-free nation to vote for liberty rather than tyranny.

Prayer and exercising the vote our forefathers built into the Constitution is still our right. Doing so in sufficient numbers will perhaps assure that we as believers continue to have the right to also carry out our Lord's Great Commission beyond this political season.

Meantime, let us also do — with increased faith and vigor — as Jesus instructed in Luke 21:28 and as Paul wrote in Titus 2:13.

Deducing Today's Delusion

The title of this week's commentary is a proper one, I think. The famous fictional detective invented by mystery author Conan Doyle, Sherlock Holmes, often used the term "deduced" in his brilliant dissection of seemingly unsolvable crimes. He would "deduce," or conclude, that the circumstances surrounding the mystery had led to the inevitable solving of the murder, theft, or whatever the crime involved.

There is no greater mystery than the "mystery of iniquity" mentioned by Paul: "For the mystery of iniquity doth already work: only he who now letteth will let, until he be taken out of the way" (2 Thessalonians 2:7).

We are now in the middle of iniquitous circumstance and behavior by a world of rebellious earth-dwellers. At the heart of the mystery of iniquity that surrounds us is a growing evil spiritual dementia that is setting the stage for the prophecy from the same section of the second letter to

---

62. Alyssa Canobbio, "Kerry: Air Conditioners as Big a Threat as ISIS," *Washington Free Beacon*, July 23, 2016.

the Thessalonians above: "And for this cause God shall send them strong delusion, that they should believe a lie: that they all might be damned who believed not the truth, but had pleasure in unrighteousness" (2 Thessalonians 2:11–12).

It is patently obvious that we are witnessing a form of spiritual dementia, of upside down thinking, every day. This evil darkening of the ability to think sanely and morally comes from the anti-God rebelliousness the great Apostle warned about in his letter to the Romans:

> And even as they did not like to retain God in their knowledge, God gave them over to a reprobate mind, to do those things which are not convenient; being filled with all unrighteousness, fornication, wickedness, covetousness, maliciousness; full of envy, murder, debate, deceit, malignity; whisperers, backbiters, haters of God, despiteful, proud, boasters, inventors of evil things, disobedient to parents, without understanding, covenant breakers, without natural affection, implacable, unmerciful: who knowing the judgment of God, that they which commit such things are worthy of death, not only do the same, but have pleasure in them that do them (Romans 1: 28–32).

It is relatively easy to deduce from things taking place all around us today that the delusion Paul forewarns will be full-blown when the Holy Spirit withdraws as restrainer of evil. As a matter of fact, my own conclusion is that the satanically inflicted dementia is already far advanced. The evidence grows hour by hour that we are in a world going mad with Luciferian rage.

Let's examine that evidence to see if we are on to something, as Sherlock Holmes might say.

• Economic Irrationality

As is often said about insanity, as attributed first to Albert Einstein, the definition of insanity is doing the same thing over and over and expecting a different result every time.

This is exactly where today's thinking is. The government runs the Treasury printing presses over and over to produce trillions of dollars with nothing to back them in order to solve the national economic woes, which only get worse and worse.

Lyndon Johnson's presidential administration conducted a War on Poverty to produce a Great Society. Since that 1964 all-out effort to solve America's differences in the plight of the have-nots versus the haves, the poverty has only increased. More than $22 trillion has been thrown at the problems. The nation is now bankrupt, for all practical purposes, and the national debt grows exponentially.

It's the same all over the world. Nations are in dire economic chaos, and the global economic structure — for the most part inextricably linked to the U.S. dollar — is on the brink of collapse. Only the staying hand of Almighty God is keeping global depression beyond any ever experienced from happening. Yet, the powers that be continue to use the same methods time and time again in their insane effort to somehow get a different result.

• *Diplomatic Dementia*

The international community of diplomats views Israel as the holdup to peace — even though Israel is a thin sliver of a nation that threatens no other nation, but provides vast goods and inventive services to the whole world.

Israel's enemies, on the other hand — the Arab nations that surround the Jewish state — threaten to annihilate the tiny nation on a daily basis. Israel offers to sit down and come to peace with those who hate them, but the Arab states won't even recognize Israel as a country. Yet the United Nations blames Israel for not being willing to give their enemies the land they want. The land Israel's antagonists want, of course, is the very buffer territory that gives Israel a degree of protection from their enemies, who have attacked them in three major wars.

The diplomats cannot understand, or refuse to recognize, the true problem in the region. It is a satanically spawned dementia that dominates their thinking.

• *Societal Insanity*

Can there be much argument that we are faced with a culture seemingly gone mad, considering things we see transpiring?

What were just a few short years ago designated as mental/psychological disorders are now proclaimed to be normal human behavior. As a matter of fact, there are now laws that demand we assign things like homosexuality, transgender identification, and other conditions formerly considered aberrant or abnormalities special status, warranting privileged treatment . . . or else.

The absolute insanity of making us agree, through legal stipulation, that men, if they feel like a woman on any given hour or day, must be allowed to go into women's restrooms, should speak for the far-advanced state of reprobate thinking. The evidence makes it a no-brainer to deduce that there is already considerable delusion in society and culture today. I'm sure you can think of dozens of activities going on in society and culture that are even more bizarre.

• *Religious Reprobate Reasoning*

Religious delusion is running wild. Jesus Himself says that the Son of God is the only way to heaven.

Even some "evangelical" ministries are now wanting to make nice with apostate religionists within Christianity. Even more deludedly, they are reaching out to embrace other religions that will have nothing to do with Jesus Christ as a spiritual factor, much less as deity who offers the only way to their perverse version of heaven.

Crislam, the combining of Christianity and Islam, is one such effort sponsored by some well-known supposed Christian leaders. Recently, Pope Francis was interviewed on a flight returning to the Vatican. He was recorded saying over and over that Islam is a religion of peace and that it presents only love, not danger, to mankind.

Following the murder of a Catholic priest in northern France by those who claimed the act was done for Allah, the pope opined the following:

> I think it is not right to identify Islam with violence. . . . This is not right, and it is not true. . . . I don't like to talk about Islamic violence because each day when I read the paper I see violence here in Italy. . . . I know it dangerous to say this, but terrorism grows when there is no other option and when money is made a god, and it, instead of the person, is put at the center of the world economy. . . . That is the first form of terrorism. That is a basic terrorism against all of humanity.[63]

Pope Francis has said on occasion that Christianity and Islam are both religions of conquest, and he has blamed Western thinking and interference in the Middle East as being responsible for the rise of Islamic extremism. "Woe unto them that call evil good, and good evil; that put darkness for light, and light for darkness; that put bitter for sweet, and sweet for bitter!" (Isaiah 5:20).

It doesn't take Sherlock Holmes to deduce that the end-times delusion Paul prophesied for the Tribulation period as recorded in 2 Thessalonians 2 has truly already infected this pre-Tribulation era.

---

63. https://www.reuters.com/article/us-pope-islam/pope-says-its-wrong-to-identify-islam-with-violence-idUSKCN10B0YO.

This Race We Face

Do you sense that time is moving faster than ever before? I must tell you that I sense the rush of everything going on becoming more intense by the hour.

We've all had the conversation that when we were younger, time seemed to move much more slowly. The older we get, the minutes, hours, days, etc., fly by at a much faster rate.

Maybe it's just that as our age increases, everything slows down within our own physiology, within our capability to match the speed with things whizzing past. The race of life in which we must participate, possibly, might simply overwhelm us, and we can no longer keep up. The perception, therefore, might be that time itself is moving ever faster, while that's not really the case.

Some physicists could likely make the case that time is actually speeding up or slowing down, or whatsoever theory science postulates these days. But the clock still moves one second at a time. We live our own given increments of life one tick at a time like all of our other fellow travelers on the planet. So, it is outside the realm of reality to suppose that the movement of time itself is any different from when we were youngsters.

Increased activities and events crowding in on our given ticks of the clock have surely colluded to alter our perception, making it seem that time is moving more swiftly. There isn't much room for argument that in America today, life's pressures have seemingly compressed our given 24 hours. We are indeed racing toward our destinations at ever-increasing speed.

This column, of course, is called "Nearing Midnight." The commentaries Todd Strandberg and I write focus as much as possible on Bible prophecy, which we place as a template over the issues and events of this generation. We hope thereby to gauge how near human history is to the Second Coming of Christ.

Progression in setting the stage for the fulfillment of prophecy is all-important in this gauging effort. How quickly issues and events line up with what Jesus and the Old and New Testament prophets foretold give some sense of when the Rapture might occur — and we know that the Rapture of the Church will happen at least seven years prior to Christ's Second Advent (Revelation 19:11). Therefore, if we consider that things are swiftly moving toward what the prophets say will happen during the post-Rapture era and Daniel's 70th week (the Tribulation), we can say with a degree of certainty that Jesus is on the very brink of calling the Church to Himself (Revelation 4:1).

For example, we have witnessed and analyzed the formation of the Gog-Magog coalition of Ezekiel 38 and 39 taking shape at a phenomenal pace. Russia, Iran (Persia), and many other entities that hate Israel are gathering.

World financial crisis is building, threatening to collapse the global economy. In that regard, the internationalist, new-world-order architects are going full steam ahead in their efforts to do away with national sovereignties and to bring the world back to Babel. We see the blatant all-out assault on the U.S. presidential candidate who opposes globalism and calls America back to the founders' vision for this country.

The mainstream media now admits, through an article by a *New York Times* former journalist who is now a news media analyst, that the mainstream news conglomerate is all in for defeating Donald Trump. The writer admits their objective is to see that Trump, whom they claim — as does Barack Obama — is unfit for the land's highest office, never gets into the White House. There's no longer any pretense of fair and balanced coverage of the candidates.

Prophetically, this fits what Daniel the prophet and John the Revelator foretold. There is to be a revived Roman Empire, a final world empire over which a beast called Antichrist will rule. We are now caught up in a race politically, prophetically, and personally, as believers.

Politically, we witness the fomenting of chaos in our nation by those who want America brought into conformation with the global blueprint. It is a Luciferian plan being carried out by Satan's human minions. The current presidential administration has taken an active part in creating this chaos through the Department of Justice (attorney general) actions and in other ways through international diplomacy.

Prophetically, we are racing toward the time when the Lord will catastrophically intervene in the affairs of rebellious mankind. All born-again believers in Jesus Christ will be removed and the most terrible time of all human history will begin.

Personally, we should all be engaged fully in the race to complete the Lord's Great Commission while there is time to do His work here on earth. There are those in heaven watching God's children. They are cheering for believers who are running the race set before us. If you've read my book *Rapture Ready . . . Or Not,* you know I'm convinced with all that is within me that I met some of these heavenly observers on Good Friday, April 22, 2011.

Wherefore, seeing we also are compassed about with so great a cloud of witnesses, let us lay aside every weight, and the sin which doth so easily beset us, and let us run with patience the race that is set before us, looking unto Jesus the author and finisher of our faith; who for the joy that was set before him endured the cross, despising the shame, and is set down at the right hand of the throne of God (Hebrews 12:1–2).

Revisiting a Fearful Future

As mentioned earlier in this book, I wrote a series of articles with the title "Scanning a Fearful Future" at the end of 2010 and the beginning of 2011. The ten-article series involved the fears people were expressing through emails. Almost all emails involved great anxiety over what well-known secular and Bible prophecy pundits were predicting for the immediate future.

The pundits were saying that the economies of the United States and the world would collapse at any moment and America would no longer be America as we've known it. A police state would develop, and there would be tremendous, martyr-like persecution for Christians. I wrote in that series that no such world-rending catastrophe would occur before the Rapture of the Church.

I believed and wrote that such a world-rending cataclysm was indeed going to occur. The world's economic disposition was (and remains) precarious. But, the Lord told me in my spirit — based on prayer and study of Bible prophecy — that no man-made crisis or action would bring America or the world into complete collapse. My conclusion, scripturally based, was that the Lord Himself will bring the world system into chaos with Christ's intervention via the Rapture.

This finding was carried through in my writing of *Rapture Ready . . . Or Not: 15 Reasons This Is the Generation That Will Be Left Behind,* in which I put excerpts of the series and gave reasons for why I believe my conclusions were validated.

The bottom line to report as of this writing is that my conclusion remains validated. We are now at a point almost six years later, and the world has not collapsed as the pundits predicted for 2011 or 2012. Yet, the situation has worsened, not gotten better, in every direction we look on the geopolitical, socioeconomic, religious, and geophysical landscapes. Evil men and seducers have gotten worse and worse, just as the Apostle Paul prophesied. His forewarning of perilous times (2 Timothy 3) is coming to pass before our eyes daily.

But God's hand of control remains upon this reeling, dangerous world of growing godlessness. Planet Earth will obviously stay on its course of destruction, but the end is not yet.

With all that said, there is now a fearfulness such as I haven't sensed, not even in the days when the pundits were predicting any-moment world economic collapse in 2010 and 2011. Christians are worried, almost frantic, as they consider things that seem about ready to come down upon their lives. The trepidation in the emails is more pronounced than ever, yet the world and life in the United States goes on pretty much as normal for these times of increasing debauchery and societal upheaval.

This year's presidential election season contributes mightily to the trepidation, I have no doubt. Another four or eight years of the sort of deliberate dismantling of the American republic that we have suffered will, people fear, end in total loss of religious liberty at best, and of personal freedom of every sort at worst.

Looking at all of this from the humanistic perspective, the reasons for fear, even panic, seem justified. But, for the Christian who has the mind of Christ at the center of his or her spiritual reasoning, a far different mindset is available. I was listening to Dr. Charles Stanley present his message that touched on the topic of fear. He gave the following passage from the Book of Isaiah that I find comforting and reassuring:

> Thou whom I have taken from the ends of the earth, and called thee from the chief men thereof, and said unto thee, thou art my servant; I have chosen thee, and not cast thee away. Fear thou not; for I am with thee: be not dismayed; for I am thy God: I will strengthen thee; yea, I will help thee; yea, I will uphold thee with the right hand of my righteousness. Behold, all they that were incensed against thee shall be ashamed and confounded: they shall be as nothing; and they that strive with thee shall perish. Thou shalt seek them, and shalt not find them, even them that contended with thee: they that war against thee shall be as nothing, and as a thing of nought. For I the LORD thy God will hold thy right hand, saying unto thee, Fear not; I will help thee (Isaiah 41:9–13).

It is true that these words were given in this instance to Israel. But the Lord of heaven doesn't change. Jesus Christ is the same yesterday, today, and forever. Those who are in God's family can rely on His promises, which are ours totally and forever, no matter the period in history in which we live.

The world has not collapsed. God is still on the throne. Prayer changes things, just as His Word tells us.

For those who don't know Christ for salvation, the future is indeed bleak. It is frightful beyond all imagination. But for the Christian alive at the end of the age, when we see all these developments begin to come to pass, we are to lift up our heads and look to Jesus. His coming for His Bride is about to take place (Luke 21:28).

23

September 2016: War
with the Beast

A time is coming, according to Bible prophecy, when the world will experience the most powerful leader to have ever lived upon the planet. He will far surpass in military capability any president of the United States of America who has yet held the reins of power.

The people of planet Earth will be awestruck by his exploits, as we see in the following:

> And they worshipped the dragon which gave power unto the beast: and they worshipped the beast, saying, Who is like unto the beast? who is able to make war with him? (Revelation 13:4).

We have looked many times at this future tyrant called "the beast." He is the first of two beasts that John, through his Revelation vision, sees coming into world history. This one will make his appearance during the period Daniel the prophet indicated will be the 70th week that will wrap up pre-millennial human history. That will be the last seven years leading up to the return of Christ at Armageddon (Revelation 19:11). We know him better, perhaps, as Antichrist.

It is good to think for a bit on that Scripture about this man-beast. The Bible says the question will be asked by the populations of the world who will actually worship him: "Who is able to make war with him?"

In other words, it will seem to everyone who witnesses Antichrist's military exploits and other miraculous accomplishments that he is a god. It will appear, the prophecy says, that he is killed by a wound in his head and then comes back to life. This is obviously a false resurrection. However, the world at that time of great delusion won't see it that way.

The question "Who can make war with him?" will be asked with mesmerized stares of eyes more glazed and glistening than those recorded on the black-and-white films of Hitler's worshipers during the 1930s.

No such leader with that kind of power is anywhere in view today. There are many, many military leaders and their armies who can and do make war with anyone and everyone in this present geopolitical climate, but that future beast will be an animal of unprecedented military capability and authority. Besides the United States military, still the most feared on the planet despite the current president's efforts to greatly diminish its strength, Russia and China continue to build tremendous war-making machines. Iran, Turkey, and others constantly aspire to more powerful militaries. Massive changes in the military power structures of the world will have to occur in order to bring about this monstrous war-making leader against whom no one is thought to be able to fight.

We often conjecture about what happens to the United States. Why isn't it in Bible prophecy? If it is there, it certainly is in a greatly changed configuration, because its military is nowhere in sight, prophetically speaking.

We believe that the militaries of Russia, China, and many others, such as Iran and Turkey, are in prophetic view. We believe we see many of these within the Gog-Magog assault into the Middle East toward Israel (Ezekiel 38 and 39).

Our own view within the pre-Trib camp concerning the Rapture holds that the great changes needed to reconfigure things in alignment with end-times Bible prophecy will unfold during the post-Rapture era. After that great Rapture event, the United States might be aligned with those entities that stand on the sideline as the Gog-Magog attack begins and simply make a diplomatic protest.

> Sheba, and Dedan, and the merchants of Tarshish, with all
> the young lions thereof, shall say unto thee, Art thou come to
> take a spoil? hast thou gathered thy company to take a prey?
> to carry away silver and gold, to take away cattle and goods, to
> take a great spoil? (Ezekiel 38:13).

At any rate, the coalition that assaults into the Holy Land environs will be powerful and unopposed — by human agencies, that is. God, of course, will destroy all but one-sixth of the Gog-Magog army in that future attack. After that destruction, only the great "kings of the East" juggernaut will remain as a force to reckon with.

So, how does the great beast of Revelation 13 accumulate such awesome strength to cause the whole world to ask, "Who is able to make war with him?"

In my own thinking — and it is supposition to be sure — there is somehow a dividing line set between the occidental and oriental worlds.

This is true to this point in history, I believe. But, in that day, there seems to be a supernatural demarcation — the Euphrates River or thereabouts. When it is "dried up" as described in Revelation 16, the kings of the East — led, no doubt, by China — will invade at the time of Armageddon. At that time, the demons appointed especially for that moment will be released from their holding places and will supernaturally indwell those hordes from the Orient. They will kill one-third of earth's inhabitants, the prophecy says. However, all of this will happen later, at the very end of the Tribulation, Daniel's 70th week.

At that earlier time of the Gog-Magog attack, I believe that Antichrist, resident within the nations who will send a note of protest (Ezekiel 38:13), will understand Bible prophecy to the point that he will think slyly to let the Gog-Magog forces go to their destruction by the God of heaven. He will then move into the military power vacuum and build his mighty army, which is supernaturally enhanced by the dark powers of Satan.

Again, it is the view of most who hold to the pre-Trib view of the Rapture and to pre-Millennialism that this beast, Antichrist, will come out of the geographical area now known as the European Union from the people who were at the heart of the ancient Roman Empire — the ones who destroyed Jerusalem and the Jewish Temple in A.D. 70. I do not believe the beast will be a Muslim, although I do believe his ethnic makeup will be from the area of ancient Assyria. He will, nonetheless, have been born and raised in the area of Europe, likely somewhere near Rome.

Today, there is movement toward beginning a military establishment in that very region. The following excerpt is interesting in that regard:

> The leaders of the Czech Republic and Hungary say a "joint European army" is needed to bolster security in the EU.
>
> They were speaking ahead of talks in Warsaw with German Chancellor Angela Merkel. They dislike her welcome for Muslim migrants from outside the EU.
>
> Hungary's Prime Minister Viktor Orban said, "We must give priority to security, so let's start setting up a joint European army."
>
> The UK government has strongly opposed any such moves outside Nato's scope.
>
> The Czech, Hungarian, Polish, and Slovak leaders are coordinating their foreign policy as the "Visegrad Group."[64]

---

64. "Czechs and Hungarians Call for EU Army Amid Security Worries," BBC News, August 27, 2016.

With the UK (Britain, possibly "the merchants of Tarshish") leaving the EU in the so-called Brexit, the way might be clear to generate great interest in such a powerful military — absent NATO — as the beast can one day build upon. One thing is sure, such a military monster will one day be constructed.

It will take the Lord Himself, returning from heaven with the saints of glory, to end Antichrist's ability to make war. Thankfully, Jesus Christ will do so. I believe our Lord will end the beast's war-making capability with the same words He used that day on the stormy Sea of Galilee: *"Peace. Be still"* (Mark 4:39).

Even so, come, Lord Jesus.

Doomsday: The Truth

Doomsday talk is on the rise. It brings to mind the 1964 movie *Dr. Strangelove,* filmed in stark black and white on the topic of nuclear war. This darkly humorous film captured the fearful times at the height of the Cold War involving America and the Soviet Union.

A U.S. general, in this fictional account, went a bit nutso and ordered a strike on the Soviet Union by the B-52 bombers under his command. (Yes, Hollywood was liberal and saw the United States as more evil than the Communist world in those days, too.)

The president, played by Peter Sellers — who also played Dr. Strangelove, the former Nazi scientist in the employ of the U.S. Department of Defense — did all he could to direct the Soviets to bring down the final B-52 as it began its assault. But, alas, the bomber, although crippled by a nearby anti-aircraft missile strike, managed to unleash a multi-megaton hydrogen bomb.

This strike set in motion all-out nuclear war because the Soviets had developed a doomsday machine nobody within the U.S. Defense Department knew about. At that point, it became a final war that could not be controlled or stopped.

Back to reality . . . President Ronald Reagan's peaceful defeat of Soviet designs for world domination was believed to bring the Cold War to an end. Immediately, the cries by the "progressives" went up to convert all of the Cold War military spending to social, do-good causes.

This call for ever-decreasing spending in America's military roared during the Clinton years and again during the Obama administrations so that the U.S. military, in many of its aspects, is now said to be at pre–World War II levels.

But it is obvious to those who view things through the lens of reality that America's old Cold War foes, Russia and China, are building military war-making machinery. They are doing so technologically, if not in war-capable hardware, and now are reaching out to achieve superpower status. Other diabolist states are doing their best to establish their niches in the world's nuclear power structure.

We know all about Iran wanting to develop nuclear weaponry and the missile capability to deliver them. The ayatollahs have even forewarned time after time just who these weapons will be used against.

North Korea makes no bones about wanting to hit any target they can when they achieve the capability to accurately launch them.

All of this has brought the world to renewed fears of the world possibly meeting its end in fiery, nuclear doom within a decade or sooner.

European doomsday worrywarts are ginning up ultra–Cold War fears by warning citizens to prepare for disaster. With the prospect of the influx of millions of hostile militants migrating to Europe, Hungarian Prime Minister Viktor Orban said, "We must give priority to security, so let's start setting up a joint European army."[65]

The German government has instructed its people to prepare for disaster by stockpiling ten days' worth of food and five days' worth of water. Berlin is also considering reinstituting conscription (a military draft) in view of the tremendous surge of Muslims entering Europe.

One thing we haven't heard much about in this volatile political season is that President Obama is also speaking in such terms. In June, he said that Americans must be prepared "by having an evacuation plan," as well as "having a fully stocked disaster supply kit."[66]

All of this comes with increasing alarm by some military analysts who report that Russia is developing and testing new "hyper-weapons." Russian TU-22M3 long-range Backfire bomber aircraft will now be armed with the new Russian Kh-32 cruise missile. The capabilities of this missile are astounding: it can fly at speeds of up to 600 miles per hour to an altitude of almost 25 miles, and when it reaches the proximity of its target, fly downward at a speed of almost 3,000 mph with a total range of almost 600 miles.

There are unsubstantiated reports that "doomsday bunkers" have been prepared for Russian citizenry. Some of the postulation is that many within

65. http://www.dw.com/en/visegrad-countries-urge-eu-to-build-a-common-army/a-19507603.
66. https://www.intellihub.com/green-beret-warns-world-governments-are-preparing-for-disaster-and-war/.

Russian officialdom are taking to the especially prepared doomsday bunkers in the Yamantau Mountain complex that has been constructed.

Add to this increasing reporting that Russian President Vladimir Putin is in the process of purging all upper-echelon officers within his military who oppose future war with Europe and the United States.

Turkey is said to be making tremendous changes within its military planning, in conjunction with Putin's own maneuverings, as preparations for an eventual war in the Middle East and beyond are becoming more manifest.

Chinese leaders are all but declaring war on China's neighbors in creating islands in the South China Sea, which it now claims for the most part to belong to China. The Chinese navy consistently challenges any commercial and other ships that want to pass through what the world still considers international waters.

China, like Russia, is believed to have produced weapons of a defensive nature designed to thwart nuclear missile strikes in retaliation for their own offensive assaults — thus in violation of longstanding agreements against such military technological development.

So, it looks like the old *Dr. Strangelove* Cold War fears are back. Despite the hyperbole and conspiracy theories, there is enough reality-based concern to be alert to the worries wrought by all this doomsday speculation.

All that said, the God of heaven will have the final say about the fate of nations and of planet Earth. He has already given us all we need to know about what this generation is now facing so far as the likelihood of doomsday is concerned.

This world is not at its end. It won't be at its end until at least 1,007 years from now . . . and that is if the Rapture occurs within the next 15 minutes.

"Doomsday" must be viewed in terms of degree. It is true, biblically, that earth's obliteration will never take place by human use of the hydrogen bomb or any other device. It is equally true, prophetically speaking, that earth as we know it will one day be done away with, then remade. That will perhaps take place through nuclear fission or some other phenomenon of natural physics. However it is done, it will be God who remakes the heavens and the earth.

To most all of those who will be left behind and live through the Tribulation era following the Rapture of the Church, it will be the time of doom. Most believers (those who accept Christ after the Rapture) will be martyred. Theirs will not be "doom" but severe persecution — and, in most cases, death. But, those who die will go instantly to an eternity of bliss beyond all imagination.

To the reader: You don't have to concern yourself with Doomsday. Jesus Christ died on the Cross at Calvary 2,000 years ago to assure that your place of heavenly safety is forever secured. Again, the following is the way God has provided for you to escape the terrors the doomed unbelievers of the ages must face:

> That if thou shalt confess with thy mouth the Lord Jesus, and shalt believe in thine heart that God hath raised him from the dead, thou shalt be saved. For with the heart man believeth unto righteousness; and with the mouth confession is made unto salvation (Romans 10:9–10).

Rapture Resistance Ramping Up

The past number of weeks has brought a ramping up of vitriol against the doctrine of the pre-Trib Rapture to my inbox. The assault seems spear-headed by one blog thrust in particular. I receive as many as three long diatribes from this source in a single day. The accusation is that those who believe in the pre-Trib Rapture are part of what this blog entity calls the "Rapture cult."

Many emails pour in from various individuals who, which close exam-ination uncovers, are likely in cahoots with the blog entity initiating this latest strategy against pre-Trib Rapture teaching. These emails, without exception, use the "Margaret McDonald" accusatory proclamation. They claim that we who believe the Bible presents a pre-Trib Rapture have been taken in by the hellish vision of the 19th-century false prophetess who is said to have also caused John Darby to fall for the lie of a pre-Trib Rapture. C. I. Scofield, the DeHaans, and the rest of us have joined and perpetuated this "Rapture cult."

The anti-pre-Trib blog writer launches an anger-tinged condemnation of ancient writings from people such as Pseudo-Ephraem who, from antiq-uity, has been studied by prophecy scholars such as Grant Jeffrey and others in order to find extrabiblical validation that the pre-Trib view of Rapture was held by the early Church fathers and the early Church in general.

The blogger insinuates that the very use of the title "pseudo" indicates this is a false teacher. The "genuine" Ephraem, he writes, apparently lived in the fourth century, while the "pseudo" lived in as late as the seventh. Yet he confuses his attempt to make his case by claiming that both, in the final analysis, write a firm denial of the pre-Trib Rapture.

The blogger writes of both Ephraems: "Both said the only thing 'remaining' is the arrival of Antichrist" — i.e., both believed, according to him, that the Antichrist coming to power is the next prophetic event to take place. No Rapture is in view.

Grant Jeffrey plainly refutes that claim through his research. Jeffrey wrote the following in a chapter for one of my books:

> 1. Ephraem's manuscript lays out the events of the last days in chronological sequence. Significantly, he began with the Rapture, using the word "imminent," then he described the Great Tribulation of three and a half years duration under the Antichrist's tyranny, followed by the second coming of Christ to earth with His saints to defeat the Antichrist.
>
> 2. Significantly, at the beginning of his treatise in section 2, Ephraem used the word "imminent" to describe the Rapture occurring before the Tribulation and the coming of the Antichrist. "We ought to understand thoroughly therefore, my brothers, which is imminent or overhanging."
>
> 3. He clearly described the pre-Tribulation Rapture: "Because all saints and the Elect of the Lord are gathered together before the tribulation which is about to come and are taken to the Lord, in order that they may not see at any time the confusion which overwhelms the world because of our sins."[67]

The writers of those earlier times used the term "pseudo" as merely a literary device to keep their names from being made public for one reason or the other. The same devices are used today in modern literature, of course.

The point is that very meticulous scholarship examining the writers of that ancient period has proven beyond doubt — to me and many others who study Bible prophecy — that many students of God's Word among the early believers held to a pre-Tribulation Rapture of the Church.

Yet the blogger calls the writings by Ephraem the Syrian (A.D. 306 to 373) "false witness" and refers to the writer as a "forger." He does this without actual proof of his charge, but with high-sounding, pseudo-scholarly phraseology.

The danger in all this is that these assaults on the Rapture deflect the study of many of the true children of God who have a desire to look into

---

67. Grant Jeffrey, "Rapture, Three Fascinating Discoveries!" Pretribulation Rapture; http://www.pretribulation.com/tag/grant-jeffrey/.

Bible prophecy these days. Believe me, these seem to constitute a group that is diminishing in number.

The bloggers that are virulently against the truth about the pre-Trib Rapture — brought to us by Paul the Apostle in his letters to the Thessalonians and the Corinthians, and indeed by Jesus Himself as given in John 14:1–3 — send their seemingly well-studied dogma in mass mailings on an ever-increasing basis. People are all too quick to take the sophistry thus delivered, usually unsolicited, as factual. Like those who get their news from cyberspace venues that twist truth that is not news at all, but fable, those marginally interested in Bible prophecy often take the lazy way and choose the blog presentations from the purveyors of anti-pre-Trib Rapture propaganda.

This is a primary reason I wrote my latest book, *Rapture Ready . . . Or Not: 15 Reasons This Is the Generation That Will Be Left Behind.* My prayerful desire has been to get the book into the hands of as many as possible in order to counter such satanically spawned attacks. My special prayer is that we get the book to pastors and teachers within churches that are still of the Philadelphian rather than of the Laodicean sort.

My thanks to all who have seen to it that your pastors and teachers now have this book in their possession. For those who haven't yet done so, I ask that you consider providing each a copy.

Time looks to be running out in this Age of Grace. Pray, if you will, that all in positions to do so will begin using their pulpits and teaching opportunities to deliver truth about Christ's imminent coming for all believers. As chapter 1 of *Rapture Ready . . . Or Not* puts it, "The end isn't near, it's here."

24

October 2016: Power

Henry Kissinger once said that political power is the ultimate aphrodisiac. He should know. For many years, he was at or near the very top on that political leadership chain that wields such power. Some believe he remains so today, even into his nineties.

Power is the one thing for which the global elitists lust. It has been that way since Nimrod first thought to establish one-world order on the plains of Shinar those millennia ago. The constant, incessant drive since the time God intervened and scattered the would-be globalist government architects at Babel has continued to be construction of humanistic world order under the absolute authority of a small number of power brokers.

Daniel the prophet and John the Revelator both saw the same composite beast coming out of the sea of humanity at the very end of history. Each vision represented a single governing, global entity. Daniel in particular saw that the monster was the composite of great world empires of the past:

> Daniel spake and said, I saw in my vision by night, and, behold, the four winds of the heaven strove upon the great sea. And four great beasts came up from the sea, diverse one from another. The first was like a lion, and had eagle's wings: I beheld till the wings thereof were plucked, and it was lifted up from the earth, and made stand upon the feet as a man, and a man's heart was given to it. And behold another beast, a second, like to a bear, and it raised up itself on one side, and it had three ribs in the mouth of it between the teeth of it: and they said thus unto it, Arise, devour much flesh. After this I beheld, and lo another, like a leopard, which had upon the back of it four wings of a fowl; the beast had also four heads; and dominion was given to it. After this I saw in the night visions, and behold a fourth beast, dreadful and terrible, and strong exceedingly;

and it had great iron teeth: it devoured and brake in pieces, and stamped the residue with the feet of it: and it was diverse from all the beasts that were before it; and it had ten horns. I considered the horns, and, behold, there came up among them another little horn, before whom there were three of the first horns plucked up by the roots: and, behold, in this horn were eyes like the eyes of man, and a mouth speaking great things (Daniel 7:2–8).

John prophesied the following through his Patmos vision:

And I stood upon the sand of the sea, and saw a beast rise up out of the sea, having seven heads and ten horns, and upon his horns ten crowns, and upon his heads the name of blasphemy. And the beast which I saw was like unto a leopard, and his feet were as the feet of a bear, and his mouth as the mouth of a lion: and the dragon gave him his power, and his seat, and great authority (Revelation 13:1–2).

It is clear that the great prophets Daniel and John were given almost identical visions of the monstrous hybrid entity that will crush all of humanity under its massively destructive power. Representing all the great humanistic empires of history, the satanically driven final world empire will have at its head a single mouth, that of Antichrist, the first beast of Revelation 13. That mouth will speak "great things," meaning it will propagandize the world's inhabitants to the extent that they will believe a great lie that will deceive all but the very elect of God, those saved during the Tribulation era (2 Thessalonians 2:11–12).

To anyone with eyes to see and especially with ears to hear, we are witnesses today of the development of that great power to deceive. The globalists are shouting with the all-in assistance of the world's media and through actions that are louder than mere words. They want to transform the world into the new Babel — a neo-Nimrod platform upon which will be erected, at least symbolically, a tower even more powerful and all-encompassing than the Tower of Babel of antiquity.

This, to me, is what is among the most troubling in this presidential election. There is a clear distinction between the directions the two major candidates want to go regarding how America will be governed for the next four years.

The power struggle is immense. One candidate claims he wants to begin returning the United States to the leadership of the world of nations, with maintenance of traditionally distinctive borders and ways of dealing internationally.

The other candidate's driving imperative is to continue taking America down the path of deconstructing national boundaries and forcing slavish adherence to more and more internationalist regulations. She is adamantly determined to bring this nation into compliance with the globalist, one-world design.

To me, this is especially troubling because Bible prophecy clearly indicates that a beastly composite world order will one day come to pass, if but for a short time. National autonomy and sovereignty will therefore at some point have to diminish and ultimately vanish.

Those of us who want to see America and other nations returning the international order to the way it has been in the recent past seem on the wrong side of Bible prophecy. The globalists seem on the winning side, in that sense.

This election will supposedly determine which direction we will go, regarding whether we will live under the U.S. Constitution or under Global Agenda 21 or 30, or whatever it's called now.

Lucifer lusted after God-like power (Isaiah 14:14). Fallen mankind, since the time of the Garden of Eden, has clamored for God-like power, which Satan promised through his original deception to Eve. Today, with a U.S. presidential candidacy that threatens to disrupt their one-world agenda, there is a desperate effort to hold to power in Washington, D.C, in the U.N., and in the echelons of principalities and powers in high places (Ephesians 6:12).

The die is cast, as Shakespeare would put it. The new world order is coming. It's just a matter of when. Will it come during this presidential election cycle?

I believe the answer to that might depend upon the *born again* of this nation.

According to Paul's prophecy in 2 Thessalonians, the Restrainer (the Holy Spirit resident within each believer in Jesus Christ) will restrain until the Holy Spirit is taken out of the way. Then all-out iniquity will fill the vacuum left in the wake of His removal.

The Church just might have at its prayerful fingertips the power to hold back or restrain absolute evil until all of Christ's born-again believers are removed.

It is incumbent upon each of us as believers, therefore, to appropriate that power of restraint against those who would bring about the Antichrist, globalist power base for as long as we serve as royal ambassadors upon this judgment-bound planet.

The power of prayer is beyond anything the finite mind can fathom. Let us use the privilege we've been given to exercise this great weapon against the ultimate evil Satan plans for humanity.

When God Promises

Every presidential election in recent times has been talked about as one of the most crucial in America's history. This election has added to it, however, anxiety among voters the likes of which I can't recall.

Not everyone is so concerned, of course. Those I'm referring to who are so concerned are those who truly see the nation as being on a pathway of rapid decline in most every aspect of society and culture. From the issues of the debauching of morality like instituting same-sex marriage and same-sex public toilet facilities, to a presidential administration that seems to have thrown the U.S. Constitution out the window of common sensibility, to the deliberate creation of an economic morass that has built to the point that the government routinely fabricates statistics to try to convince Americans that they aren't really in the economic predicament their circumstances plainly indicate, intensive fear is building.

There is genuine worry within the heartland of America that our government is no longer recognizable as founded. And the even greater worry is that this condition has been deliberately brought about by elected leaders whose primary concerns are feathering their own personal and political power nests.

Certainly, looking across America's landscape, it isn't easy to find a glimmer of hope to offer those with these concerns. Politicians cajoling votes and making great, swelling promises of the campaign stump suddenly disappear when they win elections. They join in or revert to their old Washington ways once they are put into or returned to office. It would be foolhardy to expect that this election will be any different.

Tremendous pressures exerted upon newly elected members of Congress to join the insider network or else be marginalized and rendered ineffectual have been blatantly observable over the last number of midterm elections in particular. Once the candidates have been within the D.C. Beltway for a certain time, they melt into the system. They seem to disconnect from their constituency until it's time to get out and shore up their support at home. The politicians' promises, almost without exception, fade into the canyons of lost memories, the destination for which they are intended all along by the Washington power brokers. Yet to so many among the citizenry, the government has come to demand god-like reverence. The largess that the power brokers provide from cradle to grave has replaced reliance upon provision by the true God of heaven in the mainstream of life in America — thus swiftly taking our nation in the opposite direction intended by the Founding Fathers.

Each succeeding election proves that the politicians' promises are never intended to be kept. Yet we the people continue to place trust in those who, in many cases, have been in positions of power for decades. It's a form of insanity, I think — reprobate thinking brought on by our sinful ways and activity. Again, the definition of insanity is trying the same thing time after time to solve problems even though it fails every time.

This brought to mind the distinctly defined difference between promises given by politicians and promises made by our God.

Actually, the actions of the current president of the United States in Jerusalem attending the funeral of former Israeli Prime Minister Shimon Peres brought this contrast to mind. Mr. Obama's publicity writers, while reporting on Obama's trip, made a faux pas that had to be quickly corrected.

Obama correctly stated in his prepared remarks while attending the funeral, "I could not be more honored to be in Jerusalem to say farewell to my friend Shimon Peres, who showed us that justice and hope are at the heart of the Zionist idea."

However, the White House initially put in the announcement of the president's trip that the ceremony would be in "Jerusalem, Israel." Within six hours, the embarrassed White House staff put out the corrected statement that indicated that, in fact, Jerusalem is disputed territory.

In other words, Israel, in the eyes of U.S. politicians, has no claim to the land more valid than those who claim possession among the Palestinians. The U.S. State Department has, in fact, refused to recognize Jerusalem as Israel's capital, placing the U.S. Embassy in Tel Aviv.

The same politicians who make us promises election after election and quickly forget them once they've been voted into office tell Israel that, in effect, God's promise to that nation is not valid. Yet while the politicians prove that it is *their own* promises that are not valid, the God of heaven, through the very nation of Israel, which is at the heart of so much worldwide anger and controversy, has proven beyond any doubt that He keeps His promises.

He has said that Israel, once established in the land, will never be uprooted again. He said it would be made a nation again in a single day. He said that Israel will never stop being His people. He has kept every promise. We can know, therefore, beyond any doubt, that while the politicians of this nation and world almost never keep even one promise, the God of the universe never will break a promise.

God has said to His people Israel regarding Jerusalem, "For thus saith the LORD of hosts; After the glory hath he sent me unto the nations which spoiled you: for he that toucheth you toucheth the apple of his eye" (Zechariah 2:8).

The Lord has also promised that because the politicians of this world will "divide my land," He will bring the whole world into the Valley of Jehoshaphat, Armageddon (Joel 3:2).

That's why we watch Israel so closely. Israel is absolute proof of the veracity of God's Word. He keeps His promises, and Israel is the proof! To apply this to the fear and trepidation that so many Christians are expressing today about the upcoming election and what lies beyond November 8, I urge that we consider our great, promise-keeping God.

He has told us that we will be completely kept out of the time of the soon-to-come era of horror termed the Tribulation — out of His judgment and wrath (Revelation 3:10). He will take the Bride of Christ off this condemned planet when all of the troubling signals *begin* to come to pass (Luke 21:28). When God promises, it is as good as accomplished. This promise, I hope you will sense in your spirit as do I, is about to be kept.

The Twinkling

You and many others who have chosen to read this are likely in agreement. We find ourselves at a time when the future is indeed murky. That very fact makes it a time of uneasiness — of profound uncertainty.

With so many existential threats (factors portending possible, even probable, future disruption for our lives), many look toward November 8 with a shadow of oppressiveness clouding their thoughts.

We have watched our American way, our laws and traditions, be dismantled. We have watched the process happen with the acquiescence, even the complicity, of those with whom we entrusted our votes to stop that degeneration.

More troubling is the almost certainty that if the presidential candidate presently leading in polls (according to most polls) succeeds, the tearing down of America as founded will be put on the fast track. The "promise and change" declared in January 2009 by the current president will, it is feared, soon be completed after this election. The global architects will, in that case, have removed the last roadblock from their ambition to tear down national sovereignties.

America, in the earthly sense, is that roadblock — thus the all-out effort by national and world politicians as well as media to utterly destroy the candidate in opposition to their vision for one-world order.

With most everything else in place for setting up for the Tribulation, including Israel again being in the spotlight, hounded by UNESCO in denying its historical right to the land, we have recently added some truly profound rumors of war. Russia and the American presidential administration have entered a dangerous era of international intrigue and gamesmanship. With the Clinton campaign and the administration of Barack Obama blaming Vladimir Putin and his regime for hacking emails and giving them to Wikileaks to influence the outcome of the election, not just the Cold War but a "hot war" might be forthcoming.

The Russians have moved, uncontested, into the Middle East. They have naval power and growing ground and air force capabilities in position to defend the Syrian dictator. This American administration hasn't lifted a finger to oppose this shift of Russian power into the region.

Obama has, through his ineptness — or, as I more am prone to suspect, his deliberate action — allowed the development of the forces of ISIS (ISIL, as he calls them). America has U.S. Air Force assets now in regions indicating what some believe to equate to a provocation-of-war-incident waiting to happen. Again, I'm convinced it's all part of the globalist orchestration being used by Satan himself to bring his own "son of perdition" to power.

Many who consider all this sense an incident or action in the immediate future that will explode in uncontrollable ramifications. Yet nothing, no matter the circumstances, has to this point happened to initiate the long-anticipated catastrophe.

The Russians are seemingly trying to instigate direct confrontation with American aircraft. China is trying to provoke, seemingly, a confrontation in the South China Sea. Iran is firing, through proxies, upon U.S. warships, apparently begging to be hit in return in order to start something.

The economic bubble of insanity continues to build to the bursting point. And, we have a presidential election in two weeks that some believe will bring on an even greater national schizophrenia and possible civil war, no matter who wins.

My great friend, the late Jack Kinsella, had tremendous insight, as many reading this know. He left us some God-engendered thoughts for just this time. He wrote the following in one of his *Omega Letter* commentaries:

We live in the most terrifying time of uncertainty in human history — the wrong move by the wrong guy could set off a chain of events that could potentially exterminate the human race. We have but a short time to spread the message of salvation, and it doesn't help if we are paralyzed by fear.

The Lord knew the conditions that would exist just before His return. Which is why Paul ends his explanation of the Rapture with this exhortation:

"Wherefore comfort one another with these words" (1 Thessalonians 4:16–18).[68]

Jack had just written a fabulous piece on the Rapture. The "comfort" Paul assured us was all about that "twinkling-of-an-eye" moment Jack and I — and, I hope, you — believe is about to occur based upon all of the things that have begun to come to pass (Luke 21:28).

Satan's High Anxiety

Lucifer, the ultimate rebel against everything godly, is perhaps the most brilliant being produced from the holy mind of the Creator. This proud creature has always wanted to supplant the One who created him. He has been pursuing that iniquitous, self-appointed mission since the thought came into his mind (Isaiah 14:14).

Satan, as he is now called by God, knows Bible prophecy. He believes Bible prophecy — all except the part where it says that he loses in the end.

The devil, as the Bible also refers to him, knows that God cannot lie; the Creator of all things knows every intimate detail of everything from eternity past into eternity future.

God has said that Satan loses at the end of human history. Yet the ultimate rebel believes he will still come out victorious over the omniscient, omnipresent, and omnipotent God of heaven.

Lucifer the fallen one, who was instrumental in man's downfall in Eden, serves as the best example of possessing a reprobate mind as outlined by the Apostle Paul:

> And even as they did not like to retain God in their knowledge, God gave them over to a reprobate mind, to do those things which are not convenient; being filled with all unrighteousness, fornication, wickedness, covetousness, maliciousness; full of envy, murder, debate, deceit, malignity;

---

68. http://www.omegaletter.com/articles/articles.asp?ArticleID=6604&SearchFor=rapture.

whisperers, backbiters, haters of God, despiteful, proud, boasters, inventors of evil things, disobedient to parents, without understanding, covenant breakers, without natural affection, implacable, unmerciful: who knowing the judgment of God, that they which commit such things are worthy of death, not only do the same, but have pleasure in them that do them (Romans 1:28–32).

God's Word calls Satan the "father of lies." The Bible says that unbelievers are of their father, the devil. Those who continue to refuse God's way — belief in Jesus Christ — ultimately suffer from the same insanity of their spiritual father: a reprobate mind.

This spiritual insanity cannot discern truth. It is upside down thinking in which the world is immersed. This is why we are now witnessing the insanity in most every area of human endeavor. The affliction will one day soon bring humanity to the point of annihilation. Only Jesus Christ Himself will be able to save humankind (Matthew 24:22).

So Satan, obviously insane, though brilliant in his madness, continues on a course he believes will wrest control of the earth from God Almighty. He knows and believes Bible prophecy, thus uses it to plot his overthrow of God's Kingdom.

He doesn't know, however, the intimate details of how Bible prophecy will play out. He didn't know, for example, that murdering God's Son on the Cross would result in Christ's Resurrection three days later and that this would be the formula to redeem mankind. Satan played into the Lord's holy, perfect plan that provides salvation for lost men, women, and children.

The devil, I believe with all that is within me, knows a final earthly dictator and a one-world-order regime will come upon the earth. He has, history shows, had a man ready to assume that role on many occasions throughout history.

Lucifer has been working increasingly harder with each succeeding era, with each succeeding generation, to bring about the Antichrist regime outlined in Revelation 13. The devil has worked tirelessly to bring all nations into configuration ripe for his pawns — supernatural and geopolitical human minions — to institute the new world order.

America, as I've tried to point out, is the primary national entity blocking the rest of the world from falling into line with the satanic blueprint for global order. National sovereignty, national borders, must be erased to accommodate a neo-Babel structure.

Satan cannot foresee the future but can only try to anticipate with now-perverted supernatural intelligence. He knows — as do we — that everything seems just right for removing America as that roadblock. This election presents a clear-cut demarcation between maintaining America's founding as a sovereign, God-inspired republic, and bringing the United States into the neo-Babel configuration the globalist elite are determined to inflict.

That seems to me the reason we're witnessing an astounding attack upon the presidential campaign that wants to maintain the nation's constitutional integrity as founded. The assaults, as anyone with any honesty will admit, constitute unbelievable rage from every possible quarter. They are satanic in their ferocity.

Satan knows everything is set up for his big opportunity to at last bring in his kingdom, the kingdom of Antichrist. But he is full of uncertainty that this is the time Bible prophecy has given for the development of that end-times kingdom given by Daniel the prophet and John the Revelator.

The wicked one is full of anxiety about this election, thus the over-the-top rage as we near Election Day. He doesn't want to take any chances. His minions are in full-attack mode.

Most who want a return to sanity in our beloved nation are anxious, of course. But, our nervousness doesn't compare to the obvious anxiety Satan and his forces are projecting.

The Lord has each of us here, at this volatile yet fascinating time, for His own good purposes. He will finish the work He has started in us, we are promised in His Word. We don't have to be overly concerned. We're in the mighty hand of the One who knows the outcome of this election, of America's fate, and of our glorious destiny in Jesus Christ: "For God hath not given us the spirit of fear; but of power, and of love, and of a sound mind" (2 Timothy 1:7).

25

November 2016: Prayer Wars

Never in American history has there been in presidential politics a time that fits the descriptive given in Ephesians 6:12 more than now. That spiritual battle describes succinctly the time that has led up to Tuesday, November 8, 2016:

> For we wrestle not against flesh and blood, but against principalities, against powers, against the rulers of the darkness of this world, against spiritual wickedness in high places.

For decades, it has been as if the dark, hellish forces of the ages have been turned loose against this nation, which has been so openly blessed by heaven. The cultural and social "progress" thought to have been made, according to those who want to detach America from the Judeo-Christian mooring the Founding Fathers provided, is threatened by a significant challenge. We the people of God just might have decided we don't wish that progressive agenda to proceed further. Thus, the war is on in a way perhaps unseen in the annals of U.S. presidential elections.

We are told how to fight such warfare as this. We are to "put on the whole armor of God" (Ephesians 6:11).

The Bible describes that spiritual armor and, once we are fully, spiritually armed, we are to be "praying always with all prayer and supplication in the Spirit, and watching thereunto with all perseverance and supplication for all saints" (Ephesians 6:18).

The question is: How well have most Christians these days armored up? The dumbing-down by the godlessness of the secular world and — even more troubling — by the compromising churches of recent times has taken a heavy toll. However, the one weapon Paul mentioned is in play during this war for the survival of this once-great republic.

I believe that the core of people in this nation who hold to the truth of the Word of God are "praying always with all prayer and supplication in the Spirit" that the Lord will intervene in this war that is raging. It is a "prayer war," to be sure.

I'm aware of the seminary and other positions that say 2 Chronicles 7:14 was only for Israel and doesn't apply to America. But the God of heaven does not change. Jesus Christ, who is God, is the same yesterday, today, and forever. I am trusting, therefore, that that great promise given to Israel during their direst time of need applies equally to those of this day and time who are "called by His name."

Although the nucleus of God's people who hold fast to His precepts and promises might be dwindling in number, we are still here in the hundreds of thousands, if not millions. We are engaged in this prayer war for a restoration of sanity in America's government, society, and culture.

We are praying specifically that the evil forces raging to make this nation into a state totally apart from all godliness will be, at least on an interim basis, kept from their Luciferian goal. I say "on an interim basis" because Bible prophecy plainly foretells that the satanic, globalist forces will one day establish, for a time, a one-world order as Antichrist's platform of power. It will happen; it's just a matter of time.

Meantime, however, while the Church of Jesus Christ is here, and thus the Restrainer (Holy Spirit) resident within that Body holding back evil, it is right and proper — *expected* — that God's people are to offer the prayer of 2 Chronicles 7:14: "If my people, which are called by my name, shall humble themselves, and pray, and seek my face, and turn from their wicked ways; then will I hear from heaven, and will forgive their sin, and will heal their land."

Even at this late hour just before the presidential election, millions are praying this to the best of their ability. I believe movements and revelations of corruption within the recent political processes directly reflect the Lord's attentiveness to the spiritually attuned prayer warriors.

If America is to be so blessed by a positive answer to those prayers by heaven's throne room, the battle like that described in Ephesians 6 will, after the election, intensify even more than if God's answer is otherwise. In that case, it will be this nation's final dispensation of liberty if there isn't a turning back to God in a major way.

Very shortly after this commentary is posted, we will know God's answer to those prayers — and perhaps the nation's disposition with regard to personal liberty for whatever time is left in this Age of Grace.

The war of the ages as this Church Age dispensation moves into its final stages will be fought most effectively by God's people in the prayer closets of America. Let's be sure to put on the *whole armor* before engaging in the battles we face.

Which Way, America?

July 4, 1976, brought the bicentennial celebration of America's birth. At that time, the nation was, like in most every era of modern U.S. history, facing challenges at home and abroad. The Soviet Union was at full strength and threatening to exert hegemony over territory even beyond the post–World War II nations it had dominated for more than three decades. China threatened its neighbors and the world. Our nation was considered in moral decline even then, having come out of the hippie generation, the sexual revolution, and the drug culture produced from the time before and since Woodstock in 1969. *Roe v. Wade* had just been instituted by the Supreme Court decision, and all looked to be on the fast track to degeneration into a moral abyss.

The pastors and evangelists of the time were preaching from the pulpits against the many debaucheries going on. There was pushback against the evils of the day that seemed to permeate every stratum of society and culture.

My own memory of the time is wrapped up into a single recollection. Our pastor at the time, who was an eloquent speaker — and a dyed-in-the-wool patriot — brought into our sanctuary sermons that rang with passion for restoration of the Founding Fathers' Judeo Christian–based principles. Dr. Russell J. Clearman also wrote a book, whose poignant title I chose for heading this commentary as we emerge into the post-election light — "Which Way, America?"

Dr. Clearman's book was, like his spoken words from the pulpit, a moving clarion call, through the question implicit in the title, for America to choose which way it would move. Would the nation choose to continue the road that would lead to oblivion, or the road that would return to a godly course?

Our nation went into severe economic recession shortly after that 200th birthday celebration, the Jimmy Carter years bringing fiscal distress and disrespect from nation-entities around the world. Iran turned from being an ally to, after overthrowing the shah, holding Americans hostage in the American embassy in Tehran.

Then, with God's people's appeal to heaven through movements such as the Moral Majority, with much prayer, the nation went into an era of relative peace and prosperity.

But, alas, America has again determined to walk down that descending slope of anti-godliness toward its doom. Today, with the election of 2016 just concluded, God has again answered prayers for national rescue. And, make no mistake: it was the God of heaven, listening to His people, who answered prayer and saw to the outcome of this election.

This is, of course, considered a foolish assessment by those who don't have spiritual discernment, but is true, nonetheless.

Just as the 1976 celebration of America's birthday, this election of the 45th president of the United States seems a place to ask the question, "Which way, America?"

The nation is much deeper in its descent into the abyss of anti-godliness than it was during the 1970s. Back then, homosexuality still had a moral leash. Public restrooms being shared by both sexes simultaneously was unthinkable. Same-sex marriage condoned and institutionalized by the U.S. government was unacceptable. Christians being forced to serve customers whose demands went against the business owners' Christian principles was unimaginable.

We have a much sharper turnaround to accomplish than during that earlier era. The effort will require more resolve this time. The spiritual battle is much more intense and will become even more profound as we proceed into the next four years of this new presidential administration.

Which way we choose to go will depend directly upon God's people becoming staunchly resolute in how devoted we are to heaven's directives in our prayer closets and on the front line of these satanically spawned battles we face in this end-of-the-age war.

With all that said, I sense a very possible prophetic scenario developing, which I share here with the caveat that it is only a scenario, not a "word of knowledge," as some would claim.

We have coming into the office of president on January 20, 2017, a person who has a certain degree of business genius. I have no doubt of that, having observed him over many decades of his empire building.

He is God's man for this troubled hour in this nation and world, I have absolutely no doubt. I say "God's man," not in the sense that he is devoted to godliness. I mean that I believe he is appointed to this prophetic hour for God's purposes. Profound things are afoot.

Globalism has been put briefly in the pause position upon the engine of world dynamics. The president-elect is a nationalist — one who holds firmly to national borders — to national sovereignty. He has vowed to "Make America Great Again."

Whereas I certainly don't know the future in its detailed unfolding, I can, from scripturally based exploration, speculate and postulate just a bit about things to come.

We now have one of history's proven, great builders in the business world about to take the reins of power in the United States of America — the most materially blessed nation of human history. We have in Revelation 18 a description of one of the most powerful and materially dominant entities in all human history. "Which Way, America?"

I know this flies in the face of traditional seminary teachings, but might we be witnessing the beginning of the final development of this entity that will eventuate in becoming the mystery Babylon described in that most astounding prophecy?

This is not to imply that Donald J. Trump — or anyone else — is a satanic plant. I've been a "Trumper" all the way since he won nomination.

However, God lifts kings (leaders) to power and He brings them down. Could this genius builder be about to help build a national entity that is destined to fulfill a specific prophecy? We can only stay tuned — and spiritually attuned.

But we won't see the final product, in any event, if we know the Lord Jesus Christ for salvation. There is an even greater event — that destruction of Babylon event scheduled for the tribulation era. We are looking for our blessed hope (Titus 2:13).

Even so, come, Lord Jesus.

Heaven's Post-Election Priorities

News pundits are pontificating in every direction about what President-elect Donald J. Trump's priorities will be come January 20, 2017.

We are told about building the wall on our southern border. There is much talk about repealing and replacing Obamacare. We hear about the new president's intention to power up the faded U.S. military and do away with many of the executive orders he believes helped bring the American economy and social structure to an unacceptable status.

The new president's priorities are, of course, important. We welcome new direction as we sense the reprieve this election has brought. The prayers of God's people, as I've pointed out previously, have helped win that reprieve from what seemed impending judgment.

Perhaps "correction" would be the most appropriate term. God's people prayed that God would hear them and would put the nation on a course correction.

This, He has seemingly done.

He intervened a century ago to make a profound course correction following the raucous "Gay Nineties" and the debauched era following World War I termed the "Roaring Twenties."

Writer John Steinbeck captured this corrective era in his novel *The Grapes of Wrath*. It was indeed an era when the crops of corrective judgment, whose seeds of refusing to follow the God-designed course for America had been planted more than a decade earlier, came to fruition.

Again, the tremendous Dust Bowl of the 1930s was a corrective measure while God prepared the American people for the Second World War — a conflict God didn't cause, but certainly used to temper and harden this nation to make it ready to meet its destiny.

That destiny was primarily to bring modern Israel to birth on May 14, 1948, and to spread the gospel to the world through advancing communications technologies. The United States was economically blessed from that point, making it the wealthiest and most technologically advanced nation that has ever existed.

So, while Mr. Trump's political agenda is important, even critical, to achieving worthy goals in turning America in the right direction, heaven's priorities are truly the matters for which God's reprieve has been so mercifully given.

Of course, the Church should take this as a mandate to recapture moral ground and to roll back some of the social evils the Obama administration has brought forth (most through executive fiat). That very Church has, in my estimation, allowed this slide toward the moral abyss through her acquiescence.

However, that said, the same two major issues are involved in this God-given reprieve.

Heaven's post-election priorities again involve seeing to it that (1) the gospel message is carried throughout the world, and (2) Israel continues to have the most powerful nation on the planet as an ally and protector.

God doesn't need the United States to protect Israel. But it is also beyond argument that the Lord has used America to act as midwife in birthing Israel into modernity and then as guardian during decades since that rebirth. The Lord has chosen America for this specific function, it is likely, for as long as the planet remains in the pre-Tribulation era.

A time will come when Israel will be under the wrathful hand of Antichrist and the rest of the world. God will intervene directly at that time. Daniel the prophet, passing along the angel's words, puts it this way:

> And at that time shall Michael stand up, the great prince which standeth for the children of thy people: and there shall be a time of trouble, such as never was since there was a nation even to that same time: and at that time thy people shall be delivered, every one that shall be found written in the book (Daniel 12:1).

So, while we watch the unfolding of post-election aftermath, let us view things through the prism of Bible prophecy. We are not about to go into an era that offers prospect of the Church building heaven on earth as the Kingdom-Now purveyors would have it. All is further stage-setting for the Rapture of the Church and the appearance of the "son of perdition."

But, it is a reprieve from heaven we are witnessing and living, so let's keep in mind heaven's priorities. The Great Commission is still the top priority. Bringing as many lost people as possible into God's family before the time of Tribulation is our post-election mandate.

Pre-Tribulation Ponderings

Listening to the "experts" thinking aloud on what this election means is an exercise in frustration, if not futility. The talking heads attribute Donald Trump's win to everything from the late FBI turn of events to news media's biased poll-taking and misreading of exit polling, and they throw in that those in charge of the losing campaign just didn't understand the people of middle America. They didn't see the people's pent-up rage against the Washington establishment, the D.C. insiders.

All these elements no doubt contributed to this election, as many of the pundits put it, eventuating in a totally unexpected outcome. But it is the never-mentioned aspect of this election dynamic that is frustrating to me as a Christian. It is this that produces a sense of futility.

No one in media is talking about the 81–84 percent (depending upon the figure you accept) of "evangelicals" who turned out in this election. Christian participation just isn't figured in at the highest levels of broadcast and cable punditry.

This means, to me, that the experts believe this election had nothing to do with our being fed up with the social debauchery and degradation that has been taking place, particularly over the past almost eight years. The homosexual, transsexual, same-sex marriage agenda, with mandated same-sex, multiple-occupancy public restrooms, had no influence on the voting this election year, the experts are saying with their silence. We, the voters — who are Christians and came out in numbers that have not been seen in many elections — apparently weren't (according to the pundits) making a statement that we are fed up with our White House being bathed in rainbow colors emblematic of the homosexual lobby. We aren't sick and tired of having the homosexual rainbow flag flown atop that same American presidential edifice is the message of the silence.

I guess we are to take away from this silence that this electoral landslide against the candidate and party that have crammed down America's throat all of this hellishness — mostly through presidential, executive order-fiat — had nothing to do with the social issues.

That we are disgusted with small bakery owners being publicly humiliated and fined for refusing to bake same-sex wedding cakes obviously isn't considered worth mentioning in the analysis of this election's results. The horrors and atrocities that we learned about involving Planned Parenthood and the selling of human baby body parts didn't, in the thinking of the post-election, political analysts, figure in our collective voting statement.

It was all about terrorism, wallet issues, and building back America's defense, while determining to "drain the swamp."

These were all important issues in my own thinking, as in that of many other Christians, while election day approached. But, in addition to stopping a further tearing down of America's founding structure, I have wanted a government that will stop the anti-godliness, down the road of which the administration of the last eight years has deliberately moved this nation.

As expressed previously in these commentaries, it was God's people offering up the prayer of 2 Chronicles 7:14 that turned this election so dramatically. This is the answer the pundits are seeking when they ask incessantly about what happened that the news media types missed. How could this election have turned out so differently than expected right up until 9 p.m. EST, Tuesday, November 8?

The fact is that the throne room of heaven was deluged day and night with God's people imploring Him for mercy, asking that He hear from heaven and answer our prayers. This, of course, required repentance — not of America's population, but of God's people. It is more than obvious that He did hear and answered in a spectacular way. God cannot lie, and He promised He would answer such prayer — uttered under biblically prerequisite conditions.

Now, the question is: Will we continue to pray and follow up on those prerequisite conditions? How we respond will determine how our nation — and our lives — fare over the coming days, months, and perhaps years.

We have proof that our Lord answers prayers in a spectacular way. The secular commentators will never see it, but we who did and are doing the praying certainly understand.

We can further understand God's influence in this election by the Christian people He has placed among the soon-incoming power elite.

So, in this time before the Tribulation, we have a window of opportunity to honor our Lord's merciful answer in giving us a leadership that promises a return to founding principles. Along with that merciful action, it is also obvious that we have been given a course correction, a return to the moral pathway out of the depravity foisted on us in recent years.

We don't have to wonder about how to honor His mercy and kindness in having answered our prayers. His number-one priority has always been the salvation of souls. We are expected to honor His decision to give America a reprieve in order to, first and foremost, lift Jesus Christ so that the Holy Spirit draws all to Christ for salvation.

Just beneath that all-important mission for God's people in America is to let the pastors of our churches know that the true, Christ-believing bodies of worship should be devoted to teaching and preaching truth. That is, we are, now more than ever, to be the Philadelphian church and not the Laodicean church (read Revelation 3).

There is no doubt that we see this gracious, merciful moving of God's hand in America. However, signals are growing stronger by the day that we are in times at the very end of the age.

Jesus forewarned in the Olivet Discourse that there would be great ethnic strife. We have been seeing it manifested in American cities. The seas and waves of humanity are "roaring" in America and in Europe. This election has intensified that roaring, I believe. People who refuse to accept the election results are exemplifying the Apostle Paul's "perilous times" characteristic of being "incontinent," or "out of control." Jesus said societal conditions will be exactly like now when He intervenes catastrophically into the affairs of mankind. That will happen with the Rapture.

With the United States now seeming to be headed back toward the America we once knew and loved, with the promises of the new administration, we can enjoy our moment of gratefulness this Thanksgiving season.

However, this time of national renewal is also likely to be a time like the one described by Jesus, a time that will bring His next catastrophic intervention into the affairs of mankind. That time might just be upon us:

> Therefore be ye also ready: for in such an hour as ye think
> not the Son of man cometh (Matthew 24:44).

26

December 2016: The ABC Questions

We are moving into stranger and stranger times, I sense from recent developments. Chief among those developments is the most obvious: the election of the candidate thought to have no chance at all just a few months ago. Yet here he is, poised to "Make America Great Again."

This being the case, I would ask that you indulge me just a bit, as I would like to construct a scenario or two based as much in biblically prophetic truth as in fictional cogitation.

That America has been forced toward moving into the globalist mold over the past several decades is without question, especially during the past eight years of the Obama administration. The nation's sovereignty has been in process of usurpation by the new world order builders through a series of quasi-legitimate executive orders.

It is more than obvious that the United States was moving along a seemingly unalterable course dictated by the globalists' agenda. This presidential election didn't just slow that movement; it halted it in its tracks. The president-elect is an avowed anti-globalist. He views America not as the hegemonic superpower that must be brought down to Third-World status, its wealth redistributed in order to create some insanely conceived socialistic Utopia, but as beneficent leader of a world of autonomous nations.

My idea isn't to sing the praises of the future president. He is merely a man who has been thrust into the end-times picture for God's own great purpose. My thinking here is to explore and examine the possibilities that purpose might include.

Thus, we come to the title of this commentary: "The ABC Questions."

I watch with great interest the uptick in the world's fiscal markets as the wizards of finance contemplate changes taking place in our country. The records being set in the stock markets, etc., move in sync with the strangeness of this election. The whole matter generates questions involving Bible prophecy. My questions and ruminations follow.

Question A

AMERICA — Is this nation, rather than being on the brink of imploding economically as most prophecy students thought before this election, now about to enter a time of unprecedented financial boom?

Most who have been responsible for making profit within the private sector know and lament that regulations coming out of the current presidential administration have been deadly to business development. Mr. Obama himself has boasted that he has "a pen and a phone," meaning that he could and would bypass Congress to accomplish what he wanted. This he has done prolifically. His use of his pen and phone have been particularly ruinous to the free enterprise system in this nation.

Increased taxation, added to the regulatory edicts, has resulted in horrendous job losses because of business downsizings and closings. The nation seemed poised to go much deeper into the economic abyss. The election of Donald J. Trump, a highly successful business mogul, seems to have suddenly turned things around with promises to roll back taxes and regulations and introduce a plethora of innovations.

The financial markets are apparently buying the promises, and the uptick in the stratosphere of economic anticipation shows it.

All of this just doesn't fit the thinking of Bible prophecy observers. Most seem to look for America to succumb to the forces of globalism. And, as stated before, the nation was certainly headed in that direction prior to this election.

So it is reasonable to ask whether the United States of America might be headed into another great economic boom instead of descending into depression as feared just weeks ago. This conjecture brings forth another most interesting question.

Question B

BABYLON — Could we now be witnessing the beginnings of "Babylon the Great"?

Revelation 18 presents a stunning portrait of the greatest human commercial entity of all of history. This nation and city is prophesied to dominate all the earth with its commerce and debaucheries. Here's what is said of this city-state called "Babylon the Great":

> For all nations have drunk of the wine of the wrath of her fornication, and the kings of the earth have committed fornication with her, and the merchants of the earth are waxed rich through the abundance of her delicacies (Revelation 18:3).

This Babylonian system will be destroyed in one hour, God's Word tells us. It will be a much-deserved judgment. All the world will mourn this destruction:

> And the kings of the earth, who have committed fornication and lived deliciously with her, shall bewail her, and lament for her, when they shall see the smoke of her burning, standing afar off for the fear of her torment, saying, Alas, alas, that great city Babylon, that mighty city! for in one hour is thy judgment come. And the merchants of the earth shall weep and mourn over her; for no man buyeth their merchandise any more (Revelation 18:9–11).

Here you will, I hope, indulge my postulations a bit. If this generation is at the very end of the Age of Grace, as most who are well-versed in Bible prophecy from the pre-Trib view believe, there is but one entity that could possibly be seen as doing business in the mighty way described in this prophecy.

For such a commercial power to develop from the ground up would take decades — not just 7, or even 20, years. America, if there was a massive ginning up of enterprise, could possibly reach such heights of interaction with the rest of the world in a year or two. Simply no nation on the planet has ever been so materially blessed as the USA. No other city on planet Earth has the commercial outreach and influence of New York City.

Seeing as how the timeline seems to be a major factor in this prophecy, the destruction of Babylon the Great taking place within the seven-year Tribulation, we can legitimately ask: is America going to develop into that judgment-bound entity?

Perhaps we might get a clue if the optimistic outlook of the current stock-market elites plays out as they, at least at this moment, anticipate.

Question C

CHRISTIANITY — Is Christianity about to experience a Great Awakening like in times past?

For years now, preachers and others have been saying there will be a great revival before the Rapture. Some who don't hold that there is a Rapture coming also say there will be another Great Awakening as in the past.

I've never held that belief, I must say. However, considering the strange turn of events — with the anti-God forces of the left and the globalists' ravenous desire to gobble up the United States being suddenly halted — one has to question, "Why?"

Could we be about to experience a final outpouring of God's great mercy in the form of the true Church carrying out the Great Commission in a Holy Spirit–directed outburst of supernatural witness?

Saving the World

My practice each week before beginning to think seriously on the next week's commentary for this column is to pray for guidance from on high. This week's essay, I sensed, would require especially intensive beseeching in order to receive direction toward the commentary leading up to Christmas Day. Just the opposite turned out to be the case.

An idea of what the topic should be came almost instantly. Less than an hour into the process came a message through email that validated beyond any doubt that the topic was chosen from above.

The note was from a regular family member of www.raptureready. com. Her words verified that the thought for the Christmas message wasn't mine, but that it was from the One who sent that first Christmas message two millennia ago. I quickly dashed off a reply thanking her.

I again thank her here, and will include some of her words from her most timely message to me.

As many who read these commentaries know, my recent articles have involved the lead-up to and reporting of the 2016 presidential election. I view that election, I think I have made clear, as being intervention by the Lord — for several reasons.

His intervention was, I believe, to answer the prayers of His people who are called by His name, in accordance with 2 Chronicles 7:14. His response was to begin to turn around the quick slide into the abyss of total moral decay. His action was to stop this nation's almost-certain march to globalism, which the losing candidate would have put on an even faster track than America was on, should she have been elected president.

I likened the intervention in the matter of globalism to God erecting a wall even more profound than the wall the president-elect has promised to put along America's southern border. For now, at least, America apparently will have a wall of sorts — a return to the constitutional concept of sovereignty and nationhood intended by the Founding Fathers.

That constitutional concept was formed by Washington, Adams, Jefferson, Franklin, and all the rest, based upon their strong belief in adherence to Judeo-Christian principles found in the Bible. This, the new world order architects cannot abide. Religion, they rant, is the bane of progressive thought and action. They most often champion the utopian dream fostered by Karl Marx, who wrote, "Religion is the sigh of the oppressed creature, the heart of a heartless world, and the soul of soulless conditions. It is the opium of the people."[69]

The globalist elite who hate religion and despise Christianity see communism as the route to utopia. If only they could have their blueprint for their version of socialism put fully into production, they would create heaven on earth. These have come to fanatically embrace their own version of religion called "environmentalism."

They were, until recently, calling it "global warming." The scientific sophistry behind their claim came to light through exposure to the facts, so they changed the core of their religion to "climate change."

These are of the save-the-earth cult that holds that man is destroying Mother Earth. Therefore, the globalist elite — the high priests of their religion — must see to it that all nations, all peoples, be brought under their regulation, or else we will all drown beneath the overflowing oceans because of icecap melting, etc. Greenhouse gases and carbon emissions and all of that are produced by evil Western mankind in particular, and must be governed. The globalist elitists, of course, are the only ones who can thus save the world.

Pope Francis and some within the Catholic Church have wholeheartedly joined this save-the-earth cult to add their version of religious input. The following excerpt explains:

> Catholic Online reports that new priests will be expected to be familiar with and promote efforts to reduce carbon emissions. . . .
>
> The Church has a responsibility to care for people, and the environment. And care for one is also care for the other. . . .
>
> The new guidelines suggest that in the future, priests will also have a good grasp of the global climate change problem and will share this with their congregation. . . .
>
> It must be said that some committed and prayerful Christians, with the excuse of realism and pragmatism, tend to ridicule expressions of concern for the environment. Others are passive; they choose not to change their habits and thus become inconsistent. So what they all need is an "ecological conversion," whereby the effects of their encounter with Jesus

---

69. Karl Marx, Introduction, "A Contribution to the Critique of Hegel's Philosophy of Right," Marxists Internet Archive, February 1844, https://www.marxists.org/archive/marx/works/1843/critique-hpr/intro.htm.

Christ become evidence in their relationship with the world around them. Living our vocation to be protectors of God's handiwork is essential to a life of virtue; it is not an optional or a secondary aspect of our Christian experience. Therefore, it will be necessary for future priests to be highly sensitive to this theme and, through the requisite Magisterial and theological guidance, helped to "acknowledge the appeal, immensity and urgency of the challenge we face."[70]

Since he replaced Pope Benedict, this pope hasn't reached out much to proclaim that conversion must be made to belief in Jesus Christ in order to save the souls of people of earth. But the cry at present goes out in every direction that conversion to the dogma of ecological sophistry must be instituted and enforced to save all people everywhere.

Regarding the Luciferian religion called *climate change*, the words of my emailer say it plainly:

No matter how much humans try to "improve" on God's plans, He has the last say. He allows us to experiment but then, rightly shows us that His way is the best way. No matter how much humans try to wreck Planet Earth, God always has the upper (and healing) hand.

The world belongs to God. His Creation. Wonderfully and perfectly made. There is no way He is going to allow some spiritually backward, egocentric lunatic, [to] ruin what He set up. For the RC [Roman Catholic] church to actually believe that they will influence or make a difference to what is happening to planet earth is spiritual ignorance of the highest order. They are implying that action from man can fix stuff. That they (the RC church) are running things. Astonishing!

Let me be clear in saying that I'm fully aware and agree that we are expected, as Christians, to be good stewards of the earth. However, we are not to worship the earth and make that worship the means of our salvation.

It is the reverse of the true Christmas story that we are witnessing as Christmas approaches. Globalism preaches that it is up to man to save himself by saving the planet.

---

70. Eric Worrall, "Catholic Church: New Priests Will be Expected to Preach Global Warming," http://www.clerus.va/content/dam/clerus/Ratio%20Fundamentalis/The%20 Gift%20of%20the%20Priestly%20Vocation.pdf).

Like Lucifer told Eve, we are destined to become our own gods. We are to save the world, totally apart from any deity, except, of course, for the gods — the elite — of the globalist agenda.

But the truth of the Christmas story simply, powerfully, and wonderfully tells all who will listen and believe, "For God sent not his Son into the world to condemn the world; but that the world through him might be saved" (John 3:17).

27

January 2017: Israel's 100-Year Storm

These days, it seems, we are more and more frequently given reports that a 100-year storm has occurred. These are happening about every other year, and many prophecy watchers believe that these great storms have biblically prophetic overtones.

Certainly, I admit that there appears to be some relevance of these storms to how Israel is treated. White House correspondent Bill Koening is one Bible prophecy student who writes on these kinds of weather and other occurrences with regard to, particularly, America's dealing with Israel. John McTernin is another writer on these matters that I find fascinating.

Remember Hurricane Katrina, for example, when the Bush administration had pressured the Jewish state to move Jewish Israelis in order that so-called Palestinians could move in. Katrina entered the Gulf of Mexico during this time and the result was that thousands of Americans along the Gulf Coast and beyond were forced to leave their homes. The storm was one of the worst in U.S. history.

With major tornadoes in many areas and flooding along U.S. rivers seeming to increase over the past number of years, some have attributed the virulent weather to climate change or global warming. Others have seen the significance of these 100-year-type storms as relating directly to the treatment the Obama administration has given Israel over the past eight years.

Close to the very first thing the president did was snub the Israeli prime minister, leaving him after a few minutes of their meeting in the White House to go to the family's private dining quarters. Mr. Obama has continued with his coolness to Benjamin Netanyahu since that very first meeting. At the same time, Obama has made nice at every opportunity with the leaders of the Muslim world, while giving lip service to support for the Jewish state. As a matter of fact, Obama is on record as saying right up front of his eight years in office that he intended to "put space" between America and Israel. This, ostensibly, to develop a better relationship with the Arab states to increase the chance for establishing peace in the region.

It was the old George W. Bush effort revived — trying to show the Muslims and the world that we were really their friends. The question to ask, of course, is: Have relations improved?

No, they have grown worse.

The 100-year storm of this commentary's title is the international, diplomatic storm in which Israel currently finds itself. The first such storm it faced happened almost a half century before it became a nation in 1948. Israel was promised territory for establishing a nation in the region of its traditional homeland when the British issued the Balfour Declaration, written by British Foreign Secretary Arthur Balfour and issued by the government led by Prime Minister David Lloyd George.

That promise read,

> Foreign Office, November 2nd, 1917.
> Dear Lord Rothschild,
>
> I have much pleasure in conveying to you, on behalf of His Majesty's Government, the following declaration of sympathy with Jewish Zionist aspirations which has been submitted to, and approved by, the Cabinet.
>
> "His Majesty's Government view with favour the establishment in Palestine of a national home for the Jewish people, and will use their best endeavours to facilitate the achievement of this object, it being clearly understood that nothing shall be done which may prejudice the civil and religious rights of existing non-Jewish communities in Palestine, or the rights and political status enjoyed by Jews in any other country."
>
> I should be grateful if you would bring this declaration to the knowledge of the Zionist Federation.
>
> > Yours sincerely,
> > Arthur James Balfour[71]

While there is little doubt that there was a genuine desire to establish a Zionist safe haven with the declaration, it is even more certain that the action was primarily taken to give the British access to the Suez territory for hegemonic purposes.

---

71. http://www.mfa.gov.il/mfa/foreignpolicy/peace/guide/pages/the%20balfour%20declaration.aspx.

When British General Edward Allenby entered Jerusalem, there was relative peace for a time. The Arabs of the region began to create strife against the Jews shortly thereafter, determined to not allow the British to put their geopolitical plans into action.

British General Louis Bols, put in charge of Jerusalem, disliked Zionism, and, rather than see to it that the Balfour Declaration established a Jewish homeland and protected the Jews, he looked the other way at the Arab atrocities.

The betrayal by the British instigated a regional conflict, an ethnic storm that is raging today. And now, 100 years later to the year, another storm has been set in motion, instigated by Britain — and sadly, by the United States of America.

Since 2015, the Palestinian Authority has pushed to change the language UNESCO uses to speak of Jerusalem and the holy sites, so they are referred to almost exclusively by their Muslim names. The U.N. and its Israel-hating membership has done all within their power to delegitimize Israel's historical ties to the Temple Mount or to the region, for that matter.

And now the Security Council resolution condemning settlement construction in the West Bank and East Jerusalem, unopposed by Israel's allies, America and Britain, is a betrayal of the worst sort.

Secretary of State John Kerry said on December 28 that the only chance for Israel to live in peace in the future is to accept a two-state solution. Implicit within his words is condemnation of Israel as the sticking point to peace in the region. Also, I infer, he is, along with his boss Barack Obama, threatening to abandon Israel altogether if Netanyahu refuses to give land for peace.

This last-ditch effort of the Obama administration to intimidate Israel comes too little, too late, for their nefarious plans. Donald Trump has reassured Netanyahu and the Jewish people that the betrayal will not stand. Maybe, for a time at least, there is to be a ray of sunshine beyond this 100-year storm.

Verify but Trust

Russian-American relations are front and center in the news of this new year dawning. Conflicting approaches to these relations are also very much in the headlines.

The outgoing Obama administration, it is offered for public consumption, wants Russia to be punished for hacking into the presidential election process. The incoming Trump administration, mainstream news purveyors put forth, wants to cozy up to Russia and its President Vladimir Putin because Mr. Trump is — they claim — Mr. Putin's pal. The perception they want to create is that Trump doesn't trust U.S. intelligence sources who, according to the mainstreamers, all agree that Russia hacked into the Democratic National Committee emails, etc., in order to help Trump get elected.

The fact is, however, that all the U.S. intelligence services aren't in complete agreement. They are not of the consensus opinion that Russia did the cyber-hacking, or Putin intended to help Trump's election effort. But, as we all know, the *facts* have little to do with mainstream reporting. The president-elect has embraced many of President Ronald Reagan's thoughts, particularly with regard to Russia — in Mr. Reagan's case, the Soviet Union. "Trust but verify"[72] was perhaps the most famous of Reagan's statements that best frames his position in dealing with the Soviets.

Reagan signed the Intermediate Range Nuclear Forces (INF) Treaty with Soviet leader Mikhail Gorbachev on December 8, 1987. He used the phrase "trust but verify" to explain the in-depth procedures that would make certain the treaty stayed on the up and up.

The statement was from the Russian proverb *Doveryai, no proveryai,* taught him by a Russian translator in preparation for the meetings with Gorbachev. This requirement for dealing with the Russians will be highly necessary when Trump takes the oath on January 20. It is a precautionary thought that hasn't been followed by Barack Obama for the last eight years, and the present state of disarray with regard to the cyber-hacking hubbub proves the statement's worth. Besides Israel, there is no more relevant nation than Russia in view for Bible prophecy yet to unfold. Let's pray that some within the new president's close circle of advisers can add prophetic understanding in Mr. Trump's dealings with the Russians.

With that trust-but-verify relationship between America and Russia as a foundational premise for the further thoughts I hope to present, I would like to get into the reasons the title of this commentary has Mr. Reagan's statement reversed: "Verify but trust."

I wish to apply this reversal to the personal relationship each of us has with our Lord.

I will, to hopefully make the point, reveal a small bit of relational goings-on in my own life right now. Realization of what is involved in these things completely escaped me until I began thinking on and praying about

---

72. https://www.leadergrow.com/articles/443-trust-but-verify.

this commentary. The Holy Spirit was clear and to the point in whispering to my own, more-often-than-not-dull-of-hearing, spiritual ears.

When the epiphany struck, its simplicity stunned me. My uncomfortable relationship of the moment with the uncertainties of life wasn't mere chance. It involved the things I have believed, taught, and written about most all of my Christian life.

My wife, Margaret, had just been in a car accident. Only she was involved, but it was a bad one, as far as damage to the car. Thankfully, Margaret only had her heel badly fractured from the big sedan rolling over and landing right side up.

The state police officer who worked the wreck said it easily could have been a deadly accident. The car was totaled. Needless to say, we are grateful to the Lord for His protection — and to the car manufacturer for the 16 air bags that deployed during the violent rollover.

However, I've been lamenting ever since that accident that happened on the Monday leading up to Christmas. Poor me. I've been so inconvenienced by it all. Christmas this year was, in my commercially minded self-centeredness, a disaster. Plus, I've been called into service as caregiver for Miss Margaret — and me a poor, old blind guy.

The epiphany that hit just this morning is that this was no accident in the purest sense. This was a faith- and character-tester to see how I would react to an occurrence allowed, not caused, by the Lord. His only involvement in the accident itself was that of protecting Margaret's life. What part Satan and his minions had in it, I have no way of assessing. I failed the test miserably, dwelling only on how deleteriously it affected my daily routine, which I do not, under any circumstance, want to be disrupted.

Well, that routine is continuing to be disrupted. I still don't like it, but the Lord has most assuredly let me know that it is sinful indulgence to expect the world to revolve around one's self.

I hope that from this point forward, for however much time I'm allowed in this life, I will — at the very outset of life's such disruptions — understand the spiritual implications. I hope I'll immediately verify in my spiritual understanding that nothing happens in the believer's life in which our Lord is not intimately interested. We do not believe in and serve an existential God.

Then, I hope that I will always apply this primary "trust" Scripture to my life: "Trust in the LORD with all thine heart; and lean not unto thine own understanding. In all thy ways acknowledge him, and he shall direct thy paths" (Proverbs 3:5–6).

Verify but trust. That's my prayerful New Year's wish for you as well when you face life's sometimes unpleasant surprises.

World's Greatest Threat

Global order plans are up in the air while the would-be one-world architects contemplate the installation of America's 45th president. The soon-to-be new leader of the free world has made it clear he intends to keep America, at least, free of their insidious grab for America's wealth through their climate change and other liberty-diminishing machinations.

The new-world-order builders fearmonger that America's refusal to submit to their plans is a formula for guaranteeing the demise of the planet.

Israel is, as usual, at the center of concern in the minds of the world's diplomats. The newly elected president will, he has vowed, move the American embassy from Tel Aviv to Jerusalem. This will, if it eventuates, put the U.S. stamp of validation upon Jerusalem as the undivided capital of the Jewish state.

This rates as a threat to world peace in the minds of most all U.N. leaders. Palestinian President Mahmoud Abbas has declared there will absolutely be no chance of peace between the Palestinians and Israel if this happens.

Russia has popped up as a perceived threat so great that some think Vladimir Putin could start World War III before the Trump inauguration.

Even Christian writers within pre-Trib prophecy who are touted to be highly regarded journalists — observers of tensions that might lead to war — fear that Putin is on the verge of starting a conflict that might go nuclear at some point. To me, this flies in the face of things as they are foretold to be at the time of the Rapture. The Lord said life will be going on possibly more robust than usual when He breaks in on the world like a thief in the night (Matthew 24:36–42; Luke 17:26–30).

This prophecy by Christ Himself precludes nuclear war occurring before the Rapture, from my perspective. However, the fear is expressed by some such as Joel Rosenberg that in the immediate future, we are likely to face war that will take the world out of that "think-not" time Jesus talked about in the Olivet Discourse (Matthew 24:44).

The new president-to-be himself is so feared as a threat that nearly half the nation seems to be having a collective nervous breakdown in anticipation of when he takes office.

A man was arrested in Ithaca, New York, a couple of weeks ago for shooting to death a UPS delivery man, then running over the body. He did so, he told those who interrogated him, because he thought the man was Donald Trump, the president-elect.

There are hundreds of reports of people who have become mentally unhinged over this election result. Remember, for example, the man and his "husband" who verbally assaulted the president's daughter on a commercial flight, shouting that her father was going to destroy the nation. Those who see the Trump victory as the worst possible thing for life on planet Earth, like the globalists and those who have near-phobic fears of Russia, see 2017 as a year of unprecedented threat.

Wall Street and the economic gurus, on the other hand, seem to be seeing an opposite effect regarding Mr. Trump's rise to power. The year 2017 looks pretty good to these supposed wizards of the financial world, apparently, and we know this because we can see their vote through the stock market and other forums of fiscal prognostication.

Additionally — and this is the most telling, prophetically speaking — the great, collective sigh of relief by other members of American society is obvious. The *sigh* of the evangelical Christian segment of this half of the American populace leaps out, or should, at students of Bible prophecy who have the pre-Trib view.

We are excited to get a "reprieve," as it has been termed. It appears, at least, that Christians who stand upon biblical principles and openly display their faith will experience more tolerant acceptance from the incoming administration and the federal courts that should develop as a result. However, it must be noted that, along with the sigh of relief, a settling-back into comfortable complacency is developing.

Based on the level of observation I've made and the kinds of email and news stories I receive, it seems that the fervency of the prayers of God's people and concerns for aggressively pursuing a biblically moral agenda are just about nonexistent. This, based upon prophetic Scripture, presents the greatest threat of all as we proceed into 2017.

Again, Jesus forewarned of just such a time:

> Watch therefore: for ye know not what hour your Lord doth come. But know this, that if the goodman of the house had known in what watch the thief would come, he would have watched, and would not have suffered his house to be broken up. Therefore be ye also ready: for in such an hour as ye think not the Son of man cometh (Matthew 24:42–44).

For this reason, the threat to the world, populated mostly by those who don't know Christ for salvation, is great. A complacent Church is a threat greater in this way, perhaps, than the ones we most often consider.

Let us vow to dedicate 2017 as a year to actively carry out the Great Commission (Matthew 28:19–20).

Red Lights Flashing!

Questions pour in these days from those who have consistently read these commentaries over the years. Although phrased differently to one extent or the other, the tone and thrust of the questions are the same. Serious students of Bible prophecy, particularly those with the pre-Trib perspective, view geopolitical matters taking place as profoundly significant. They see the red, flashing lights of alert.

"What do you think this means?" Most queries ask this in one form or another. Developments last week in Paris, France, stir intensive interest. Israel being at the heart of the matters involved generates the inquiries I receive almost hourly.

I completely agree with those who email me. Things transpiring are like seeing the flashing red lights at train crossings. *Imminent danger exists — time to pay close attention!*

Seventy-two nations, most overtly antagonistic to Israel, gathered during the past inaugural week, ostensibly to determine the Jewish nation's fate. Their intent, in the opinion of many Bible prophecy students, was to force Israel to give up all claims to the land.

Intervention by the incoming Trump administration seems to have preempted full implementation of the anti-Israel agenda. Great Britain also added its conference-dampening input.

Israel, with its constant vigilance against ever-present attempts to destroy the nation reportedly has managed to thwart much of its U.N. enemy efforts in the Paris conference matter.

United Nations globalists' agenda, under the Resolution 2334 rubric they want to establish, is to declare Israel an occupier, the oppressor of the Palestinians who — Israel's antagonists say — have legitimate claim to the land.

While angry losers in America's presidential election continue to sniffle and sob, and in some cases rage, that Donald J. Trump is an illegitimate occupier of Obama's White House, the U.N. Israel-haters go through their own sort of whining and moaning. We have witnessed a constant diatribe of last-days antics, orchestrated by Satan himself, I'm convinced, to rearrange the geopolitical and socioeconomic landscape. Pope Francis, meeting with Palestinian Authority President Mahmoud Abbas, intruding into the Israeli-Palestinian land-for-peace thrust by the U.N., also, I believe, made observable Satan's hand being inserted into the religious arena in his attempt to set the international stage for Antichrist's eventual rule.

Israeli Prime Minister Benjamin Netanyahu called the Paris peace conference, devised by the Palestinian Authority and hosted by France, a "fraud." He said the conference was "anti-Israel." He warned the phony summit was a fraud "whose goal is to lead to the adoption of additional anti-Israel positions."[73] Critics of the so-called Paris summit for peace between Israel and the Palestinians say that the conference and U.N. R2334 constituted an effort to lock Israel into the borders as they were in 1949. A document produced from the meetings might, it was feared, mean that Israel would have no claim to the Temple Mount, Mount Olivet, and all other sites revered as holy by Jews and Christians. Such a document would, it was thought, be designed to give the territory to the new Palestinian state if the so-called two-state solution comes to fruition. Representatives of Israel weren't part of the conference. Netanyahu has vowed to ignore anything coming out of the "summit." The ramifications of this attempted globalist grab in Middle East power politics remain to be seen.

Immediately upon release of information about R2334, U.S. Secretary of State John Kerry made his now infamous, obviously anti-Israel statement as part of his speech. Kerry said that Israel could be either Jewish or Democratic; it cannot be both.[74]

The Trump administration will undoubtedly have much to say in changing America's course as stated by Kerry. However, the secretary of state's utterly audacious declaration thus laid out for the world to see the fact that the Obama administration views Israel as an oppressive regime intent upon treating Palestinians cruelly if the Jewish state doesn't go along with allowing the Palestinians all they want and deserve.

Ignoring all the atrocities and terrorism spawned daily by enemies who have vowed to destroy Israel, Kerry went on to imply that America would recommend punitive repercussions for Israel's refusal to make peace under terms of the Paris meetings.

---

73. https://www.theguardian.com/world/2017/jan/12/netanyahu-middle-east-peace-conference-rigged-move-against-israel-paris-trump.
74. https://www.washingtontimes.com/news/2016/dec/28/john-kerry-israel-can-be-jewish-or-democratic-not-/.

Even though the conference in France seems to have been neutralized in large part, such statements by America's (now former) top representative on the world diplomatic stage raises red flags and sets those red lights flashing to be sure. Our thoughts immediately go to Genesis 12 about those who bless Israel and those who curse Israel.

Zechariah 12 and 14, Joel 3:2, and many other prophetic passages involving God's pronouncements about Israel at the end of the age leap at us. The red lights flash brightly. There are no more powerful signals to be found in Scripture on the nearness of Christ's return at Armageddon following the seven-year Tribulation.

We know, according to God's Word, too, that Christ will call all believers into heaven at least seven years before His Second Advent at the time of Armageddon.

Israel, the false peace process, all nations turned against God's chosen nation — these are flashing red lights to be sure. However, I sense that for the moment, God's mighty hand has again intervened in this matter of the deck being stacked in favor of the Palestinians against God's chosen people.

Forewarning to Our New President

A Fox News person — I can't remember who — reported that Paul Anka, who wrote the song "My Way," had withdrawn from performing at one of the events scheduled during the inaugural festivities.

Anka reportedly said the inauguration gig conflicted with his schedule. He thus joined a long list of celebrities and performers who said they would not be a part of the Trump victory celebration.

CNN gave a news flash that Nancy Sinatra, daughter of the late crooner Frank Sinatra, was furious that Mr. Trump would use the song in the presidential celebration. She was, it was reported, incensed because it was the song her father had made famous by recording it.[75]

Ms. Sinatra, however, it became clear, was incensed not at Mr. Trump, but at CNN for what has become known as a "fake news" story. She reportedly was angry because the story was not true, and she was said to have responded, "That's not true. I never said that. Why do you lie, CNN?"[76]

That's a question many voters asked themselves before the vote by the electorate was cast in this presidential election. The diatribes by mainstream news hounds, favoring one candidate over the other, included lying the

---

75. https://www.cnn.com/2017/01/19/politics/nancy-sinatra-donald-trump-my-way/index.html.

76. http://www.foxnews.com/entertainment/2017/01/20/nancy-sinatra-slams-cnn-for-anti-trump-spin-on-story-about-her-humorous-tweet.html.

likes of which has rarely if ever reached the level it did in this election cycle.

The song "My Way" and the lies surrounding it open the way for me to issue this warning to our new president, as suggested by the commentary's title.

I'll say this at the outset: I can't help but like the song. I've always, Lord help me, liked it, particularly the way ol' Elvis sang it. However, it is one of the most anti-God songs ever created. It is straight from the mind of the old serpent himself, I have no doubt. That's why it is so appealing to the human mind and why even believers such as myself — weak in many ways because of our fallen nature — can't help but like the song.

"My Way" tells the story of the singer living totally on his own terms, without listening to or bowing the knee to anyone. He did it all — *his way.*

It's not just a matter of the song boasting about one's own greatness; it is a repudiation of God Himself. That might not have been Mr. Anka's thought in writing it, but if you study the words, it is hubris that reflects Lucifer's own words in Isaiah 14:14.

Getting back to our new president and his choosing the song for inclusion in his celebratory festivities, such hubris is likely, one hopes, not Mr. Trump's own attitude. We should prayerfully hope and believe that he doesn't, by making this song a part of his celebration, harbor the thought that he is now president only because of his own greatness and ability.

We have heard him state his thanks to so many, including the national voting public that cast their votes for him, in fact. I've heard him say that God is the one who made America "great" in the first place, and will do so again.

Still, I'm concerned when I know that he, like myself, can't help but like this song. It appeals to the pride that can so easily swell within each human being.

The Lord tells us in His Word that he hates "a proud look" (Proverbs 6:17). He further says, "Him that hath an high look and a proud heart will not I suffer" (Psalm 101:5). And, again, "An high look, and a proud heart . . . is sin" (Proverbs 21:4).

God tells the end of all such pride in one's self: "Pride goeth before destruction, and an haughty spirit before a fall" (Proverbs 16:18).

Being blind, I, of course, couldn't see any of the presidential ball festivities. I did hear them, and the song "My Way" seemed to be the central theme song at each of the three. I was told that at one point the new president, while dancing with the new first lady, looked into a nearby camera and mouthed the words, "I did it my way."

So, it is hearsay, not a firsthand account. Perhaps some of the readers of this commentary witnessed this silent comment by the president.

I was a supporter of Donald Trump and continue to be so as he promises to move America forward and lead us out of the slide into the abyss into which we are headed. Mr. Trump is often audacious and outspoken, and to be frank, it is one of the traits that endeared him to many, myself included, that is, to the extent that I like his pushing back against the pay-no-attention-to-the-American-people arrogance of Washington, D.C., insiders and mainstream media types.

That said, I must issue this warning, Mr. President. You, I, and America must do it "God's way," not "my way," as Mr. Anka, Mr. Sinatra, or even ol' Elvis would have it. Our very national existence depends upon this truth.

28

February 2017: Doomsdayers' Diatribe

Six days into the presidency of Donald J. Trump, the humanistic gurus of the community known as the "atomic scientists" raised a ruckus. They lamented that we are within two and a half minutes of nuclear midnight. This is supposed to mean that global catastrophe is closer, perhaps, than it has ever been.

The atomic scientists' perception that the unthinking, bumbling, or perhaps deliberate evil of the new president makes the doomsday clock time-setters nervous indeed.

Their joint declaration states,

> Both his statements and his actions as president-elect have broken with historical precedent in unsettling ways. He has made ill-considered comments about expanding the U.S. nuclear arsenal. He has shown a troubling propensity to discount or outright reject expert advice related to international security, including the conclusions of intelligence experts. And his nominees to head the Energy Department and the Environmental Protection Agency dispute the basics of climate science.[77]

I have written in these commentaries for many months that the globalists' key rallying point for trying to bring about the new world order they seek has been global warming, which is now called climate change. The Luciferian rant is ratcheting up in every aspect of geopolitical atmospherics. However, we can expect an even more massive uptick in the assault. Climate change will be the spear tip of the campaign against God's order of things as we move deeper into this administration.

The scientists in question issued the accusation — highly disturbing, in their view — that Trump, during the presidential campaign, talked

---

77. https://thebulletin.org/press-release/it-now-two-and-a-half-minutes-midnight10432.

about the need to increase and upgrade nuclear weapons capability. At the same time, they ranted that he spoke against the scientific community's overwhelming consensus that climate change poses a threat beyond any other to the well-being of the planet.

All the while they've said nothing of former President Obama trying to anger Russia's Vladimir Putin in the last months of the Obama administration — a thing that gave Putin fodder to proclaim the need to further increase the Russian nuclear arsenal.

Like in every other instance of hypocritical treatment by media and by the humanistic, scientific community, Obama gets a pass, while their collective ire descends full force on the one who defeated them in the American electoral process.

They ignored that international relations have deteriorated dangerously during the Obama years; rather, they noted fawningly that the former president in 2010 called for a nuclear-free world.

At the same time, they pointed out angrily their convoluted and quasi-accurate assessment that Trump suggested South Korea and Japan might consider developing nuclear weapons since North Korea and even China represent growing threats. They berated Trump and his six-day-old administration for having no "firm plans" to extend the controversial "Iran nuclear deal."

The doomsdayers further castigated Trump and laid out their great fear his winning the American presidency has wrought:

> The political situation in the United States is of particular concern. The Trump transition team has put forward candidates for cabinet-level positions (especially at the Environmental Protection Agency and Energy Department) who foreshadow the possibility that the new administration will be openly hostile to progress toward even the most modest efforts to avert catastrophic climate disruption.[78]

Please believe me. This is not the last we will hear of the climate-change madness.

Those of the "million-woman march" and the "if-it-feels-good-do-it" crowd lost their "political fast-track to succeeding" they were previously on. These, as we have witnessed, are furious to the point of displaying mental instability. But the globalist elite of this world, working to bring in

---

78. https://www.coursehero.com/file/p4kbsvu/The-relationship-between-increased-atmospheric-carbon-dioxide-levels-and/.

Antichrist's regime — even if unknowingly — are exceedingly angrier and more determined that this president will be removed by hook or crook.

We already hear the volume increase in the talk of impeaching him. There are more than mere hints that a *coup d'état* is in the wishful thinking of the angriest of the nation's power brokers.

It does not, nor should it, surprise that this level of rebellion is raising its ugly, serpent-like head. We only need to go to the great Book of Revelation to understand the extremes to which fallen man will go when he doesn't get his way.

A rebellion of the most horrific magnitude ever will occur at the end of the Millennium, the thousand-year reign of Jesus Christ. This uprising will happen, we are told through prophecy, after the reign of the only perfect Ruler in all of human history.

And, this gets us back to the Doomsday Clock scientists' forewarning. They claim Trump will cause the destruction of the earth because he declares their climate-change mantra to be lunacy. Well, maybe it's me, not Trump, who calls it lunacy, but he adamantly opposes it and them nonetheless.

That Revelation 20:7–9 tells us there will be this last, satanically led rebellion in an attempt to dethrone the Creator of all things lets us know that there will still be a planet Earth, despite President Donald Trump and even seven years of Tribulation.

Also, it proves, in my estimation, the lunacy of the doomsdayers' diatribe.

Trump and God's Purpose

Mention has been made many times of opinions that go something like this: Trump isn't a godly person, yet neither was Nebuchadnezzar and other kings and leaders the Lord chose down through the centuries to do great things and serve great purposes. So, God can use Donald Trump to accomplish what He wants accomplished.

Considering the 180-degree course change this nation has embarked upon in this presidential election, it is an understatement to say that God must be up to something profound with the election of Donald J. Trump.

The abrupt turn away from advocating for the homosexual agenda and other forms of aberrant behavior, and toward championing protection of moral values and Judeo-Christian principles upon which the nation was founded, is amazing to say the least. No one would have imagined strongly, during the early days of the past election season, that the Christian faith would come under the protective hand of a presidential administration so soon. This was especially unthinkable because the previous administration adamantly embraced the Muslim faith in ways that baffled those who aren't a part of the extreme political left.

That political left has been completely driven to acting in maniacal ways in response to the Donald Trump victory. It is astounding that the fever pitch of enragement continues to build with each succeeding day Trump is in office.

Psychiatrists and psychologists who study mass hysteria conclude for the most part that such a level of rage is impossible to maintain over an extended time. Yet we daily observe the opposite. The furious, even lunatic, behavior continues and even grows over anything that involves President Donald Trump.

Those who demonstrate the slightest support for this president have the political hounds of the netherworld descend upon their lives. It is astounding to witness. And, as often as not, it is somewhat amusing, as long as the insane rants are kept to the verbal and not the physical level, such as the violence that took place in Berkley and surrounding other universities. The corporate world is infected and affected by the lunacy. CEOs, such as that of Starbucks, for example, climb eagerly onto the anti-Trump hate wagon at the risk of alienating half of their customer base or clientele. Amidst all the silliness, clothing designers refuse to design the new first lady's apparel. The fashions produced by the president's daughter are ripped from the lines of clothiers.

In the halls of government, we have the likes of Democrat Senator Charles Schumer weeping on the Senate floor. He tells sobbingly how it breaks his heart that people are detained at the airports because of President Trump's temporary ban of people coming in from the seven nations that Schumer's own Democrat President Obama put on the banned list several years ago. The senator himself wholeheartedly backed the banning of such entrants into America under Obama's executive order.

We watch the Democrat committee members throw temper tantrums, refusing to attend Cabinet committee hearings and undertaking other childish actions to hold up proceedings.

We listened to the attempted grilling of New England Patriot quarterback Tom Brady about why he was a friend to President Trump. They ignored relevant football questions in anticipation of the upcoming Super Bowl and went for the jugular to, hopefully, score hate-filled political points.

But, all this theater, both entertaining and troubling to the process of our representative democracy, pales in comparison to the intrigues to be analyzed on the international level.

The new president's breathtaking movement toward fulfilling campaign promises makes it clear that the Lord of heaven put Trump in place for developments that are going to stagger the world. Prophetic fulfillment — rather, preparation for the fulfillment of Bible prophecy — is, of course, much more significant than the just-mentioned fulfillment of campaign promises.

We can, if attuned to God's Word on the wind-up of the age, see things developing that, as I said, will stagger the world.

One example is the fact that the enemies of Israel who had curried favor with the Obama administration are dumbfounded that their position relative to having the favorable attention of the U.S. president has drastically and abruptly changed.

Speaking to *Newsweek* last week, Saeb Erekat, go-between for PLO chief Mahmoud Abbas in dealing with Israel and the U.S., found that a totally different relationship is now in effect. Indicating the PLO is almost in panic, he said, "I don't know any of them [Trump's advisers]. We have sent them letters, written messages. They don't even bother to respond to us."[79]

Trump is at the same time apparently considering moving the U.S. embassy from Tel Aviv to Jerusalem, which many say will cause an immediate Islamist uprising. The president, additionally, has installed a thoroughly pro-Israel ambassador within the U.N. and has reached out warmly to Israel's Prime Minister Benjamin Netanyahu.

Third only to the change in attitude toward Christianity and return to constitutional sanity and the 180-degree turnaround on treatment of Israel are the actions President Trump is undertaking to restore America as leader of the free world.

Trump's geopolitical and fiscal aggressiveness thus far is affecting global alliances militarily. The new president's actions are having profound effects on the world economy.

I wonder whether all this means we might be seeing a specific stage-setting given by Jesus Himself. Again, that prophecy is found in Matthew 24:36–42 and Luke 17:26–30. The question: Are we on the verge of witnessing an economic boom in the midst of which the Rapture will occur?

Something big is up. God has Trump here at this time for some great purpose.

79. https://www.jpost.com/Opinion/Column-one-The-Trump-way-of-war-480439.

29

March 2017: Catalyst for Cataclysm

Anxiety continues over the political chasm now dividing this nation. And the break involves much more than politics; it is a separation of worldview unlike any yet known in this nation.

We've all heard, particularly recently, Lincoln's words reflecting off Jesus' declaration that "a house divided cannot stand." Yet these United States, clearly a house not so *united,* as this presidential election showed, not only continues to stand, but seemingly is on the brink of entering boom times, economically speaking at least.

For many years leading up to the 2016 presidential election, America appeared to be moving more and more toward unification. From our perspective on the Christian right, however, that coming together looked to be leading to disaster for religious freedom. Not only was religious liberty being cast aside, we thought, but all vestiges of morality and constitutional principles were being trashed at every turn. The libertines were having their way, and hope to ever regain our national sanity seemed all but lost.

Those who prefer America to be detached from moorings the Founding Fathers provided thought the political left had won the presidency. They thought they had won right up until late that night when poll results proved the opposite. The rage hasn't stopped since that moment of epiphany.

The *progressives* were certain they had won the day and that Bob Dylan's lyrics, taken from the poetry of his self-chosen namesake, Dylan Thomas, were proving prophetic:

> Come mothers and fathers
> Throughout the land
> And don't criticize
> What you can't understand
> Your sons and your daughters
> Are beyond your command

Your old road is
Rapidly agin'.
Please get out of the new one
If you can't lend your hand
For the times they are a-changin'.
The line it is drawn
The curse it is cast
The slow one now
Will later be fast
As the present now
Will later be past
The order is
Rapidly fadin'.
And the first one now
Will later be last
For the times they are a-changin'.[80]

The oft-quoted mantra during the Woodstock era was about to find its declaration chiseled upon the marbled, governmental walls of earth's only superpower: "Do not go gentle into that sweet goodnight. Rage, rage, for the times they are a-changin'."

The "rage," as I said, is still raging. The losers of the election — Mrs. Clinton and Mr. Obama — are reportedly leading the charge from the shadows with their opposition community organization efforts, in collusion with the so-called *deep state*. The manufactured, paid-for rage is manifest in Republican town hall meetings across the nation.

I continue to maintain that it is the satanically engendered globalist agenda that is driving the rage. George Soros funding is unabashedly admitted by the liberal side to be adding inspirational fire to the vitriol and anger. America must be brought under control of the one-world minions. The Trump victory jolted the new world architects' incessant drive to knock America off its constitutional foundation.

The new president, with each mention of rolling back regulations, of reformulating tax structures to make things friendlier to the business world and middle-class taxpayers, inspires the financial markets to record heights. Rather than America and the world collapsing into the deepest depression in history like many experts were predicting, the economic indicators are soaring in the opposite direction.

---

80. Bob Dylan, "The Times They Are A-Changin'," recorded October 24, 1963, track 1 on *The Times They Are A-Changin'*, Columbia, Vinyl LP.

We are now heading into fiscal territory like that prophesied by Jesus. The Lord said the buying, selling, building, etc., would be going along quite nicely at the time He next catastrophically intervenes into the wicked affairs of mankind. I'm convinced that those times of buying, selling, building, etc., were referring not to just "business as usual," but to a coming boom that is unprecedented.

So, we have all the major elements in view that Jesus predicted when foretelling what the times of His next intervention into human affairs would involve.

He said the nations would be "in distress with perplexity." The "seas and waves" (people of the nations) would be "roaring." He said that people will, at the same time, be buying, selling, building, planting, and marrying. It will be a "think not" generation at the time of Christ's sudden intervention, according to Matthew 24:44.

World conditions will be just like in the days of Noah and Lot. It will be during this time of both anxiety and apparent affluence that He will suddenly break in on an unsuspecting world.

We are, I firmly believe, swiftly entering just such a time. The Rapture of the Church will be, I'm convinced, the catalyst for cataclysm for those left behind.

Presidential Prophecy Briefing

This president is doing his best to fulfill campaign promises. His "best" is something to behold. He is getting it done at breakneck speed despite opposition, much of which is satanically inspired.

The hatred toward him and even his family is unlike anything witnessed in our nation's post-election history. Donald J. Trump forges ahead as if he doesn't notice the fierceness and threats of the haters screaming their vitriol from every quarter. At least the rage doesn't seem to bother him much.

He doesn't turn the other cheek, of course. His tweets can be as devastating as slaps across the face.

For example, his tweet that asked the question: Isn't it terrible the way Obama had my phones tapped in the Trump Tower?

He responds immediately in most cases to the written words of the hostile news media and spoken words of political antagonists. He is a New York City street fighter, and can obviously handle himself among the political and media street brawlers even though he is a political neophyte, but one who is quickly attaching himself to the learning curve.

Mr. Trump can be very kind, generous, and compassionate, as well as tough. We have seen these traits demonstrated on many occasions before and since he became president. He gets no notice of approval for this side of his personal deportment from any of his opposition, of course. Neither does he seek it. He just . . . well . . . forges ahead and accomplishes what he has promised.

Although I've received criticism even from brothers and sisters in Christ who read this column for being "too caught up in worldly politics," I don't mind being overly transparent that I'm an ardent supporter of our new president. This doesn't mean I approve of some of his NYC street jargon or his every word uttered or action taken. But for the most part, I think he is a man of honor, determined to do exactly what he promised the voters who supported him. I have no doubt that he is God's chosen man for the job at this critical time in history.

The larger part of what makes this a critical time is Israel's position on the world stage. That stance is becoming more front and center with every hour that passes. This, as we have said many times in these essays, is a prime indicator, if not the prime indicator of where this generation stands on God's prophetic timeline.

I believe this, in conjunction with the convergence of many prophetic indicators at this late hour, constitutes the number-one signal that the Rapture of the Church is very near.

After all that positive assessment of President Trump to this point, I must project an exhortation, almost an admonishment, in his direction. More to the point, I am issuing such to a select few people who orbit him, on a personal basis, I'm presuming.

I'll mention five men specifically. These, I believe, have a responsibility the Lord Himself appointed for influencing this president. Each, I know absolutely, has biblical knowledge of God's Word regarding the wind-up of human history. They must, if they have opportunity — and I have no doubt they do — inform Mr. Trump, in detail, what Bible prophecy has to say about anyone dealing with Israel.

These men whom I believe have this responsibility are Franklin Graham, Robert Jeffress, David Jeremiah, and Mike Huckabee. One other might be Jerry Falwell Jr. Each is thoroughly familiar with the futurist view of biblical prophecy. Each understands Israel's role in the final disposition of prophetic fulfillment.

I'm not certain about Huckabee as to how in-depth is his stance on prophetic details regarding Israel. Sadly, Southern Baptist seminaries are now egregiously weak in prophecy teaching. Huckabee, however, was inculcated as a budding Southern Baptist minister when that denomination was on the money in God's truth surrounding eschatology. Falwell surely must adhere to his late father's viewpoint in matters concerning Israel's future.

These people have apparently been embraced as evangelical leaders friendly to and accepted by the president. Thus, their responsibility to advise him is profound.

My reason for addressing the matter stems from President Trump's meeting with Palestinian Authority President Mahmoud Abbas and Trump's subsequent comments. The following excerpt frames my concern:

> US President Donald Trump is mulling the option to hold a peace conference in the Middle East in an effort to resolve the Israeli-Palestinian conflict, after speaking on Friday with Palestinian President Mahmoud Abbas. . . . "The president emphasized his personal belief that peace is possible and that the time has come to make a deal," the White House said. . . .
>
> "The president noted that such a deal would not only give Israelis and Palestinians the peace and security they deserve, but that it would reverberate positively throughout the region and the world," the White House clarified.[81]

So, the question comes: What's wrong with the president of the United States trying to make peace?

Another question: Didn't Jesus say, "Blessed are the peacemakers, for they will inherit the earth"?

The problem isn't the effort at peacemaking by Mr. Trump or anyone else. The problem is that the attempt at making peace between Israel and her enemies always involves Israel having to give up its land for peace, something God says will bring mankind to the battle of Armageddon:

> For, behold, in those days, and in that time, when I shall bring again the captivity of Judah and Jerusalem, I will also gather all nations, and will bring them down into the valley of Jehoshaphat, and will plead with them there for my people and for my heritage Israel, whom they have scattered among the nations, and parted my land (Joel 3:1–2).

---

81. Orly Azoulay and Elior Levy, "Trump Mulls Middle East Peace Conference," Annette News — Israel News, March 12, 2017.

God will not abide dividing His land, which the world, in effect, has already done. To further divide the land, after God has brought the Jews back from dispersion, will undoubtedly be the proverbial straw that breaks the camel's back.

God's Word prophesies peace deals that involve His chosen people and nation:

> Because ye have said, We have made a covenant with death, and with hell are we at agreement; when the overflowing scourge shall pass through, it shall not come unto us: for we have made lies our refuge, and under falsehood have we hid ourselves. . . . And your covenant with death shall be disannulled, and your agreement with hell shall not stand; when the overflowing scourge shall pass through, then ye shall be trodden down by it (Isaiah 28:15–18).

Antichrist will make that final peace deal with Israel (read Daniel 9:26–27). The results, as you see from Isaiah's prophecy, will be catastrophic for Israel. Joel, in his prophecy, makes it clear that it will be equally disastrous for the whole world.

President Trump, like all presidents before him, receives daily briefings on the important matters he must consider. Nothing is more important than the way he deals with this nation so close to God's great heart.

The gentlemen I've mentioned have an awesome responsibility to give the president the most important briefing he will ever receive: forewarning from God's prophetic Word regarding Israel.

30

April 2017: New World Order Throwing Fit

Senator John McCain (R-Arizona) was quick to get behind mainstream media microphones and cameras. He did so immediately after President Trump pulled the bill to repeal and replace the Affordable Healthcare Act (Obamacare) from consideration of the House of Representatives.

The former presidential candidate, acknowledged as a severe critic and opponent of the new president, presumed to instruct Mr. Trump on how he might approach Democrats to improve the soon-to-implode health system President Obama ramrodded through Congress. McCain then launched into his thoughts on how he and Trump are on opposite ends of the ideological spectrum with regard to America's rightful place in world leadership.

The senator talked about how he believes the United States should come closer to the European Union (EU) and totally embrace NATO as part of a new world order. He implied that Trump foolishly rejects this approach, wanting America to be isolationist in its approach to dealings with the world around our nation.

McCain said, "The new world order is under tremendous strain." While speaking at the Brussels Forum, he went on to say that the world "cries out for American and European leadership" through the EU and NATO, and said that the EU and the United States needed to develop "more cooperation, more connectivity."

McCain, chairman of the U.S. Senate Armed Services Committee, said, "I trust the EU." He said further that the EU was "one of the most important alliances" for the U.S. and that the EU and NATO were the "[most effective organizations] in history" in maintaining the peace for the last 70 years.[82]

---

82. https://www.zerohedge.com/news/2017-03-25/mccain-new-world-order-under-enormous-strain.

McCain's strong implication was that Trump's idea of moving away from the so-called new world order was opposite of the direction America should move. The nation must, he implied, embrace this alliance in order to save the world in keeping peace and security in view.

I am reminded of Psalm 2 about the end-times powers that be that will have no deity to rule over them, but declare that humanist effort will prevail. I believe the tremendous upheaval we have seen, particularly since Trump's election, is minion-driven enragement. The insane statements and movements are centered in the fact that God has intervened, for whatever reason, into Satan's plans to install world government.

It is just a postponement — a temporary setback — for the new world order builders, but it has driven them into manifesting the insanity that reprobate minds come to, as indicated in Romans 1.

All this involves two of the end-times characteristics the Apostle Paul prophesied in 2 Timothy 3.

I wrote about this in-depth in my latest book, *Rapture Ready . . . Or Not: 15 Reasons Why This Is the Generation That Will Be Left Behind.* I include a portion of that here.

Heady/High-Minded

The powerful and elite would-be new world order builders fit well within this perilous-times category. They sell out their nations and even their families for the sake of building the new world they desire — apart from any governance by God. Psalm 2 calls out these earth-dwellers as the KJV of the Bible defines them. They are driven by the powers and principalities outlined in Ephesians 6.

This self-uplifting, while ascending on the misfortune of others, is symptomatic of headiness or high-mindedness. Satan was and is the highest-minded of all. He sought and still has the audacity to believe he can lift himself to a position above the one, true, eternal God. Those who reject the truth of Jesus Christ are, through omission, heirs to the fallen ones — Lucifer's great high-mindedness.

All who seek, through their great intellect, their desire, or their superiority in the realm of power-brokerage, to put themselves upon the pinnacle of god-likeness in the world they have chosen to conquer are inheritors of Satan's pridefulness. They are exhilarated by the cutthroat struggle to vanquish all obstacles, all foes.

The high-minded intellectuals of academia, of the sciences, or of the liberal clergy seek more than at any time in history to erase all mention of

God the Almighty, even at the temporary expedient of tolerating many religions and allowing those religions their many various ways to godhood.

With the intellectual exercise of plotting the planet's physical and social salvation, they are sacrificing their eternal souls on the altar of "Evolutional Theory." God's Word tells that the last generation will be as was the generation that perished in the Flood of Noah's day. Of that people, God says,

> Because that, when they knew God, they glorified him not as God, neither were thankful; but became vain in their imaginations, and their foolish heart was darkened. Professing themselves to be wise, they became fools, and changed the glory of the uncorruptible God into an image made like to corruptible man, and to birds, and fourfooted beasts, and creeping things (Romans 1:21–23).

What is this, if not a description of modern intellectual man and his attempts to rationalize away all vestiges of the true God? It perfectly describes the writings of Charles Darwin and those who have reworked, reformulated, and totally fallen for, in one form or another, the evolution lie. These, like the antediluvians, "changed the truth of God into a lie, and worshipped and served the creature more than the Creator" (Romans 1:25). These foolish, soul-darkened "intellects" join forces with those they would once have termed superstitious idiots, the occultists, and New Age adherents, to deify Mother Earth for the sake of ecological purity.

Headiness and high-mindedness are encapsulated within the climate change, radical environmentalism that is being used to destroy national sovereignty and autonomy, thus to bring all within one-world rule. The Antichrist regime will be the penultimate outgrowth of that drive toward global order.

The headiness and high-mindedness of the new world order builders — and the rage we are witnessing, I believe — are prime reasons why believers in Christ should be more than ever "looking up" — as we are exhorted in Luke 21:28.

Case of the Missing Millions

Erle Stanley Gardner, creator of Perry Mason, the fictional criminal defense attorney, had nothing on the Apostle Paul. Gardner reported on the great lawyer as he solved all his cases, winning acquittal for his clients at every turn. But Paul, the former Saul of Tarsus, brought the world the story of resolution to what will be the greatest mystery of all time — that wrapped up in the case of the missing millions.

We find some interesting interplay here, believe me. While Perry's mysteries were to entertain us as he got his innocent clients off the proverbial hook within human courtrooms, Paul's "mystery" involves us as the subjects of all being guilty in God's court of righteousness. Paul explains how each of us can be gotten off that hook, even though we are already proven *guilty*!

Perry always carefully defined the crime of which his client was accused. We knew the client was innocent . . . well . . . because of the very fact that Perry Mason was defending him or her. Paul places the crime we're all accused of within one simple statement: "For the mystery of iniquity doth already work" (2 Thessalonians 2:7).

We know that we are all guilty as charged under this "mystery of iniquity" because of Paul's words that report condemnation by the God of heaven: "For all have sinned, and come short of the glory of God" (Romans 3:23).

So, sin is at the heart of this "mystery," which is working in the world today as it always has. It is scheduled to get much worse as the dispensation of Grace (Church Age) nears its end: "But evil men and seducers shall [become] worse and worse, deceiving, and being deceived" (2 Timothy 3:13).

So, whereas the fictional Mr. Mason's clients were presumed innocent, each of us is, in fact, guilty as charged. This is because of original sin: "Wherefore, as by one man sin entered into the world, and death by sin; and so death passed upon all men, for that all have sinned" (Romans 5:12).

The original man, Adam, ate the forbidden fruit from the Tree of the Knowledge of Good and Evil. That act of rebellion started the mystery called "iniquity" upon planet Earth. Apparently, that mystery was already present in Lucifer, one of the Lord's most majestic angels. This is what God says about that long-ago mystery:

> Thou hast been in Eden the garden of God; every precious stone was thy covering, the sardius, topaz, and the diamond, the beryl, the onyx, and the jasper, the sapphire, the emerald, and the carbuncle, and gold: the workmanship of thy tabrets and of thy pipes was prepared in thee in the day that thou wast created. Thou art the anointed cherub that covereth; and I have set thee so: thou wast upon the holy mountain of God; thou hast walked up and down in the midst of the stones of fire. Thou wast perfect in thy ways from the day that thou wast created, till iniquity was found in thee. By the multitude of thy merchandise they have filled the midst of thee with violence,

and thou hast sinned: therefore I will cast thee as profane out
of the mountain of God: and I will destroy thee, O covering
cherub, from the midst of the stones of fire. Thine heart was
lifted up because of thy beauty, thou hast corrupted thy wisdom by reason of thy brightness: I will cast thee to the ground,
I will lay thee before kings, that they may behold thee (Ezekiel
28:13–17).

This magnificent creature became full of pride (read Isaiah 14:14). He
came to the planet prepared for man. Ever since, Lucifer — now called
Satan — has conducted his iniquitous work effectively. Man is therefore as
guilty in the court of God's righteousness as the fallen angels who rebelled
with Lucifer all those eons ago.

Paul the Apostle — a mere man, fallen like the rest of us until he was
declared "not guilty" — is only the Supreme's court reporter. He tells us of
the one and only attorney who can successfully handle each case involving
the mystery of iniquity before the eternal bench of God the Judge.

Here are John the Apostle's words on that Great Advocate:

My little children, these things write I unto you, that ye sin
not. And if any man sin, we have an advocate with the Father,
Jesus Christ the righteous: and he is the propitiation for our
sins: and not for ours only, but also for the sins of the whole
world (1 John 2:1–2).

Our attorney is far superior to Perry Mason or any earthly attorney. He is
Jesus Christ, the very Son of the Supreme Judge, God the Father. When
Jesus defends, it is a guaranteed "not guilty" verdict! Our defense rests upon
our plea that we believe in the death, burial, and Resurrection of our advocate, the Lord Jesus Christ.

Paul, the court reporter, says of that plea, which each of us must make as
we turn our desperate case over to our attorney, whom we trust completely,

That if thou shalt confess with thy mouth the Lord Jesus,
and shalt believe in thine heart that God hath raised him from
the dead, thou shalt be saved. For with the heart man believeth
unto righteousness; and with the mouth confession is made
unto salvation (Romans 10:9–10).

Jesus, the Christ, stands between us and eternal punishment. He is our only
hope. And He never fails to win our acquittal: "For there is one God, and
one mediator between God and men, the man Christ Jesus" (1 Timothy 2:5).

Paul expounds on a further "mystery" that will be handled by the Lord Jesus Christ. This eternal legal action will not only keep us from God the Judge's courtroom of condemnation, the action will get all of Jesus Christ's clients completely off this condemned planet at some stupendous moment just ahead!

Paul tells us of this all-important action:

> Behold, I shew you a mystery; We shall not all sleep, but we shall all be changed, in a moment, in the twinkling of an eye, at the last trump: for the trumpet shall sound, and the dead shall be raised incorruptible, and we shall be changed (1 Corinthians 15:51–52).

He states further,

> For the Lord himself shall descend from heaven with a shout, with the voice of the archangel, and with the trump of God: and the dead in Christ shall rise first: then we which are alive and remain shall be caught up together with them in the clouds, to meet the Lord in the air: and so shall we ever be with the Lord. Wherefore comfort one another with these words (1 Thessalonians 4:16–18).

Thus the case of the missing millions will conclude. Mystery will be solved. Comforting words indeed! *Even so, come, Lord Jesus!*

Posthumous Post Profoundly Personal

Please indulge me as I yet again share a personal memory of Easter season six years ago. It is a memory that I couldn't put out of the forefront of my thoughts even if I wanted to — which I don't.

Good Friday, April 22, 2011, was the day that, after a workout session, I felt as if my chest would explode. It was a widow-maker heart attack.

Once the emergency guys got me to the hospital about two miles from our home, my heart stopped. I was instantly in the presence of a throng of beautiful young men and women who cheered vigorously, all the while bidding me to join them.

I started to do so, but everything grew dark around me and I was on the gurney being whisked toward the cath lab.

I heard a young man say he had to "hit him with the paddles."

I asked, "What paddles?" and he replied, "Your heart stopped, and I had to use the defib paddles."

My heart stopped two more times that afternoon. Each time I was instantaneously in front of the same wildly cheering group of young men and women who bid me to join them.

The third time I joined them, we were running a victory lap of some sort. They were looking over at me and laughing joyously, their hands extended at full arm's length into the air.

The sensation was . . . well . . . heavenly. I have no other way of describing it. We were running, without any physical exertion whatsoever, toward some wonderful destination. (I have, in reflecting on this experience for years, concluded that we were headed toward the throne of God.)

I know these people were the "cloud of witnesses" of Hebrews 12:1–3.

But things grew dark again, and I was again, after seemingly several seconds, on the cath lab table, and the cardiologist interventionist was working on me. He had removed the arterial blockage.

Astonishingly, I had no permanent heart damage and have had absolutely no problem with my engine since. My life, however, continues to be affected every waking moment by that Good Friday trip to somewhere on the heavenly property that I will someday inherit, as will you, if you know the Lord Jesus Christ as Savior. (We are "joint heirs with Christ," God's Word promises.)

So, with that memory indelibly etched in my spirit, I naturally — perhaps "supernaturally" would be a better term — was reflecting on my trip of six years ago the other day as Easter 2017 approached.

One thing I do every morning is read *The Omega Letter*. This email newsletter sent daily to subscribers is well-known by most who love Bible prophecy, of course. It was written by Jack Kinsella, perhaps the most prolific such writer I've known.

Jack was a dear friend who went to claim his heavenly inheritance in 2013. I miss him immensely, as do all who knew him. He was indeed a special Christian brother. More than that, he was a special teacher of all things biblical, especially regarding the prophetic Word of God. In that respect, I don't miss him because his hundreds of articles continue to instruct, implore, exhort, admonish, and inspire on a daily basis. His writing is, amazingly, as fresh as the day he wrote it.

So it was on Saturday before this past Easter Sunday that I opened my *Omega Letter*. There it was: Jack's inspiration and exhortation for this Easter. Only it was originally written April 23, 2011. That's right. It was written one day after my trip onto the heavenly property that Jack now owns for all of eternity. I probably shouldn't, but I envy him that fact. . . .

Jack's words were poignant and personal that day as he waxed eloquent yet simply in his own inimitable, communicative style.

Since the word "coincidence" is not in God's vocabulary according to Jack's dear friend Hal Lindsey, I know the Lord somehow used my close friendship with Jack to convey this special message.

In closing that issue of the *Omega Letter,* Jack addressed the question: What happens when we die?

He wrote,

> If the Bible is true and Jesus can be believed, then when a saved person closes his eyes in this life, he awakes fully conscious in the next — where he is whisked by the angels into heaven. . . . There is a choice. But it is admittedly limited. One can repent and trust Jesus or one can face God clothed in one's own righteousness and see how things work out.[83]

Jack pointed out that, tragically, the rich man Jesus told about in the story of the rich man and Lazarus is still in the place of torment, eternally regretting that he depended on his own righteousness to get him to heaven. Jack's posthumous words deliver to me the profoundly personal exhortation to do more to reach the lost with the gospel at every opportunity — chances I've been given by having been returned to earth for a while longer.

---

83. Jack Kinsella, *The Omega Letter,* April 23, 2011.

31

May 2017: America's Schizophrenia

The United States is divided today as much as it was during the Civil War. We aren't shedding blood in furious, literal warfare, but the hatreds — the differences in thought — divide as surely as did the North-versus-South issues of the mid-1800s.

Our name "United" is no longer applicable in the truest sense. We are split in many ways, from political ideology with regard to constitutional authority to worldview on geopolitics, socioeconomics, and religion. In terms of the discipline of human psychology, we are a schizophrenic country. We have severe split-personality disorder, at the very least.

National schizophrenia continues to manifest in ways that indicate mental disorder within some factions of American society and culture. Anger, unfounded — i.e., unprovable as to reasons it is warranted — is growing. Denial of reality, in that much of the population refuses to accept the legitimacy of a constitutionally conducted presidential election, is a prime symptom of the nation's psychological illness.

Members among that faction talk openly in social media about wanting to see the newly elected president murdered. It's a psychological — even psychotic — revisitation, some might say, of those long-ago, Southern-like sympathizers in the mold of John Wilkes Booth.

Their mindset is not unlike that of the dastardly assassin who so resented Abraham Lincoln after he directed the Civil War victory to preserve the Union that he could abide nothing less than the 16th president's murder.

Voters have spoken within the rational, constitutional process. They put the current president in office. Mainstream media, entertainment media, higher educational institutions, and leftists of every stripe refuse to accept the legitimate election. They are observably driven to a form of madness. They are the ones who show the signs of the mental illness they accuse the new president of having.

We review just a few of the schizophrenic symptoms manifest in the United States. It all stems from reprobate or upside down thinking, about which the Apostle Paul warned in Romans 1. It's what happens when any people move in a direction other than the one God prescribes.

- Muslims are called peaceful while Christians are called homophobic, Islamophobic, etc.

- The liberals' mindset is that we should do all for the children, yet they are responsible for 58 million being murdered in their mothers' wombs.

- This mindset calls homosexuality an acceptable alternate lifestyle, while God's Word calls it an abomination.

- Marriage is between one man and one woman, and this culture now says it also is legally a marriage between man and man and woman and woman.

- The mindset is to say, "God Bless America," yet the government has kicked God out of public affairs in 1963 and since.

- Schizophrenia exists as Islamists commit heinous attacks out of hatred for anyone who doesn't see things their way (bow to Allah), yet the mindset is that we must have open arms and welcome people from those countries, without questioning and examining (vetting) them.

- Christians are called intolerant, yet the progressives won't tolerate the Christian worldview; they see it as intolerant and hateful.

- Men want to become women, women want to become men . . . and now men want to be made into women who can have babies.

- Presidential administration always looks for a "motive" when it is obviously Islamists who murder. Never call them Islamic terrorists.

- Socialism is literally impoverishing all societies around the world, yet capitalism is called the system that demeans people — examples being Venezuela and other places of late.

- Israel has only a sliver of land and the Arab nations have vast lands, yet the world diplomatic community (and many among the ideological left in America) demands that the Jewish state divide its land and give it to make a Palestinian state — to people blood-vowed to kill all Jews.

The final bulleted point in this list is the most troubling. It holds the very fate of America within its grip, if one believes God's Word as given in Genesis 12 — and we do.

The schizophrenia is seen to be a perhaps unresolvable spiritual malady in this regard. America has for the last couple of decades, particularly over the past eight years, exhibited a split over support of Israel.

The former administration "put light" between the United States and Israel, something one of the Obama administration spokespersons vowed would happen as stated at the very outset. The Trump administration has promised to do just the opposite. It has indeed to this point embraced the Jewish state and even is seriously considering moving the American embassy to Jerusalem from Tel Aviv. Yet, at the same time that the American government is again befriending Israel, a faction of domestic terrorists are exhibiting psychotic hatred reminiscent of that found in the Germany of the 1930s:

NEW YORK — Antisemitic incidents in the United States surged by 34 percent in 2016 compared to 2015, and have jumped 86 percent in the first quarter of 2017, new data released by the Anti-Defamation League on Monday showed.

In its annual "Audit of Antisemitic Incidents," the ADL reported that there has been a "massive increase" in the amount of harassment of American Jews, particularly since November, the month of the US presidential election.

The report stated that there was a total of 1,266 acts targeting Jews and Jewish institutions in 2016, nearly 30% of which occurred in November and December. These incidents included 720 incidents of harassment and threats, 510 vandalism acts and 36 physical assault incidents.

During the first three months of 2017, another 541 incidents took place including 380 harassments and 161 bomb threats. In addition, the beginning of the year saw 155 vandalism acts — including three cemetery desecrations — and six physical assault incidents. Among the latest incidents, included one last month, in which a New York rabbi received a threatening email, which read in part: "Things will start getting bloodier for the Jew boys, I know where you live."

According to the data, if anti-Semitic occurrences continue at this rate, 2017 could end with over 2,000 incidents.[84]

For the moment, it seems that the current administration wants to apply healing balm to the rift with Israeli Prime Minister Benjamin Netanyahu and his nation that was caused by the previous administration. But the American schizophrenia remains a most serious spiritual disease that grows within. Believers must continue praying as hundreds of thousands did leading up to the presidential election just past. It is the only prescription that will spare this nation the demise the Lord says will befall all individuals and nations who choose to defy His divine order for mankind.

Israel's Identity Crisis

It seems strange that the one nation on earth that God Himself calls His "chosen" suffers such low self-esteem. I use the term in the sense that there is an internal, national uncertainty concerning where the nation fits within the international scheme of things. There projects from Israel an aura of not belonging.

I suppose this shouldn't surprise, considering that most countries making up the United Nations vote against Israel in almost every case that is brought against the nation. The history of such anti-Israel voting is stunning.

Israel completely outperforms all its neighbors in productivity. Its ingenuity benefits not only the region but all the world. That tiny sliver of land encompasses only a fraction of the land grant the Lord says is theirs. Yet it is an island of technological, agricultural, and societal creativity that is second only to that generated by the United States. And, fact is, much of America's creativity and activity is directly due to the brilliance of U.S. Jewish citizenry.

Its tentativeness in national confidence has long been the concern of Israeli thinkers and innovators. Just this past week, initiatives to deal with Israel's identity crisis came to the surface as breaking news:

> A proposal to anchor Israel's status as a Jewish state in a Basic Law was approved by the Ministerial Committee for Legislation Sunday.
>
> MK Avi Dichter (Likud), who proposed the bill, called the vote "a big step towards establishing our identity, not only

---

84. Danielle Ziri, "US Antisemitic Incidents Jump 86% at Start of 2017," *Jerusalem Post*, April 24, 2017.

universally, but mainly towards ourselves, the Israelis, to be a free nation in our land," a line from Hatikva. . . .

"I've been working on the Jewish State bill for six years," Dichter recounted. "Six years to establish the simple and most basic truth: Israel is the nation-state of the Jewish People." . . .

The legislation states that "the State of Israel is the national home of the Jewish people, in which it realizes its aspirations for self-determination according to its cultural and historic traditions. The realization of national self-determination in the State of Israel is unique to the Jewish people." . . .

It also mentions the Law of Return, and calls for the government to work to strengthen Israel-Diaspora ties.

It states that Hebrew is Israel's official language and Arabic has a special status, requiring all government services to be available in Arabic.[85]

The bill, if approved, was set for a preliminary vote on Wednesday. It will thus take place in the first week of the Knesset's summer session. The Justice Ministry will be charged with drafting its own version of the bill within 60 days. The two bills will then be combined.

The bill is receiving pushback by those who see it as a racist action that puts too much emphasis on Israel being Jewish and not enough on democracy. Such an accusation has some validity. But, with things going on lately, it is action that is warranted, in my view.

One example of the world doing all possible to strip Israel of its sovereignty and even its right to exist is that perpetrated by the U.N.:

> The UNESCO Executive Board passed a resolution in Paris that disavowed Israeli sovereignty in Jerusalem. The organization insists, thereby, that Israel should no longer have authority in the city. The vote was meant to delegitimize Israel's right to the city governance that was won during the 1967 Six Day War.
>
> Because of continuing such actions by the U.N. against Israel, the Israeli government is considering ousting that organization from its facilities within the city of Jerusalem.
>
> The government on Sunday is set to debate the question whether or not to oust the United Nations from its Jerusalem headquarters, but is not expected to take any action on the matter at this time. . . .

85. Lahav Harkov, "Israeli Ministers Approve Controversial Jewish State Bill." Israel News, *Jerusalem Post*, May 7, 2017.

In a statement to Channel 2, [Miri] Regev [Culture and Sports Minister] said that clearly there was no longer any logic to the UN remaining at that location.

"We've been sovereign in the city for 50 years, so there is no need for UN monitors. They were given use of the compound to oversee the cease-fire agreement from the Six-Day war, it's an agreement that is no longer relevant. This saga has to end," she said.[86]

Israel's identity crisis is destined to become much more acute. Zechariah the prophet and other prophets foretold a time when all nations will seek to kill all Jews. Haven't we heard that before?

Anti-Semitism on the rise is only one symptom of the great hatred that Antichrist will foment, especially during the second three and one-half years of the Tribulation: "Alas! for that day is great, so that there is none like it: it is even the time of Jacob's trouble; but he shall be saved out of it" (Jeremiah 30:7).

Israel's identity will one day be firmly established, however. God has promised to make it the head of the nations when Christ rules and reigns from atop Zion in Jerusalem as King of kings and Lord of lords.

God's Next Catastrophic Intervention

North Korean leader Kim Jong-un continues to fire off missiles that fail shortly after lifting off. But there are enough successes to portend a time when he can arm them with nuclear devices to kill hundreds of thousands. The ayatollahs and military of Iran remain on course to produce deliverable nuclear weapons to rain upon the hated Israel. Russian President Putin becomes more bellicose by the day, sending his bombers near America's Alaskan shores. He has fighter jets buzzing American aircraft within 20 feet in some cases.

Syrian dictator Assad continues to inflict genocide in the region, no doubt causing Israel's military to consider preemptive action to protect the Jewish state.

China, despite some minor, peaceful overtures to President Trump and America, continues to build its military and new bases in waters that are considered international rather than Chinese territorial waters. ISIS and the many Israel-hating terrorist entities continue to plan and carry out murderous assaults around the world.

---

86. Tovah Lazaroff, "Israeli Minister Calls to Oust UN from Jerusalem Headquarters," *Jerusalem Post*, May 3, 2017.

This is a time when there is a cry for peace and safety, while there seems to be little peace upon the planet.

Our president is going to the Middle East to have a go at formulating a peace deal between Israel and the Palestinians — a thing many diplomats of every stripe have tried but failed to achieve.

Everything regarding those geopolitical exigencies seem to point to just how near this generation is to the time of Tribulation, the final seven years immediately preceding Christ's Second Advent. But those represent only one side of the equation that makes up the signals we are to look for in being watchmen on the wall as Bible prophecy fulfillment draws near.

While the volatility and violence that will be part of end-times indicators are certainly something to consider, Jesus painted a much different picture that will be on the scene when He next catastrophically intervenes into the affairs of fallen mankind.

We know that God's prophets never contradict one another. If we search deeply enough and long enough, we will see the interconnectedness and the absolute integrity of prophetic truth. So, how, as God's Word says, does Paul's prophecy, "evil men and seducers shall [get] worse and worse, deceiving, and being deceived" (2 Timothy 3:13), comport with Jesus' own words about the moment He will next break in upon this rebellious world?

How does, for example, the Lord's own declaration make sense? He prophesies that people will be buying, selling, marrying, and building — doing all the things of everyday life. How does that declaration not conflict with the Revelation foretelling of 21 devastating judgments that were given to John on Patmos?

That is, how does such a not-unpleasant set of circumstances like Jesus describes using the days of Noah and of Lot not contradict the Olivet Discourse? The Lord's words describe conditions *so horrific* when Christ comes back that no flesh will be saved if He doesn't return at that moment (Matthew 24:21).

The only reason for these diametrically different prophetic descriptions is, of course, wrapped up in the Apostle Paul's words: "Behold, I shew you a mystery; we shall not all sleep, but we shall all be changed, in a moment, in the twinkling of an eye, at the last trump: for the trumpet shall sound, and the dead shall be raised incorruptible, and we shall be changed" (1 Corinthians 15:51–52).

The premillennial, pre-Tribulation view of Christ's return is the only view that answers the big questions about the apparent contradictions.

God's next catastrophic intervention into the affairs of rebellious mankind's evil doings will take place in two phases. The first involves the "mystery" Paul describes in 1 Corinthians 15:51–55. All born-again believers who have died or are living will in one stunning moment be translated into supernatural bodies and instantly appear with Jesus Christ above the earth.

Jesus tells that, at the time of that event, the Rapture, things will be relatively normal for most people living on the earth. As a matter of fact, I believe His words say that it will be business even better than usual.

The second phase of Christ's Second Coming will, of course, be that moment when He comes back with all the saints to put an end to man's most terrible war — Armageddon (Revelation 19:11–12).

At that time, the earth will have been devastated by war and God's wrath. Again, Jesus said that all flesh would die if He didn't intervene at that moment.

God's judgment will begin, Jesus said, the very day He is next "revealed." That will be at the Rapture, when all the earth will know there has been a tremendous event that made millions simply vanish. Like in Lot's day, God's judgment will begin that very day, Jesus says as recorded in Luke 17:26–30. God's wrath won't begin until the covenant of Daniel 9:27 is confirmed. But judgment will begin immediately, we are told by the Lord Himself.

It will be a catastrophic intervention right from that "twinkling-of-an-eye" moment!

I believe we, as watchmen, should be observing the times to see if the near future holds a noticeable upswing in national and international economies — in conjunction with considering all the traditional signals that the Bible describes.

32

June 2017: Restrainer Working Overtime

Over the past year, I have received emails castigating me for writing on politics and matters surrounding government and things of the world. The main irritation with me seems to come from those who believe I'm paying too much attention to this world and not thinking enough on the spiritual. I should, in their opinion, drop supporting one political position or the other and dwell strictly on biblical/spiritual issues — no politics or support for politicians. That I should support and focus only on what God's Word has to say about the end times is foundational to these critics' primary exhortation.

The problem is, the two are not mutually exclusive, to my way of thinking. Politics and the machinations of politicians these days are, in my estimation, linked to Bible prophecy in ways I cannot ignore. To do so would be to neglect the "watchman" commission I believe I've been given.

It is with this admission to you that I begin yet another rant, as my critics would have it, on what is going on in the political world as connected to the spiritual. I make no apologies that I come down on one side of the issue that I wish to address. Actually, the "rant" involves a number of issues under the wider problem of the evil that pervades our nation's capital and other power centers here and abroad.

Satan has always worked in the power centers of the world. His record of success can't be denied for the most part. Every man-made government that has ever existed has harbored evil at every level. The fallen one has brought every empire to destruction in one way or the other through his seduction and deception. The masses of people under the various regimes throughout history have suffered by the billions. They have died by the multiplied millions.

Purists among the scholars who observe the rise and fall of great nations and empires would, if they are biblical in their analysis, say God brings those entities down. But it is Satan who has led them to their demise as they get further and further away from God in comportment.

In getting back to my dwelling on present political realities and the media and politicians who have created this incendiary atmosphere of hatred for America's current president, I would like to offer the following.

As stated above, Lucifer has managed, through corruption, seduction, and every other way of his evil methodologies, to bring down great nations and even empires. Anyone who has the good sensibility to admit the in-our-faces truth of things going on in opposition to President Donald Trump can testify to the hatred at its center. Washington, D.C., is the greatest power center, perhaps, of all of history. The evil doings there are staggering.

I find myself agreeing with President Trump's words when he said recently that no president has been subjected to the degree of hateful treatment to which he has been subjected. Not even Richard Nixon had media so blatantly arrayed against him during the time of Watergate. It is an assault of unprecedented virulence we are witnessing. It is going to get much worse, and I've pointed out before why that is the case.

Satan's plan to install a one-world order has been disrupted. He is as determined as ever to put his man — the "son of perdition" — into power. The American electorate voted the anti-globalist Mr. Trump into office, and the end-times war began in earnest.

The minions, both demonic and human, are looking for any crime and anything else that might rise to the level of impeachable offense so that they can carry out another Watergate-type *coup d'état*. Short of that, they obviously intend to keep the vitriol flowing, even if there is no offense to be found. They have proven capable of creating charges — lies, out of whole cloth.

Trump's election has brought on the observable manifestation of a specific end-times signal. The Restrainer, I am convinced, can almost visibly be seen going about His office of holding back the evil onslaught.

The Restrainer and His work in this Age of Grace (Church Age) are explained by my good friend Ron Graham, in an excellent article posted a couple of years ago. Ron, before he died in 2013, partially wrote the following, and his wife, Nathele, completed it in 2015. The article is in relationship to prophecy Paul the Apostle gave in 2 Thessalonians 2: "For the mystery of iniquity doth already work: only he who now letteth will let, until he be taken out of the way" (2 Thessalonians 2:7).

The Greek word translated into English for "letteth" is *kat-echō*, and the definition of this Greek word is somewhat different than the definition of our English word "let," which means "to allow or permit." The Greek word is actually just the opposite; it means "to restrain, to hold back, detain, retain." What we must ask ourselves is "Who is the 'He' that Paul is referring to in this verse?"

First of all we find the apostle referring to the "who now letteth" as a "He" and secondly that this "He" is currently holding back a flood of wickedness which is straining at the bit to be loosed. Who could be so powerful to be able to hold back worldwide wickedness but the Holy Spirit?[87]

One, if spiritually attuned to the current political climate, senses the constant surge of anger and hatred trying to excise the president from office. This will not happen as long as God the Holy Spirit says otherwise. Christians must pray as diligently as they did before the 2016 election that the Restrainer continues to hold back the evil that is intended to bring about the installation of human history's final dictator. (And, yes . . . I've gotten the notes from those who think Donald Trump could be that man — a thing his actions thus far refute, in my view.)

Soon, Christ will call His Church to Himself. The Restrainer will at the same time remove from acting on the consciences of mankind. Meanwhile, thankfully, He is working overtime.

The U.S. Embassy–Jerusalem Decision

U.S. presidential candidate Donald J. Trump's declaration was loud and clear: "We will move the American Embassy from Tel Aviv to Israel's capital, Jerusalem!"

This was the candidate's core promise involving Israel throughout the long, disputatious campaign season. It was at least a part of why many within the religious right supported the Trump candidacy.

So it was that, when President Trump made the announcement after his trip to the Middle East and Jerusalem, a cry of betrayal went up from his base of support. His administration will not for the foreseeable future move the American Embassy from Tel Aviv to Israel's capital:

> WASHINGTON — President Donald Trump signed a temporary order on Thursday to keep the U.S. embassy in

---

87. Ron and Nathele Graham, "Restrainer," Rapture Ready; raptureready.com, 2015.

Israel in Tel Aviv instead of relocating it to Jerusalem, despite his campaign pledge to go ahead with the controversial move.

After months of fierce debate within his administration, Trump chose to continue his predecessors' policy of signing a six-month waiver overriding a 1995 law requiring that the embassy be transferred to Jerusalem, an action that would have complicated his efforts to restart Israeli-Palestinian peace talks.[88]

The White House was quick to report that the president was by no means lessening his support for Israel. Also, it made clear that the move of the embassy is only delayed. It will still be moved to Jerusalem is the word that continues to come from the administration — even though no time table has been set for such a move.

White House sources said, "The question is not if that move happens, but only when." The statement further said that the president's decision to defer the move for now was made "to maximize the chances of successfully negotiating a deal between Israel and the Palestinians, fulfilling his solemn obligation to defend America's national security interests."[89]

President Trump said at the 2016 AIPAC conference in Washington, D.C., "We will move the American embassy to the eternal capital of the Jewish people, Jerusalem."[90] He remained silent about his pledge to make the move, however, following his November 8 election.

Many within the Christian community who supported him are worried that this means Trump is a wolf in sheep's clothing. I am even getting emails, as I wrote last week, from those who are beginning to say he has Antichrist characteristics. Some (prophetic observers) especially look at his son-in-law, Jared Kushner, with suspicion in that regard.[91]

Some believe that the entire matter involving Trump's decision to remove the United States from the Paris Accords on climate change was to

---

88. Matt Spetalnick, "Trump Delays Moving U.S. Embassy to Jerusalem Despite Campaign Pledge," Reuters, June 1, 2017.

89. https://www.whitehouse.gov/briefings-statements/statement-american-embassy-israel/.

90. http://www.politifact.com/truth-o-meter/promises/trumpometer/promise/1377/move-us-embassy-tel-aviv-jerusalem/.

91. This suspicion is because of reports of possible peace talks in the future and concerns rooted in the prophetic event mentioned in Joel 3:2, saying God will bring all to Armageddon because they have "divided my land." There are those that fear that Kushner is trying to get Israel to fall for a false peace plan in a two-state solution to the problems between Israel and their enemies. Prophetic observers are wary of anyone trying to initiate a peace deal involving Israel and its land.

create a diversion from the supposed fact that he was betraying his campaign promise regarding the embassy move to Jerusalem.

I harbor no such suspicions — at least not to this point. He has proven a man of his word up to now. He hasn't *not* moved the embassy — he's only delayed that move.

Considering the current climate of distrust and animosity between the Jews and their enemy Muslim neighbors, it is wise to proceed cautiously, while intending fully to move the embassy at the best possible diplomatic moment. At the same time, I urge the president to move the embassy. It will show the desire to *bless* Israel — never the wrong thing to do.

Trump has, in my estimation, been very forthright in stating why he made the decision to delay. We will see if he follows through on his White House promise: "The question is not if that move happens, but only when."

One thing is absolutely certain: God's touchstone city to the entire world will one day be the capital of the millennial earth. God has reserved great things for this place He calls "the apple of my eye":

> Again the word of the LORD of hosts came to me, saying, Thus saith the LORD of hosts; I was jealous for Zion with great jealousy, and I was jealous for her with great fury. Thus saith the LORD; I am returned unto Zion, and will dwell in the midst of Jerusalem: and Jerusalem shall be called a city of truth; and the mountain of the LORD of hosts the holy mountain. . . . And I will bring them, and they shall dwell in the midst of Jerusalem: and they shall be my people, and I will be their God, in truth and in righteousness (Zechariah 8:1–8).

Conditional Security and Rapture

Truth about what God promises those who are "saved" continues to be mistaught and misunderstood. Nothing is more important to lost humanity than truth regarding the disposition of the soul in relationship to Jesus Christ and to God the Father.

Religionists of the world teach a variety of pathways through life. These propagate many false teachings about how to attain their various ideas of life after death. Most such ministers advocate conducting one's life in a way that displays good works. A *social gospel* of works is perhaps the most common thread found throughout this sort of religiosity.

Good works, however, like is said of beauty, are in the eye of the beholder. Good works are one thing to someone who is a Hari Krishna devotee. Good works mean something quite different to a follower of Allah who holds strictly to sharia law. One might hold out flowers to another person in his or her version of peace and love in an attempt to evangelize. The other too often whips out a scimitar and threatens decapitation if the one being witnessed to doesn't bow the knee to Allah. Point is, each effort to make new converts is, in that religion's view, considered "good works."

But the erroneous teaching on the topic of salvation within Christianity is the most problematic to the true believer in Christ's death, burial, and Resurrection, as I see it.

Most of God's children can recognize the cults and isms of the world's religions as false. Christians who fail to study and pray over the Holy Scripture, however, are, sadly, all too often easily misled about doctrinal truth found in the Bible. Even otherwise solid teachers of biblical truth are sometimes egregiously wrong when instructing on salvation and the security of the believer.

Again, nothing is more important than our soul's relationship to Jesus Christ and God the Father. While one who teaches *conditional security* of the believer isn't necessarily in the same classification as the false religionists of the world who preach and teach "another gospel" than Jesus Christ crucified, the error is very serious because it, like the false religions of the world, holds up *works* as necessary for salvation.

They teach that believers, after accepting Christ, as given in Romans 10:9–10, must then work to maintain their salvation. They must live holy lives throughout their remaining time in this flesh. They must, through their own devices — assisted by constantly being filled with the Holy Spirit — hold on to the salvation or else risk losing it. Thus, their salvation — in this system of teaching — is conditional upon the work of the believer.

Being holy and being filled with the Holy Spirit are, of course, ideal. We must all aspire to live such a life as Christians. But we all sin, and we are told in 1 John 1:6–8 that if we say we don't sin, we are liars. The truth is not in us.

We certainly should constantly repent of wrong to be cleansed of all unrighteousness, we are told in 1 John 1:9. But nowhere in Scripture are we told that, once saved, we can lose our salvation through sin and then be reborn again.

Rapture Not Conditional

Like in the matter of salvation, the believer is unconditionally secure in that he or she will go to be with Christ in the Rapture. This is true no matter the Christian's walk with the Lord at the time of that great event. Some years ago, I wrote the following in this regard:

> Going to Christ when He calls as Paul outlines in 1 Corinthians 15:51–55 and 1 Thessalonians 4:13–18, and given by John in Revelation 4:1–2, is a salvation matter. We know that from the overall gospel message and from the total context of God's dealing with His family. Remember when Jesus prayed that beautiful prayer to His Father, as the Lord faced the Cross (John 17)? Read it again, and you will see that it is absolutely clear that born-again believers are forever secure in the Father's hand, based upon what Jesus did on the Cross.

We know with absolute certainty that we are once and forever in God's family because of the words of the One who created all that exists: "My Father, which gave them me, is greater than all; and no man is able to pluck them out of my Father's hand" (John 10:29).

Paul confirms that the Rapture is a salvation matter as follows: "For God hath not appointed us to wrath, but to obtain salvation by our Lord Jesus Christ, who died for us, that, whether we wake or sleep, we should live together with him. Wherefore comfort yourselves together, and edify one another, even as also ye do" (1 Thessalonians 5:9–11).

The Rapture will be Christ keeping us from the hour of temptation or Tribulation (read Revelation 3:10). The Tribulation is the time of God's wrath, to which Paul tells us we are "not appointed." However, many insist that Christians who haven't properly confessed their sins will go through that time of God's wrath (and the entire seven years of the Tribulation will be God's judgment and wrath). They use the following verse to make their case: "Watch ye therefore, and pray always, that ye may be accounted worthy to escape all these things that shall come to pass, and to stand before the Son of man" (Luke 21:36).

The key word they hold forth as relevant here is the word "worthy." Does this word not mean that we as born-again believers must be good enough to stand before Jesus in that raptured throng? Does this word not mean, therefore, that if we fail to live up to God's standards while on this earth, we will (at some point in God's holy view of what it takes to fall from being Rapture ready) lose our ticket in that translation moment, thus not be taken when the shout is heard, "Come up hither"?

Like in examining the issue of salvation itself, we now look at the word "worthy." What does it mean to be "worthy," as given in this Rapture example? Again, the answer is wrapped up in the same name as before: "Jesus." Jesus is the only person "worthy," in God's holy eyes, to be in the heavenly realm.

Remember what Jesus said to a man who addressed Him as "Good Master"? "And Jesus said unto him, Why callest thou me good? none is good, save one, that is, God" (Luke 18:19).

Jesus, the second person of the Godhead, was not seeking to chastise the man for addressing Him in this way. The Lord was confirming through this question that He is indeed God, the only good, the only righteousness. Righteousness is the only ticket to heaven — either through the portal of death or through the Rapture. Only through Jesus can a person enter the heavenly realm.

Jesus spoke to this all-important matter by addressing Nicodemus: "Jesus answered and said unto him, Verily, verily, I say unto thee, Except a man be born again, he cannot see the kingdom of God" (John 3:3).

God's Word says about fallen mankind, "As it is written, There is none righteous, no not one" (Romans 3:10) and, "For all have sinned and come short of the glory of God" (Romans 3:23).

So, Jesus is the only person "worthy" to enter heaven. Only through Him are any of us worthy to stand before Him in that heavenly realm. That is the truth found in the Scripture in question.

On a less magnificent scale, the word "worthy" in this passage means that we should be in a constant mindset of prayerful repentance. We should always want to be found "worthy" — cleansed of all unrighteousness, as stated in 1 John 1:9, so that we will hear our Lord say to us on that day, "Well done, good and faithful servant" (Matthew 25:23).

That said, if you have in your heart (in the deepest reaches of your spirit/soul) believed in the death, burial, and Resurrection of the Lord Jesus Christ and have confessed that He is your Savior, your salvation is sure. You're going to be with Him when He calls, either through death or in the Rapture. That is certain.

33

July 2017: Kings of East Nuclear Factor

All directions in God's Word to humanity point outward from God's touchstone city to the human race. That is, Jerusalem is the topographical center of the world from God's holy perspective.

Therefore, north, south, east, and west, in terms of Bible prophecy, can be determined by considering that all-important city as the starting point.

We will look in this commentary at the "kings of the east" prophecy. That prophesied group of potentates, then, must be viewed as if we are standing, perhaps, on the Temple Mount in Jerusalem and looking eastward. This is how we can know that the "kings of the east" referred to in prophecy yet to happen are kings or national entities of China and the Orient in general.

Here are the nucleus scriptural references to the prophecy:

> And the sixth angel sounded, and I heard a voice from the four horns of the golden altar which is before God, saying to the sixth angel which had the trumpet, Loose the four angels which are bound in the great river Euphrates. And the four angels were loosed, which were prepared for an hour, and a day, and a month, and a year, for to slay the third part of men. And the number of the army of the horsemen were two hundred thousand thousand: and I heard the number of them (Revelation 9:13–16).

> And the sixth angel poured out his vial upon the great river Euphrates; and the water thereof was dried up, that the way of the kings of the east might be prepared (Revelation 16:12).

We note with interest that the Euphrates River seems to be the boundary dividing the Occidental world from the Oriental. God tells through prophecy that this boundary harbors some powerful and tremendously evil demonic actors that are incarcerated until time for the prophesied invasion from that world. As a matter of fact, these are so powerful that they will imbue this 200-million-member military force with the capability of killing one-third of the people of the world.

I'm aware that there is a train of thought that puts forth that one-third of a specific number of combatants who are to die in the overall campaign of Armageddon will be killed by this force from the Orient. To me, it reads that one-third of those living on the planet will be killed.

That there are supernatural elements involved within this murderous capability cannot be denied. It is reasonable to presume, however, that nuclear weaponry might be employed in accomplishing that grisly task.

The prophecy concerning the "kings of the east" becomes particularly fascinating when looking at geopolitical military rearrangements taking place today.

To preface these considerations, I urge us to remember that the demonic minions that will be the catalyst to galvanize the destructive "kings of the east" force are presently under God's restraining power. These evil entities are held back until a particular "hour, and a day." There is a specific moment when they will be unleashed to cause the 200-million-man force to kill one-third of everyone living on the planet.

I have always considered it a point of fascination that since the atomic attacks on Hiroshima and Nagasaki, Japan, in 1945, there hasn't been a single incident of a nuclear weapon discharged in any sort of military conflict. There have been nuclear tests of every sort, above ground and below, but not a single nuclear warhead of any sort has been fired as part of military action.

My friends, this lack of employing nuclear weaponry has taken far more than diplomacy, human fear, intrepidation, or whatsoever else. This has been the obvious, restraining hand of the God of heaven. Just like in the case of the evil angels being restrained somewhere beneath the Euphrates, the nuclear war-making genie has been kept in the bottle marked "For Tribulation Only."

As a matter of fact, the nuclear factor has been used, I'm convinced, by the Lord Himself to prevent man from self-destruction. If nuclear weapons were not at the ready at every moment of every day, the human race might have long ago ended most, if not all, life on earth with conventional weapons only slightly less horrific. Man has — some would surmise — retained the common sensibility, at least to this point, to refrain from all-out war, since those two small-by-comparison nuclear bombs that ended World War II.

North Korea forges ahead, producing nuclear weapons and the means to deliver them to distant points, despite a U.S. president who has vowed that such development will not be allowed to be brought to the point that the NK weapons can be used against the United States. A showdown of monumental magnitude seems to be shaping up at some point soon.

Yet, as many who read these commentaries know, I'm convinced there will be no earth-shattering event such as nuclear war until the Rapture has occurred. Jesus' words in the "days of Noah" and "days of Lot" prophecy in Matthew 24:36–42 and Luke 17:26–30 indicate it will be business as usual — even better than usual — right up until He next "reveals" Himself to a rebellious world. This will be Rapture, not the Second Advent, when He comes back to earth to end Armageddon and the threatened, complete destruction of all life on earth.

In the meantime, it is almost a certainty in my spirit-mind that there will be no complete disarmament of the nuclear powers. These weapons of mass destruction will doubtless be used during the Tribulation as part of judgment and wrath poured upon the evil and rebellion that will be against the God of heaven.

The North Koreans might be restrained in some fashion from unleashing their nukes on the rest of us for now. They will, however, likely have them at their disposal when they rage across the dried-up Euphrates under demonic influence. China and the rest of the Oriental diabolists will, the prophecy says, kill a third of the people left on the planet at that time. Certainly, nuclear weaponry could fulfill that prophecy.

It is interesting that there seems to be no nuclear weaponry used on Israel as the Gog-Magog forces descend like a cloud to take great spoil. It is a conventional force that makes the assault, apparently. At that point, there is either great restraint so they can enjoy the "spoils" they intend to take or there is restraint on the Gog-Magog forces of some other sort, preventing use of nuclear weaponry. Some believe this is because there has been nuclear disarmament at this juncture, and there are no nuclear weapons available. I do not agree.

God Himself will unleash His own form of "nukes" at that time, destroying all but one-sixth of the invading force.

The assault from the "kings of the east" seems to have no such encumbrances of nuclear restraint. The attack seems to come later than the Gog-Magog attack as the wind-up of the campaign of Armageddon looms.

One thing is sure: we are witnessing things shaping up for prophetic fulfillment in the arena of the "kings of the east" in regard to the nuclear factor.

End-Times Trending

Setting the stage for prophetic fulfillment continues at a quickening pace. Progression related to end-times matters spreads across the eschatological horizon, making choosing which particular topic to write about somewhat of an exertion — but not an unwelcome exercise.

News of the hour presents some fascinating directions in which to aim our attention. I've chosen three items for consideration in this commentary.

The first area of possible, even probable, prophetic relevance is China's increasingly hegemonic activity. Sino-expansionism is among the most blatant signals of stage-setting for prophetic fulfillment.

Chinese leadership is projecting two-faced influence and manipulation through its newfound power as "king" of the "kings of the east." They are employing their usual, inscrutable methodologies to convince the world community they are reliable partners with which to do business. On the other hand, the leadership — Communists all — are not only building an enormous military capability but making moves to intimidate their neighbors through provocative bullying encounters upon the high seas.

This bullying even includes flying military aircraft from the China Sea island bases they are creating in deliberate, near-miss incidents with American aircraft. China's increasingly powerful navy moves more and more near the point of ramming some of our naval ships in the region — as the U.S. military challenges China's obvious intention to increasingly claim territorial waters that are not theirs.

The following gives a flavor of China's recent, dangerous activity:

> The expansion of China's military is no secret. Beijing raised the People's Liberation Army budget by 7% this year, typical of its annual increases. . . .
>
> On Wednesday, the PLA Navy announced it had finished work on a destroyer warship that can displace 10,000 tons, according to the state-run *China Daily News* website. This is a particularly major advance. The extra-hardy, domestically built destroyer not only helps Beijing double down on its disputed claims in the East and South China Seas but also gives it new

deterrent weight against its most powerful Asian rivals such as Japan and India.[92]

Chinese President Xi Jinping, despite meetings with American President Donald Trump while smiling, promising to make an effort to corral the North Korean dictator Kim Jong-un, is presenting his own dictatorial propensities these days. Xi Jinping has warned against "impermissible" challenges to Beijing's authority over Hong Kong.

Mr. Xi Jinping was speaking at the swearing-in of the territory's new leader, Carrie Lam, as Hong Kong marked 20 years since its handover to China from Britain. In a speech, he said that Hong Kong needed to "improve its systems to uphold national sovereignty, security and development interests. . . . Any attempt to endanger China's sovereignty and security, challenge the power of the central government . . . or use Hong Kong to carry out infiltration and sabotage activities against the mainland is an act that crosses the red line and is absolutely impermissible."[93]

There is growing concern that the Chinese central government is undermining Hong Kong's more politically liberal traditions, despite its promise to give it a high degree of autonomy.[94] Secondly, in the matter of end-times trending, we look briefly at the coalescing Turkey-Iran relationship. It is a most fascinating element of the prophetic, stage-setting development in these closing days of this dispensation.

It is more than curiosity to me that the new American president appears to have been, wittingly or unwittingly, again a catalyst for development of key biblically prophetic preparation.

Donald Trump's recent visit to Saudi during his Middle East trip and his more-or-less pledge to come down on the side of the Saudi Kingdom as they face increasing threats from the likes of Iran has set in motion a closer tie of two key Gog-Magog partners. The newly forming closeness between Turkey and Iran is in view as they deal with the controversy over Qatar. The following excerpt enlightens this situation a bit:

> The latest Iranian comments, as well as Turkey's decision
> to send troops to Qatar amid a dispute with Saudi Arabia rep-
> resent the creation of a new Qatar-Turkey-Iranian sphere of

92. "New Chinese Navy Destroyer Can Best Japan, India and Maybe the United States," Rapture Ready News, July 2, 2017.
93. http://www.scmp.com/news/hong-kong/politics/article/2100856/full-text-president-xi-jinpings-speech-one-country-two.
94. "Xi Jinping Warns Hong Kong over Sovereignty 'Red Line,'" BBC News.

influence that has potential to influence the region and Israel. Qatar and Turkey have both had close relations with Hamas over the last decade. The creation of a warmer relationship between Doha, Ankara and Tehran could threaten Israel and could bring Jerusalem closer to Riyadh and Cairo.[95]

Turkey, under the almost overnight dictatorship formed by Tayyip Erdogan, seems headed in the direction of becoming, at some point, the entity that Ezekiel the prophet called Togormah. His regime is embraced, apparently, by the ayatollahs of Iran (Persia). It is a most interesting development that presents even more interesting possibilities.

The third and last item I would like to look at in considering end-times trending is the matter of the slap-down it looks as if President Trump is in process of giving the globalists within his administration. This, if it has legs — as they say — is, in my opinion, key to stage-setting for the "days of Noah, days of Lot" prophecy by the Lord Jesus. Again, that prophecy is found in Christ's Olivet discourse in Matthew 24:36–42 and in Luke 17:26–30.

In brief, I continue to believe that America — and much of the world — is about to experience not an economic meltdown, but an economic boom, based upon Jesus' words in that prophecy.

The globalists, I sense, were feeling as if they about had Mr. Trump pulled over to their sides in the matter of America's trade relations. It looked very much like the president would put their agenda, rather than America, first — continuing to let America's wealth drift out without *quid pro quo*. Now, because of the president's recent action, the Wall Street types are fearing a global trade war that would end their grasp on U.S. wealth in particular.

This news excerpt gives more information:

> While one of Trump's recurring campaign promises was that he would "punish" China and other key U.S. trade counterparties if elected, for taking advantage of free-trade by imposing steep tariffs and duties on foreign imports to "level the playing field," the president's stance changed drastically after the election, U-turning following his amicable meeting with China's President Xi Jinping in March, but mostly as a result of pressure by his ex-Goldman advisors to keep existing trade arrangements in place and not "rock the boat."

95. Seth J. Frantzman, "Turkey's Power-Play in Qatar Leads to Warmer Relations with Iran," *Jerusalem Post*, July 1, 2017.

Now, all that may be about to fall apart.

And what may be even more striking is that Trump over-ruled his cabinet, as "the sentiment in the room was 22 against, and 3 in favor — but since one of the three is named Donald Trump, it was case closed." Axios adds that while "no decision has been made, the President is leaning toward imposing tariffs, despite opposition from nearly all his Cabinet."[96]

Needless to say, if Trump follows through, the outcome would have a profound effect on U.S. economic and foreign policy; Trump will formalize his decision in the coming days.

Donald J. Trump might just be president at this moment for the end-times buying, selling, building, etc., prophesied by the Lord Himself. It is at just such a time Jesus tells us the following: "Likewise also as it was in the days of Lot; they did eat, they drank, they bought, they sold, they planted, they builded; but the same day that Lot went out of Sodom it rained fire and brimstone from heaven, and destroyed them all. Even thus shall it be in the day when the Son of man is revealed" (Luke 17:28–30).

Heaven's Awards Ceremony

Christians could suddenly be called before Jesus Christ in any given moment of time:

> Behold, I shew you a mystery; We shall not all sleep, but we shall all be changed, in a moment, in the twinkling of an eye, at the last trump: for the trumpet shall sound, and the dead shall be raised incorruptible, and we shall be changed (1 Corinthians 15:51–52).

> For the Lord himself shall descend from heaven with a shout, with the voice of the archangel, and with the trump of God: and the dead in Christ shall rise first: then we which are alive and remain shall be caught up together with them in the clouds, to meet the Lord in the air: and so shall we ever be with the Lord (1 Thessalonians 4:16–17).

For years in these commentaries, we have been chronicling how close the world is to that spectacular moment. Using God's Word, we have shown over and over that the lost of the world — all who have not accepted Jesus Christ as their Savior — will be left behind to suffer unimaginable horror.

---

96. "Trump 'Overrules' Cabinet, Prepares to Unleash Global Trade War," Zero Hedge.

It doesn't have to be that way for anyone. God tells all who will listen that He is not willing that any should perish, but that all should come to repentance. He gives His plan of salvation for escaping eternity in hell and the way to escape this terrible time that is about to begin on earth once the Rapture occurs. The Apostle Paul wrote the following:

> That if thou shalt confess with thy mouth the Lord Jesus, and shalt believe in thine heart that God hath raised him from the dead, thou shalt be saved. For with the heart man believeth unto righteousness; and with the mouth confession is made unto salvation (Romans 10:9–10).

Accepting Christ for salvation must be made before, not after, the Rapture in order to escape the Tribulation. Now is the day of accepting Christ for salvation, the Bible says. Few who have rejected Christ before the Rapture will come to salvation after the Rapture, is how I believe the Scriptures have it.

I'm going to prayerfully presume you don't want to go to that place of torment called the lake of fire, or go through the hell on planet Earth called Tribulation, the last seven years leading up to Christ's Second Coming. I'm presuming that you will accept God's plan of salvation as given above.

Now we will look at what God's Word tells us is wrapped up in His plans for all who have been wise enough to humble themselves and accept His Son, Jesus the Christ, for the salvation of their eternal souls — that is, we will look at what I will term here as "Heaven's Awards Ceremony."

The great promises for Christians that follow have been put together by many astute Bible scholars and students over many years. I have long ago forgotten the sources in particular. I will just say here that mixed in with my own thoughts is the scholarship of many folks whose thoughts are much elevated above my own. I do know that many of these thoughts on the bema (judgment seat of Christ) are from Dr. Harold Wilmington of Liberty University.

Immediately upon the Church being called into heaven in the Rapture, all will stand before the bema. Jesus Christ will judge each person, not for punishment, but for eternal rewards. This judgment will be for giving awards for the ways in which individual Christians have contributed to God's glorious kingdom living on planet Earth.

Things on which Christians Will Be Judged at the Judgment Seat of Christ

1. How we treat other believers: Hebrews 6:10; Matthew 10:41–42.

2. How we exercise our authority over others: Hebrews 13:17; James 3:1.

3. How we employ our God-given abilities: 1 Corinthians 12:4, 12; 2 Timothy 1:6; 1 Peter 4:10. Add to these Scriptures Jesus' teaching of the parables of the ten pounds (Luke 19:11–26) and the talents (Matthew 25:14–29).

Each believer has at least one talent: 1 Corinthians 7:7, 12:7–11; Ephesians 4:7; 1 Peter 4:10.

There are 18 of these gifts: Romans 12; 1 Corinthians 12; Ephesians 4. It's up to each believer to find/discern his or her gifts.

4. How we use our money: 1 Corinthians 16:2; 2 Corinthians 9:6–7; 1 Timothy 6:17–19. All belongs to God: 1 Peter 18–19.

5. How we spend our time: Psalm 90:12; Ephesians 5:16; Colossians 4:5; 1 Peter 1:17.

6. How much we suffer for Jesus: Matthew 5:11–12; Mark 10:29–30; Romans 8:18; 2 Corinthians 4:17; 1 Peter 4:12–13.

7. How we run that particular race God has chosen for us: 1 Corinthians 9:24; Philippians 2:16, 3:13–14; Hebrews 12:1.

8. How effectively we control the old nature: 1 Corinthians 9:25–27; Greek word *adokimos*, "castaway," means "disapproved." It means self is disapproved. Paul wanted to keep his old nature in check — seen in 2 Timothy 2:15; 1 Corinthians 16:3; Philippians 1:10; 1 Thessalonians 2:4.

9. How many souls we witness to and win to Christ: Proverbs 11:30; Daniel 12:3; 1 Thessalonians 2:19–20.

10. How we react to temptation: James 1:2–3; Revelation 3:10.

11. How much the doctrine of the Rapture means to us: 2 Timothy 4:8.

12. How faithful we are to the Word of God and the flock of God: Acts 20:26–28; 2 Timothy 4:1–2; 1 Peter 5:2–4.

The results of the judgment seat of Christ — some will receive rewards: 1 Corinthians 3:14.

At Least Five Rewards Mentioned in the Bible

1. The incorruptible crown, given to those who master the old nature: 1 Corinthians 9:25–27.

2. The crown of rejoicing given to soul-winners: Proverbs 11:30; Daniel 12:31; 1 Thessalonians 2:19–20.

3. The crown of life, given to those who successfully endure temptation: James 1:2–3; Revelation 2:10.

4. The crown of righteousness for those who especially love the doctrine of the Rapture: 2 Timothy 4:8.

5. The crown of glory, given to faithful preachers and teachers: Acts 20:26–28; 2 Timothy 4:1–2; 1 Peter 5:2–4.

If Heaven's Awards Ceremony sounds just a bit intimidating, it doesn't have to. God's holy view of what constitutes acceptable, even superior, service as His royal ambassadors is almost assuredly different to the way awards are given out by award-givers of the human variety here on earth.

Jesus told us that the last shall be first, and the first shall be last: "And he sat down, and called the twelve, and saith unto them, If any man desire to be first, the same shall be last of all, and servant of all" (Mark 9:35).

A truly humble spirit in serving the Lord by serving others — putting others first and ourselves last — will bring believers to front and center of the bema seat in Heaven's Awards Ceremony.

Temple Mount Movement

Rapture Ready News headlines tell the story. Things are shaking on and around Moriah, the Temple Mount in Jerusalem. It is the geographical area most central to Bible prophecy yet to occur.

Those headlines are:

- Muslim Authority Protests Temple Mount Security Measures, Blocks Entrance; Ministers Approve Bill Aiming to Take Jerusalem off the Negotiating Table

- Arab-Israeli Lawmaker Warns of Third Intifada after Friday Attack

- Closing the Aksa Mosque

- Jordan's King Abdullah Calls for Calm after Temple Mount Attack

No doubt about it, things are moving and shaking on and around the Temple Mount. Considering all the other signals taking place in the world today, the import of this activity should alert the student of Bible prophecy to the lateness of the hour.

The Temple Mount is not only the nucleus problem of the historical, Arab/Israeli ages-long conflict. That place in the middle of the Temple where the Holy of Holies sat, housing the *shekinah* glory of God within the Ark of the Covenant, is at the heart of the spiritual warfare that began with man's Fall in the Garden.

It is where the ram was provided for the sacrifice God required, sparing Abraham's son Isaac from serving that purpose. It is very near where God's own Son hung suspended between heaven and hell as sacrifice for the sin of mankind to provide eternal salvation.

Mount Moriah is where the Tribulation Temple will be built and where Satan's evil one, the son of perdition, will claim himself to be God.

A great, planetary spiritual earthquake is coming, and its epicenter is the very spot that is smack in the middle of our headlines today.

The rumblings from that spiritual seismic area are growing daily.

When three terrorists murdered two Israeli police officers, the latest quivering of Moriah began.

The officers were killed near the gates of the Temple Mount, and the Israeli prime minister took action that infuriated the Muslims of the region and around the world. Netanyahu closed the Temple Mount to Muslim worship at the religion's sites there, which brought immediate anger and threats of a third intifada, or violent uprising.

The Israeli prime minister eventually agreed to gradually open some areas for worship on the Temple Mount. (Only Muslims are allowed to worship there; the Jews are forbidden.)

Netanyahu, however, placed detection devices — metal detectors and specially placed surveillance cameras — to restrict possible terrorist activity. King Abdullah phoned the Israeli prime minister to lobby for the gates to be fully opened, thus restoring access to the worship places.

Before leaving on his trip to France and Hungary, Netanyahu dismissed the oft-repeated charge that the Israeli government was "disrupting the status quo" in Jerusalem and at the Temple Mount. This is a charge that has brought on violent rampages from the Arabs in the past.

"I decided that as of tomorrow, in the framework of our policy of maintaining the status-quo, we will gradually open the Temple Mount, but with increased security measures," Netanyahu said.

"This evening, I held a discussion with the top security leadership and I instructed that metal detectors be placed at the entrance gates to the Temple Mount. We will also install security cameras on poles outside the Temple Mount but which give almost complete control over what goes on there," the prime minister added.[97]

The action threw the Muslim element into a frenzy of threatened violence. The crowds could be heard shouting, "Disgrace, enough with that, you are suffocating us! Al-Aksa belongs to Muslims!"[98]

The anger is directed at the new safeguards against terrorists bringing weapons into the Temple Mount area. Apparently, the safeguards Netanyahu installed are doing a good job of keeping out those tools of the Muslim militants who plan for future such actions as took the lives of the policemen.

Tremors spawned from the rage that continues to build in and around this most critical promontory on the map of prophecy are scheduled to grow stronger, not weaker. We know that it is all moving toward the time Jesus prophesied nearly two millennia ago:

> When ye therefore shall see the abomination of desolation, spoken of by Daniel the prophet, stand in the holy place, (whoso readeth, let him understand:) then let them which be in Judaea flee into the mountains: let him which is on the housetop not come down to take any thing out of his house: neither let him which is in the field return back to take his clothes. And woe unto them that are with child, and to them that give suck in those days! But pray ye that your flight be not in the winter, neither on the sabbath day: for then shall be great tribulation, such as was not since the beginning of the world to this time, no, nor ever shall be (Matthew 24:15–21).

---

97. https://www.jpost.com/Arab-Israeli-Conflict/Temple-Mount-metal-detector-saga-first-began-with-innocuous-statement-500540.

98. http://www.breitbart.com/jerusalem/2017/07/16/watch-islamic-activists-instigate-scuffles-block-entrances-temple-mount/.

34

August 2017: Mr. President — Cursing or Blessing?

There continues to be much turbulence stirred within the American government and America in general. I've written a number of times that I believe God intervened in the 2016 presidential election. He, I'm convinced, answered the prayers of the *people called by His name* — Christians. He turned the American ship of state around, or at least began that process of steering in a better direction.

Donald J. Trump, a man who was and continues to be far from a godly man, in my view, was nonetheless chosen by the Almighty to head the project to slow, if not completely halt, globalism's takeover of the United States.

Globalism, I believe, is how Satan intends to take America down the pathway to the eventual installation of his man of sin, Antichrist. That intention has been greatly slowed with the election of Mr. Trump, and the fallen one isn't happy. The uproar among his many minions, both demonic and human, is witness that gives testimony to Lucifer's enragement.

Donald Trump is God's man of the hour, even though not a godly man. In that regard, I support God's decision totally, as anyone who reads these commentaries knows. I continue to believe that if the other candidate had won the election, the effects, especially for those of us who value American ideals as founded and who believe that the Bible is truth, would have been terrible.

One day, perhaps soon, the United States and the world will experience those feared results of losing such elections. For now, however, there is a heaven-sent reprieve, and we must support godliness and a movement back toward God's way, rather than continue on the path to destruction.

This is why I — we, as Christians — must call out ungodliness when it pops up its ugly head, no matter where it does so.

That brings me to the title of this article, "Mr. President — Cursing or Blessing?"

The turbulence I mentioned at the outset was full-blown in the White House the week of July 14. It was no doubt stirred and fanned by the breath of the old serpent, the devil. The winds of inter–White House turf war continued this week just past.

President Trump, always one to keep the mainstream media and the rest of us off-balance with his actions and tweets, did so in his own inimitable fashion. He removed his chief of staff, Reince Priebus, and replaced him with Ret. Gen. John Kelly. But, it wasn't that cut and dried.

Mixed in with the shakeup of White House staff was the matter of the desire (the necessity, in my view) of getting rid of the so-called leakers. These holdover personnel from the previous administration were wreaking havoc on the president's efforts to move forward with his agenda.

Sean Spicer, the communications director, was also let go. In his place came one Anthony Scaramucci. We know now that this mouthpiece seems to have no boundaries on usage of language. And that is what inspired this commentary. Mr. Scaramucci, chosen by the president to clean out the leakers, began his new job by talking with a reporter of *The New Yorker,* the hip New York City magazine that looks down on the rest of us as most generally just not "with it."

The president's new man in the communication director's seat indeed began to communicate. He did so in a cursing rant he thought was, but actually was not, "off the record." It was so bad that it apparently caused Chris Wallace of Fox News to blush when he read it. Wallace said, "I am no choir boy. But I have never heard anybody . . . in private say some of the things that Scaramucci said in public about Reince Priebus and Steve Bannon."[99]

It was anger, framed in sewer language, whether real or feigned for impact, that to this point we hadn't had a close associate of a sitting president use. I'm no choirboy, either, having grown up among my male peers as a youngster in junior high school, high school, university, and even the U.S. military. The report of Scaramucci's vulgar tirade made me feel uneasy. I don't like one so closely associated with my president using such ungodly language. It somehow sullies the office.

Of course, I realize that this president sometimes uses less than godly language himself. I don't like that, either. This I say for those of you who were about to ask, "Well, how about Trump's language?"

When I first heard the report of Anthony Scaramucci spewing forth as he did, my mind began searching for words I once heard reported as spoken by our first president on the use of vile language.

---

99. http://thehill.com/homenews/media/344315-foxs-wallace-calls-mccain-unplugged.

I soon found the quote. It was George Washington, then the head general of the Continental Army during the Revolutionary War, issuing a written command that said the following:

> The General is sorry to be informed — that the foolish and wicked practice of profane cursing and swearing, a vice heretofore little known in an American army, is growing into a fashion — he hopes the officers will, by example as well as influence, endeavor to check it, and that both they and the men will reflect that we can have little hope of the blessing of Heaven on our arms, if we insult it by impiety and folly; added to this, it is a vice so mean and low, without any temptation, that every man of sense and character detests and despises it.[100]

We have, of course, become a profane nation in ways that would make our first president wonder, no doubt, how the Lord of heaven could let us proceed further as a country. As much as I back Donald J. Trump and his much-beleaguered presidency, I must ask: Mr. President — cursing or blessing?

How can we expect the continued blessings of the Almighty when we allow such cesspool thinking and expression as Mr. Scaramucci used representing a president of the United States, therefore representing us?

Anthony Scaramucci might be a tough New York guy who uses street language to get things done. He did not have the right to use it while in an office that represents the rest of us, many of whom still prefer a godlier means of expression.

It is good that another general of excellent reputation, General John Kelly, evidently feels the same way. Scaramucci's vulgar tirade to *The New Yorker,* in concert with his demand to be allowed to bypass the new chief of staff, General Kelly, resulted in him being asked to leave the communications position he had occupied for only ten days.

Wise decision, Mr. President. Please consider the following regarding your own language.

God's Word says the following: "Let no corrupt communication proceed out of your mouth, but that which is good to the use of edifying, that it may minister grace unto the hearers" (Ephesians 4:29).

Even more to the point, James put it this way:

---

100. George Washington, Extract from the Orderly Book of the Army under Command of Washington, dated at Head Quarters, in the city of New York, August 1770; reported in *American Masonic Register and Literary Companion,* Volume 1, 1829.

But the tongue can no man tame; it is an unruly evil, full of deadly poison. Therewith bless we God, even the Father; and therewith curse we men, which are made after the similitude of God. Out of the same mouth proceedeth blessing and cursing. My brethren, these things ought not so to be. Doth a fountain send forth at the same place sweet water and bitter? Can the fig tree, my brethren, bear olive berries? either a vine, figs? so can no fountain both yield salt water and fresh. Who is a wise man and endued with knowledge among you? let him shew out of a good conversation his works with meekness of wisdom. But if ye have bitter envying and strife in your hearts, glory not, and lie not against the truth. This wisdom descendeth not from above, but is earthly, sensual, devilish (James 3:8–15).

Ezekiel 38–39 and Nukes

Today's sense of impending nuclear exchange hearkens somewhat back to when I was a teenager. I remember sitting in the high school library looking at a daily newspaper. The headline was about Nikita Khrushchev, the Soviet premiere, threatening the use of hydrogen bombs if his plans for eastern Europe were resisted by the West.

Rumor had it among us high schoolers that nuclear war would commence on this particular Friday. I was in the library thinking on such possibility. The world would end this very day, so the tale was told.

I guess I was sort of into issues and events of the times, just as I am these many decades later. Although a kid, I was concerned, but certainly couldn't let on to my fellow students — especially not my macho pals, who all were saying "bring it on" to the Ruskies. They seemed to have no fear or regard for what would happen if ol' Khrushchev decided to nuke America. I did think about it and was, frankly, quite worried.

Now we have a 30-year-old North Korean despot even uglier than Nikita threatening to send his newly developed, nuclear-tipped missiles to Guam and even to somewhere within the U.S. homeland. I haven't paid much attention to the threat during the current "crisis," even though it was issued by a true lunatic rather than the calculating, totally aware Khrushchev — i.e., the Soviet dictator realized what it would mean for him, personally, should he be so foolhardy as to initiate nuclear war. I'm not certain Kim Jong-un has the same degree of realization.

Being three-quarters of a century old currently might make the difference in my degree of concern then, in 1958, versus now. Even though sense of my own mortality at 16 was almost nonexistent, I was fearful. The present threat has many people today thinking like I did back then. The current nuclear threat doesn't concern me at all, although my knowledge of my own mortality now is with me every waking hour.

What's the difference in the young Terry's concern and the old Terry's lack thereof, do you think? It must be more than merely naïveté about geopolitical, diplomatic interaction that might bring on or avert nuclear catastrophe that caused me to worry. It can't just be that I can now, through reasoning ability guided by experience, assuage fear because I'm much wiser at this age about how nuclear-armed states always pull up short of using those weapons of mass destruction.

One thing is sure: I have no such confidence in human agents who have their fingers on the nuclear triggers. I have no doubt that one day those triggers will be pulled. Preparation is underway in every direction we look. Nuclear war is looming like the mystical sword of Damocles over this powder-keg world.

Pakistan and India threaten each other with their nuclear stockpiles. The big, nuclear-muscle boys — America, China, and Russia — look warily at each other through satellite-computer guardians 24/7.

Israel stands ready to invoke the Samson Option. If it looks like the use of nuclear weapons is all that will stop an attack that would mean the end of the Jewish state, they will go to any such length necessary.

And this brings us to the title of our commentary today. Iran stands on the brink of developing nuclear capability even more threatening than that of the North Koreans. Previous U.S. presidential administrations — particularly those of Bill Clinton and Barack Obama — made "deals" they promised would make the whole world safer from nuclear war. The deals they made with both North Korea and with the Iranian regimes, however, have brought us to now having to act perhaps precipitously, or else face certain nuclear war in the not-too-distant future.

Iran, as Bible prophecy students know, is the nation that occupies the area that was ancient Persia. Persia is foretold by the prophet Ezekiel to mount an all-out assault against Israel as part of the Gog-Magog coalition.

It is strongly expected that North Korea has provided the Iranians with nuclear warheads or with the technology necessary to produce nuclear weapons. Iran is far advanced in missile technology, and it is only a matter of time until it is able to fit nuclear warheads to those missiles, presuming it hasn't done so already.

The Trump administration has led the way in imposing sanctions on Iran to stop development of the missile program. If it can't be halted, Israel will almost certainly take military action to try to destroy Iran's nuclear development capability.

America's most recent action has caused the Iranian regime to ramp up its call for the destruction of America and Israel. The following tells of that rogue nation's anger:

> DUBAI — Iran's parliament gave initial approval on Sunday to a bill to boost spending on Tehran's missile program and the elite Revolutionary Guards in retaliation for new sanctions imposed by the United States.
>
> Lawmakers overwhelmingly approved the outlines of the bill to "counter America's terrorist and adventurist actions" as some chanted "Death to America," the state broadcaster IRIB reported.
>
> The measure came in retaliation to legislation passed by US Congress and signed by US President Donald Trump in early August to impose new sanctions on Iran over its missile program.[101]

With one of the primary Gog-Magog force members about to go nuclear, there should be reason for greatly increased worry. Like the North Koreans, they are a regime blood-vowed to destroy its enemy. In the case of North Korea, it is South Korea and America that constitute the enemies who inspire the blood vow. With Iran, of course, it's Israel and America that must be obliterated.

However, in the case of Iran, we know from prophecy that it is going to act on that blood oath. In North Korea, if they are a factor in bringing the world to nuclear Armageddon, it will be much later, in consort with the "kings of the east" of Revelation chapters 9 and 16.

So, why am I "calm (old) Terry" as opposed to "16-year-old, fearful Terry" in the high school library, reading magazines and newspapers instead of studying in study hall? The danger is imminently graver now than then.

The answer, of course, is Bible prophecy. The old Terry knows and believes what God's Word has to say about the outcome of all this nuclear saber-rattling. Bible prophecy tells me that Iran is not destroyed by the

---

101. "Iran Eyes More Funds for Missiles, Troops after US Sanctions — Middle East," *Jerusalem Post*, August 13, 2017.

time of the Gog-Magog attack, which is yet future. Israel is not destroyed at that time, or ever.

Bible prophecy tells me that Iran, Russia, Turkey, and all the others of that force come in a conventional, not nuclear, attack. Something has obviously happened by that time to cause nuclear weaponry to not be used — at least not in a world-rending way.

The other nations, we are told by Ezekiel in chapters 38 and 39, are there, too. They send only a diplomatic note of protest when they see that great, satanic, Gog-led force descend toward Israel. Nuclear weaponry, again it is obvious, hasn't yet been used in a world-destroying way by that time.

Again, Jesus said it will be business as usual at the time of His "revealing." That is, people will be doing business as usual, according to the Lord's "days of Noah, days of Lot" prophecy (Matthew 24:36–42 and Luke 17:26–30). At the time of the Rapture, therefore, there will have been no world-shattering nuclear conflict or major catastrophic event on a global scale, either.

If only that worried 16-year-old Terry had studied Ezekiel 38–39 in that study hall in 1958. . . .

Bannon Versus Globalists and Bible Prophecy

Observers of end-times events who believe there is an advancing power grab by the globalist elite look with interest at Steve Bannon's exit as President Trump's chief strategist. National politics that make up part of the intrigues going on in the White House are secondary at most, so the thinking goes. Matters involving the long-sought changed world order are all-important in considering the most recent developments in Washington, D.C.

On the secular side, many — perhaps most — media pundits speculate that the Republican *establishment* types have succeeded in convincing Trump to get rid of the ultranationalist Bannon (as they view him), so Congress will work with Trump in achieving a more rational legislative agenda. These, of course, have no concept that there is a much deeper meaning to all of this.

I take that back to some extent. They do have a strangely twisted thought process that touches on Bible prophecy yet to unfold.

Bannon, it seems, according to a number of these pundits, has an *apocalyptic* view of the world. He believes that Trump and America somehow are destined to be involved in world history as it winds up.

The media types who purport this to be the case don't go far into this accusation. That is, they don't give us details about how Mr. Bannon's end-times view might have affected any outcome he personally desired to achieve while advising the president.

It is indeed strange . . . the secular media types sensing and commenting that there is some weird connection to apocalyptic matters in all these goings-on.

There is such visceral hatred for this president that when anything bad happens, his enemies in media and everyone else find ways to link Trump to the evil involved. For example, this was the case in the recent white supremacist activities and the clashes over confederate statues in Charlottesville. Trump's statements on the matters involved were made to look by mainstream news types like the president took the side of the KKK and the neo-Nazis. Anyone who heard the president's remarks knows the opposite is true. He plainly called out the evil. But he made the mistake of saying there was evil on both sides. That gave the haters all the fodder needed to link him directly to the skinheads and all the rest.

In the same sense, Steve Bannon is linked by the mainstream news types to a mindset like the ayatollahs who want to bring on their version of the apocalypse. That is as deeply into Bannon's "apocalyptic" worldview of geopolitics as they wish to delve. If they can make that linkage in the mind of the American voters — the evil of Steve Bannon to the Iranian religious madmen — their mission is achieved.

Evil that lurks within the mainstream media as it currently exists, in my view, is the real linkage to the chaos now being perpetrated. It is Luciferian. It is part of the Saul Alinsky blueprint being utilized by the George Soros-globalist types to bring America down so her power to influence is diminished . . . so her wealth can be redistributed to the have-nots in order to secure power bases for the globalists constructing the changed world order they desire.

Something seems to me to be boiling beneath the obvious dismissal of Bannon from Trump's advisory team in the White House. I have no idea of what that might be. Steve Bannon made the following statement shortly after leaving his post: "The Trump presidency that we fought for, and won, is over." Bannon said further, "We still have a huge movement, and we will make something of this Trump presidency. But that presidency is over. It'll be something else. And there'll be all kinds of fights, and there'll be good days and bad days, but *that* presidency is over."[102] He said also, in a statement unfortunately laced with profanity, that he was going

102. https://www.weeklystandard.com/peter-j-boyer/bannon-the-trump-presidency-that-we-fought-for-and-won-is-over.

to fight the globalists every step of the way. Well, you had better have the Lord at your side in that effort, Mr. Bannon. The globalists, knowingly or not, have the most powerful being ever to be created as their leader. Lucifer is determined to prepare the planet for the coming of his man of sin.

There is no political strategy, even by a top strategist like yourself, that can alter Satan's plan for his Antichrist regime.

But the Lord did so, and with ease, in this last presidential election. He is still in complete control. Trump is God's man for this troubled hour as we move swiftly toward the Rapture of the Church.

Meantime, prayer by God's people is the primary tool that must lead the fight against the globalists. Prophetically speaking, the battle is already won!

> He that sitteth in the heavens shall laugh: the LORD shall have them in derision. Then shall he speak unto them in his wrath, and vex them in his sore displeasure. Yet have I set my king upon my holy hill of Zion. I will declare the decree: the LORD hath said unto me, Thou art my Son; this day have I begotten thee. Ask of me, and I shall give thee the heathen for thine inheritance, and the uttermost parts of the earth for thy possession. Thou shalt break them with a rod of iron; thou shalt dash them in pieces like a potter's vessel (Psalm 2:4–9).

35

September 2017: Prelude to Planetary Madness

News reports forewarn a nation descending toward chaos. Forces have obviously been set in motion that threaten to tear America apart. This instigation is purposeful, I have no doubt, and is spawned by Satan.

Saul Alinsky's blueprint to bring about chaos so the one-world-order builders' perfect, utopian plan can eventually rise from the ashes of this republic is well underway. George Soros and all the other globalist elite have little trouble finding minions to carry out the carnage. Lucifer's demonic followers throw fuel of hatred on the fires of anarchy, and we see the incendiary results in our hourly headlines.

A 1979 Hollywood production remade in 1980, 1985, and 2015, I believe, gives a fictionalized look at the real world to come when God the Holy Spirit removes from acting as restrainer on the already half-crazed minds of earth-dwellers.

Mad Max is the disturbing foreshadowing of things to come when the Body of Christ — the Church — is removed in the Rapture.

Although made in Australia, the movie was Americanized in that the Aussie accents were dubbed over in the American-English accent to give the sense of the carnage taking place in the United States. The storyline, set in the near future, portrayed a world gone mad with evil. The dystopian film presented in graphic terms people's unrestrained actions against their fellow human beings.

Of course, the creators of the film had no idea that Bible prophecy presents just such a scenario — at least, I don't think that entered their thinking.

We find the *real* story of things to come in this regard in the following Scripture:

> And now ye know what withholdeth that he might be revealed in his time. For the mystery of iniquity doth already

work: only he who now [restrains] will [restrain], until he be taken out of the way. And then shall that Wicked be revealed, whom the Lord shall consume with the spirit of his mouth, and shall destroy with the brightness of his coming (2 Thessalonians 2:6–8).

When the Holy Spirit withdraws from restraining wickedness perpetrated by fallen mankind, the world will instantly become worse than the fictional world of *Mad Max*. The present hostilities and chaos being churned by the would-be masters — both human and demonic — will swiftly result in destructiveness beyond description. We are indeed currently enduring a prelude to planetary madness.

But the Creator has not left us in a state of hopelessness despite the rioting and insanity going on in our nation and world. The Lord has provided a way to escape the carnage so vividly described in Revelation by John the Apostle while exiled on Patmos two thousand years ago.

I wrote the following for the book, *The Departure: God's Next Catastrophic Intervention into Earth's History*:

First, the Departure

Before God's wrath falls, in the twinkling of an eye (an atomos of time), millions of Christians — those born again by believing in the shed blood of Christ on the cross two millennia ago for salvation — will vanish from the earth's surface. The departure — the Rapture — will bring planet-rending disturbances to an already reeling world of nonbelievers.

God has been patient in allowing the world to see the Tribulation storm alerts. He has shown mercy and grace, as there is no prophecy given that must be fulfilled in order for the Rapture to happen. The departure can take place at any moment.

Getting out the warnings is the duty of spiritual meteorologists. This is a commission each author in *The Departure: God's Next Catastrophic Intervention into Earth's History* takes most seriously. We prayerfully hope many, upon reading the book, will take to heart the call of the only Lord and God of all Creation, who prompted the Apostle Peter to write: "The Lord is not slack concerning His promise, as some men count slackness; but is longsuffering to us-ward, not willing that any should perish, but that all should come to repentance" (2 Peter 3:9).

This is the only way to be saved from the sin that separates the sinner from the Heavenly Father. This is the only way to be secure from the approaching Tribulation storm.

> If thou shalt confess with thy mouth the Lord Jesus, and shalt believe in thine heart that God hath raised Him from the dead, thou shalt be saved. For with the heart man believeth unto righteousness; and with the mouth confession is made unto salvation (Romans 10:9–10).

We join with the prophet John, who wrote, "He which testifieth these things saith, Surely I come quickly. Amen. Even so, come, Lord Jesus" (Revelation 22:20).

Putin Predicts Coming Prince

One would almost think that Russian President Vladimir Putin has been studying prophetic Scripture in the Bible. He has predicted that the entity that becomes the ultimate leader in Artificial Intelligence (AI) will rule planet Earth. His is a most interesting prognostication. Here's an excerpt from the news item laying out ol' Vlad's foretelling.

> MOSCOW (AP) — Russian President Vladimir Putin says that whoever reaches a breakthrough in developing artificial intelligence will come to dominate the world.
>
> Putin, speaking Friday at a meeting with students, said the development of AI raises "colossal opportunities and threats that are difficult to predict now."[103]

The former KGB operative turned dictator/oligarch of the nucleus of what was the Soviet Union before *perestroika, glasnost,* the fall of the Berlin Wall, and finally the dissolution of the U.S.S.R., said further that "the one who becomes the leader in this sphere will be the ruler of the world."

The Russian warned that "it would be strongly undesirable if someone wins a monopolist position." He pledged that Russia would share its knowhow in artificial intelligence with other nations. Putin predicted that drones will fight future wars. He said, "When one party's drones are destroyed by drones of another, it will have no other choice but to surrender."

The Putin prediction would be amusing, if not so much on the eerie side — kind of like Gog of Ezekiel 38–39 "prophesying" the emergence of "the prince that shall come" of Daniel 9:26–27.

---

103. "Putin: Leader in Artificial Intelligence Will Rule World," *Houston Chronicle,* September 2, 2017.

We have mentioned numerous times that Vladimir Putin displays characteristics the future leader of the Gog-Magog attack will possess, according to the prophet Ezekiel. Putin, here, is delving into perhaps not the characteristics of Antichrist, but certainly into the technological realm Revelation seems to indicate that the future führer will have at his disposal.

The Russian says that the leader in such advanced technology will eventually rule the world. To be sure, Antichrist is prophesied to rule over most of the world at a point during the seven-year Tribulation era. His rule will be brief and chaotic, but it will be brutal and, according to Jesus Himself, will bring a time upon the people of the planet worse than any before or after.

Artificial Intelligence will mark his despotic control. He will, through the most advanced AI technology, do the following:

> And he causeth all, both small and great, rich and poor, free and bond, to receive a mark in their right hand, or in their foreheads: and that no man might buy or sell, save he that had the mark, or the name of the beast, or the number of his name (Revelation 13:16–17).

But AI is, perhaps, prophesied to go much deeper than Antichrist's 666 computer controls. Some would say there will come a destructive military force that appears to be completely robotic, commanded through AI to assault Jerusalem during the time known as the Day of the Lord. It is a terrifying description of a superhuman — or perhaps hybrid or robotic — force destined to riffle the city and ravish its women, according to prophecy. Read about what some call Joel's Army (Joel 2:1–11).[104]

> AI is a hot topic, causing an uproar even among some of the well-known leaders in its development.
>
> SpaceX and Tesla CEO Elon Musk got into a spat recently on Twitter with Facebook's Mark Zuckerberg over the dangers of artificial intelligence.
>
> Musk urged a group of governors to proactively regulate AI, which he views as a "fundamental risk to the existence of human civilization."
>
> "Until people see robots going down the street killing people, they don't know how to react because it seems so ethereal," Musk said.

---

104. I wrote a short story of a fictional nature about Joel's Army years ago for a filmmaker, http://www.raptureready.com/2017/09/09/joels-army-a-short-story/.

Zuckerberg shot back, saying fearmongering about AI is "irresponsible."[105]

Many scientists and futurists are declaring that at some point, major wars will be waged by beings of intelligence superior to that of mere mortals. However, Bible prophecy tells that, ultimately, it is human blood that will flow to the bridle reins following the fighting at Armageddon. The corpses of millions of human beings will have to be buried following the battle of Gog and Magog.

Seduction in the Storm

We are currently writing a book called *Deceivers: Exposing Evil Seducers and Their Last-Days Deception.* I say "we" are writing it because it is to be one of my books that presents a compilation of chapters by some of the most recognizable names. These include Todd Strandberg, Jan Markell, Dr. Dave Reagan, Gary Stearman, Dr. Gary Frazier, and others.

Jesus, while sitting on the Mount of Olives with His disciples nearly two millennia ago, gave as His first forewarning that, in the last days, deceivers will be in abundance. Certainly, there is deception at every level at this present time in human history.

Ruminating over the book we are in process of writing, the thought came that we have on the front burner of headline news a storm-like combination of signals harboring seduction and deception that begs exposure.

The primary foretellings I would like to look at that Jesus gave while answering His disciples' question — "What will be the sign of your coming and of the end of the age?" — include the following:

1. There will be distress of nations with perplexity.
2. There will be wars and rumors of wars.
3. There will be earthquakes in various places.
4. The seas and waves will be roaring.
5. Nation will rise against nation.

During this last-days storminess, Jesus said, there will be deceivers and great deception. I would like to consider for our purposes here a peculiar seduction within the end-of-days storm that is assaulting this generation:

---

105. Rosalie Chan, "Humanlike Robots Provoke Questions about our Humanity," Religion News Service, https://www.houstonchronicle.com/life/houston-belief/article/Houston-features-headline-The-uncanny-valley-11998150.php, August 26, 2017.

1. There will be distress of nations with perplexity.

We have only to consider recent news to validate this Olivet prophecy by the Lord.

The national and world economic distresses are phenomenal. America's own national debt is right at $20 trillion. The unfunded liabilities for the nation exceed $200 trillion. The world at large has economic circumstances that might not be as large, but that are just as perplexing to those trying to deal with the problem.

2. There will be wars and rumors of wars.

At present, we see one of the most troubling confrontations since the Cuban missile crisis of 1962.

The North Korean dictator Kim Jong-un threatens to launch hydrogen-bomb-tipped ICBMs at the United States and our possessions and allies. Whether he has this capability is a matter of conjecture. But the threat is there.

Other rumors of potential wars can be found without effort simply by thinking on Israel and those blood-vowed to remove the Jewish state from the planet.

The cold war might again become reality soon — with Russia and China building massive military forces even at the expense of Russia's already-dire economic circumstances on the one hand and China's desire to, for its own benefit, interact commercially with other nations on the other.

Rumors of war are everywhere we look on the geopolitical horizon.

3. There will be earthquakes in various places.

Most recently, while hurricanes Harvey and Irma devastated portions of the U.S. mainland, an 8.2 earthquake struck Mexico.

Swarms of earthquakes up to 5.3 on the Richter Scale continue to shake the infamous Yellowstone Caldera region, causing alarm even among seasoned, professional seismologists.

Earthquakes make much of the Middle East quiver on a regular basis. They are occurring in "various places" at most every hour of every day.

4. The seas and waves will be roaring.

There's no question that the literal seas and waves have been roaring as of late. Again, Harvey and Irma were given 24/7 coverage on practically every news channel over recent days.

But I believe the Lord was prophesying mainly about figurative seas and waves roaring. The peoples of the world are indeed in tumult. Europe is rioting because of economic turbulence. The Arab world is often in uproar against the hated Israel and against each other. America boils with clashes fomented, in many cases, by thugs paid to stir trouble in our city streets.

The seas and waves, both figurative and literal, are roaring.

5. Nation will rise against nation.

We have looked many times at the term "nation" in this prophecy Jesus gave. The root of the word for "nation," here, is the Greek word *ethnos*. This means that in the days just before Christ's Second Advent (Revelation 19:1), there will be great strife of one racial group against another.

Certainly, these kinds of conflicts exist everywhere across the planet — including within our own borders. All we must do to understand this is to look at the white supremacist and Black Lives Matter groups to see the reality of this prophecy taking place in our own time. And we are at least seven years away from Christ's Second Advent when Armageddon will be raging.

So, we can conclude that we are in the beginning of the great, end-times storm about which Jesus forewarned. Now, to look at the peculiar seduction that I believe is taking place as part of Satan's deception that is, perhaps, at the eye of this prophetic storm.

The following news story helps make my point:

> Sure, the US has a National Flood Insurance Program, but who's covered by it? Besides, the Program was already $24 billion in debt by 2014 largely due to hurricanes Katrina and Sandy. With total costs of Harvey estimated at $200 billion or more, and Irma threatening to cause far more damage than that, where's the money going to come from?
>
> It took an actual fight just to push the first few billion dollars in emergency aid for Houston through Congress, with four Texan senators voting against of all people. Who then will vote for half a trillion or so in aid? And even if they do, where would it come from?
>
> Trump's plans for an infrastructure fund were never going to be an easy sell in Washington, and every single penny he might have gotten for it would now have to go towards repairing existing roads and bridges, not updating them — necessary as that may be — let alone new construction.

Towns, cities, states, they're all maxed out as things are, with hugely underfunded pension obligations and crumbling infrastructure of their own. They're going to come calling on the feds, but Washington is hitting its debt ceiling. All the numbers are stacked against any serious efforts at rebuilding whatever Harvey and Irma have blown to pieces or drowned.[106]

The author paints the direst portrait of the results the storms will bring to America. (Read the complete piece via information in the endnote to get the full impact.) And I agree completely with the writer's assessment of the situation — that is, if I didn't know "the rest of the story," as Paul Harvey used to say.

The world's economies, as I have written many times, are intricately, inextricably linked to that of America. That's why I build my thoughts on things that are likely to happen — prophetically speaking — upon the American model. If this nation comes crashing down, the whole world will be sucked into the vortex caused by the collapse.

Jesus tells us that, like in the days of Noah and of Lot, people at the time of His next catastrophic intervention into history will be buying, selling, planting, and marrying — doing all the normal activities of life. I believe, because it is Jesus who predicts the buying, selling, etc., that it will be far more than normal in its reality. I believe we are about to see an economic boom.

Somehow, some way — I don't presume to know how — all the destruction taking place now because of the hurricane damage might well turn out to be a catalyst for the prophesied building, buying, and selling Jesus foretold that day atop the Mount of Olives.

The "seduction" I believe wrapped up in all of this might well reside within the good economic times that could result from the rebuilding — that is, the economic boom that might be on its way might take people's thoughts even further from God. The seduction just might produce the "think-not generation" that Jesus prophesied will be doing anything but giving consideration to God and eternity: "Therefore be ye also ready: for in such an hour as ye think not the Son of man cometh" (Matthew 24:44).

Donald Trump is a builder perhaps unparalleled in history. Could it be that he is president of the United States for just this moment in regard to Jesus' "days of Noah, days of Lot" prophecy?

---

106. Raul Illargi Meijer, "After the Storms Are Over: America Can't Afford to Rebuild, Zero Hedge," September 10, 2017, https://www.zerohedge.com/news/2017-09-09/after-storms-are-over-america-cant-afford-rebuild.

36

October 2017: Rapture and Watching

Recently I listened to a well-known preacher on his TV program saying something to the effect that only those "watching" for Jesus will go to be with Christ in the Rapture. He defined "watching" as Christians who truly want Jesus to return and who believe with great faith that He will call them to Himself in that great Rapture event.

This didn't totally surprise me, because this preacher has, in my opinion, never been clear in his thoughts on the *security* of the believer — that is, the "once saved, always saved" doctrine, as the sometimes hotly debated term goes.

While his remark that "to be watching is commanded by the Lord" is scripturally correct, I reject that it is possible for even one truly born-again person to be left behind when Christ says, "Come up hither" (Revelation 4:1). I believe the Apostle Paul made very clear who will be taken in the Rapture when Jesus calls the Church. Paul, in revealing the "mystery" of the Rapture, said the following:

> Behold, I shew you a mystery; We shall not all sleep, but we shall all be changed, in a moment, in the twinkling of an eye, at the last trump: for the trumpet shall sound, and the dead shall be raised incorruptible, and we shall be changed (1 Corinthians 15:51–52).

Paul, given the key to this mystery by the Lord Jesus Himself, tells us clearly that *all* will be changed. It will take place in less than a microsecond. That's the Rapture!

The pronoun "we" is all-inclusive as given in this context. It means all who are born again — the Church.

There is no room for any believer to be left behind in Paul's declaration. Those who are truly *saved* will go in that twinkling-of-an-eye moment.

Paul, under divine inspiration, further enlightens concerning the security of the believer:

> For I am persuaded, that neither death, nor life, nor angels, nor principalities, nor powers, nor things present, nor things to come, nor height, nor depth, nor any other creature, shall be able to separate us from the love of God, which is in Christ Jesus our Lord (Romans 8:38–39).

Again, Paul uses a pronoun that includes all those who believe in God's way to salvation — Jesus Christ — the only *righteousness* God the Father recognizes. Paul, under that divine inspiration, says that nothing and no one will ever be able to separate "us" from the love of God. Paul is undeniably talking about the born again because he goes on to say that the "love" of which he speaks is "in Christ Jesus our Lord."

The pronoun this time is "our," meaning those he is talking about — including Paul himself — who are born again. The TV preacher then said that watching for Christ means one is "worthy" to stand before the Lord on that Rapture day — again implying strongly that unless one is watching, he or she is not going to go in the Rapture.

He used the following Scripture in that declaration: "Watch ye therefore, and pray always, that ye may be accounted worthy to escape all these things that shall come to pass, and to stand before the Son of man" (Luke 21:36).

Some years ago, I addressed the matter of being "worthy" in God's holy eyes.

What does it mean to be "worthy," as given in this Rapture example? Again, the answer is wrapped up in the same name as before: Jesus. Jesus is the only person "worthy," in God's holy eyes, to be in the heavenly realm.

Remember what Jesus said to a man who addressed Him as "Good Master"? "And Jesus said unto him, Why callest thou me good? none is good, save one, that is, God" (Luke 18:19).

Jesus, the second person of the Godhead, was not seeking to chastise the man for addressing Him this way. The Lord was confirming that He is indeed God, the only good, the only righteousness. Righteousness is the only ticket to heaven — either through the portal of death or the Rapture. Only through Jesus can a person enter the heavenly realm.

Jesus spoke of this all-important matter when he addressed Nicodemus: "Jesus answered and said unto him, Verily, verily, I say unto thee, Except a man be born again, he cannot see the kingdom of God" (John 3:3).

God's Word says about fallen mankind, "As it is written, There is none righteous, no, not one" (Romans 3:10) and "For all have sinned and come short of the glory of God" (Romans 3:23).

So Jesus is the only person "worthy" to enter heaven. It is through Him that any of us are worthy to stand before Him in that heavenly realm. That is the truth found in the Scripture in question.

On a less magnificent scale, the word "worthy" in this passage means that we should be in a constant mindset of prayerful repentance. We should always want to be found "worthy" — cleansed of all unrighteousness, as stated in 1 John 1:9, so that we will hear our Lord say to us on that day, "Well done, good and faithful servant" (Matthew 25:23).

Many of God's children will doubtlessly lose rewards at the bema, also called the judgment seat of Christ, for not being watchful and not listening for their Lord's call in the Rapture. But, they will make that fantastic trip into heaven, every single one, because of the Lamb of God who redeemed them.

Trump: "Peace Has to Happen"

It is inevitable. Peace in the Middle East must happen, according to President Donald Trump.

The president, while being interviewed on former Governor Mike Huckabee's initial TBN program, made the declaration: "I want to give that a shot before I even think about moving the embassy to Jerusalem." He said further, "If we can make peace between the Palestinians and Israel, I think it'll lead to ultimately peace in the Middle East, which has to happen."[107]

In June of 2017, Trump signed a temporary order keeping the American embassy in Tel Aviv. This follows the actions of presidents preceding him. Some see this as breaking a promise he made while on the 2016 presidential campaign trail. He received rousing ovations every time he declared he would move the U.S. embassy to Jerusalem, the city Israel claims as its capital.

Mr. Trump has said on numerous occasions that his administration is working on a peace plan between Israel and the Palestinians that will result in peace for the whole region. He has appointed his son-in-law, Jared Kushner, as unofficial diplomat in charge of working to accomplish peace in the Middle East.

Others — including the Benjamin Netanyahu-led government — deny that the president has abandoned the idea of moving the embassy. In his statement that he wants to give peace a chance before moving the

---

107. https://www.jpost.com/Israel-News/Politics-And-Diplomacy/Israeli-politi-
    cians-bash-Trump-for-delaying-embassy-move-506946.

embassy, Trump simply means, in their view, that the move is postponed. To force such an action at this moment in the current volatile geopolitical climate would likely ramp up hostilities.

To those who view the world through the prism of Bible prophecy from the pre-Millennial, pre-Tribulation perspective, the president's declaration and decision on the embassy move should not come as surprise.

Like every other prophetic indicator on the world horizon, the fact that there is a continuing drive to force peace between Israel and its enemy neighbors is simply something that must be in view while final prophecies near fulfillment. Like Mr. Trump says, peace between Israel and its closest enemy neighbor "has to happen," from the human point of view.

Like all the world has cried for decades, as wrapped neatly in the lyrics of the song by John Lennon, we must "give peace a chance."

But that much-ballyhooed peace process leaves out the one essential ingredient that can make it come to pass. God is ignored. The very Prince of Peace, the Lord Jesus Christ, is not even considered in the humanistic effort. As a matter of fact, His holy name is ridiculed and mocked at every turn by most of the diplomatic world. Christ is viewed in most instances as the holdup to peace rather than the solution to the hatred and war-making that has dominated human history.

Mr. President, much of your political — electoral — base is made up of those of us who support Israel. We want peace for Israel, the Middle East, the United States, and the world. We know, however, from God's prophetic Word, that there will be no peace until the Prince of Peace rules and reigns in the hearts and minds of mankind.

The present call for peace is addressed by the Apostle Paul as follows: "For when they shall say, Peace and safety; then sudden destruction cometh upon them, as travail upon a woman with child; and they shall not escape" (1 Thessalonians 5:3).

Mr. President, peace will happen. It will come in two distinctively opposite forms.

The first peace will be a false peace brought about by the man of sin, the son of perdition: Antichrist. Daniel the prophet said the following about this false prince: "And through his policy also he shall cause craft to prosper in his hand; and he shall magnify himself in his heart, and by peace shall destroy many" (Daniel 8:25).

The other peace, the real peace, will be brought upon the planet at Christ's return to make all things right again. Jesus, the Prince of Peace, said the following just before leaving this sin-corrupted world: "Peace I leave with you, my peace I give unto you: not as the world giveth, give I unto you. Let not your heart be troubled, neither let it be afraid" (John 14:27).

Prophetic Indicators in View

Those who are watchful for Christ's soon return see this present time as inundated with significant signs. We often these days hear the term "convergence" bandied about. "Convergence" is used to define the coming together at once of most of the indicators the prophets, particularly Jesus, gave for the end of the Church Age (Age of Grace).

Two signals fitting within that definition, I believe, are in the news while we continue to observe these troubled but exciting times. I say "exciting" because the signs indicate that our Lord must be very near the moment when He shouts from the clouds of heaven, "Come up hither" (Revelation 4:1–2).

First, I would like to again look at the prophecy Jesus gave about when He will next be revealed to mankind in a dramatic way. As most readers probably know, I believe Christ was talking about our present time very near the end of the Church Age in this prophecy.

The Lord, as recorded in Matthew 24:36–42 and Luke 17:26–30, said it would be just like the days of Noah and the days of Lot when He intervenes or is revealed. I believe this must be the time of the Rapture. He said people will be buying, selling, building, planting, and marrying, etc. It will be business even *better* than usual when the Rapture occurs.

But, we have to look into other aspects of the way it was in Noah's day in order to find reference to the prophetic signal I wish to examine here. We go to Genesis 6 for that perspective:

> And God saw that the wickedness of man was great in the earth, and that every imagination of the thoughts of his heart was only evil continually. And it repented the LORD that he had made man on the earth, and it grieved him at his heart (Genesis 6:5–6).

Paul, the great Apostle, further enlightens on how it was in Noah's day:

> Because that, when they knew God, they glorified him not as God, neither were thankful; but became vain in their imaginations, and their foolish heart was darkened. Professing themselves to be wise, they became fools, and changed the glory of the incorruptible God into an image made like to corruptible man, and to birds, and fourfooted beasts, and creeping things.

Wherefore God also gave them up to uncleanness through the lusts of their own hearts, to dishonour their own bodies between themselves: who changed the truth of God into a lie, and worshipped and served the creature more than the Creator, who is blessed for ever. Amen (Romans 1:21–25).

The following item in the news is quite telling regarding how this generation fits within God's prophetic timeline:

"So many millennials read their horoscopes every day and believe them," [Coco] Layne, who is involved in a number of nonreligious spiritual practices, said. "It is a good reference point to identify and place people in the world."

Interest in spirituality has been booming in recent years while interest in religion plummets, especially among millennials. The majority of Americans now believe it is not necessary to believe in God to have good morals, a study from Pew Research Center released Wednesday found. The percentage of people between the ages of 18 and 29 who "never doubt existence of God" fell from 81% in 2007 to 67% in 2012.

Meanwhile, more than half of young adults in the U.S. believe astrology is a science. . . .

Melissa Jayne, owner of Brooklyn-based "metaphysical boutique" Catland, said she has seen a major uptick in interest in the occult in the past five years, especially among New Yorkers in their 20s. The store offers workshops like "Witchcraft 101," "Astrology 101," and a "Spirit Seance."

"Whether it be spell-casting, tarot, astrology, meditation and trance, or herbalism, these traditions offer tangible ways for people to enact change in their lives," she said.

Astrology isn't the only spiritual field overwhelmed by demand: Danielle Ayoka, the founder of spiritual subscription service Mystic Lipstick, said her customer base is growing exponentially. The self-described astrologer sells a "mystic box" subscription, which includes crystals, "reiki-infused bath salts," and incense customized to the unique energy of the current moon cycle for $14.99 a month. She says she's seen 75% increase in her audience in the past year.[108]

108. "Why Millennials Are Ditching Religion for Witchcraft and Astrology," MarketWatch, Rapture Ready News, October 21, 2017.

Second of the prophetic indicators appropriate to mention here involves the incessant assault by the globalist elite.

The drive to construct the New World Order, as President George Herbert Walker Bush termed it, continues at a stepped-up pace. President Donald J. Trump's call to "Make America Great Again" has sent the one-worlders into a frantic effort to get our thinking back on track . . . the track upon which President Obama faithfully took the United States, in line with recent presidents who came after Ronald Reagan, who, for the most part, was a staunch advocate for American sovereignty.

Now, the son of the first President Bush has weighed in, demonstrating where his strongest allegiance lies. Without mention of Trump's name, George W. Bush unloaded on any thought of America being given first place over the more important globalist agenda:

> Former President George W. Bush delivered a public repudiation of President Donald Trump's political identity, suggesting many aspects of the current administration are fueling division in the United States and around the world. . . .
>
> "We cannot wish globalism away," Bush said, noting that the United States must sustain "wise and sustained global engagement" for the future of the country.
>
> Bush indirectly accused Trump of fueling dangerous ideologies that threatened the unity of the United States and global stability, spending a large portion of his speech complaining about social ills in the country. . . .
>
> Bush urged Americans to "recover our own identity," citing a commitment to global engagement, free and international trade, and immigration.
>
> "We've seen nationalism distorted into nativism, and forgotten the dynamism that immigration has always brought to America," he lamented. . . .
>
> Bush's decision to publicly criticize Trump's presidency is unusual after he made a point of rarely challenging President Barack Obama while he was in office.[109]

George W. Bush had qualities I admired in a president. Holding to his father's desire to bring the world back to configuration like it was during the days of Babel is not one of them. Globalism is a satanic, not a godly,

109. Charlie Spiering, "George W. Bush Emerges to Bash Trump, 'Nativism': 'We Cannot Wish Globalism Away,' " Breitbart, October 21, 2017.

concept. It will eventuate, however. We are seeing the stage being set for producing the platform from which Antichrist's regime will rule with an iron fist.

Here's what the Lord says about the effort we see developing:

> The kings of the earth set themselves, and the rulers take counsel together, against the LORD, and against his anointed, saying, Let us break their bands asunder, and cast away their cords from us. He that sitteth in the heavens shall laugh: the LORD shall have them in derision. Then shall he speak unto them in his wrath, and vex them in his sore displeasure. Yet have I set my king upon my holy hill of Zion. I will declare the decree: the LORD hath said unto me, Thou art my Son; this day have I begotten thee. Ask of me, and I shall give thee the heathen for thine inheritance, and the uttermost parts of the earth for thy possession. Thou shalt break them with a rod of iron; thou shalt dash them in pieces like a potter's vessel (Psalm 2:2–9).

37

November 2017: Departure Near

(Author's note: Because I'm convicted that we are so near the time when Jesus will say "Come up hither," I wanted to again present an article, somewhat revised, from my past commentaries. It is vital that the Church be aware of the nearness of our departure.)

The Scripture is haunting. It echoes and reverberates throughout the spiritual hallways of the Church with each passing hour.

"Now the Spirit speaketh expressly, that in the latter times some shall depart from the faith, giving heed to seducing spirits, and doctrines of devils" (1 Timothy 4:1). This forewarning fits into the last-days pattern, also given by the Apostle Paul, in the familiar prophetic passage: "Let no man deceive you by any means: for that day shall not come, except there come a falling away first, and that man of sin be revealed, the son of Perdition" (2 Thessalonians 2:3).

The "falling away," *apostasia* in Greek, means a "departure from." Paul prophesied in 2 Timothy 4:1 that at the end of the Church Age, people will depart from the "faith." He foretells in 2 Thessalonians that this will be a general "falling away," the apostasy of the end time. What is this "faith" away from which people will fall, and who will fall away? Can the departure that God forewarned be recognized when it occurs?

"Faith," as here defined, must, by context, be the faith in the One who is at the heart of the gospel — faith in the Lord Jesus Christ as the Lamb of God, chosen from the foundation of the world to be the propitiation for the sin that separates fallen man from God. It is the faith you and I must have to confess that Jesus is the only begotten Son of God, and to believe in the deepest part of our spirits that God raised Him from the dead: "That if thou shalt confess with thy mouth the Lord Jesus, and shalt believe in thine heart that God hath raised him from the dead, thou shalt be saved" (Romans 10:9).

A person can't fall from a position (doctrinally speaking in this case) he never has attained. The "people," then, whom Paul the Apostle is writing about in 1 Timothy 4:1 and 2 Thessalonians 2:3 are those who have believed in Jesus Christ for salvation of their souls.

This brings us to the question: Can the departure be recognized when it occurs? To recognize that "falling away" when it begins to happen will almost certainly give the Christian attuned to God's will a heads-up on the nearness of the Tribulation era, thus to the nearness of the Rapture of the Church.

We have looked at the "faith" as faith in Jesus for salvation, and at the "people" who will "depart" from the faith as being the Church. Although there are those who think this departure includes the possibility of losing one's salvation, the "falling away" of 2 Thessalonians 2:3 cannot include that meaning. A quick look at Romans 8:38 and 39, to name just one security-of-the-believer passage, shows that God's Word teaches that the believer can't depart from the Heavenly Father to the point of losing his or her family status. Jesus, in John 17, makes that clear. I suggest that if you have questions about this, read the Scriptures I just mentioned.

What, then, is meant by "departing" from the "faith"? Glad you asked. The "faith" mentioned in 2 Thessalonians and 1 Timothy 2:3 is a collection of faith principles wrapped up in the Lord Jesus Christ. These are doctrines put forth by the Word of God, which is none other than the Lord Jesus: "In the beginning was the Word, and the Word was with God, and the Word was God" (John 1:1).

"People" at the time of the "falling away" will "depart" from the "faith" — the doctrines put forth by the Word of God, who is Jesus Christ. This departure will mark the generation of Christians at the very end of the Church Age.

The question most relevant to us today is: Are we seeing signals of the departure?

We have dissected and examined every end-time signal found in God's Word many times on the RaptureReady.com webpages: Israel again being in the land of promise; the European Union looking to be the reviving Roman Empire; Russia, Persia (modern Iran), and other nations shaping up as a nucleus that will one day form the Gog-Magog force of Ezekiel chapters 38 and 39; plus, all the other end-time characteristics of this generation.

However, I believe the most insidious of all that's taking place under the clever, devious hand of the devil is the departure from the faith currently being orchestrated by Lucifer, the fallen one. This falling away is evident to the spiritually discerning when looking at the church growth movement. This "seeker-friendly" approach to both the saved and the lost (all who don't know Christ) through New Age, corporation-type seminar seductiveness and brainwashing techniques that water down or completely eliminate true Bible doctrine is leading in a profound departure from the "faith once delivered" (see Jude 1:3).

The new paradigm instituted by the champions of the church-growth movement is the shift from New Testament Christianity to "New Spirituality-Driven Christianity."

Like in the modern corporate organization, invented in large part by German economic guru Peter Drucker, who mentored some of the leading designers of the church-growth movement, the system is more an organism than an organization adopting Drucker's model based upon Freudian psychology and Darwinian evolutionary principles. The individual is assigned a value and must fit in or be removed from the system. I heard one person of the movement say, "Pillars just hold things up. So, they need to be moved out of the way." Thus, those who hold to doctrine must get out of the way so no one will have their feelings hurt by talk of sin, blood atonement, and eternal punishment in the place called hell, if repentance is not forthcoming. Again, the Apostle Paul wrote God's view of this watering down of doctrine: "But though we, or an angel from heaven, preach any other gospel unto you than that which we have preached unto you, let him be accursed" (Galatians 1:8).

Are we at the point of departure from the faith that is prophesied for the very end of the Church Age? Maybe we can get a better sense by looking at one more area of Scripture pertaining to the matter:

> I charge thee therefore before God, and the Lord Jesus Christ, who shall judge the quick and the dead at his appearing and his kingdom; preach the word; be instant in season, out of season; reprove, rebuke, exhort with all longsuffering and doctrine. For the time will come when they will not endure sound doctrine; but after their own lusts shall they heap to themselves teachers, having itching ears; and they shall turn away their ears from the truth, and shall be turned unto fables (2 Timothy 4:1–4).

There is another prophetically scheduled departure to consider. It's the one to which we should be looking forward. It is a God-ordained departure that will remove every child of God of the Church Age — living and dead

— from the planet in one millisecond of time: "Looking for that blessed hope, and the glorious appearing of the great God and our Savior Jesus Christ" (Titus 2:13).

In God's Face

One of the pleasures in life at my advancing age is what I call conflab sessions. Yes, I know the legitimate word would be confab, not conflab, but the sessions are so informal that I use the urban rather than the mainstream dictionary term.

These conflab sessions are especially enjoyable between my sons and myself or between myself and my partner in the www.raptureready.com website, Todd Strandberg — "the Toddster," as I sometimes call him. He is like one of my boys — thus the informality.

We often go over the most pressing news of the day. Most always we discuss things from the prophetic perspective. When discussing the seemingly endless string of absurd, anti-God things going on, the bottom line usually expressed by these younger gentlemen is that it's a good thing they don't have divine power and authority, else — well — there would be a quick resolution to the absurdity and evil.

Being considerably more mature and mellow, I usually say things like, "Yes. I, too, am thankful you don't have such power and authority."

They, of course, realizing my wisdom from this senior vantage point, ignore my usual remark. I'm sure they remain unresponsive to the opinion because they so profoundly respect my . . . *ahemmm* . . . even temperament and sound judgment.

We do get deeply into the issues of the day, and there are plenty to explore, to be sure. More often than not, we end up talking about how the Lord seems to be putting up with so much, with people, in effect, telling Him, "In your face."

We discuss, for example, things like the actress who held up the award she had won, saying Jesus didn't give it to her. She then made a salacious remark involving the Lord that my boys thought should have brought an instant lightning bolt to the top of her lovely head.

Before that, there was the crucifix submerged in urine, for which the art critics gave great accolades. Since then, the former New York City mayor said when he reaches the pearly gates of heaven, he will walk right in and demand his reward because he's earned a face to face with God — if there is one. Before him, a famous billionaire asked about Christianity said that he didn't need anyone to die for him.

In the 1960s, we had people kicking God out of classrooms and throwing Bibles out the doors of those classrooms. We had a generation of "if it feels good, do it" trying to strip society and culture of all morality. In the 1970s, we began to legalize the murder of babies by the millions while still in their mothers' wombs.

We later had — and continue to have — men-with-men and women-with-women sexual-relations advocates. Much of the anti-biblical, anti-God activity was written into our laws or issued through governmental authorization by presidential edict. One president even gave a White House party, bathing the presidential residence in the rainbow colors.

All of this happened, even though the vast majority of Americans disapprove of such debauched activity.

Then came the official governmental declaration that homosexual marriage is the equivalent of heterosexual marriage, saying to God, in effect, "In your face!"

Now, we have the latest movement of the anti-God insanity down the broad way that leads into the abyss. Transgender, transsexual advocacy has trans-morphed into an even more rebellious, anti-God, anti-biblical proposal by the earth-dwellers.

There are those within the scientific and medical communities who see men carrying babies in the womb at some future date. The following news excerpt tells the story:

> WOMB transplants could allow men to have babies "tomorrow," an expert claims. They would not be able to deliver the baby naturally, but could give birth by cesarean.
>
> Richard Paulson, president of the American Society for Reproductive Medicine, said eight children had already been born to women after transplants.
>
> And he told a meeting in San Antonio, Texas: "There's plenty of room to put a uterus in there. Men and women have the same blood vessels."
>
> He said the next step would be trials involving transgender women to help them become natural mothers. . . .
>
> Doctors hope to perform the first UK womb transplant in 2018.[110]

Remember that movie with Arnold Schwarzenegger? His character was pregnant. The shocking movie poster had him, with his Mr. Universe body,

---

110. Victoria Fletcher, "Womb Transplants Could Allow Men to Have Babies 'Tomorrow,'" Rapture Ready News, November 5, 2017.

with a swollen abdomen. He was smiling, being proudly with child. Well, that might not be mere fiction for too much longer.

Come to think of it, I'm glad I don't have my finger on the trigger of divine power and authority, either! We can all be thankful that the Lord does!

Evil-Day Seducers

A flood of stories continues to pour upon us. It's as if a cesspool of salaciousness is in process of being purged and it's all gushing into our eyes and ears.

If the things with which we are deluged aren't true — and there is more than enough that is true — then the news media will make it up and throw it into the mix for their own nefarious purposes. I'll let you think on what you consider to be real sludge and fake news.

Hollywood has always provided fodder for the tabloids to fill ears and eyes more than willing to take it all in. Now, however, even Hollywood seems to be regurgitating the sick things that have become worse and worse.

Wait! There's a prophecy about such sickness: "But evil men and seducers shall [become] worse and worse, deceiving, and being deceived" (2 Timothy 3:13).

The Apostle, in his second letter to Timothy, seems to have been pointing to a time near the end of the dispensation of grace that would see an increase in the number of evil people who become worse by the day. He called them "evil men and seducers." At the same time, he said they would be being deceived while deceiving others.

The rumors have been around for ages about the so-called *casting couch*. This is the term for those in the acting profession who misuse their power to give job-seeking actresses roles in exchange for sexual favors. Until a few weeks back, this was all kind of looked at by the public and by the acting industry as something that elicited a wink and a chuckle. It was all a consensual thing . . . no harm done. Just compromise herself a time or two, and many a budding starlet was on her way to fame and fortune.

The Harvey Weinstein story has suddenly changed all that. Now, we know details of the alleged crimes involved. Underage sexual contact, abuse, blackmail, and a number of other criminal actions make the *casting couch* no longer a thing about which to only give a wink and a chuckle.

It is as if the Lord Himself has taken the cover between thumb and index finger and peeled back the lasciviousness. Suddenly, the evil of Hollywood has been exposed for what it is. Bible prophecy again is validated in our time, as the world sees the evil-day seduction that has been going on among the much-worshipped elite — the idols media and fans have made of those under this blanket of iniquity.

Pulling back this blanket has exposed such debauched evil at every level. It is exposing politicians at every level.

Some used to chuckle, wink, and revel in stories such as when Senator Edward Kennedy, the lion of the Senate, and Senator Christopher Dodd reportedly visited a certain D.C. restaurant and made "waitress sandwiches" in private dining rooms. Many other stories of orgiastic activities in D.C. and other halls of power have entertained the news-consuming public for decades.

But it is no longer funny. And the same entertainment and news media types who have for those many decades secretly enjoyed knowing about the debauchery and/or engaged in it themselves now find it all an outrage — especially when an avowed Christian is accused by supposed victims from some 30 or more years ago.

Indeed, it is not funny. It is evil that will add to the horrors of God's wrath and judgment in the near future. The following excerpt illuminates the evil-day seduction taking place worldwide:

> It's not just pimps and escaped convicts involved. It's the people we're expected to respect or "look up to" the most: the politicians, the elite, the wealthy businessmen, your neighbours, and oftentimes the people that you'd least expect.
>
> In this particularly devastating case, it's the people we're supposed to trust to help others: the United Nations' peacekeepers. As it turns out, these people are anything but "peacekeepers." Instead, they're the ones wreaking havoc in these villages and causing children to have nightmares for the rest of their lives. . . .
>
> Many of the children living in poverty in Port-au-Prince, Haiti, are left to fend for themselves, scavenging for food and struggling with hunger on a daily basis. Their lives drastically changed when the UN peacekeepers moved to their village, as they were offered snacks and cookies.
>
> However, this food came with a heavy price no one should ever have to pay. In exchange for food, the UN peacekeepers demanded sex from children as young as 12. In regard to the child sex ring run by UN peacekeepers in Haiti, nine children were being passed around from 2004 to 2007. . . .

There was another pedophile ring in the Democratic Republic of Congo that the UN was involved in — UN police officers in Bosnia paid for prostitutes and were caught trafficking young women from Eastern Europe — and the UN was involved with child sexual abuse and rape in the Central African Republic as well.[111]

Many stories contain reports much more graphic, disgusting, and heart-wrenching. They are quite difficult for me to read, much less bring before you in this column.

Evil men and seducers are becoming worse and worse, to be sure. They have been deceiving and being deceived by hiding much of the evil going on in America and the world. The uncovering of these things taking place now is long overdue. I believe the exposure is the Lord revealing exactly how far along this generation is on God's prophetic timeline.

> These be they who separate themselves, sensual, having not the Spirit. But ye, beloved, building up yourselves on your most holy faith, praying in the Holy Ghost, keep yourselves in the love of God, looking for the mercy of our Lord Jesus Christ unto eternal life (Jude 1:19–21).

Persia Prophecy Preparation?

My good friend Bill Salus published a book a few years back that continues to hold my fascination: *Nuclear Showdown in Iran: The Ancient Prophecy of Elam*. He presented a thorough treatment of a topic few, if any, writers about Bible prophecy have, to my knowledge, explored in recent times.

Today's news headlines are dealing in serious concern with the most volatile area of the world. It is the same area that has been the center of war, anger, and bloodshed for millennia. Bill Salus's book, in my view of things that are developing, demonstrates a certain degree of prescience.

We have watched for many years the coalescing of military powers that look very much like the Gog-Magog force described by Ezekiel the prophet in chapters 38 and 39. We point out incessantly that this gathering to the north of Jerusalem and Israel looks to be a major part of preparation for fulfillment of Bible prophecy. This forming of Russia, Iran, and Turkey into an agglomeration that is an existential threat to the Jewish state, in

---

111. Kaylee Brown, "United Nations 'Peacekeepers' Caught Running a Child Sex Ring: 2,000+ Cases of Sexual Abuse Reported," Collective Evolution, April 13, 2017; https://www.collective-evolution.com/2017/04/13/united-nations-peacekeepers-caught-running-a-child-sex-ring-2000-cases-of-sexual-abuse-reported/.

combination with the convergence of many other prophetic signals, is well worth examination.

Ezekiel tells us this region of the Middle East he calls Persia will constitute a primary partner within the Gog-Magog coalition. The news at the moment is particularly pointing the prophetic finger at Iran, ancient Persia. We begin by having a look at the forming alliance between the major players of the Gog-Magog force:

> Moscow, Turkey, and Iran are all sending symbolic messages to Washington that the Americans are out in the cold and the post-ISIS era may well be dictated by regional powers. . . .
>
> Turkish, Russian, and Iranian diplomats will meet in Antalya on Sunday in the run-up to a major get-together in Sochi on November 22. The meeting is supposed to focus on Syria, but its real purpose is part of a larger effort by Moscow to illustrate its influence in the region. . . .
>
> According to *Hurried Daily News*, the foreign ministers from Moscow, Ankara, and Tehran will meet in Antalya, followed a few days later by a meeting in Sochi between Vladimir Putin, Recep Tayyip Erdogan, and Hassan Rouhani that is being billed as a "trilateral summit."[112]

The meetings between the prophesied powers is over the disposition of another prophesied power — Syria. The whole matter has Prime Minister Benjamin Netanyahu exercised considerably regarding the threat to Israel, another nation in prophecy you may have heard about:

> Prime Minister Benjamin Netanyahu promised on Tuesday that Iran would not gain a foothold in Syria by which to attack Israel. The premier spoke via video to American Jewish leaders just hours after Russia clarified it had no intention of pushing Tehran's military forces out of the country.
>
> "Iran is scheming to entrench itself militarily in Syria. They want to create a permanent air, land and sea military presence, with the declared intent of using Syria as a base from which to destroy Israel. We are not going to agree to that. I have said very clearly that Israel will work to stop this," Netanyahu told the Jewish Federation of North America's General Assembly which is meeting in Los Angeles.

---

112. "Analysis: Russia-Iran-Turkey Meeting Is Message to US — Middle East," Israel News, *Jerusalem Post*, November 19, 2017.

"We must all work together to stop Iran's aggression and its
pursuit of nuclear weapons. If we stand together we will achieve
it. But if we have to we'll stand alone. Iran will not get nuclear
weapons. It will not turn Syria into a military base against Israel," the premier asserted.[113]

And that brings us to my admiration for Bill Salus' expansive work on what
looks to be a fulfillment of Bible prophecy in the making. Much of the
book involves the following prophetic passage: "But it shall come to pass
in the latter days: I will bring back the captives of Elam, says the LORD"
(Jeremiah 49:39).

Bill believes this is a prophecy that's yet to happen. God will make it
possible for Christians to escape from this, one of the most hateful regimes
on earth against those who follow Christ. He believes the forewarning is
dire for those of Iran (Persia/Elam) who refuse to let God's people go. He
describes the land of Elam:

> The prophet Jeremiah issued an interesting prophecy that
> could involve Iran's highly controversial nuclear program. The
> subject of Jeremiah's prophetic utterances is Elam. During the
> prophet's time, Elam comprised what consists of the central
> western portions of Iran today. Elam basically hugged much of
> the northeastern coastline of the Persian Gulf, while Persia en-
> compassed much of today's southern and eastern parts of Iran.
> It was bounded by Elam to the west and Media to the north.[114]

The author believes the prophecy indicates Iran's prime nuclear facilities in
Bushehr, a mountainous region, could be struck by Israel's military force.
He also thinks it could be struck by a major earthquake, nuclear disaster,
or directly by the hand of God in a supernatural cataclysm. In any case, he
believes, as I take it, that believers of the region will be freed to go into the
world to carry the gospel in a mighty way.

Bill sees the prophecy about this region also as proclaiming that
Elam's military will suffer destruction. This, he believes, is found in Jer-
emiah 49:34–39. The prophecy says that Elam's "bow" will be broken.
He believes this might mean that the missile-launching capabilities might

---

113. "Beware Iran: PM Netanyahu Vows Israel Will Act Alone against Iran to Destroy Their
Nuclear Capability If Given No Choice," *Jews News*, November 13, 2017.
114. Bill Salus, *Nuclear Showdown in Iran: The Ancient Prophecy of Elam* (Prophecy Depot
Publishing, 2014), chapter 3.

be destroyed. The arrows (missiles) can't fly to their targets if there are no launch facilities.

We've looked before at how the Gog-Magog force comes to destroy Israel, but it seems to be a conventional force, not one that involves nuclear weaponry. Certainly, to today's Israeli prime minister and the Israeli people, this prophecy should be welcome news. It is fascinating — and reassuring — to be a "watchman" while the Persian prophecy is in process of preparing for fulfillment.

38

December 2017: God Declared Out of Order

Anti-God forces are still on the move, forging ahead with even increased intensity in their madness. We read about it every day or see it on our television and/or computer monitors. Anti-God forces' determination to unseat the Creator of all things has not abated. It is, as said, intensifying.

We can go back much further, but a modern starting point to see this intensification involves the 1962–63 decision by the Supreme Court to attempt to kick God out of classrooms by banning Bible reading and prayer from public schools. Then, we consider most often the *Roe v. Wade* decision in 1973 that gave us not only the right, but the commission, to allow the murder of babies in their mothers' wombs.

God was, in these cases, ruled "out of order" by the Supreme Court justices. They, we can infer, believe they know better than the Founding Fathers of America — and better than God, as well. The humanists continue in their incessant drive to remove all influence by the One who gives and allows each heartbeat, each breath for every living being upon the planet.

As example, it is interesting that, while Sweden has allowed so many Muslims into their country that they are taking over, the most prominent Christian body in that nation, at the same time, seeks to rule God "out of order." Many among the Lutheran Church — more than six million membership among ten million citizens of that country — are declaring, in effect, that the order God established is wrong and they are out to rectify the situation.

The following excerpt explains:

> The Church of Sweden is encouraging its clergy to use the gender-neutral term "God" instead of referring to the deity as "he" or "the Lord."

The decision was made on Thursday, wrapping up an eight-day meeting of the church's 251-member decision-making body. The decision will take effect on May 20 during Pentecost.

It is the latest move by the national Evangelical Lutheran church to modernise its 31-year-old handbook setting out how services should be conducted.

The decision to update the book of worship gives priests new options on how to refer to God during their services.

Priests can now open their services by referring to the traditional "Father, son and Holy Ghost" or the gender-neutral phrase "in the name of God and the Holy Trinity." Other gender-neutral options are available for other parts of the Church of Sweden liturgy.[115]

God is thereby ruled out of order by the high, ecclesiastical body in the nation that seems to have developed spiritual dementia. God's Holy Scripture refers to Him as "He." But, Sweden's Lutheran top echelon, now led by Archbishop Antje Jackelen, who was elected Sweden's first female archbishop in 2013, says it is wrong to refer to the Lord in the masculine gender.

Obviously, the radical feminist agenda is on track and growing in Europe. That agenda, instigated and fueled by the same creature who first beguiled the first woman, continues to seduce and deceive. "God is out of order" is Satan's number-one accusation.

He told Eve, "Yea, hath God said?" He continues to whisper, even shout, the same question. He thus declares on every continent, at every opportunity, "God is out of order!"

Again, in Sweden, Muslims are taking over. Swedish women, it is reported, are dyeing their hair black in many instances and even wearing burkas to keep radical Muslim men from raping them — because blonde hair and blue eyes, to these radicals, gives license to rape, since the women are obviously, in their view, infidels.

That mankind has come to such a reprobate mindset should not surprise. Insanity has set in on a planetary scale. The lines between truth and lie, good and evil, have become so blurred as to make God Himself almost unrecognizable. Paul, the great Apostle, wrote the following prophetic truth, which we've looked at a number of times:

---

115. "Church of Sweden to Stop Clergy Calling God 'He' or 'the Lord' in Bid to Crack Down on Gendered Language," *The Telegraph*, November 26, 2017.

> And even as they did not like to retain God in their knowledge, God gave them over to a reprobate mind, to do those things which are not convenient; being filled with all unrighteousness, fornication, wickedness, covetousness, maliciousness; full of envy, murder, debate, deceit, malignity; whisperers, backbiters, haters of God, despiteful, proud, boasters, inventors of evil things, disobedient to parents, without understanding, covenant breakers, without natural affection, implacable, unmerciful: who knowing the judgment of God, that they which commit such things are worthy of death, not only do the same, but have pleasure in them that do them (Romans 1:28–32).

The reprobate thinking has set in across the globe. The radical, feminist mindset is one proof. Those who hold to such upside down thinking have ruled God "out of order." Paul writes concerning those who rule God "out of order," and who instead do things that are right in their own eyes: "But we are sure that the judgment of God is according to truth against them which commit such things" (Romans 2:2).

Drunken World about to Sip

To my way of thinking, things going on regarding Israel are most significant in light of Bible prophecy. Intrigues involving the status of Jerusalem are profound beyond any others in recent times. A strange setting of the prophetic stage is in process, with Saudi and Israel engaging in unprecedented overtures to each other. A key prophetic player is the chief cause of the strange bedfellows climbing between the geopolitical, diplomatic sheets. We get a flavor of the Bible prophecy stage-setting from the following excerpt:

> Imagine an Israeli taking a direct flight on El Al airlines to Riyadh, or the House of Saud establishing an embassy in Jerusalem. Previously unthinkable, rumors abound of a desire by Crown Prince Mohammad bin Salman (MBS) to normalize ties between the two countries. . . .
>
> Israel's relationship with the Saudis appears to be warming, with the countries allied in the struggle against a common enemy, Iran. . . .
>
> There are a number of reasons Riyadh and Jerusalem may be cozying up, outside of the desire to stop Iran's expansionism. Both

countries agree, for example, that the "Arab Spring" revolutions were destabilizing and unleashed dangerous forces. They likewise believe that a reduction in American influence in the Middle East left a power vacuum that risks being filled by enemies.[116]

Many prophetic observers, including yours truly, believe that Sheba and Dedan of Ezekiel 38:13 likely refer to the area possessed by present-day Saudi and surrounding territory. These will not be part of the Gog-Magog assault against Israel given by the prophet Ezekiel.

Instead, they will apparently stand on the sideline and issue a note of diplomatic protest, along with others. Certainly, recent developments, with Iran (ancient Persia) being the chief nemesis of both Israel and Saudi, have the Jews and Arabs coming together. They are doing so, at least, in their desire to promote their common defense.

At the same time, the Arab/Muslim world as a conglomerate is making sounds of war. The reason: rumors that American President Donald J. Trump will move the U.S. embassy from Tel Aviv to Jerusalem.

Another news article frames the situation:

> The Trump administration has notified U.S. embassies around the world that it plans to formally recognize Jerusalem as the undivided capital of Israel, according to a report published Thursday by *The Wall Street Journal.* The plan includes the future relocation of the U.S. Embassy from Tel Aviv to Jerusalem.
>
> According to the report, the plan has not been finalized, but envoys were being notified so that they can inform their host governments and prepare for possible protests. . . .
>
> "The president has always said it is a matter of when, not if, [the embassy will relocate to Jerusalem]," a White House spokesperson said.[117]

It seems that we are about to witness the world's geopolitical players take a sip from the cup prophesied by Zechariah:

> Behold, I will make Jerusalem a cup of trembling unto all the people round about, when they shall be in the siege both against Judah and against Jerusalem.

---

116. Ian May/The Media Line, "Inside the Prospective Israel-Saudi Arabia Rapprochement," Israel News, *Jerusalem Post*, December 2, 2017.

117. Hana Levi Julian, "White House Notifies US Embassies Around the World of Plan to Recognize Jerusalem as Capital of Israel," The Jewish Press, JewishPress.com, December 1, 2017.

> And in that day will I make Jerusalem a burdensome stone for all people: all that burden themselves with it shall be cut in pieces, though all the people of the earth be gathered together against it (Zechariah 12:2–3).

Giving Jerusalem validation as the rightful capital of Israel should be done. The president is right to do so, if he does move the American embassy to God's touchstone city of the world.

But doing so would almost without a doubt bring consequences — consequences no American president has been willing to risk since Congress declared Jerusalem the capital of Israel with The Jerusalem Embassy and Recognition Act of 1995.

God said He Himself will make Jerusalem a "cup of trembling" to those who deal treacherously with His chosen city and people. The world today is drunk with hatred for God and for the nation of Israel. Perhaps this American president is chosen to be God's instrument for leading the world to take a sip from that prophesied deadly cup.

Trump Prophetically Enlightened?

Presidents of the recent past have made statements I recall as having Bible prophecy in view. I haven't researched to find these statements in their exact verbiage, but they were made and could be easily found with today's search engines.

I remember that Jimmy Carter referred to the Holy Land as having biblical and historical importance according to Israel's prophets. Ronald Reagan sometimes would refer to the Second Coming of Christ and the reality of Armageddon. Bill Clinton once said that when he was governor of Arkansas, his pastor, Dr. W.O. Vaught, told him that if Bill ever became president, he had better treat Israel according to Genesis 12, regarding the blessings or curses to be given by the Lord Himself, depending upon whether one blessed or cursed Israel.

President Donald Trump, in talking about his decision declaring Jerusalem as Israel's eternal capital and announcing he will move the U.S. Embassy from Tel Aviv to Jerusalem, said something of profound significance. He announced a number of important reasons for his decision, then said, "This is . . . a recognition of reality. It is also the right thing to do."[118] One must wonder how much of this president's words are based upon true understanding of why it's "the right thing to do."

---

118. https://www.ynetnews.com/articles/0,7340,L-5052940,00.html.

A considerable amount of the criticism I've heard about Trump's decision comes from a specific, leftist diatribe who say it's the crazy evangelical Zionists who base Israel's right to the land they "occupy" upon the Bible. The word "Bible" is dripping with vitriol, even when read rather than heard. It's like they are saying, "The Bible! Ugh!"

Trump is listening to the Bible thumpers and doing it for their votes. That is the rant. Yet, the following Bible truth is exactly what makes Mr. Trump's decision the "right thing to do."

Jerusalem is, in fact, chosen by the Lord of heaven to be at the center of His chosen land for His chosen people:

> But I have chosen Jerusalem, that my name might be there; and have chosen David to be over my people Israel. Now it was in the heart of David my father to build an house for the name of the LORD God of Israel. But the LORD said to David my father, Forasmuch as it was in thine heart to build an house for my name, thou didst well in that it was in thine heart: notwithstanding thou shalt not build the house; but thy son which shall come forth out of thy loins, he shall build the house for my name. The LORD therefore hath performed his word that he hath spoken: for I am risen up in the room of David my father, and am set on the throne of Israel, as the LORD promised, and have built the house for the name of the LORD God of Israel. And in it have I put the ark, wherein is the covenant of the LORD, that he made with the children of Israel (2 Chronicles 6:6–11).

Almost every leader on the world stage is against the decision. Even our closest allies, like British Prime Minister Theresa May, are adamantly against the declaration and the move. Yet this president is unmoved. He seems determined to carry out the promise that presidents preceding him didn't have the political will or courage to honor.

Trump has proven that he keeps promises, even bucking the heavy resistance of opposition from outside his own political party and from within. He forges ahead, despite the world's opposition to this decision. He doesn't wither under the fire of the fanaticism of the Islamic world that rages with hatred for Israel.

It is not possible for me to know for certain, but I strongly suspect that Christian counsel from people such as Dr. Robert Jeffress, pastor of First Baptist Church of Dallas, has made it known to the president the truth about Israel from God's perspective. Thankfully, Mr. Trump has wisely listened to such counsel, it appears. America stands in much better stead with the Almighty with this fulfilled, presidential promise.

Happy Holidays!?

The secularists, those who demand that we not be exclusive at this time of year, have done all they can do to replace the greeting "Merry Christmas" with "Happy Holidays." They don't want us to hurt the feelings or offend the sensibilities of people by using the name of the One for whom we celebrate the season.

The politically correct insist that we all use the term "Happy Holidays" as we send out greetings. They cringe at the sight of nativity scenes and become disturbed at the sounds of songs that name the One whose birthday we celebrate on December 25.

While it is true that the larger portion of American citizenry doesn't think it's wrong to proclaim "Merry Christmas," the politically correct Nazis, many of whom speak loudly through their social activist, bully pulpits, try to make it miserable for those of us who use the greeting we cannot and will never abandon.

These of the "Happy Holiday"–only crowd — the militant types who genuinely hate the moral authority that Christianity represents — see "Merry Christmas" as equivalent of the evil that they themselves most often champion. They accuse, for example, in many cases, that Adolf Hitler's Nazi regime celebrated Christmas during those horrific years in Germany by saying "Merry Christmas" right after saying "Heil Hitler."

They themselves act like Nazi thugs in many cases. They are the types who demand that Christians who own bakeries be forced to bake cakes for same-sex couples or lose their businesses through fines and court costs. They demand that taxpayers, in a nation that claims to be more than 70 percent Christian in population, subsidize the arts, which often display most salacious, even anti-God, presentations. They expect Christian taxpayers to fund abortion through support of organizations like Planned Parenthood.

The fact is, there is little "happy" within the ranks of those who want to do away with the term "Merry Christmas." They are in constant turmoil, and are often found among those who foment rioting and claim it in the name of social justice. They form, in my opinion, the nucleus of the Apostle Paul's perilous-times characteristic, "false accusers" (2 Timothy 3:3).

Those with the no-more-"Merry Christmas" rant fall in line with every effort to remove God from every public venue. It is just a matter of time, it is obvious to anyone with the ability to observe, that when they come to full power, they will demand that Christ be taken out of our private lives as well.

Let's look for a moment at the mindset that wants to break the bond between mankind and the Creator, a thing that will bring severe ramifications and wrath from heaven, according to God's Word (read Psalm 2:1–9).

Beginning with our government allowing Madelyn Murray O'Hair to achieve her enraged, singular goal of getting God out of public schools, we have witnessed a rush to national insanity. We have watched entire generations be subjected to revisionist history and inculcated by anti-God education. The results have, in these days of bizarre behavior and brainwashing by anti-God forces — primarily through social media — brought this nation to the brink of change that cannot be reversed.

I believe it took the God of heaven Himself intervening in the 2016 presidential election to stop America from being shoved into the godless, grasping arms of the globalists.

The rage that intervention produced is self-evident. We have witnessed those who have been raised through O'Hair's insane achievement go completely out of their minds. They believe what the mainstream media, the entertainment world, and the social media liars have told them. They are miserable, and even when they get what they want, it just throws fuel on the fires of their anger against an America that, under God's gracious hand, has allowed them to live better than any people on earth.

There is nothing "happy" about the mindset that demands we say "Happy Holidays" rather than "Merry Christmas." This fallen attitude has made this the most unhappy generation in American history.

Satan is at the core of the movement to push God out of this magnificent desire by true Christians to honor their Lord's incarnation. The secularists' "Happy Holidays" offers nothing but misery in a future apart from God and heaven's influence.

Bible prophecy foretells a time that will be as far from happiness as we can imagine. Apart from God, this planet is destined to become hell on earth.

Jesus Christ, the reason for our celebration, on the other hand, promises to save mankind individually and collectively (as the human race) so that we may live for eternity in the most blissful conditions beyond imagination. This is why we don't say "Happy Holidays" — rather, we proclaim "Merry Christmas!"

Conclusion

End-of-Days Drama

Globalism was dealt a stunning blow on November 8, 2016. The effects of that trauma became instantly evident. The left side of the geopolitical spectrum literally lost all sensibility, in my opinion.

Evidence of the collective nervous breakdown as the result of the election of Donald J. Trump continues to be seen in every direction we look across the national and international landscapes.

Secretive collusion to steal the election remains the primary suspicion of the left. I say "suspicion" because, despite exhaustive efforts by everyone on the left, including all of mainstream media, there hasn't been even the hint of fact showing that the Trump campaign colluded with the Russians or anyone else.

All evidence shows that the people of middle America were simply fed up with the antics of the previous presidential administration and those who joined in its madness. Plus, that political party's candidate was overwhelmingly unacceptable to the voting public. The nation gave Donald Trump a wide electoral victory, and that was that.

Still, the so-called mainstream media leads the charge, stirring the anger of the political left. They feed the flames of irrationality of the opposition party. They stoke the viciousness of the entertainment industry and the treasonous intrigues of the globalist elite.

Donald Trump stole the election from the rightful heir to the presidency is the ongoing propaganda rant. Instead of using factual evidence of any sort, this mantra uses nonspecific, nonsensical insinuation and hyperbolic supposition to fill the minds of Trump-haters with rage.

This book's foregoing essays have delineated much of this. We need, however, to look deeper, here, into what it all means for these "end of days," as the secular world terms the time near the end of human history.

Two primary elements make up the last of the last days leading to Christ's Second Coming. There are many elements of lesser importance, and we will look very briefly at those. But we must first consider the most prominent end-of-days signals before analyzing the whole prophetic picture in synopsized fashion.

Israel is the number-one indicator of how near is the time when Christ will come back to establish God's Kingdom on earth. Secondary only to Israel's place on the Bible prophecy timeline is the rapidly developing movement toward establishing a one-world or *global* order. Let us look at these separately and at how they fit together in prophetic fulfillment.

Israel the Key

Throughout history, the people of earth have been offended by Israel or the Jewish race being called God's chosen nation. Jewish people themselves have often misunderstood the meaning of those designations. They have often been the hated and hunted people throughout history because of this biblical pronouncement by the God of heaven: "For thou art an holy people unto the LORD thy God, and the LORD hath chosen thee to be a peculiar people unto himself, above all the nations that are upon the earth" (Deuteronomy 14:2).

They are indeed a "peculiar" people in that while God calls them His chosen, the world and even much of Christendom now think of today's Jews as different from the people "chosen" by God in antiquity. Some evangelical denominations deny that Israel has any tie whatsoever to the nation of Israel of those ancient times.

This being the case, it is a head-scratcher as to why modern Jewry is so demeaned during this present hour, exactly as they have most always been throughout time. If the Jews aren't special in any way, why pick them out for marginalization and even hatred? There must certainly be something that engenders such vitriol against them and the modern state of Israel.

Much of the invective against the Jews centers around the claim that they are "Christ killers" — they collaborated with the Roman Empire to put the Lord to death. This is one of the charges the Nazis of Hitler's day made to incite hatred for the Jews.

But that indictment doesn't explain fully the nearly universal hatred since time predating the crucifixion. The Jews — the nation Israel since ancient times — have been assaulted, have endured genocide, and have been exiled as well as enslaved throughout their history. Pharaoh, remember, used them as slave labor until the Exodus. The Egyptians then tried to destroy them once they had left Egypt.

If the Jews are not "peculiar" people chosen by God for His own purposes, why the hatred and persecution down through time? Why the hatred and building anti-Semitism that we see today if, as the world claims, there is nothing special about the Jews?

The world of philosophers, politicians, statesmen, psychiatrists, and even most religionists have no answers as to why there is hatred, except to join the mantra that the Jews are occupying land rightfully belonging to the Palestinians. But, again, the hatred was there long before the Jews began returning to the so-called Holy Land in the late 1800s and Israel was founded as a modern nation in the mid-20th century.

The truth is that the answer can only be found in God's Word. One writer frames the matter of Israel's right to the land in a way I find satisfying:

> The Land of Israel is the only place on earth which God says He owns in terms of property ownership that can be transferred. (Of course, we know the whole world is His, yet this one parcel of land on the earth has a unique relationship to Him.) About Israel, He says, "The land shall not be sold for ever: for the land is mine, for ye are strangers and sojourners with me" (Leviticus 25:23).
>
> Exactly what does the Bible say about God's parcel of land, and who has a right to it?
>
> When we come to the modern-day Israel-Palestine issue, people often ask the question, "Just what right do Israel and the Jewish people have to this land?"
>
> Arguments are continually brought forth concerning the rights of the Palestinians and the rights of the Israelis that seem logical to the people who present them. But a basic question still remains in my mind as I listen to the many conflicting viewpoints concerning this parcel of land: "Who has the ultimate authority to determine rights concerning this special piece of real estate?"
>
> The biblical answer to that question is that God alone determines the "rights" that any of us have. Something is right or wrong because of Divine decree, not human feeling or human reason. The existence of God previous to the creation of the universe and mankind gives Him the right to determine our "rights."
>
> Morality exists because God exists. Authority exists because God exists. And, Almighty God has already determined the

rights of Israel and the Jewish people to the land God owns and has deeded over to them.[119]

This adequately explains Israel's right to the land to most who believe Israel is God's chosen in perpetuity. We can know that the hatred, the anti-Semitism, is wrapped up in God dealing with Israel in this special way. But Israel's God-given promises of possession of the land He gave the Jews is only a secondary cause of the world's anger against Jewry and against the present Jewish state.

To truly get to the root of the insane attitude toward God's chosen, we must look at the very earliest part of the instruction manual God gave humankind for living on planet Earth.

The answer we seek to the question of why the hatred has its genesis is found in, well, the Book of Genesis:

> And the LORD God said unto the serpent, Because thou hast done this, thou art cursed above all cattle, and above every beast of the field; upon thy belly shalt thou go, and dust shalt thou eat all the days of thy life: and I will put enmity between thee and the woman, and between thy seed and her seed; it shall bruise thy head, and thou shalt bruise his heel (Genesis 3:14–15).

The following briefly outlines the beginning of the cause and effect of the trouble mankind has generated and thus suffered down through human history. It is the beginning of the reason why Israel is so hated today.

Salvation is rescue from something that is death-dealing in nature. That is, it is the plucking from a deadly situation or circumstance and placing in a position of safety. This is what God offers to all of mankind. He offers salvation through His Son, Jesus Christ. (And remember, the *Savior* was born into the Jewish race. This is most important to consider.)

Salvation from What?

Each human has been born under the penalty of sin, since Eve was seduced into eating of the forbidden fruit from the tree of the knowledge of good and evil, and Adam knowingly disobeyed by joining the woman in partaking of that fruit.

God forewarned the first two people that if they disobeyed by eating from this tree, they would surely die. Lucifer, in the form of the serpent,

---

119. Clarence H. Wagner Jr., "12 Keys to Understanding Israel in the Bible," Lambert Dolphin's Place; http://www.ldolphin.org/twelvekeys.html.

put the question of whether to believe the Creator in their minds by asking, "Yea, hath God said?"

> Now the serpent was more subtil than any beast of the field which the LORD God had made. And he said unto the woman, Yea, hath God said, Ye shall not eat of every tree of the garden? And the woman said unto the serpent, We may eat of the fruit of the trees of the garden: but of the fruit of the tree which is in the midst of the garden, God hath said, Ye shall not eat of it, neither shall ye touch it, lest ye die. And the serpent said unto the woman, Ye shall not surely die: for God doth know that in the day ye eat thereof, then your eyes shall be opened, and ye shall be as gods, knowing good and evil (Genesis 3:1–5).

With that disobedience, just as God forewarned, sin and its consequence, death, entered the world. The man and woman lost fellowship with God. They began aging and degenerating toward death. Humans now needed salvation from sin and death.

God loves His creation called *man* and desired to have mankind become part of His eternal family, to live with Him forever in heaven. The Creator, in His grace and mercy, said He would redeem his human creation, would bring One who would save mankind from sin and death into the world.

He cursed the serpent, Lucifer, who became known as Satan and the devil, and said to him, "And I will put enmity between thee and the woman, and between thy seed and her seed; it shall bruise thy head, and thou shalt bruise his heel" (Genesis 3:15).

With that declaration, God sealed Lucifer's doom. The Lord would raise "seed" that would crush the head of the serpent (the form Satan assumed in the temptation of Eve). That means God would produce, through Adam and Eve, a Savior who would redeem mankind and who would put an end to Satan and his evil.

The Jewish race is the one the Lord chose to be the people through whom the Christ, the Savior, was brought into the world.

When Jesus Christ died on the terrible Roman cross on Golgotha in Jerusalem, He said, "It is finished." He had completed the salvation process begun way back in human history (Genesis 3:15) and finished His program for the redemption of man. Satan's fate was sealed at the moment Jesus said those three words.

Lucifer, the angel who led a third of heaven's angels to rebel, thus making himself and those with him in the rebellion unredeemable, hates

God's chosen race who produced the "seed" that will end his career. The "seed," Jesus Christ, will "crush" the serpent.

The serpent, sentenced to eternal torment by heaven's court, must believe that if he can keep God from honoring His promises to Israel, his own fate can be changed. Satan has thus turned many nations against Israel down through the centuries in an attempt to destroy the chosen people. If the serpent can erase Israel from the earth when God said they are His people forever, he can make God a liar. His own doom can, he must believe, thereby be avoided.

Today, we hear the constant cry from the Middle East enemies of the Jews: "Death to Israel!" Almost every nation within the U.N. votes against the Jewish state at every opportunity. Arab leaders made it their mission since Israel's birth into modernity to erase it from the map.

Israel isn't even on the maps of the classrooms within the Muslim, Arab world.

The hatred for the Jews and for Israel is satanically inspired. It is obvious just in our daily headlines. The Jewish state is at the center of all controversy regarding the call for world peace. In many cases, the nation is held up as the reason there is no peace in the region and even in the world.

Israel is the link to the wind-up to history while the Second Coming of Christ nears.

Globalism the Goal

Tied in closely to hatred for the Jews in Satan's plan to change his own fate is his blueprint for one-world order. Many in the diplomatic community term this plan for construction the "new world order." But, there is nothing *new* about the chief architect's design. It is as old as human history.

The effort to remove the Creator God from humanity's governance was made on the plain of Shinar following the worldwide flood of Noah's time. Rather than give the full scriptural account here, I direct you to Genesis 11:1–9. These passages encompass the entire story of the Tower of Babel.

Satan convinced the people of that day to establish a power center where they could govern their own affairs. The purpose was to remove God from ruling over them. It was Lucifer who wanted to be worshiped, of course, and it ultimately would have come to pass except for the Lord's direct intervention.

God catastrophically did just that: He intervened by confounding their language so that they could no longer work together and by scattering them abroad. With this first attempt at new world order stopped by heaven's action, the serpent began working down through the eons of time to again establish global order.

Every civilization since has had, to one degree or another, elements of Lucifer's blueprint to again bring the world to Babel.

Nimrod was the evil leader chosen by Satan to attempt that first one-world order. The serpent, not knowing the precise timing of God's prophetic utterances, has since that time had a man ready at every juncture in history to pick up the mantle of the fallen Nimrod. Antichrist will be the man who will finally be allowed to put together Satan's attempt to establish world order. Instead, however, it will be world "disorder" that will produce hell on earth.

The result of this move back to Babel and away from God's governance is prophesied in the words of the Lord Jesus Christ: "For then shall be great tribulation, such as was not since the beginning of the world to this time, no, nor ever shall be" (Matthew 24:21).

Sin-fallen people will thus have their time of almost absolute self-rule. Instead of having God to rule over them, they will have a man, indwelt by Satan himself, falsely claiming to be God. He will enslave them and consign them to a future doomed for an eternity in the Lake of Fire.

Here is what the Lord says about this satanically inspired movement back to Babel:

> Why do the heathen rage, and the people imagine a vain thing?
>
> The kings of the earth set themselves, and the rulers take counsel together, against the LORD, and against his anointed, saying,
>
> Let us break their bands asunder, and cast away their cords from us.
>
> He that sitteth in the heavens shall laugh: the LORD shall have them in derision.
>
> Then shall he speak unto them in his wrath, and vex them in his sore displeasure (Psalm 2:1–5).

Globalism, then, is the vehicle Lucifer is using to drive this present generation back to Babel. He is seducing, inducing, and inciting the so-called international community to construct, diplomatically speaking, a neo-tower that will reach into heaven to usurp the throne of God, which he has wanted to accomplish since his original rebellion (read Isaiah 14:14).

The Tribulation that will result from the serpent's effort to rebuild that structure will bring horrific carnage upon earth. Jesus said that if He didn't return when He does at the Second Advent, no flesh will be saved. All that breathe air will die.

At the same time, however, that era of Tribulation will cause the spiritual hearts of a remnant of His chosen people to believe in Jesus the Christ:

> And I will pour upon the house of David, and upon the inhabitants of Jerusalem, the spirit of grace and of supplications: and they shall look upon me whom they have pierced, and they shall mourn for him, as one mourneth for his only son, and shall be in bitterness for him, as one that is in bitterness for his firstborn (Zechariah 12:10).

During this seven-year period, the Lord will return the spiritual hearts of a remnant of His people back to Himself while He is pouring out wrath on all who will continue to reject him. This will be a time when God again deals with His chosen people, Israel, because Christ's bride — the Church that consists of all born-again believers (John 3:3) — will have been moved from earth to their heavenly home.

The Church Age, or Age of Grace, will end, and the Lord will begin dealing with Israel as in days of old. This instantaneous change that will renew God's interrupted program for His chosen nation will be through the Rapture (read 2 Corinthians 15:51–55 and 1 Thessalonians 4:13–18).

Signals abound that this generation is on the very cusp of experiencing this transition from the Church Age into the Tribulation. I believe there is no more dramatic proof that this sudden change is about to happen than what has resulted from the election of Donald J. Trump as president of the United States.

As mentioned in a previous chapter and above, the anger and irrationality that erupted immediately upon Trump's election continue to be nothing short of extraordinary. At the heart of the phenomenon is the fact that the almost uncontested drive toward globalism was slowed to a crawl with the election. The new president says he is determined to be a champion of national sovereignty, among other anti-globalist goals and aspirations. I'm convinced that the near-insanity we have witnessed since November 8, 2016, is satanically driven rage. Lucifer's construction project, the neo-Babel plan, had the proverbial monkey wrench thrown into its machinery. The Lord Himself threw that monkey wrench, and the effect was stunning.

American government, the moving economic force used to that point to put forth the globalist agenda, was suddenly on a course that was 180 degrees opposite. The minions, both spiritual and human, were driven by their master into the near-lunatic frenzy we continue to witness.

In addition to being staunchly anti-globalism, Trump is stridently pro-Israel; moving the American Embassy from Tel Aviv to Jerusalem is proof. Satan wants to destroy Israel, the nation and its people, in order to thwart God's covenant promises. The serpent must do so — he must think in his sin delusion — in order to be victorious.

It is reprobate thinking in its most emblazoned presentation. Satan knows God cannot lie. He knows that God is omnipotent — cannot be defeated. He knows God has pronounced his fate in the Lake of Fire. Yet he still thinks he will win this great, cosmic battle.

Paul the Apostle wrote the result of turning one's back on God: "And even as they did not like to retain God in their knowledge, God gave them over to a reprobate mind, to do those things which are not convenient" (Romans 1:28).

Lucifer has infected most of humanity with his anti-God sin sickness. This is why we are witnessing the mind-boggling, upside down thinking of recent days, months, and years. This is why we have been force fed the insanity that homosexuality is a loving, alternative lifestyle rather than aberrant behavior, as the psychology books have told us for years. This is why the courts of America — even pastors in some pulpits — equate gay marriage to heterosexual marriages.

Reprobate infection is why babies in the wombs are slaughtered by the millions in our nation while fish and animals, and even plants and other vegetation, are protected by federal law. God-denial and rejection have brought this generation to these last of the last days reprobate mindset.

That is why we who believe in Jesus Christ as our Redeemer, like Lot in the days just before Sodom was destroyed, are "sore vexed" as God's Word terms Lot's perplexed state of mind.

The end-of-days drama has this generation on the fast track to the consummation of the age. Signals of Christ's coming again to change this wicked planet into His righteous kingdom are in every direction we look. Even so, come, Lord Jesus!